QUESTIONING
— the —
MUSIC EDUCATION PARADIGM

Lee R. Bartel, Editor

Dedicatory Foreword by Charles Leonhard

PUBLISHED BY THE CANADIAN MUSIC EDUCATORS' ASSOCIATION
AS VOLUME 2 OF THE BIENNIAL SERIES, *RESEARCH TO PRACTICE*,
LEE R. BARTEL, SERIES EDITOR
2004

Cover and Book Design: Melanie Bartel
Printed and Bound in Canada by Britannia Printers, Toronto

Library and Archives Canada Cataloguing in Publication

Questioning the music education paradigm / Lee R. Bartel, editor ; dedicatory foreword, Charles Leonhard.

(Research to practice ; 2)
ISBN 0-920630-90-1

1. Music--Instruction and study. I. Bartel, Lee Roy II. Series.

MT1.Q55 2004780'.7
C2004-905206-3

Published by CMEA:

Canadian Music Educators' Association National Office
Faculty of Music
Wilfrid Laurier University
Waterloo ON Canada N2L 3C5

QUESTIONING
—— the ——
MUSIC EDUCATION PARADIGM

Lee R. Bartel, Editor
Dedicatory Foreword by Charles Leonhard

CONTENTS

SECTION 1: QUESTIONING HOW WE TEACH

SECTION 2: QUESTIONING WHAT WE TEACH AND FOR WHAT WE TEACH

SECTION 3: QUESTIONING WHAT IS EXPECTED OF TEACHERS AND HOW WE TEACH THEM

CONTENTS

SECTION 4: QUESTIONING WHOM WE SHOULD BE TEACHING

SECTION 5: QUESTIONING OUR ASSUMPTIONS AND STRUCTURES

RESEARCH TO PRACTICE

Series Preface

LEE R. BARTEL, SERIES EDITOR

From research to practice – making that connection is the hope of most music education researchers. As a profession music education is a profession of practitioners. Even university music education professors are generally first music teachers and have a strong sense of the applied. Consequently, music education as a field finds research – both the conduct and the application – a challenge. But if there is to be growth and development in the field, research is critically important, especially research that has strong implication for practice and that is communicated to practitioners. Such is the hope of this biennial series of books: to allow researchers to "speak" to practitioners about the implications of research and how it really matters to the important issues of music education.

What counts as research is debated in some music education circles. A narrow view excludes philosophical inquiry, questions all but the most linear of qualitative research, and prefers "scientific" quantitative research. In this series I take a broad view of research. The fundamental "motor" of research is an important question. Research is systematic inquiry, it is data acquisition and knowledge development. If the data are a set of pre-existing philosophical concepts and new knowledge is developed from it, that counts as research. Whether the data are the thoughts of a group of students or teachers, or test scores, or notated observations, it is the analytic approach that transforms these into new knowledge. In addition to a broad approach to research, this series places emphasis on the implication and application of research knowledge to pedagogic contexts.

The first volume of the Research to Practice series was entitled, *Creativity* and *Music Education* edited by Timothy Sullivan and Lee Willingham. It presented an international group of seventeen scholars bridging the theory to practice gap in relation to fostering creativity in students. This second volume again presents an international cast of twenty three contributors. These scholars have theoretically problematized aspects of music education but do not merely raise criticisms. Rather, they address these problems with practical solutions and suggestions. That is the goal and mandate of the *Research to Practice* series.

DEDICATORY PREFACE

The Great Masquerade: Means Become Ends

CHARLES LEONHARD

Today I have chosen to address a weakness in focus and methodology which plagues the contemporary music education program—the confusion of means and ends.

The strength of music as an art and the reason every society has nurtured and valued its music lie in the strong appeal of music to the life of feeling. The potential strength and value of the music education program lie in the development of responsiveness to the expressive import of music. Without its expressive function and aesthetic quality music has nothing unique to offer to the education of children and young people. With consistent emphasis on its expressive function, however, music in the school fills a unique role in the development of the human potential of people of all ages. This should be our dominant objective, the overriding end toward which we strive and toward which the entire program is directed.

We have come to the place where we emphasize the means to the expressive import of music at the expense of the expressive import itself. Many of us have taken refuge in any one of a number of false havens: organized approaches to musical learning such as Orff and Kodaly, elaborate teaching strategies, notions about concept develop-ment, behavioral objectives, emphasis on technique, emphasis on the externals of the structure of music. As a result, the means have become ends. We have become so involved with the approach, the strategy, the concepts, the behavioral objectives, the techniques, the externals, that we ignore or give only secondary attention to the essence of music, its expressive import with its affect on the sentient life and spirit of the people. Means are masquerading as ends. When means masquerade as ends, music loses its heart and the music program loses its life and its reason for being.

The masquerade begins early in the elementary school. In children's early years and, perhaps, even in kindergarten, music is a source of delight, an avenue for self-expression, a spur to a high level of feeling. As children move through successive years of schools, however, they find less and less in music to feel good about and more and more to learn about it; and much of what they are expected to learn has little or nothing to do with the enchantment they found in music originally. Children are flooded with cognitive considerations—key signatures, scales, the names of lines and spaces on the staff, meter signatures, different kinds of notes and other vagaries of the abstract notation system, form and all the rest of the so-called "fundamentals of music."

Music, that marvelous force that seemed so wondrous to children, begins to recede in their consciousness and that of their teachers. What was once a source of delight becomes increasingly a source of drudgery and boredom. Children are subjected to the trivia of music at the expense of its essence. They do not learn to shape a phrase, to project and respond to the expressive line in music, the real fundamental of music. They are expected, on the other hand, to learn technical trivia which they are usually not in a position to use and which they quickly forget if they learn them at all. The technical and cognitive matters are devoid of musical meaning, divorced from the expressive effect of the music and do not serve as essential instruments to learnings that are important to children.

Unfortunately this focus on means at the expense of ends is continued as children assay other forms of the study of music. In listening the focus is on recognition of form, recognition of instruments, recognition of themes, and facts about the composer's lives, all of which come to intrude on children's responses to the expressive import of the music. Seldom if ever are children permitted to listen to music and respond to it in their own creative and imaginative ways without the encumbrance and interference of musical and technical trivia. Is it any wonder that the high point of interest, attitude, and achievement in music comes in the fourth grade?

With the beginning of instrumental instruction, another means becomes the end — technique. Children dredge through instruction books filled with exercises, scales, contrived melodies and tunes that have little or no expressive appeal. Little that they play has expressive import and, even if a piece they are playing does have expressive import, they are perforce so involved with technique that they are likely to miss the expressive import. There is no time for listening to artistic performances on their instruments, no time to play by ear tunes that they know and like, no time to improvise. There is only time for technical study and drill. Again, the means have become the end.

When students become members of a performing group, they find that means, though different than previously, still function as ends. Indeed, students often find themselves serving as means to the conductor's own musical ends. Conductors work on such means as precision in tuning and precision in rhythm, but these means too often become ends in themselves. Such means are legitimate if they are viewed by both teacher and students as means to an end and if they do, in truth, eventuate in an artistic and expressive performance. Often, however, they are not so viewed and they do not so eventuate; instead they lead to a precise, well-tuned, leaden and mechanical performance devoid of expressive import and appeal.

Marching and half-time shows which formerly functioned as an attractive adjunct to the music program and served as means to public support of the music program have, in many schools, become ends in themselves and represent the dominant features of the instrumental program. Marching and playing competition which formerly served as a means to motivation for students has, in many instances, become an end in itself. I have been shocked to find many high schools in which marching band is a year long obsession, high schools in which the band begins work on contest compositions at the close of the football season and does little else until the close of school, junior high schools which emphasize marching, high schools in which the band has become ancillary to majorettes, baton twirlers, and dancing girls. These practices represent perversions of means and ends which are unconscionable, immoral, unethical, and positively detrimental to the purposes of music education. An unfortunate by-product of these developments is that skilled music educators all over the country are leaving the profession because they can no longer countenance the demands of the flimsy program to which they have fallen heir.

The time has come for you and me as music educators to return to the basics of music education, the true fundamentals of music— emphasis on the expressive import of the music we involve students in and the cultivation of responsiveness to that expressive import. We must reject the flights of fancy that have moved music education away from the essence of the art of music — the idea of music as an academic discipline, dominant emphasis on behavioral definition of objectives, and the conceptual approach to teaching music, all of which lead to emphasis on cognitive considerations, the memorization of abstract information and the minutiae of musical behavior.

We must realize that the appropriate subject matter of music study is music itself. We must select music for study that is expressive and appealing to students and emphasize its expressive import. We must begin instruction with the expressive import of the music we are dealing with, relate everything we do or ask the students to do to that expressive import and end with that expressive import. Expressive import is truly the alpha and omega of music learning and music teaching.

We must view knowledge, information and technique as instruments to enable students to do what they desire to do with and about music. We must present information about music only when it is going to be used directly to refine musical responsiveness and musical behavior. We must develop technique in the context of a piece of music the student desires to play. We must involve students in experiences with music—experiences with the quality of undergoing, of doing, of being involved with the music. The focus of instruction must be upon the composer's expressive intentions and the means he used to achieve those intentions.

I move now to some specific suggestions designed to place the expressive import of music at the heart of the program.

To teachers of general music, the following suggestions seem pertinent.

1. Simplify your program. Choose a few objectives that are feasible in terms of your time with the children and the resources at hand. I suggest concentration on teaching children to sing and play classroom and folk instruments, to sing parts and play instruments by ear, to sing in three parts by the end of the sixth grade, and on developing a repertory of songs they like to sing and sing well.

2. Choose music that is attractive and appealing to the children and easy enough for them to sing it with a degree of artistry. This will undoubtedly mean supplementing the series books, too many of which have deemphasized performance in favor of listening, related arts and abstract concepts. The best of traditional folk and classic and contemporary popular music provide a rich source of repertory. Emphasize the shaping of phrases for expressive purposes in all performance and bring in recorded songs that exemplify expressive phrasing and artistic performance of folk and popular music. Many of our currently popular folk and popular singers are true musical artists and qualify as exemplars for children. Listening to recordings by [editor's note – this was written in

1981. Mentally insert the popular performers of today] Diana Ross, Anne Murray, Crystal Gayle, Debbie Boone, Barbara Mandrell, Melissa Manchester, and Carly Simon provides a far richer musical and expressive experience than listening to the lifeless over-trained and colorless recordings of children which accompany series books. Introduce information about music only when it is needed for use in helping children develop insight into and independence with the music they are singing and playing.

To teachers of beginning instrument classes, I make the following suggestions:

1. Realize that true musical technique involves projecting the expressive import of music and not playing scales and exercises. Teach basic beginning technique as quickly as possible and then move directly to having children play by ear tunes that they know, like, and can sing. Pentatonic songs represent the ideal material for beginning instrument instruction. Not only are they easy to sing, comprehend, and play, but they also provide an early avenue for improvisation of simple descants, bordons, and other independent parts.

2. Provide beginners with regular experience in hearing their instrument played beautifully and expressively through your own performance or from recordings and tapes of both the music they are learning and compositions beyond their present level of technique.

3. Emphasize playing by ear at all times. One of the great strengths of the Suzuki approach is the reliance on the ear and on immersion in hearing the instrument well played. It is high time, in my opinion, that teachers of wind instruments take a cue from Suzuki and get away from the rigid plodding through instrument methods books. Encourage the young player to play by ear and from the notation music that he likes and selects for himself.

For conductors of choral and instrumental performance groups, I make the following suggestions.

As a conductor, you are intimately involved with music, you reflect, you image, you create; you make discriminations about musical style; you experiment with varying interpretations of the score; you make judgments about the performance; you listen to authoritative recordings; you analyze the structure of compositions. As a result, you have authentic experiences which lead to significant musical learning and an enhanced level of aesthetic responsiveness. Why not involve your students in these same experiences on a level appropriate to their level of advancement?

1. Make the projection of the expressive import of music the central focus of your rehearsals and your public presentations, and involve your students in the decisions that any musician has to make in refining performance. Involve them in such experiences as:
    a. finding cues in the score for interpreting a composition;
    b. locating lines of rising and falling intensity and identifying the peak of intensity in the expressive line; labeling the feeling generated by different sections of a composition (expectation-uncertainty-resolution-confirmation);
    c. serving as critics of the performance of the group;
    d. hearing two performances of the same composition, selecting the preferable interpretation and justifying the preference;

e. (for interested advanced students) directing the development of the performance of a small group or the large ensemble.

2. In developing repertory for your group, choose for the most part compositions that are sufficiently within the technical grasp of the performers to make an artistic and expressive performance possible.

3. Provide your group with opportunities for copious reading of music at sight.

4. Play recordings and tapes of artistic performances for your group and discuss with your students the factors that contribute to expressive performance.

5. Involve students in all the avenues to musical experience: Stir their imaginations to cultivate responsiveness to the expressive import of music; involve them in making judgments of their own and others' performances; judgments about the style of music, and judgments about its form.

6. Emphasize the development of precise listening skills—hearing their own part in relation to other parts, hearing repetitions and contrast in melodic, rhythmic, and harmonic motion, relating tonal motion to tonality and recognizing the elaboration and development of thematic material.

All music educators, regardless of specialization, should promote a return to the real basics of music education, the development of the ability of all students in the school, to use their own performance for expressive purposes and a return to the real fundamental of music, its expressive import. The primary role of the music program, as for all arts programs, is to stimulate feelingful thought and thoughtful feeling, processes in which the imagination is freed, stimulated, and takes flight. In this role, music education will be in a position to counter the sterility, the depersonalization, the retreat into isolation which pervades contemporary society. In this role, music education will be valued and supported by students and by the public.

Finally, I remind you that responsiveness to music is taught by example and learned by contagion. Only to the extent that we, as music teachers, are moved by the expressive import of music can we lead our students to responsiveness to that import. We must have a firm belief in and demonstrate in our own lives the power and beauty of the art of music. Only then can we fulfill our mission as music educators — to touch the hearts, stir the feeling, and kindle the imaginations of our students.

If we accept this mission and put it into practice, if we realize that music education operates in the realm of feeling and can educate for humanness in an increasingly mechanistic and depersonalized society, music will no longer be considered a frill; but can indeed operate as a core subject lying at the heart of the school curriculum. Music will truly be basic.

Editor's Note: This speech was first published in the Missouri School Music Magazine, Volume 35, Spring 1981, pages 30-31, 40.
Dr. Charles Leonhard (1915-2002) died January 31, 2002
For more information please see: www.charlesleonhardlegacy.com

INTRODUCTION

What is the Music Education Paradigm?

LEE BARTEL

In this book twenty three authors "question the music education paradigm." But, what is it that they are questioning? What is a paradigm? Is there a music education paradigm? And what do these authors believe the music education paradigm to be?

A paradigm is a set of assumptions, concepts, values, and practices that constitutes a way of viewing reality for the community that shares them. In other words, a paradigm leads a group of people to agree "this is how it is and this how it should be." What then is the music education paradigm? Is there a common set of assumptions, concepts, values, and practices that the "music education profession" holds? For example, what is it that we count as music education? Is it what generalist teachers do? Most music educators speak disparagingly about the music efforts of classroom teachers. There seems to be general agreement by the music education profession that music education is that which music specialists do. There may be some disagreement about what specialists should do but not that they should do it. Another fundamental concept and assumption is that if someone is really serious about developing music making proficiency they need to take music lessons – which usually means private, one-on-one music lessons.

This book is divided into sections that are a means to examining the music education paradigm: how we teach, what we teach, for what we teach, what is expected of teachers and how we should teach them, whom we should be teaching, and more generally what are our assumptions and structures. With limited space and a variety of opinion, these areas are not necessarily comprehensive in their examination of these aspects of the paradigm. However, crucial questions are raised and some possibilities are explored. I hope that this exercise in what can be called "applied philosophy," because it is basically issues- driven thinking about "what ought to be," will stimulate more questions and a re-examination of what we understand as "music education."

How we teach

The music education paradigm may be best characterized by the rehearsal model – a teacher/conductor in front of a group of music makers controlling the starts and the stops, correctly diagnosing problems, and effectively prescribing remedies to reach the goal of a flawless performance. Music education today is perhaps more teacher directed than any other aspect of schooling. The reason commonly given for this is sound: music making is noisy and, if all participants are not under central control, classrooms quickly degenerate into chaos. But music education also chooses the rehearsal model because our culture values music making and in the classical tradition the large ensemble is the most prestigious. Consequently we value highly the large symphony orchestras and they are driven by conductors and efficient rehearsal. Music teachers are trained in the tradition and literature and adopt the "model" as the one to aspire to. It becomes a pillar in our paradigm structure.

The macro-structures of school building design influence our possibilities and, therefore, our paradigm as well. Typically music teachers are given less space in the building than physical education teachers. This is of course because we have been perpetuating the large ensemble approach and so do not need very large amounts of square footage except for a concert hall. But if we had the space equivalent of a school gymnasium, we could have adequate sound proof practice rooms to have a program allowing for small group and individual music-making activity. Our present structures perpetuate the rehearsal model of education.

Another "structural" feature of music education is the division between grade levels and school buildings—students undergo major transitions from level to level by moving from one school to another. The present music education paradigm is aligned with the structural divisions and compounds the problem of articulation and transition by introducing very different approaches to music instruction.

Although elementary music is often not conceived as ensemble music, music teachers most commonly use a teacher directed approach derivative of the rehearsal model. Whether it be Orff, Kodaly, a general singing approach, or more varied conceptual programs, classes tend to be traditionally teacher directed.

Music education is proud of the "discipline" created by participation. Music educators have high expectation for promptness, attention, repetitive practice, pursuit of excellence, and perfection (practice makes perfect). We believe the art demands it and justifies the means to achieve it. Consequently, music teachers are often demanding teachers and more than other teachers are "allowed" (and we allow ourselves) to be passionately demanding in ways that may at times approach abuse. The great artistic experience and reward of the wonderful performance justifies the means to achieve it. This fits with the image of the passionate maestro of the great orchestra to whom, until recently, was essentially granted the right to be a psychological and administrative tyrant. This approach, so accepted within the music education paradigm, may also owe something to the militaristic legacy of the band.

What we teach

Another fundamental concept, assumption, and practice of music education is that music is learned formally in school or in lessons. The assumption is that when children enter school or start piano lessons they are essentially a blank slate. So what we teach is a skill sequence, a curriculum, that starts at zero and builds in a continuous spiral to the highest level of performance. Although the reality may not be so in particular schools, districts or regions, we espouse this ideal as seen in any given set of national standards. Programs that do not have this characteristic are considered weak.

Although a continuous curriculum ladder may be an ideal within music education, there is no doubt that the most dominant aspect of what we teach is replication of existing music prescriptions – i.e., learning to read and perform music created by someone else. The converse is what we do not teach – we rarely teach composition. To the extent that jazz has "gone mainstream" in music education, improvisation may be taught at secondary levels, but in general, improvisation and composition have little place within music education as practiced, especially in North America.

If one sees music education essentially as a continuous sequence with a common goal from first grade to the end of high school, whether in school, community, church, or private lessons, one must see the culmination, what it leads to, as the defining characteristic. In this light, the music education paradigm in North America teaches performance. Despite the paranoid protestations of some philosophers that it isn't so although they insist it should be, music education is essentially about developing performance ability.

Consequently, what music education is not about, does not give place to, and does not legitimize within the process of schooling is listening for pleasure. Music educators feel obligated to listen for something. The music education paradigm assumes we will teach children to identify, label, describe, compare, analyze, criticize, but not to allow them to revel, emote, respond, relish, cherish, treasure, or enjoy. Music educators seem to believe that teaching the first list will lead to the second, although it rarely seems to. A related curricular reality is the emphasis on cognitive knowledge and skill and the attendant lack of focus on affective response in all aspects of the music program, including performance.

The music education paradigm is strongly aligned with "classical music" which today includes jazz as concert music, and music theatre. However, there is still an implicit hierarchy of "taste" and, consequently, program definition that favours real (serious) classical music. Along with this is a general intolerance of popular music (which usually means currently popular music – music of the Beatles is now old enough to be acceptable for arrangement and performance, especially by large ensembles in arrangements that "sanitize" it for school use).

The music education paradigm features a strong commitment to the beautiful in music. Beautiful tone, beautiful compositions, beautiful harmony, balance, form, control, clarity. We admit as legitimate the domesticated and socialized sounds of commercially engineered and fabricated instruments. Even human voices are exercised and trained to be acceptable. We have no place for the ugly, the wild sounds, for noise.

For what we teach

Already alluded to in discussing what we teach, music educators consciously or unconsciously assume that they are playing a role in the education of students who will go on to a professional career in music or at least to do what they themselves do. Our curriculum is designed for this. One of the highest compliments we can receive is that someone we taught was inspired to "go into music."

The goal we teach for, and of which we are more conscious, is the student's continuation in the school music program. We "prepare" the student for the next level – for band, choir, or orchestra. There is a considerable aspect of elementary general music that does pursue a general education in music as well as music making in its own right. But, we hope and expect that students will select music in intermediate and secondary school, will participate in the performance ensembles, and so we need to provide the preparation expected of "feeder schools." In this sense we work with primarily short-term goals. We do not seriously consider what a life-long involvement with music might be and design our curriculum and program for this goal.

What is expected of teachers and how we teach them

In general the music education profession expects universities and colleges to prepare teachers to conform to and contribute to the paradigm as already described. The way we do this is to select them on the basis of their success in the music programs, on the basis of their ability to perform on the "authorized" school instruments. Then we teach them in teacher directed classes to do what music teachers do. People tend to teach the way they were taught. For musicians this has often been a long exposure. They value their large performance ensemble experiences highly and see them as their ideal professional involvement. Then typically student teachers are assigned to "apprentice" with experienced teachers considered successful within the paradigm. And when these new teachers graduate and are hired into a system, they are either left to prove themselves through evaluation reinforced conformity or they may be "mentored" by experienced teachers who may well make it their duty to "cure" the novice of any impractical new ideas perpetrated on them by idealists within the university.

One of the fundamental expectations of music educators is that they will get their students to perform – whether it is the kindergarten class at a school assembly, a 4th grade recorder ensemble at a spring concert, or a concert band on tour. This seems to be a cultural norm foisted on us and perpetuated by us in a reciprocal manner. In many places, especially at the high school level, the big performance is the focus of much of the content of music education. Added to this is competition – either blatant within the ensemble or the ensemble in regional or national contests, or subtle in the comparisons with previous ensembles or those in other schools. In many ways strong parallels exist between high school music ensembles that constitute the heart of the program and competitive sports.

Whom we should be teaching

The question of whom we should be teaching applies primarily to intermediate and secondary levels where students are given a choice about participation and, therefore, where music educators are free to design programs that appeal to a particular type of learner. Music educators, administrators, and society in general has come to expect that music beyond elementary school is primarily for the "talented." Music program offerings and expectations are such that there are few entry points because of skill demands. Music educators are not thrilled about teaching the "general student," meaning the student not interested or prepared to participate in the band or choir, and consequently create less than welcoming opportunities for these students. The creation and acceptance of magnet arts schools further shifts the paradigm's evident priority toward the elite performers. The elite teachers, the ones we aspire to become, the "stars" of the paradigm, teach in the elite school contexts.

What are our Foundational Assumptions

A full declaration of the philosophical values and assumption of music education is well beyond the scope here. However, it can be observed that music educators and the prominent philosophers influencing music education have sought philosophical certainty in all matters of relevance. The recent focus by Reimer on experience is an excellent shift. But in general music educators seem to prefer dogma to an ongoing dialectic process and indeterminacy.

The music education paradigm has strong assumptions about gender and music. Music is essentially gendered feminine and, consequently, boys are almost expected to withdraw in greater numbers than girls. However, since societal power structures favour the male, leadership within music – e.g., conducting major ensembles – has been strongly dominated by men. Consequently, feminists have focused on the legitimate needs of girls, but in the process have created another gender imbalance and have ignored the plight of boys in relation to music in our culture.

Conclusion

I have tried to give a general overview of the music education paradigm. I have drawn on the definitions and characterizations given by the authors in this book. Of course no general description is true of everyone in every place. If we define the paradigm in one way, there will be teachers who will say, but that is not what I do. With most paradigms there are exceptions, people on the fringe. Many of the music teachers who say "that is not the music education paradigm because it does not describe what I do" are very self conscious of being "alternative," of being different, of being innovative. The fact that innovation is considered "innovation" simply reinforces the idea that in fact there is a dominant "right way" or accepted way to teach music – the paradigm. And upon examination, most teachers considering themselves different from the paradigm, in fact conform to a substantial portion of it. Just because some people and programs differ from what we describe as "the paradigm" does not negate the definition – it only shows that cracks are appearing in the paradigm, that here and there individuals in practice are questioning the applicability of the paradigm.

I invite you to think about what we do. I invite you to read the various authors and begin an argument with them in your mind. I invite you to open discussions with your colleagues on these issues. I invite you to question the paradigm as defined here. And I invite you to question the paradigm as you understand it yourself.

SECTION 1:

QUESTIONING HOW WE TEACH

JENNIFER BULLER PETERS
THEY ARE NOT A BLANK SCORE

LINDA CAMERON & KATIE CARLISLE
WHAT KIND OF SOCIAL CLIMATE DO WE CREATE IN OUR MUSIC CLASSROOMS?

LEE BARTEL & LINDA CAMERON
FROM DILEMMAS TO EXPERIENCE: SHAPING THE CONDITIONS OF LEARNING.

MARY KENNEDY
PUT THE "PLAY" BACK IN MUSIC EDUCATION

KATHARINE SMITHRIM & RENA UPITIS
MUSIC FOR LIFE: CONTAMINATED BY PEACEFUL FEELINGS

CHAPTER ONE

They Are Not A Blank Score

JENNIFER BULLER PETERS

Abstract

Current music education practice has been criticized for its lack of power, its disconnect between institutional musical experience and musical experience in every day life, and an over emphasis on large performance models of education. Music educators struggle to incorporate principles of constructivism and cooperative learning in their classrooms as learned and accepted pedagogical practice is often rigid and encourages passivity on the parts of teachers and students alike. In order to create life affirming and transforming music education programs, music educators need to develop a deep respect for the process of musical enculturation, the role of informal learning in the classroom, and the complex, chaotic, and non-linear nature of learning. We cannot do this if we do not step back and examine fully the music curriculum that is offered to our students via the media, and the role the media plays in, not only the building of identity, but also the contemporary culture of our students and the musical fabric of society as a whole. Music educators need to become media educators and in doing so will bring new ideas and refreshing, relevant, and engaging concepts into the classroom for students to explore.

Introduction

My interest in the media and its relationship to music education began while working as a summer arts camp instructor. I was fascinated by, on the one hand, the over-arching presence of music and the media on the camp as a whole, and on the other, the initial refusal of students to connect the music "class" I was teaching to all of this music in their lives. The very moment students entered my classroom they went from kids who were excited about summer and being at camp to kids who were wary and suspicious. It was as if they had already decided that whatever it was we were going to be doing in music class, it was certainly not going to be fun. At the very time that this was going on, I discovered that the karaoke room down the hall was one of the most popular spots on campus. There one could find singing voices, moving and swaying bodies, laughter and enthusiasm. I realized that there was something very wrong with this picture and I spent the rest of my summer trying to (as many others in the music education profession have) readjust it.

A few years later my nephew Zachary was born and I have since watched him grow into a very intelligent musical being, all without the assistance of any kind of formal education. Zachary has built his musical knowledge through informal learning experiences, and day-to-day interactions with the world. He has become an avid music and media consumer – his world filled with television programs, videos, DVD's, music recordings, computer games, books, radio, and the list goes on. These media sources will become powerful and complex forces in Zach's life and cannot be defined so much by their value (because the media cannot be simply delineated as "good" or "bad") but by their very pervasiveness. The mass media, in fact, has been defined as the "Second God...everywhere and nowhere" (Ying, 2003, p. 1). Still, when Zach first enters a school music classroom at age 6 or 7, he will be treated (despite well meaning lip-service to the opposite) that he knows nothing about music. The music teacher will assume he is a blank slate. He will have to begin at the beginning, instead of in the middle, as he is used to in his complex media environment with sounds, images, and knowledge coming at him from every direction. He will have to start with the basics, even though he may already have a working knowledge of them. In time, this musical being may become like the four out of five boys who believ(e) that they are "not" good at singing and music, like the one out of two boys who does not even like singing, like the group of students who wish for more visual arts (56%), but not more music in school (Upitis, Smithrim, Patteson & Meban, 2000). The truth music educators must face is that when Zachary, and every other child, comes to school, he is not a blank slate. He is already musically educated.

Zachary is not an unusual child and is by no means alone in his media use; an important and recent study by the Kaiser Foundation and the Children's Digital Media Centers (2003) found that children as young as nine months old are being targeted by major entertainment media conglomerates. Very little is known, though, about how children this young actually engage with the media, or how it effects their social, physical, and academic development. Rideout, Vandewater & Wartella, (2003) explain:

> The rapid changes in our media environment have not been accompanied by a similar growth in our knowledge of how media may impact children's cognitive, social emotional or physical development. These issues are of great importance not only to parents, but also to educators, health providers, policy-makers and advocates. Many experts have argued that it is especially critical to understand media use by the youngest children, noting that because social and intellectual and (musical) development are more malleable in these early years, media use at this age could have an especially significant impact. (p. 3)

I would argue that the issue of media and its impact on children of all ages is also of great importance to music educators. Children learn *about* music through the mass media; they also *experience* music through the mass media. For many children the media will be their first music teacher, and because the media plays such an integral role in our lives, perhaps their most important music teacher. If we put any stock at all in Marshall McLuhan's words, who suggested that all forms of media are technological extensions of the human body, and that all, "like poetry" ingrain in the user their own subtle assumptions (Marchand, 2002), music educators will realize that experiencing music through the mass media potentially alters and changes our students' musical perceptions. And yet music educators seem to singularly ignore the media, if what *actually* happens in a music classroom is used as any indication. We might think about the media, we might try to include a few popular selections from the Disney movies our students know so well, but do we make any real changes in our practice based on the music education that is already being delivered to our students via the media?

School music educators face many complex struggles in the current political and educational climate today (Woodford, in press, Hanley, 2000). We will have to start making

3

changes if we are going to successfully meet these challenges. Perhaps we can even strive beyond the goal of making music programs merely relevant in students' lives, to creating music programs that are truly life affirming and life lasting. If this is to happen, we must take into account the media, its influence on children's musical lives, and the potential role it can play in the classroom.

Talking about the media and music education is complex and before going any further with my critique of music education as it is experienced by many (not all) students in schools today, I must offer a definition of the media and how I use that term in relation to music education throughout the rest of this chapter. The media can be thought of as "all systematic ways of representing who we are individually and collectively" (Fisherkeller, 2000, p. 597). In other words, the media (plural of medium) refers to all the ways that human beings have developed in order to communicate with one another including the invention of the alphabet, language, the printing press, music, recorded music on CD's, DVD's newspapers, magazines, television, radio, film, video, internet, all digital technology, computers, the telephone, fax machines...the list goes on and continues to change along with the growth and speed of technology, every day. We learn about and experience music through the media (on television or in a film, for example) and at the same time can consider music its own medium. The educational strategies, pedagogies, and methodologies that we use as music educators can also be considered media, because through them we teach students and communicate certain messages about music. If we place any merit in McLuhan's "the medium is the message," a statement that communicates perfectly the idea that how we do something greatly influences the results we obtain, regardless of our initial intent (Strate, 2003), this is tremendously important. Further, the development of new digital media will continue to change and affect how we experience music (Gouzouasis, 1995).

Finally, the world of the media is complex, multifaceted, and involving multiple and conflicting value systems. Media messages, whether about music or not, are necessarily contradictory and chaotic. That the media is affecting children is unquestionable, but the how and why are not so easily ascertained. Media effects and influences have to be seen as multi-directional, not linear and uni-directional as so many in the media effects field would have us believe. The media involves individuals, as well as political and social institutions that both consume and produce media, sometimes critically and actively and at other times, thoughtlessly and inactively. On its largest level, "media defines cultures and cultures define media" (Gouzouasis, 1995, p. 16).

Critique of Music Education

An awareness of the media and its role in the musical fabric of society is vital if we are going to both understand the contemporary culture and identity of our students and design meaningful and engaging music education programs. The purpose of this chapter, then, is twofold: to explore the influence of the media on music education and musical enculturation and to examine potential implications for classroom practice. Though discussions involving change require a critique of current practice, I do not wish to make the unfortunate assumption that everything that has come before and is going on now is completely faulty and in need of fixing. While there are many issues, both theoretical and practical that music educators need to address, there are also places where music in the lives of children and their teachers is alive and flourishing. Music is a human activity, involving relationships on many levels, and like any human endeavor, is rarely fixed in an unmoving state. Music education is always changing, shifting, and evolving and this can be difficult to capture in a paper critique like the one that I am about to offer.

The Power of Music

An examination of the music education literature reveals two important issues relevant to this discussion on the media. On the one hand the power of music is demonstrated over and over again. Music allows us to express our humanness in a way like no other. Bowman (2002) explains:

> One of the most important reasons people are musical is that such experience restores unity and wholeness to body and mind, drawing upon human powers and experiential dimensions that lie dormant and neglected where sound figures marginally or does not figure at all. People are musical because the unique phenomenal nature of music...fosters experience with a richness and complexity found almost nowhere else in the world (p. 59).

We come "hard-wired" for music (Cohen & Trehub, 1999) and share, as humans, a compulsion to communicate, to share meanings, to participate, and to explore the possibilities of life. We can do things metaphorically through the language of music (Small, 2000). Musical experiences allow us to play, providing opportunities to experience life and even ourselves in new and unique ways (Stubley, 1993). Such experiences can lead to a dynamic restructuring on both individual and cultural levels (Stubley, 1993, Attali, 1985). Musical experiences also connect us to our evolutionary roots – humans have been making music for over 40,000 years. This collective consciousness is a very powerful and compelling force and we continue to make music and experiment with sound. We do this, says Anthony Palmer (2002), "...not because it is nice to do so, or because we have spare time, but because it is a psychic imperative" (p. 46).

On the other hand, and very ironically, the power expressed by these words does not seem to be reflected in the school classroom. Research by Kennedy (2000) has shown that a very small number of high school students are involved in arts education in Canada and an even smaller number (in comparison to visual arts) are involved in music education. At the same time, non-music students are actively using and consuming music outside of school (Ross, 1995, Gembris, 2002). As Smithrim & Upitis (2003) note, though the students who are involved in school music programs may well remember their musical experiences warmly "any tangible value-added to graduates' musical lives is not evident" (Regelski, 2002, 114). I have often wondered, as likely others have in the music education profession, how many school band students are still musically active and playing their instruments years after graduation.

A similar situation emerges in the lives of elementary school students. Upitis, Smithrim, Patteson & Meban (2001) found that of 7000 elementary school students surveyed in Canada, only 21% of fourth graders wanted more music in school. The researchers explain that while this could mean students were "satisfied" with their music programs, it was more likely that most of the students neither found much value in their music classes nor wanted to spend more time in similar musical activity. This explanation makes sense in light of other statistics that emerged in the study. By grade four only one in five boys thinks he is good at singing, and only 27% of both girls and boys think they are good at music. Yet listening to music is reported as the "most favored" after school activity by 83% of the students. Looking at these statistics I find myself asking the identical questions authors Smithrim and Upitis asked at the conclusion of their study (2003): "Where is the power of music in our lives? Is it ever in school? And when it is in school, what does it look like? Taste like? Feel like? Sound like?" (p. 12).

Part of the problem may lie in the fact that we cannot, as a profession, decide what music education should be for (Regelski, 2002, Jorgensen, 1997). We tend to ask questions about methodology and pedagogy before asking why we are teaching music in the first place. What kind of values do we want to instill in our students? What are our musical long-term life goals for students? When we fail to answer these questions, methods and teaching strategies can become narrow and aimless, hurting teachers and limiting the strength and influence of our music education programs. Jorgensen (1997) explains:

> The fact that instructional methods have been worked out to a high degree of sophistication and defended as dogma is oppressive to teachers. It fosters their dependence on methods and those who promote them on passivity, timidity, meritocracy, technocratic attitudes and behaviors, and even anti-intellectualism construed as a lack of interest in and reflection about questions that underlie practice (p 91).

If music teachers cannot practice critical thinking, music students should not be expected to either!

Enculturation

In our preoccupation with questions of pedagogy and methodology we not only neglect to consider what music education is for; we also neglect the role of enculturation and informal learning in student's musical lives. Martin Buber (1965) once observed that a teacher is "only one element amidst the fullness of life" (in Bresler & Thompson, 2002, p. 9). In other words, children will learn from everything that they experience – "nature and the social context, the house and the street, language and custom, the world of history and the world of daily news in the form of rumour, of broadcast and newspaper (and media), music and technical science, play and dream – everything together..." (Buber, p. 9). In this respect, music education can be seen as going on all the time, everywhere, not just in school. The process of enculturation and the musical development of children are frequently discussed in the music education literature (Nettl, 2002, Campbell, 2002, 1998, Harwood, 1994, 1987, Merrill Mirsky, 1988, Ridell, 1996). Research by Zenatti (1993) has shown that, because of the enculturative aspects of the mass media, progressively younger and younger children are able to distinguish between major and minor harmonies, as well as elements of melody. Experiments by Lamont (1998) also reveal that informal, enculturative musical experiences (like those provided through the media, family and friends) may be more important in young children's musical lives than formal instrument training. Serafine (1988) comes to a similar conclusion:

> What is amazing about the acquisition of music by the young is not that they eventually play instruments and pieces on which they have been instructed by their elders, but rather that they know the subtler things which no one has told them about: what counts as order of music, what features should be attended to, what makes melodies similar and different, what properly makes a tune end, and so forth (p. 5).

6

In her experiments with children Serafine found, like Lamont, that age, general cognitive growth, and normal everyday music experience were better predictors of success on musical tasks (like pitch discrimination, or patterning) than formal instrumental training.

The process of enculturation ensures that all children will be, in many ways, fully functioning musical beings by the time they get to school. Enculturation will also remain an integral source of knowledge and values as they grow into adulthood (Campbell, 1988). If music educators want their programs to matter in the lives of their students they will have to do more then pay lip service to the enculturation process. Truly embracing a constructivist framework of education which will take into account personal experience, the social contexts of learning, and all the knowledge, meanings and understandings a child comes to school with will require nothing more (Wiggins, 2001, Vitale, 2002, Smithrim, 2002). This has been discussed frequently in the music education literature by researchers including Bartel & Cameron 2001, Campbell, 1998, Smithrim, 2002, Wiggins, 2001, and Rinaldo, 2003. Music educators tend to talk a good game, but how are we doing in practice?

Pedagogical Practice

An appropriate first step in respecting the process of enculturation would be to ensure that the sounds that first greet our students when they walk through our classroom doors are sounds they are most accustomed to hearing – the music of their everyday lives. Elliott (1995) explains:

> The musical practices we select for music teaching and learning at the outset of a child's musical education ought to make the most of the tacit dimensions of musicianship - prodecural, informal, impressionistic, and supervisory musical knowings - that children begin to develop themselves through early musicing and listening in their own cultural contexts...teachers ought to take account of a student's *musical memosphere*. For the musical knowings that infants and young children achieve on their own amount to a bridge between young brains and young musical minds." (p. 211)

The most familiar sounds to our students will be popular or Afro-American in style, yet a study on vernacular music reveals that our teaching methodologies do not reflect this content (McCarthy, unpublished). Many music educators in North America feel that popular music is vastly inferior to other musics and is virtually a waste of time in the classroom (Woodford, in press). When we do teach popular music it is often because we feel that we have to in order to pacify students and "progress" to music we consider more worthwhile (better known as the stepping stone strategy, or "bait and switch"). It is unusual for popular music to be taught authentically, as if it warranted intensive criticism and examination (Woodford, in press). If music education is going to be meaningful and relevant to students' lives, music educators will need to come to terms with the simple fact that people are rarely enculturated into classical music with the same kind of strength they are popular music (Green, 2001). This acknowledgment must be reflected in our teaching practices and not just our words.

As music educators we will also have to examine our pedagogical practices and strategies if we are to fully take into account the process of enculturation. In general, music educators tend to rely heavily on teacher directed, carefully sequenced, and overly prescriptive methodologies like those of Orff, Kodaly, and many influential instrumental music educators. We seem to feel that formal music education should begin at square one and proceed from there. This is in part due to the fact that we feel we have to make music as academic as any other subject in order to justify its position in the school curriculum. Our good intentions aside, what often results is that many students are treated as if they know very little about music when they enter a classroom for the first time. For example, a student from Toronto experiencing an early Kodaly lesson and learning to sing doh-mi-so etc. will most likely have heard this particular progression hundreds of times (on the radio, the music from their computer games, even from the familiar ring to the subway doors opening and closing) and might even know what kind of musical context to place it in, if given the chance.

Further, beliefs that music learning will always universally progress most effectively when instruction is organized in a sequence of linear steps that supposedly match students' developmental needs (Montgomery, 2000) while pervasive and difficult to counter, are not necessarily true. It is certainly not how students naturally learn outside of the classroom and the complexity of their outside musical expressions reflect this (Green, 2001, Campbell, 1998). When students have the freedom to play and to choose what it is they want to do in their classroom, their activities look very little like the typically planned music experiences of most teachers (Smithrim, 1997, Littleton, 1991). As Smithrim observes, students neither march with their instruments, play traditional singing games, nor sing any ta-ta-ti-ti-tas. Students learn through immersion and experimentation; they do not follow peer instructions; they do not try to impose a logical order from the outside on what it is they are doing.

Small (1977) suggests that music educators need to embrace the idea that "there are as many ways into knowledge as there are people, that the logical, straight-line arrangement of syllabuses, with their linear progression from one stage to another, is based on a fantasy about the way humans learn" (p. 219). I find his suggestion very applicable to music education today. Children's minds and natural learning patterns are often at odds with current educational materials and practices; this may be the reason why many children do not succeed at school and why even successful students have difficulty transferring their knowledge in new situations (Gardner, 1995, Campbell, 2002).

When we acknowledge that learning is a haphazard and chaotic process, and that there can be "method in madness," we will gain the confidence to allow our students to play and experiment (Green, 2001). We will no longer miss out on the multiple teaching moments that arise when students have some freedom to decide what they would like to do in music class – the ones that we cannot predict with our scripts and lesson plans (Eisner, 1997). Students might even reflect more musical ability than we give them credit for. I would also suggest that such an acknowledgement could potentially breathe some life into the sometimes "endulling" process of music education (Shore, 1992).

Music educators are not only guilty of teaching music as if there were only one way to learn, they are also guilty of emphasizing learning products and outcomes at the expense of honouring the learning process. It may well be helpful to teachers to identify broad learning outcomes and objectives, but if we continually focus on these products, rather than process, we run the risk of neglecting, rather than nurturing, student learning. Further, "by focusing learning on specific objectives there exists the inherent danger of limiting the learning of concepts that may be tangential to the expectation" (Rinaldo, 2002, p. 24). This is so obviously counterproductive that I wonder why we even bother with wanting to develop national standards in music education in the first place. My thoughts are echoed by Smithrim and Upitis (2003) who claim that standardization of curricula is actually doing the opposite of what it was meant to do – "making music an academically important subject" (p. 16).

We work so hard at ensuring that our students can produce the skills and knowledge outlined in provincial curriculum documents, and yet somehow we are still left questioning why music education does not seem to have any lasting influence on our students. I suggest this is because we continually (and perhaps inadvertently) give our students the wrong sorts of tools (Campbell, 2002). In our narrow practice of emphasizing rote learning, performance over composition, and the development of basic musical skills unconnected to real music practice, we fail to "engage students in those kinds of discourses and creative activities that contribute significantly to the construction of their individualized musical selves" (Woodford, 1997, p 16) and I would add, the development of genuine musical understanding. Students leave our classrooms not really knowing what all that music was really for. And after all, what is the point of knowing various conceptual elements of music and not being able to use them (Green 2001)?

On the other hand, when we allow our students the freedom to explore what it means to learn and how to learn, when we present students problems and projects that will draw meaningfully on their more basic skills, when they can enjoy the journey and have some fun along the way, students will leave our classrooms with the tools that they need to be successful, life long music learners and makers.

We also need to take into account the fact that our pedagogical practices seem mostly geared towards "enabling" students to play in large performance ensembles. I use the word "enabling" ironically, because such ensembles are usually teacher directed and based on a "rehearsal model" rather than a collaborative model of education. Bartel (2000) explains:

> In the music class the large ensemble still rules. The teacher is the conductor. The teacher must know all the music and be able to make all musical decisions. The students obey, conform, and "recite" the correct answers (or musical phrases). Otherwise the band will not be ready for the required concerts, the standard will not be up to collegial expectation, and the reputation of the teacher (conductor) and ensemble (symphony orchestra) will not be noteworthy (p. 25).

The problem with this model is that it is often considered elitist, miseducative (Bartel & Cameron, 2001) and even violent (O'Toole, 1997, Lamb, 1996). Bartel & Cameron (2000) suggest that in the quest for excellence, music teachers may also potentially send the message to students that, because of a lack of talent and musical ability, they are not welcome in music-making activities. Overall, as researchers and teachers we are hearing far too many stories about children being told to "mouth the words" in choir practices, about teachers who do not allow their students the freedom to either express, or discover how to express themselves musically. It is no wonder that school music programs lack the power to make a difference in students' lives in the long term.

When we fail to link school music to students' lives beyond the classroom, when we forget that it is the process rather than products of musical learning that will stay with our students for life (and allow them to become active musical participants in their adult lives), when we do not respect the process of enculturation and the role of informal learning in education music in school loses its life affirming qualities. Music class, to use what some educators might consider a trite word, is no longer *fun*. Smithrim (1997) includes a profound quote in her study on play in preschool music education: "Dare to err and to dream; a higher meaning often lies in childish play" and I think we need to keep her words in mind, whether we are teaching four and five year-olds, or fifteen and sixteen year-olds. Even the most successful artists need to have a little fun. Respected dance choreographer Twyla Tharp (2003) explains:

> The call to the creative life is not supposed to be torture. Yes, it's hard work and you have to make sacrifices. Yes, it's a noble calling; you're volunteering in an army of sorts, alongside a phalanx of artists who have preceded you, many of whom are your mentors and guides...They form a tradition that you have implicitly sworn to protect, even while you aim to refashion it and sometimes even shatter it. But, it's also suppose to be fun. (p. 201)

To play, to have fun, and to be entertained (or to entertain oneself) are qualities that have to be palpable in a music class from the moment a student walks through the door (Green, 2001). The word entertainment is an equally dangerous term for educators; keep in mind it also means to be *engaged*. When children are engaged the notions of agonizing discipline, practice, and hard work, which seem to be such an integral part of the school performance experience (and a turn off to many students), need not even enter into the equation. As Small (1997) has explained: "Anyone who wants badly enough to do something will discipline himself to do it, and in fact will scarcely think in terms of discipline at all." His assertion is supported by research, particularly in Green's (2001) study on popular musicians in England. These musicians, as young students, practiced and explored their instruments for five or six hours a day in the early stages of their development. They found this "work" to be stimulating, highly enjoyable, and fun - qualities that are at times underrated or even missing from many a music education class.

I do not want to believe that Swanwick was right when he said "music is not a problem until it is institutionalized" (in Campbell, 1998, p. 183), but music educators have many challenges to address in order to prove him wrong. An important first step to take is to acknowledge that there are many sources of music education in a child's life and that formal education may not necessarily offer the most favorable environment. Runfola and Swanwick (2002) write:

> Much work remains to be done on musical learning outside of instructional programs as a part of lifelong enculturation and on the effect of different levels of instructional framing, especially less-directive and more loosely sequenced or informal teaching and learning in the early stages of ones development. The future of music education may not depend so much on schools as we know them, but on things such as opportunities in local communities and the global communities of the Web. (p. 393)

Perhaps, music educators can learn from these "different opportunities" and offer students a more dynamic and relevant kind of music education within our classrooms.

Media and Enculturation

Of course, one of these "different" learning opportunities is found in the media. We cannot neglect the fact that the body of knowledge represented by popular culture and the mass media is significant, on many levels, in the lives of our students (Giroux, 1989, Willis, 1990). Those involved in media related fields are as much educators as are school-teachers. Take the example of television, for a moment:

> Television is everywhere in our lives, widening our world, and shaping our outlook. Television is America's home entertainer, instant informer, a living room salesman, a babysitter, a time waster, and mass marketer of culture. Familiar as we are with television we consistently overlook one of the functions it performs relentlessly, day in and day out: education. Television is America's (most) neglected teacher. (Morrisset, cited in Berry, 1993, p. 103)

Media decision makers influence what music children will hear and at what age they will hear it. They introduce children to a variety of musical heritages and styles; they instruct children in the forms, conventions, and uses of music in everyday life. Most importantly, they impart specific musical values whether they are consciously aware of those values or not. Many are also aware of the role that they play as educators. They want to get the message out to children that music is powerful, and that music is something one can engage in at every stage of life (Buller, 2003). As one television personality expressed it: "Music is not a spectator sport" (Buller, 2003, p. 34).

Of course, these are not the only messages that are being communicated to children – the media music curriculum is, as previously discussed chaotic, inconsistent, and offering multiple and conflicting messages (Cortes, 2000). It is because of these very qualities, however, that the media's messages and music should be critically explored in the classroom. It is clear that those involved in the media do not always program "high quality" music. And yet, whatever teachers may personally feel about the media music curriculum, their feelings may be irrelevant in the eyes of students. Children will put their creativity to work when they listen to music, whether or not it is considered prepackaged, mindless drivel by adults, and that is something we, as educators, cannot deny. Campbell (1998) aptly describes in *Songs in their Heads* the role mediated commercial music plays in children's lives. They "sing, move and groove" to it, but also use it in their games and activities on the playground. Not surprisingly, children also combine the commercial music they are exposed to through the media with the musical lore handed down through the generations to create new kinds of interactions and musical cross-fertilizations (Harwood, 1994). It could even be said that popular music, as delivered by the mass media, is the folk music of today (Campbell, 1998). So why do we ignore it and continue to teach using only folksongs of the past?

In the end, to force children to separate media culture and personal experience from the school classroom is to turn a world of color into a world of black and white, in essence, denying that children have expressions and thoughts about their lives and their place in contemporary society. This denial sends a message to students that music in school is not for or about them – their ideas, their relationships, their identity, and everyday life. Music is a disconnected and arbitrary activity taught by a teacher out of a movable cart.

What is music education for?

Before I go any further in my discussion on how an awareness of the media and its role in the music education of children can positively change music education in our classrooms, I have to return, for a moment, to the question of what music education should be for (otherwise I am guilty of the same criticisms I have made in my critique). Regelski (2002) suggests that students graduating from music programs should possess the ability to be able to "musically self actualize independently of the teacher" (p. 113). In other words, students should leave our programs being able to make and enjoy music, whatever music that may be. We need to as, Small (1998) describes, "provide that kind of social context for informal as well as formal music interaction that leads to real development and to the musicalizing of the society as a whole" (p. 208). Students should be able to think critically and musically for themselves and understand the many diverse roles that music plays in our culture. As mentioned before, this is just one of the reasons why the media's musical messages must be included in our classes. We are bombarded by sound and music in our lives, and that music and sound does not just provide a benign wallpapering or back drop to the more important issues in life. Woodford explains: "Music can be used to celebrate love, sex, religion or patriotism, but it can just as easily be used to stoke excessive, patriotic, nationalistic, religious, or sexual fervor and thus channel, distort, or wipe out thought. It can even literally be used as a weapon of humiliation and torture..." (in press, p.49). He quotes examples of US marines using the music of AC/DC to aid in the forced surrender of General Noriega, of Croat prisoners being coerced to sing Serb songs by their captors and of American soldiers forcing continuous rock music on Al Queda prisoners to cause disorientation before interrogation to make his case. If we want students to not only be critical consumers of music, but also freely acting participants in the musical society in which we live in, we will have to explore all of music's diverse uses within the walls of the school classroom. We will have to become media educators as well as music educators. In our fast paced, and ever- changing media environment, the two can hardly be separated.

Implications

The most important question to be asked, of course, is what does all of this mean? What would a classroom look like where the media, the process of enculturation and informal learning, and the principles of constructivism played an integral and foundational role? In his book, *The Unschooled Mind*, Gardner (1991) asks his readers to imagine students attending museums and science centers (where children would explore various "exhibitions" and disciplines, all the while learning alongside adult practitioners and older students) instead of formal schools. He understands that his suggestion may be met with some disbelief. After all, Gardner explains, "the connotations of the two types of institutions could scarcely be more different. 'Museum' means an occasional, casual, entertaining and enjoyable outing...school in contrast connotes a serious, regular, formal, deliberately decontextualized institution" (p. 202). His suggestions are radical, but necessary. The educational power of children's museums and art galleries, in contrast to many formal schools, is obvious to any one walking into, for example the, Art Gallery of Ontario, the Royal Ontario Museum, or The Smithsonian on a typical Saturday afternoon. Gardner explains this "dramatic" reversal by looking directly towards the world of the media:

> On the one hand, youngsters live in a time of unparalleled excitement, where even the less privileged are exposed daily to attractive media and technologies, ranging from video games to space exploration, from high speed transportation to direct and immediate means of communication. In many cases, these media can be used to create compelling products. Activities that might once have engaged youngsters –

reading in classrooms or hearing teachers lecture about remote subjects – seem hopelessly tepid and unmotivating to most of them. On the other hand, science museums and children's museums have become the loci for exhibitions, activities, and role models drawn precisely from those domains that do engage youngsters; their customary wares represent the kinds of vocations, skills, and aspirations that legitimately animate and motivate students. (p. 202)

If students look like they are having a great deal of fun while at the museum or science center, they are also learning a tremendous amount about the world and themselves. "Fun" leads to a profound sense of personal involvement and engagement – the very qualities we want students to experience in music class. Project-based learning programs, incidentally, like the ones Gardner explores, are being implemented in schools across Canada by governments and other private institution initiatives (like the *Royal Conservatory of Music's Learning Through the Arts* program) and are experiencing great success. One particular school, James Ling, in Montreal has had a complete turn around in drop out rates, and absenteeism after a three year pilot program. Students at James Ling report their school as being very artistic, the classrooms decorated much like their own bedrooms. Because students are active and engaged in learning, school has become relevant to their lives. They feel a sense of pride and fulfillment, something many have never experienced (High Hopes, CBC Special Report).

If project-based learning can have such an effect on a student body as whole, think of what it will do for music education programs specifically. Music educators may feel strongly that music education programs, by their very nature are already "project-based" – students learn and perform various pieces, for example, on a variety of instruments. They may be active working on their own compositions, or doing research on a listening topic. I would suggest, however, that students are not always aware that they are working on a project. They might not have a strong sense of the role that they play, or feel that they had a part in deciding what projects were going to be worked on and in which direction they were going to go. Music students need to get up out of their chairs, away from their "conductor" teachers and even the physical space of the music room itself. They need to get out into the wider musical world whether that be within the confines of the school, or outside of it. They need to experience the links between music, their outside lives, and topics they may be learning about in other classes. In other words, music learning needs to be integrated, involving multiple skills and knowledge sets.

So what would a music "museum" look like? What kinds of exhibits and hands on activities would we include for our students? What kind of sound "sculptures" would fill the air? What if students were involved in putting together the exhibits, in deciding what it was about music, and how music is experienced that they could share with their teachers and peers? Certainly the media would play a role. Children's emotional investments in the mass media cannot be underestimated, a fact easily demonstrated by any parent trying to tear a three year old away from a riveting episode of *Bob the Builder*, or a teenager from a computer game. Students would naturally turn to their most major and emotionally connected source of musical experience in putting together exhibits and activity centers; in doing so, music education would be infused with some of the power it so desperately needs. Because students would be involved alongside teachers in deciding what it was they wanted to learn, their musical memospheres, including popular or other forms of world music, would have a better chance of being authentically represented. Exhibits and activities would also be holistic – encompassing and reflecting the real world. Basic musical skills would have to be taught and explored because they would be necessary for undertaking long-term projects and explorations. Teachers would have the important role of offering guidance, of pointing out musical possibilities, of finding musical projects (because students do not in every case know what it is they want or ought to learn), of encouraging students on their musical journeys and helping students manage the highs and lows of learning.

Let me take a step further, and make a suggestion that is perhaps more surprising than the one Gardner makes. What if a music education classroom looked like the production of a really well put together children's TV show? A show that, much like Mr. Dress-up, Sesame Street, or Street Cents, for older students, leaves a lasting legacy in the lives of its viewers? A show in which the students of the class were not only the actors on the set, but also the producers and directors? Educational television shows for kids are usually organized around some sort of plot or narrative background. Programs for preschool children, for example, typically involve a few central characters (that might be either adults, or puppets) and children from the "neighborhood" who come over to visit. They spend the "day" in various activities – playing, learning, making music, or just plain old fooling around etc. The purpose is to create a sense of adventure and a magical world in which kids can, as one children's television actor, described it "play and sing all day long" (Buller, 2003, 35) and at the same time, learn the kinds of social or academic skills they will need when they enter school. Programs for middle school children and teenagers have to be designed with more atmosphere – they look and sound cool if they are successful. A show like Street Cents depicts young adults critically analyzing the ways in which money, marketing, and consumerism work in our society. After watching, kids walk away with a sense of empowerment and the self-confidence to use their own skills and abilities. They can "be" every bit as smart as adults, perhaps even smarter, and still have fun!

With these ideas in mind, what kind of plot or narrative structure can teachers use when designing their music education programs? How can teachers create the same sense of adventure and magic that are such an integral part to the most successful shows? Narrative and story telling forms of media are enormously powerful forces that both shape identity and culture. We need to, not to take the emphasis away from *music*, put them to use in the music education classroom. At the start of learning teacher and student must have a vision for what is going to happen in the classroom; a narrative structure can help form this vision. The creation of this vision answers the essential education questions: "What is this music class going to taste like? Feel like? Sound like?" (Smithrim & Upitis 2003, p. 12) What roles are students and teachers going to play? Will there be any outside guests? Which parts of the musical world will be explored? How will we present what we have found and created? The same questions that a children's television producer must answer, a teacher must answer also. In answering these questions, we might also find ourselves moving away from the just "large" performance ensemble model of music education (a limited narrative structure, indeed, in light of the roles that can be played as composers, producers, listeners and other kinds of performers).

A television model of education also gives teachers the opportunity to explore how musical basics can be taught in an engaging and entertaining manner. Basics often form the foundation for many children's education programs. They are, however, usually put to some meaningful use, or are explored in a colorful, game-like manner (like learning the order of numbers through a song, and brightly animated shapes and pictures on Sesame Street). I am not in any way suggesting that music education should be about gimmicks and cheap tricks. I believe that music is a profound expression of what it means to be human in particular cultures, at particular points in time; this needs to be honestly reflected in our programs. That said, I do not find anything wrong with adding a bit of colour, zip, and spice in order to get things going. Making music education more fun is part of making music education more relevant in students' lives. In this respect there is much that teachers can glean from children's programs and vice versa, much that children's television producers can learn from music educators.

My personal vision of a school music classroom is one where students focus on creating and experiencing music similar to the ways they do outside of the classroom - through a media context. I want my students to see themselves as powerful creators equal to the same people who target them with advertisements, films, popular music, music videos, and commercial goods. Projects could include recording and producing their own CD's and DVD's (down to liner notes and the art on the cover), creating soundscapes and soundtracks to their own video and film productions, creating music to go along with their favorite picture books, or even writing their own stories along with music, producing television commercials, exploring the sounds and music of different cultures, and presenting their findings through a variety of representations (through music, language etc. – all media sources). The list can go on and is limited only by the imagination. In order to reflect the emotional investments and connections my students experience in the media on an everyday basis outside of school, my pedagogical strategies would naturally have to include the kinds of media sources students are acculturated through beyond the walls of the classroom (Gouzouasis, 1995). Since there is every chance that my students may be even more adept at dealing with technology than I am, we would have to find ways to work together and share knowledge. I would be forced to make a commitment to lifelong learning in order to keep up with or stay ahead of my students.

If I had a problem with popular music I would likely end up acknowledging that popular music in the classroom is nothing to fear or dread. I might even find that, as Nicholls (1976) describes, when popular music is used creatively and explored in a contextualized manner "...children (and teachers) will find that they are capable of producing more interesting pop music than is sold to them." He goes on to explain that "this could provide a formidable rival to the 'establishment pop,' pop of the mass media!" (in Green, 2001, p. 201). As my students learned to use music basics in entertaining and meaningful ways, they would, at the same time, learn to critically reflect on the music that is "fed" to them via the mass media and mechanical commercialism.

This is what the "story" of my classroom looks like. Which brings me to another point. Authentic changes in music education will not emerge if we continue to impose a linear and sequential order of learning on our students. Using a television, museum, or apprenticeship model of education might make our programs look different on the outside, but internally there is the possibility that they will remain much the same.

To make an alternative suggestion let me return for a moment to the description I gave of my nephew Zachary at the beginning of this chapter – learning in the "middle" as he does in his complex media environment with sights and sounds coming at him from every direction. When I think of Zachary and how he learns I think of chaos, complexity, and simplicity all at the same time. My thoughts, appropriately, find resonance and explanation in the theories of complexity and chaos. Complexity and chaos theory deal with the study and explanation of changes generated within dynamic systems – the search for order in disorder. As Bartel and Radocy (2002) note, complexity can be defined by the interconnectedness of multiple elements, layers and dimensions, "all of which may depend on or influence the other, neither of which is in a fixed relationship or quantity, nor is related to a fixed behavior" (p. 1112).

Zachary is a complex system; he lives within multiple complex systems. And yet somehow within this chaotic and non-linear environment he searches out patterns, relations, and forms – the order embedded in the chaos. New experiences, which, in essence, teach Zach his place in the world, musical or otherwise, require him to construct constructs, or what Bartel (2002) refers to as " bits of knowledge" (p. 54). Constructs can be simple, or more complex, but whatever their form, they will have to organized within larger systems in order to create understanding. Constructs also grow in complexity with new experiences – links between different constructs are formed which continue to spiral out in a kind of three-dimensional spider web. The directions in which Zach's spider web are going to grow on any given day are impossible to predict because all of the elements of his life are interdependent. Like all complex systems, regulation (or a change) at one level will lead to emergent global properties on another level, and these emergent properties in turn will influence the components that produced them in the first place, altering the entire system. I catch glimpses of these processes every day in Zachary's life – when I talk to him, make music with him, watch him draw pictures, and play imaginary games. It is these processes that make learning such a joy. As Reynolds (2003) describes: "Emergent order is one of the delights of thinking...the experience of the elements of an idea coming together to form a new coherence is one of the satisfactions of human life" (p. 2).

To tap into this joy music educators need to acknowledge not only the classroom as a complex system, but also their students as complex systems. Teachers will also need to, at times and with discretion, invite the complexity and chaos of the outside musical world, the whirlwind, into the classroom. It is only then that we will carve out a space for that powerful "spurt and gap" kind of learning characterized by its "surprises and seemingly random connections, for the dynamic bubbling up of ideas that form themselves into relationships" in our classrooms (Reynolds, p. 4). This is not to say that teachers do not have a role to play, or that classroom activities should dissolve into anarchy; order and self-organization emerge only when there is a proper balance between flexibility and formal structure (Doll, 2003). In order to create this balance the principles of centralized control, which work against creativity and self-regulation, and diffused control, which work for creativity and self-regulation, can be used as guidelines.

Admittedly, questions regarding curriculum and pedagogy are difficult to answer when viewed through the lens of complexity and chaos theory. Even Doll (2003), a leading complexity and educational theorist questions how curriculum and instructional procedures can be designed if learning is, in fact, non-linear. Solutions will depend on one's teaching situation, the life experiences of one's students, and of course, will need a great deal more exploration than that which is within the scope of this paper.

That said, teachers can focus on a few elements as outlined by Bartel (2002) which remain true to the idea of learning as a non-linear process and that are necessary for the development of musical understanding: "Learning involves (1) increasing the complexity of constructs – "bits of knowledge" (adding web pages to a web site), (2), increasing the associations among constructs (creating more links between sites), (3) increasing the complexity of explanatory constructs, (4), increasing the extent of construct conscious-ness or clarity, (5), making associations more readily accessible, and (6) increasing facili-ty at accessing and using the links, thereby (7) increasing the accuracy of explanatory constructs to anticipate and predict the future" (p. 66).

Teachers can create a process-folio environment within the classroom to ensure that these processes are alive and at work in student learning. For example, for every project a child is involved in, whether it involves performance, composition, or other multi-media skills, a project box is created (Tharp, 2003). Tharp explains in her book, *The Creative Habit*, the role project boxes play in the process of creating dance choreography:

> A box is like soil to me. It's basic, earthy, elemental. It's home. It's where I can always go back to when I need to regroup and keep my bearings. Knowing that the box is always there gives me the freedom to venture out, be bold, dare to fall flat on my face. Before you can think *out* of the box, you have to start with a box. (p. 80, italics mine)

Inside a box is everything encountered from the conception of a project through to its fruition. For students this would include, brainstorming sheets, pre- ideas, early sketch-es, relevant research, creative inspirations, practice on the basic skills required for a pro-ject, recordings, comments from teachers and peers – everything goes into the box. While the box is not a substitute for the actual product of creating (whether it be a composition, a poem, or a dance step), it is a powerful tool that allows students to look back and reflect on their creative process. In essence, the box physically demonstrates the haphazard process of their creativity come alive; a deeper understanding of this process makes it all the more likely that students will want to embark on another adventure. As they trace the path of their thinking, making conscious all the constructs and links involved, they also learn that in a complex world the empty page and sound-less air can be filled with many things. What was intended at the beginning is not always what emerges in the end! Looking back, they can ask themselves the important assessment and reflective questions: "How did I do?" "Did I achieve my goal"? "How could I do things differently the next time" "What skills do I need to improve on," and so forth. Further, the box provides students an opportunity to explore multiple representations of knowledge (since that is, essentially, what is going into the box)! For example, if a stu-dent is working on a thematic composition they could also include poetry or artwork, which explores similar ideas.

In the end, incorporating ideas from complexity theory is not as much about the media as it is creating a contextualized classroom environment for our students. That said, "contextualized" today has everything to do with the mass media (incidentally, if music educators want to find out what it is that students are learning musically from the media for research purposes, they will need to involve students in media related pro-jects). One of the great challenges facing music educators today is to keep up to date with the fast paced changes that so characterize the fields of media and technology. We need to become media educators and cannot afford to be left behind. Gouzouasis (1995) suggests that educators only have a limited window in which to get involved in the media world, or our place will be taken over by others. His comment might sound dire, even fatalistic, but it comes with positive intentions. He believes, as I do, that the world of music, media and digital technology can only be better for our students if we are involved. There is much potential to be discovered, much to be sorted out. An awareness of the media and how it shapes our musical lives offers music educators a valuable opportunity to make changes in pedagogical and curriculum practice. It may inspire us to find new ideas, and bring refreshing, relevant and engaging concepts into the classroom for students of all levels to explore.

References

Attali, J. (1985). *Noise: The political economy of music.* Minneapolis, MN: University of Minnesota Press.

Bartel, L. (2000). The rehearsal model. *Orbit,* 31(1), 25.

Bartel, L. (2002). Meaning and understanding in music: The role of complex constructs. In B. Hanley and T. W. Goolsby (eds.) *Musical understanding: Perspectives in theory and practice.* Victoria, B.C.: Canadian Music Educators Association.

Bartel, L & Cameron, L. (2001). *Facing the music in education: A report on a study in progress.* Paper presented at the American Educational Research Association, Annual Conference. Seattle, April 13.

Bartel, L. & Radocy, R. (2002). Trends in data acquisition and knowledge development. *The new handbook of music teaching and learning.* Colwell, R. and Richardson, P. (Eds.). Oxford University Press: New York. pp. 1108-1127.

Berry, G. L. & Asamen, J. K. Eds. (1993). *Children and television: Images in a changing sociocultural world.* California: Sage Publications.

Bresler, L. & Thompson, C. M. (2002). *The arts in children's lives.* Netherlands: Kluwer Academic Publishers.

Buckingham, D. & Sefton-Green, J. Eds. (1994). *Cultural studies goes to school: Readings and teaching popular media.* London: Taylor & Francis.

Buller, J. (2003). *Music and childrens' television.* Canadian Music Educator 44(3), 32-36.

Cameron, L. & Bartel, L. (2000). Engage or disengage: An inquiry into lasting response to music teaching. *Orbit,* 3 (1), 22-25.

Campbell, P.S. (2002). The musical cultures of children. In L. Bresler & C.M. Thompson (Eds.). *The arts in children's lives.* Netherlands: Kluwer Academic Publishers.

Campbell, P.S. (1998). *Songs in their heads: music and its meaning in children's lives.* New York: Oxford University Press.

Campbell, P.S. (1999). The many-splendored worlds of our musical children. *Update: Applications in Music Research.* Fall/Winter, 7-13.

Cohen, V. & Trehub, S. (1999). The kinaesthetic source of musical schemes: Infants' reaction to descending versus ascending tonal patters. Presented at the International Research in Music Education Conference, University of Exeter, April 1999.

Cortes, C. (2000). *The children are watching: How the media teach about diversity.* New York: Teacher's College Press.

Doll, W. (2003). Chaos and complexity theories. *Special Interest Group Newsletter.* Retrieved January 17, 2004. http://www.udel.edu.

Eisner, E. (1997). Educational objectives – help or hindrance. In D. Flinders & S. Thompson (Eds.). *The Curriculum Studies Reader.* New York: Routledge, pp. 69-75.

Elliott, D. (1995). *Music matters: A new philosophy of music education.* Toronto: Oxford University Press.

Fisherkeller, J. (2000). The writers are getting desperate: Young adolescents, television and literacy. *Journal of Adolescent and Adult Literacy,* 43(7), 596-606.

Gardner, H. (1995). *The unschooled mind: How children think & how schools should teach.* New York: Basic Books.

Gardner, H. (1999). *Intelligence reframed: Multiple intelligences for the 21st century.* New York: Basic Books.

Gauntlett, D. (1998). Ten things wrong with the 'effects' model. Retrieved October 10, 2003. http://www.theory.org.uk/effects.html.

Gembris, H. (2002). The development of musical abilities. *The New Handbook of Music Teaching and Learning.* Colwell, R. and Richardson, P. (Eds.) Oxford University Press: New York, pp. 487-508.

Gouzouasis, P. (1995). Music is the medium: What's the message? *Canadian Music Educator,* 36(6), 15-20.

Gouzouasis, P. (2001). Understanding music media: Digital (re)genesis or cultural meltdown in the 21st century. In B. Hanley & B.A. Roberts (Eds.). *Looking forward: Challenges to Canadian music education.* Toronto: The Canadian Music Educators Association, pp. 225-250.

Green, L. (2001). *How popular musicians learn: A new way for music education.* Aldershot, England: Ashgate.

Hanley, B. (2000). What's ahead? Challenges for music education in Canadian Schools. In B. Hanley & B.A. Roberts (Eds.). *Looking forward: Challenges to Canadian music education.* Toronto: The Canadian Music Educators Association, pp. 81-101.

Hart, A. (1991). *Understanding the media: A practical guide.* New York: Routledge.

Harwood, E. E. (1987). *The memorized song repertoire of children in grades four and five in Champaign, Ilinois.* Unpublished doctoral dissertation, University of Illinois.

Harwood, E.E. (1994). Miss Lucy meets Dr. Pepper: Mass Media and children's traditional playground song and chant. In H. Lees (Ed.), *Musical connections tradition and change* (pp. 187-193). Proceedings of the 21st World Conference Of the International Society for Music Education, Tampa, Fl.

Hawke, N. S. (1998). *Morphin' tansformin' mutatin': The dynamic interaction between media culture and children's lives.* Unpublished Ph.D. Dissertation, State University of Oklahoma.

Hendershot, H. (1998). *Saturday Morning Censors.* London: Duke University Press.

High Hopes. By Lynn Robson. CBC National News Special Report. January 23, 2004.

Jorgensen, E. (1997). *In search of music education.* Urbana: University of Illinois Press.

Kennedy, M. (2000). Music for all Canadians: Dream or reality at the high school level. In B. Hanley & B.A. Roberts (Eds.). *Looking forward: Challenges to Canadian music education.* Toronto: The Canadian Music Educators Association, pp. 139-149.

Lamb, R. (1996). Discords: Feminist pedagogy in music education. *Theory into Practice,* 35(2), 124-131.

Lamont, A. (1998). Music, education and the development of pitch perception: The role of context, age and musical experience. *Psychology of Music,* 26, 7-25.

Littleton, J.D. (1991). Influence of play settings on preschool children's music and play behaviours. Doctoral dissertation, University of Texas at Austin, University Microfilms No. 9128924.

Marchand, P. (2002). Marshall McLuhan. Retrieved October 10, 2003, http://www.marshallmcluhan.com/marchand.html.

McCarthy, L. *An analysis of radio commercials in Toronto: The vocabulary of vernacular music.* Unpublished manuscript.

McGuire, K. M. (2001). The use of music on Barney & Friends: Implications for music therapy practice and research. *Journal of Music Therapy,* 38 (2), 114-148.

Merrill-Mirsky, C. (1988). Eeny meeny pesadeeny: Ethnicity and gender in children's musical play. *Dissertation Abstracts International,* 57 09A.

Montgomery, A. (2000). Elementary school music: Reflections for the future. In B. Hanley & B.A. Roberts (Eds.). *Looking forward: Challenges to Canadian music education.* Toronto: The Canadian Music Educators Association, pp. 81-101.

Morisset, L. (1993). The medium of television and the school curriculum. In G. Berry & J. K. Asamen, (Eds.). *Children and Television: Images in a Changing Sociocultural World.* California: Sage Publications.

Nettl, B. (2002). What's to be learned? Comments on teaching music in the world and teaching world music at home. In L. Bresler & C.M. Thompson (Eds.). *The arts in children's lives.* Netherlands: Kluwer Academic Publishers.

O'Toole, P. (1997). I sing in a choir but I have "no voice!" *Quarterly Journal of Music Teaching and Learning,* 4(4), 65-76.

Regelski, T. (2002). On "methodolatry" and music teaching as critical and reflective praxis. *Philosophy of Music Education Review,* 10(2), 102-123.

Reimer, B., Palmer, A., Regelski, T. & Bowman, W. (2002). Symposium: Why do humans value music? *Philosophy of Music Education Review* 10(1), 41-63.

Reynolds, S. (2002). Modernism's devastating impact on learning: The tyranny of consciousness. Paper presented at the American Educational Research Association, Annual Conference, April. Retrieved December 28, 2003. http://www.udel.edu/aeracc/papers/02/Index.html.

Ridell, C. (1990). *Traditional singing games of elementary school children in Los Angeles.* Unpublished doctoral dissertation, University of California.

Rinaldo, V. (2003). A fragmentary view of education. *Canadian Music Educator,* 44(3), 23-25.

Ross, M. (1995). What's wrong with school music. *British Journal of Music Education,* 12 (3), 185-201.

Runfola, M. & Swanwick, K. (2002). Developmental characteristics of music learners. *The new handbook of music teaching and learning.* Colwell, R. and Richardson, P. (Eds.) Oxford University Press: New York, pp. 373-393.

Serafine, M.L. (1988). *Music as cognition: The development of thought in sound.* New York: Columbia University Press.

Shor, I. (1992). *Empowering education: Critical teaching for social change.* Chicago: University of Chicago Press.

Small, C. (1977). *Music, society and education.* London: John Calder.

Small, C. (1998). *Musicking: The meanings of performing and listening.* Hanover, NH: Wesleyan University Press.

Smithrin, K. (1994). Preschool children's responses to music on television. Canadian *Journal of Research in Music Education,* 35 (7), 38-48.

Smithrim, K. (1997). Free musical play in early childhood. *Canadian Music Educator*, 38(4), pp. 17-24.

Smithrim, K. (2002). Review: "Teaching towards musical understanding: A handbook for the elementary grades" by A. Montgomery. *Canadian Music Educator* 44(1), 40-41.

Smithrim, K. & Upitis, R. (2003). Contaminated by peaceful feelings: The power of music. *Canadian Music Educator*, 44(3), 15-17.

Statistics Canada. (2000). *Focus on culture: Quarterly bulletin from the culture statistics program*, 12, (4).

Strate, L. (2003). *Media Transcendence. McLuhan Studies* 1(3). Retrieved October 16, 2003. http://www.epas.utoronto.ca/mcluhan-studies/vl_iss3/1_3art8.html.

Stubley, E. (1993). Musical performance, play and constructive knowledge: Experiences of self and culture. *Philosophy of Music Education Review*, 4(1), 94-102.

Szego, C. K. (2002). A conspectus of ethnographic research in ethnomusicology and music education. *The new handbook of music teaching and learning.* Colwell, R. and Richardson, P. (eds.) Oxford University Press: New York, pp. 707-727.

Upitis, R., Smithrim, K., Patteson, A. & Meban, M. (2001). The effects of an enriched elementary arts education program on teacher development, artist practices, and student achievement: Baseline student data achievement and teacher data from six Canadian sites. *International Journal of Education and the Arts*, 2(8), http://ijea.asu.edu/v2n8.

Vandewater, E. & Wartella, E. (2003). *Zero to six: Electronic media in the lives of infants, toddlers and preschoolers.* Research report published by the Henry J. Kaiser Foundation and the Children's Digital Media Center. Retrieved November 15, 2003. http://www.digital-kids.net/

Vitale, John. (2002). *The effect of music on the meanings students gain from film.* Paper presented at American Educational Research Association, Annual Conference, New Orleans.

Wiggins, J. (2001). *Teaching for musical understanding.* McGraw Hill: Boston.

Winn, M. (1987). *Unplugging the plug-in drug.* New York: Penguin Books.

Wolfe, D. E. & Stambaugh, S. (1993). Musical analysis of Sesame Street: Implications for music therapy practice and research. *Journal of Music Therapy*, 30 (4), 224-235.

Wolfe, D. E. & Jellison, J. (1995). Interviews with preschool children about music videos. *Journal of Music Therapy.* 32 (4), 265-285.

Woodford, P. (1997). Music education, culture and democracy: Sociality and Individuality. *Canadian Music Educator*, 39(1), 15-18.

Woodford, P. (In Press). *Democracy and Music Education.* Urbana: Indiana University Press.

Ying, Kong. (2003). Effects of electronic media on advertising. *McLuhan Studies* 1(6), 1-12. Retrieved November 12, 2003. http://www.epas.utoronto.ca/mcluhan-studies/vl_iss6/1_6art4.html.

CHAPTER TWO

What Kind of Social Climate Do We Create in Our Music Classrooms?

LINDA CAMERON & KATIE CARLISLE

Abstract

This chapter explores the effect of the macro structures and micro interactions of music education on the social/emotional climate and hence on the very being of the musician. Micro interactions are defined as the varied interactions between teacher and student(s) or among students. Macro interactions are defined as persistent power relations and macro structures as the systems, traditions, and constraints of music education. Following a conceptual analysis of social climate and social-emotional climate, we explore how we can improve micro interactions in the music classroom. Music educators need to shift their focus from the music and the performance to their students. They need to experience how their students interact with their environment and their classmates. Improvement lies in interacting positively with our students as individuals and on a collective level, while working to broaden their relationship with sound. In a progressive music education paradigm the teacher embraces many identities such as: learner, music maker, resource, teacher, real person in the community, performer, and responsible leader. We conclude with a summary application of transformative music pedagogy.

Introduction

Questioning what we know, believe, and do is a tough challenge especially when the systemic macro structures are set to reinforce tradition and habit. We are exploring the effect of the **macro structures** and our **micro interactions** on music education with a careful look at the effect these phenomena have on the social/emotional climate and hence on the very being of the musician.

What are the teaching and learning conditions that are fundamental to your learning and musical development? Learning and living grows, develops, and is sustained in a safe and caring place, nurtured in the context of care, in a positive social/emotional climate. We could cite studies that validate this claim, and will refer to many later in this chapter, but at the outset we would rather ask **you** to **STOP** before reading further, to consider the variables that make **the most significant difference in your ability to concentrate, focus, comprehend, take risks, make attempts, problem solve, approximate, attend, remember, thrive, to enjoy learning...to really enjoy making music.**

The tone of teaching and the trust between the members of the learning community is a basic condition for success, for effective learning. Stress, criticism, competition, verbal abuse, ornery unpredictable leadership, physical abuse, loneliness, fear...don't inspire nor do they really help you reach your aspirations and fulfill your dreams. In the Face the Music study, Bartel and Cameron (2002b) found that subjects initially reported that they needed the critical, demanding teacher in order to succeed...until they unraveled the emotional issues that ensued and recognized the pain and stress that it had inflicted on them, deleteriously affecting them forever. We question, did the negative really support and challenge learning? There were many who reported that the best teaching/learning experiences were with teachers who cared and provided them with a safe and caring place to learn, a social/emotional climate that grew them and drew them. Small (1998) suggests that we need to "provide that kind of social context for informal as well as formal music interaction that leads to real development and to the musicalizing of the society as a whole" (p. 208). The role of the **micro interactions** (the varied interactions between teacher and student(s) or among students) in the music education context is very significant.

Glimpses into the micro interactions in music education contexts will offer you an opportunity to look, reflect, and hopefully question the music education paradigm related to the social emotional climate and its impact on learning...life-long learning and music making.

First:

> Mr. Nice Guy welcomes the students warmly into the large band room, inquiring how they are and encourages individuals to get their instruments to warm up before class begins. He knows their names and a little about all of them, he responds with appropriate repartee to the chatter and cluttering about. He questions if they have practiced and tries to inspire responsibility with praise, teasing, and support. There is a slight tension as time clicks by, Mr. Nice Guy's eyes glance noticeably at the clock. Then class begins: the group has efficiently settled in specific chairs and behind music stands, he steps onto the podium, announces the title for the piece to be played at the competition on Saturday, and raises his baton linking eyes with those not quite ready. Students play 8 bars before they are stopped. He says, "Good start." "Please note the articulation." He cues the next entry and students play more precisely. He stops them at the next rehearsal letter and says, "That is much better, you are going to win!" "Please play from Letter B, and watch the crescendo coming" (feedback, instruction, students play, feedback, instruction, students play, feedback, instruction, students play -- the essence of efficient rehearsal Yarbrough and Price (1989) and if you add Sang's notions (1982) instruction would include modeling.)

We notice in this vignette that the teacher is truly a "nice guy" who knows his students and cares about them, treats them with respect, wants them to succeed and perform well, gives them guidance and support. Looking at this, we are satisfied with the program, at least the surface micro interactions.

However...it is recognized that there are **macro interactions** (or persistent power relations) and **macro structures** (systems, traditions, and constraints...) apparent here that affect the very nature of pedagogy that force and restrict what happens or could develop, that affect the micro interactions. First and foremost in this vignette we see things familiar, it is how we have experienced and witnessed music education and so we feel comfortable with the program. It is how we have been trained. Time allocation, room design, the need to prepare for performance/competition (often the measure of a teacher's effectiveness in the system), a repertoire chosen by others in order to compare in competition, fund raising, the podium and power of that position, the baton always in the same hand, the responsibility resting there as well...these illustrations of the macro structure also impact. Is this the way it could or should be? Are there other possibilities?

Second:

> Stephen leads Marcus to the music office. Mr. J, the band director, looks up and says, "Oh hello! You must be Marcus. Well, you came just in time because band class starts in 10 minutes." There is an assortment of instruments on the desk: trumpets, trombones, flutes, clarinets, and saxophones. "You ever played one of these before?" Marcus shakes his head. "Okay, here's a clarinet, same as what Stephen plays. He'll show you what to do. Your music folder is in the slot behind the door."

> "He seems nice, but I don't want to play this. I play guitar."

> "I know, but we're not allowed guitars in band class...We gotta' hurry because Mr. J.'ll come in soon and we gotta' be ready. Here, I'll put your clarinet together." Thank goodness for Stephen, Marcus thinks.

> Marcus looks around the band room. There are posters everywhere of people dressed-up in black holding orchestral instruments. On the bulletin board is a detective peering accusingly through a large magnifying glass with the caption, "Let's see who's been practicing" and a star-filled chart beside it. Students with furrowed brows play their instruments, their noses close to their music stands. Latecomers dart in, giggling nervously as they anxiously unpack their instruments.

> All of the sudden, a "foghorn" sounds as two students stand playing with their saxophone bells touching. There is a laughter explosion, then silence! The band director appears at the door.

> Without a word, Mr. J ascends the podium, lifts his arms, and the class begins its warm-up routine. Not knowing what to do, Marcus just listens. When Stephen looks over at him, bug-eyed, Marcus shrugs. Stephen hisses, "Pretend." Marcus rolls his eyes.

> After the warm-up, Mr. J. asks Christine, a flute player, to come stand by the podium. "I've decided to give Christine a solo in the trio section of 'Winchester March.' Make sure you play softly so we can hear her." Mr. J. beams at Christine while the girls in the front row glare in her direction.

> After the band starts playing again, Marcus sneaks out to go to the bathroom. Quietly closing the door, he jumps when Mr. J. stops the band and shouts, "Look! We have festival in three weeks and I can't bring in a band sounding like this! Christine plays her part so well. Why can't all of you?"

> Marcus wanders over to the auditorium. Peering inside, he sees students in raised rows practicing standing and sitting. The girls keep losing their balance as their long choir robes get caught under their shoes. "Eyes on me...watch your robes, girls..." sings the choir director, continually gesturing students to stand and sit. Marcus listens to the whooshing sound as they practice moving as one. Reward finally comes from their teacher: "...Perfect!"

Does any part of this vignette sound familiar to you? This scene is an amalgam based on our experiences as students in the traditional music education paradigm and from our interactions with many music teachers embroiled in these practices. Considering the micro interactions, how would you feel in that classroom context? What if you were Marcus? Christine? Mr. J.? One of the students? A parent of one of the students? One of the kids who were tapped on the head and didn't even get a chance to participate at all? Could you call this classroom a safe and caring learning place? The emotional tone created by the various micro interactions and relationships seeps through this scene and looks like, feels like, and too often depicts a "social-emotional climate" in the music classes we have witnessed. Does this social context affect learning? Does this affect life-long learning and interest? Does this matter to everyone? We contend that it affects all of these. And incidentally...who makes the decisions, who has choice, who is doing the real work of music, who is fully engaged and why? There are persistent issues of power in this pedagogy that are not inclusive, not democratic, not really that productive.

There are likely some macro elements that may have eluded you. Notice the room arrangement, the instrument selection, the music "office," the expectation of performance, the "orchestral room arrangement," the number of students in one room, the risers. Someone somewhere designed the music room to service the music program expected by the Board of Education. You see music rooms like this in many schools. What is in the music library?...what is the curriculum?....what are the expectations both for short and long-range results? What is valued and how is it evaluated? These decisions are part of the systemic macro choices that affect the micro interactions in the classroom. Who is the head of music in the system and what is the philosophy? Did you see that in the vignette? It was hidden by our expectations. It is the micro interactions we suggest that have the greatest effect on the individual and create and sustain the social/emotional climate, but macro structures are often causal or foundational to the micro elements. The features of our music classrooms that music educators often find most reassuring are the ones that we recognize from our own prior experiences. What we do, how we teach, is motivated by what we believe and this set of beliefs is an inheritance passed down over time. Brian Cambourne (1988) says that we are all "prisoners of a model of learning" (p.17) and it is hard to break out of that paradigm. "Just as prisoners are locked into a context which permits a very limited range of behavioural options, so they are locked into a range of teaching behaviours which, while they may vary in **emphasis** from time to time, will not vary in **substance**" (p.18). This dilemma is at the heart of educational reform. When non-traditional methods of instruction and structures are practiced in classrooms, many of us become suspicious, defensive, critical and even hostile. We argue from the perspective that the traditional music education system worked for us....just look at us! Or did it? Let's not consider all of those students who were tapped on the head and told to just mouth the words or those who were ridiculed out of class, or the myriad of people whose musical self-efficacy is flawed to the negative scale, or those who simply decided they were not able or interested enough to persist in music because of the subtle messages they received. What about students who were not considered talented enough to be moved into first chair...are they worth the challenge? What is this theory or model of learning/teaching that has imprisoned music teachers?

Alfie Kohn in *The Schools Our Children Deserve* suggests that, "It's not easy to acknowledge these possibilities, which may help to explain the aggressive nostalgia that is loose in the land. Any number of people subscribe to the Listerine theory of education: the old ways may be distasteful, but they're effective. ...Traditional schooling turns out to be as unproductive as it is unappealing" (1999, p. 2). He challenges us to question why our children aren't spending more time thinking about what they are learning and playing a more active role in the process. We are asking how we can make music education real, meaningful, and relevant for all.

If we don't stop to consider that we might be somehow trapped in a theory and model of teaching that might not be as effective as it could be, then music education classes, programs and productions are destined to continue to be teacher centred, controlled, controlling, competitive, and focussed on performance perfection. This *unintentional* reality is very apparent across the spectrum of music education. It is what is expected by parents, it is taught and reinforced in many teacher education programs, it is celebrated at the many competitions, it is how the resources are allocated and how music rooms are designed—it is the way it has established itself and has become Establishment. The structure of the paradigm is hierarchical with teacher not only at the front but often elevated on a podium, gesturing and verbalizing what he or she expects. There is minimal collaboration at best, sometimes there is little consultation and cooperation, and compliance is demanded. How else can you control all of those students and all of that noise? How else can you get a product that will not embarrass you, that will make you proud? The large ensemble has inevitable demands.

What seems to describe many traditional music educators in their quest for perfection is the "stormy" behaviour (Bartel and Cameron, 2002a) that is the hallmark of their teaching. We've observed that radical shifts in temperament are "normal" in traditional music teachers' day-to-day classroom demeanour and behaviour, and are also too often what students remember of their school music experience. Interactions between music teachers and students form lasting impressions of classroom experiences and shape life-long attitudes towards music-making. This chapter explores the impact of **social-emotional climate** in both traditional and more progressive music education settings and focuses on the importance of the micro interactions as a barometer in those contexts.

Conceptual Analysis of Social Climate and Social-*Emotional* Climate

In music education research, little attention has focused on the construct of social climate in the music classroom. It is a construct that lies beneath the surface of other foci such as teachers' concern for student motivation, class control, or the development of positive attitudes towards music. Because the concept of social climate is not well defined in music education, we will begin with some basic conceptual analysis and construct definition.

"Social" and "climate" evoke immediate associations. "Social" relates to "sociable" or "sociability" which refers to group relations or, more informally, "food, fun, and fellowship." It also has strong association with the larger structure of "society," as in social science or social services. The term "climate" conjures up images of weather environments such as tropical, coastal, moderate, arctic, etc. However, in "social climate" it has a much more immediate and local meaning for the psychological tenor and tone of the relationship among people, the warmth and comfort of temperate situations. Perhaps it is more like the sudden shifts from sunny to cloudy to rainy in a particular locale at a particular time. Have you experienced a chilly social environment? It limits your comfort to be and do.

The term "social climate" incorporates two foci – the macro and the micro. The macro focus is on society, social structures, social policy, and on social values—the systemic. The micro focus is on the personal experience of the psychological dynamic emanating from the essence of relationship. It is the nature of the interaction. We borrow and extend upon Jim Cummins' definitions of macro and micro interactions (Cummins, 1996). By macro interactions, we mean the persistent power relations in the wider society and how they influence teaching and learning. By micro interactions within the traditional music education paradigm, we mean the interactions between a teacher and his or her students and also among students. This refers to all of the decisive verbal communication as well as the minute non-verbal gestures, the various reflectors of attitude, the body language, that have just as much, if not more, impact upon students and their learning. It is the "stuff" of relationship and relating.

The construct, social-emotional climate, places social climate within an affective context. When we think about emotions, we sense either immediate response to or a closing off of an environment, depending on its climate and the individual. Emotions are deeply personal and, therefore, allow us to experience an individual perspective. Indeed, the power of emotion can either bind people to, or alienate people from, their environment and community. It can open one up for total engagement in learning or block any potential. Emotion can preoccupy. Students who feel alienated or choose to disassociate from their educational environment suffer cognitive, academic, social, and emotional consequences. Indeed, the social-emotional climate of a classroom can be a wonderful or disastrous determinant of students' growth, learning potential, and self-esteem. Daniel Goleman (1995) suggests that, "...the emotional areas are intertwined via myriad connecting circuits to all parts of the neocortex. This gives the emotional centres immense power to influence the functioning of the rest of the brain—including its centres for thought" (p.12).

In recent years, teachers and researchers have rediscovered what good teachers and parents have known for many years: that knowledge of ourselves and others as well as the capacity to use this knowledge to solve problems creatively provides an essential foundation for both academic learning and the capacity to become an active, constructive citizen (Gardner, 1983; Goleman, 1995; Sternberg, 1997). Promoting social and emotional learning (SEL) helps students to learn and develop, and it helps teachers to be even more effective educators (Salovey & Sluyter, 1997). Mental health professionals who work with the young have for over a century been acutely aware of how social and emotional experience profoundly affects and even determines children's ability to learn and develop. This is not new knowledge, Aichhorn and Freud saw the significance.

There is a significant research body that suggests that a "safe and caring environment" is paramount for learning to occur. The development of positive personal relationships with and fostering it among students is recognized as a valued and extremely important part of the role of the teacher (Goodlad, 1990; Lieberman & Miller, 1984, Deiro, 1996). It seems that the bottom line in this research is the creation of the kind of place where care abounds and, therefore, the academic/music development of students along with social and emotional growth is nurtured. That means providing support along with challenge and criticism, being sensitive to one another, working alongside not 'on top' of others, being collaborative and co-operative rather than competitive, and being motivated not by pride but rather hope. Sergiovanni (1998) suggests that the curriculum and learning experience should "provide pupils with opportunities to develop loyalty, fidelity, kinship, sense of identity, obligation, duty, responsibility, and reciprocity" (p.44). The curriculum could provide opportunities for communities to develop learning experiences that reflect students' interests, needs, values, aspirations, and that are responsive to the local context.

The Macro Perspective

To look closely at *micro* interactions (which will extend into a second definition later in this chapter), we will attempt to peel away the layers of *macro* interactions. "Macro" (as in macro interactions) is inherently tied to meanings of "social" and the emotional (as in social/emotional climate). These meanings let us examine how society supports or does not support its members, how society sorts its members, and the effect both aspects have on individuals. It has to do with the social systems within the context.

One way to look at how macro elements impact music programs is to examine school music programs or any kind of select music performing ensemble that seeks to recruit the "best" music students. The macro factors involved here are competition, technique and, of course, performance. Students are "driven" to be accepted, because they perceive the program or the ensemble to be the best and the most challenging. More often than not, they leave behind at the door their identity outside of school. There is no room inside the select group for individual differences. Students trade one macro identity (their life outside school) for another (the performance/competition arena). When students seek or are forced to fit a mould, they shut off what gives rise to individuality, creativity, and indeed their soul.

The problem with macro forces that have ensconced traditional school music programs is that there is little room for positive personal and caring micro interactions to occur. The relationship of teacher (conductor) is essentially to the whole group and unless the participants are completely compliant, submissive, convergent, and hopefully enthusiastic the teacher cannot accomplish the "program," and program is almost always paramount. The macro system predetermines the conditions for learning: teachers are too busy preparing for performances that will top last year's, classroom contexts are designed to function only as large ensemble sites, traditional teacher training models reproduce clones, fund raising is a necessity, cultural expectations defy change, notions that it is only technically difficult pieces that challenge students, image maintenance ("we *have* to be the best") preoccupies, and the question of whether real learning and growth is taking place is avoided. These macro issues of podium, power, and position sustain the system as it was by usurping the possibility for thoughtful transformative pedagogy.

Indeed, "social" forces are woven into the fabric of schooling. When they impact on micro interactions, it is evident whether they serve to stratify or equalize students. In traditional education, the "haves" may be in held in high esteem by their teacher, but these students have little say over their learning and growth. They simply are a "good fit" in the macro organization mold. To have freedom is to be able to make choices and make mistakes. When students are encouraged to make choices for themselves and take responsibility on a continual basis, they have the freedom to *become*, to grow toward their potential. Indeed, their macro identity (their life outside of school) is ready to comingle on the level of micro interactions. This kind of environment sets the stage for deep levels of learning and engagement (as defined by Bartel and Cameron, 2000).

The Micro Perspective

An examination of social climate from a micro perspective requires a closer look at the meanings of "climate." In terms of weather and emotional tone, we interact with climate on the basis of comfort and discomfort. People like to be able to predict climate, whether it is the weather or people's behaviour. They engage themselves most when the climate is comfortable rather than chilly.

Emotional tone affects relationship. A person's tone, attitude, demeanour, or body language communicates whether they are welcoming, caring, trusting or trustworthy. People tend to receive these messages immediately. The climate of relationship is in constant flux unless participants are sensitive to micro interactions. Social-emotional climate is the environmental product of the macro and micro interactions between members of a group and the perceptions members hold of those interactions.

Our discussion places micro interactions (student/teacher, student/student, teacher/students and student/students) at the forefront of social-emotional climate. The problem this chapter proposes lies in how teachers and students experience and perceive those interactions.

The classroom is a hotbed of recursive interpersonal communication and most children are acutely aware of the social dynamics embedded in classroom relationships. Teachers do determine the quality of relationship they have with students. Indeed, teachers play a role in determining the depth of learning that occurs by the relationships they foster. Traditional education pedagogy ignores the impact of teacher-student relationship and instead focuses on student product and performance, skill development, and knowledge acquisition. Traditional music education pedagogy is particularly guilty of this. Many music educators believe they have fulfilled their role as educators if students master the performance literature. They are happy when one more trophy is won, one more performance has received adequate accolades, and when the show goes on. For the emotional cost involved teachers too often invoke the justification of the art—the "elevation of spirit," the aesthetic delight, the movement of the soul. *Ends* clearly justify *means* in the arts. But, in their quest for perfection, do traditional music educators give pause to reflect on the quality of interactions they have with their students and the effect that has on significant learning and life long enjoyment of music making? Are they willing to allow "performance standards" to become secondary to "relationship standards"?

Paulo Freire (1998) challenges teachers to try to keep hope alive and to live part of their dreams within their educational space. The importance of a dialogical relationship which merges teacher and student is reaffirmed in *Pedagogy of Hope* through Freire's defence of popular discourse and the democratization of content in education. Our music classrooms need to be places of hope and democracy, where we can all catch glimpses of the possibilities of the kind of world, the place, where students learn and live the competencies, capacities, and creativity of music.

Let's take a broader view of this question and, indeed, of interactions. Interactions (both micro and macro) over time affect relationships. The nature of these relationships determines the kind of community or feeling that evolves within a group of individuals. Social-emotional climate stems from the idea of community. This makes us wonder:

How do traditional music educators perceive community? Does community really matter? In the *Face the Music* research project (Bartel and Cameron, 2002b) respondents alluded to the impact and import that community had on the desire to participate (or not), the social potential for like-minded people to enjoy each other (or not), and the support (or not) of the group in their learning experiences. The "group" can make or break the learning potential and, indeed, the person.

Do music educators develop *authentic* community which "requires us to do more than pepper our language with the word 'community,' label ourselves as a community in our mission statement, ..." (Sergiovanni, 1994, xiii)? Or do they only organize group experiences? Being part of a group does not necessarily mean that it is a community in which students and teachers, conductor and ensemble, are bound together in special ways that are significant and that fulfill the individual, giving an enduring sense of identity, belonging, and most of all, an empowered place to each member. You could sing in a choir and feel lost and alone as you comply and perform, and most critically, be without real voice (O'Toole, 1993-94).

Music educators in the traditional paradigm take their cue from professional musicians and their rehearsal environment. In the rehearsal model (Bartel, 2000, p. 25), the conductor (or teacher) is the power center. Borrowing from its scientific meaning, the teacher acts as a formal "conductor" of what transmits to students. Although participants may claim to enjoy the experience, a group joined with purpose, does that constitute community? It matches encultured students' expectations of how things should be done. It is said that people love a benevolent dictator – for the "lazy" person it allows a positive life without the discomfort of responsibility. The ensemble where every important decision is dominated by the "director," allows people to "participate" without thought or real effort. It creates and perpetuates the model of the docile happy masses dominated by the elite (Gatto, 2003).

Traditional music education has been outstanding and exemplary at capturing and pursuing the primary goals of public education in North America described by Alexander Inglis's 1918 book, *Principles of Secondary Education.* Gatto (2003), quoting Inglis and elaborating upon him, argues that these six functions of schooling are still the dominant functions of schooling today. He outlines the purpose of schooling in America as follows:

(1) *The adjustive or adaptive function. Schools are to establish fixed habits of reaction to authority... [and] precludes critical judgment completely. (2) The integrating function. This might well be called "the conformity function," because its intention is to make children as alike as possible. (3) The diagnostic and directive function. School is meant to determine each student's proper social role. (4) The differentiating function. Once their social role has been "diagnosed," children are to be sorted by role and trained only so far as their destination in the social machine merits - and not one step further. So much for making kids their personal best. (5) The selective function. This refers ... to Darwin's theory of natural selection ...Schools are meant to tag the unfit [in music this means untalented]. That's what all those little humiliations from first grade onward were intended to do: wash the dirt down the drain. (6) The propaedeutic function. The societal system implied by these rules will require an elite group of caretakers. To that end, a small fraction of the kids will quietly be taught how to manage this continuing project, [is that what we do when we give some of the "talented" students the opportunity to also "conduct" the ensemble that makes us believe we are actually "democratizing" our classroom?]*

Although possibly completely inadvertently, music teachers, through the micro interactions within the context of the macro structures of the traditional music education paradigm, perpetuate "group" activity that can masquerade as community without really being so. When we analyze the sense of community fostered in the typical large music ensemble, what appears on the surface to be a united group with a sole purpose is in fact often quite counterfeit. Authentic community requires a binding together in special ways that serves each member significantly as well as the group. It requires authentic involvement and investment with empowered responsibility. Students and teachers within a traditional context may strongly defend the "community" they feel in rehearsal. Yet, the "ultimate" euphoria they may experience may not come from "community" as much as from group adhesion and conformity orchestrated by the director. The euphoria experienced and demonstrated in Hitler's mass rallies was palpable. Yet was it a demonstration of true community?

Another subtle aspect of our music education ensemble model that is driven by the fierce competitive individuality of our western culture is the "hope" and expectation of individual achievement and success we instil in the "talented" within our groups. The reverence and awe we have for "talent" in our culture gives those students demonstrating it an indisputable "elite" status within any ensemble and requires a competitiveness among individuals within that elite group. Because most music educators emerge from within that group as "successes" we find the system quite acceptable without recognizing the fundamental effect this has on community and individual musical identity. By contrast, Minette Mans (2000) tells us that: "One of the main differences between Western music and dance and the spirit of *ngoma* (Music/dance as ngoma emphasizes communal performance), is the shift of emphasis from individual performance to the synergy of group performance where everybody participates. This does not imply that individual excellence is of no consequence in *ngoma*. On the contrary, excellence in terms of balance, clarity of purpose, precision and originality are valued, but within the context of improving the performance of the whole group. Performers gain identity through their cohesion and merger with others. Hence, performance as *ngoma* demands the ability to function in a complex interactive environment in harmony with other individuals."

In this context, "the talented" do not try to stand out in the group but rather to encourage others to join into the performance with you...this is the ngoma spirit where everyone gains. "Communal performance also means that a particular aspect of performance, for example the drumming, the dance or the masks, is never emphasized over another in performance. The principles of equity and balance are therefore brought to the fore in this kind of performance" (Mans, 2000). This collaborative, cooperative, and consensual community is a good example of the possible rhythm of community in contrast to the competitive model in Western music dominated by the conductor.

With these ideas, we propose the problem: traditional music educators are not generally aware of the impact their perspective on community has upon micro interactions and the conditions of learning. In their efforts to fulfil their role, established by the macro structures of tradition, music educators do not take into account their student's perspective, causing the quality of micro interactions to suffer. In a traditional view of community, teachers are generally oblivious to students' interests and experiences. Students respond and interact: they read facial expressions; they listen for the degree of tension in voices; they sense mood. These cue the child to the environment helping him or her determine whether with that particular teacher, it is a safe and comfortable place to be and to learn. These cues – and the behavioural decisions children make from them – imprint upon their minds and are difficult, if not impossible, to change. So the importance of micro interactions is critical. They determine children's relationship with their music teacher and their peers, and their attitude towards music. Unpredictable or unfriendly teacher behaviour sets up a climate of mistrust. Children shut themselves off from the wonder that comes from curiosity, creativity, spontaneity, experimentation, and discovery. This lack of deep experience in music class suppresses children's' musical, social, and emotional growth.

A dominant goal of traditional music education is to create an exceptional product. Teachers strive for perfection and aim to impress their audience (and their funders). Interactions with students revolve around the teacher's needs (often attributed to the needs of the demands and potential of the art). Ways in which many music teachers interact with students tend to create a chilly climate of mistrust. Excessive rehearsing and supervision of practice habits are ways teachers distance themselves from students and students from each other. The rigour that traditional music teachers espouse masks the sterile nature of their teaching. This affects students in different ways. Musically, students develop "tunnel vision." They tend to favour only their part, or a particular genre, or come to believe they are incapable of composition and improvisation. Socially, they are discouraged from interacting with their teacher and peers on a personal level. Emotionally, they may respond to the music, but in an environment of obedience and compliance. Students learn not to initiate musical ideas or social behaviour. They tend not to collaborate or co-operate as autonomous agents but rather engage in the appearance of collaboration within the control and motivation parameters of the conductor/teacher. Since music-making in a traditional environment is quite restrictive and, for most participants, does not result from personal and meaningful interaction, most students do not experience lasting engagement. As a result, many participants (even among that select group that chooses to participate in high school music) are unlikely to explore their musicality throughout their lives, and many do not develop positive relationships with their music teacher and with their peers.

How can we improve micro interactions in the music classroom? Music educators need to shift their focus from the music and the performance to their students. They need to experience how their students interact with their environment and their classmates. Improvement lies in interacting positively with our students as individuals and on a collective level, while working to broaden their relationship with sound.

The structure of traditional music learning virtually buries the affective side of learning. Teachers enforce their methodologies and repertoire on students in order to mould them into desirable performers. This is control over minds rather than a meeting of minds. The affective or "feeling" domain in learning is where students and teacher meet and come to know each other. It is where positive micro interactions are developed and fostered.

So far we've looked at micro interactions through the lens of the traditional music education paradigm, where the teacher is responsible for decision-making, transmits information, and controls the psychological tenor of relationship within the classroom.

Music teachers need to be more sensitive and tactful (van Manen, 1986) about the interactions they have with students.

In a progressive music education paradigm, micro interactions take on more meaning. First, the teacher embraces many identities such as: learner, music maker, resource, teacher, real person in the community, performer, and responsible leader. Positively meaningful micro interactions take place between teacher and student, teacher and students, student and student, and student and curriculum. Progressive teaching recognizes that learning occurs from these kinds of multiple interactions. Traditional teacher-student interactions are behaviourist and based on learning outcomes. Students fail if they don't master what is presented to them. Encouraging multiple kinds of interactions allows students to find their own way into learning and engagement. This kind of positive and deep experience encourages students to grow musically, intellectually, socially, and emotionally. Teacher and students are encouraged to develop healthy respect and esteem—to care for and about themselves and each other.

There is more to uncover about our broadening view of micro interactions. Right now, let's take a glimpse into the Music Producers' Studio to see a different vision of school music-making:

Room 101 is the music room, the hub of the music program in a large urban middle school. As you approach Room 101, you can hear a cacophony of sound emanating down the hall reverberating against the busy sound of school. It is the sound of laughter, sound exploration, bits of melody emanating from a small ensemble, instruments (guitars, keyboards, steel pans, synthesizers, drums) being worked on, problems posed by sight reading a new score being sung through, kids talking, teacher responding to a small group suggesting that she will be with them momentarily...music work.

When you enter the bright room you are greeted by an energetic student who welcomes you with an enthusiastic smile to "The Music Producers' Studio" and points to the teacher across the room warning that she is busy working with some kids but promising you that she will be with you shortly. As you head towards the teacher through diverse groups of students engaged in a variety of music making activities you will: eavesdrop into conversations about the best sound to make a particular piece work, how it should be played, what the right rhythm is or what key works; witness a variety of musical problem solving (Wiggins, 2000); hear segments of pieces being played, strummed, hummed or clapped; see kids with noses pressed against scores thinking through the phrase and rhythm while checking their musical predictions; see someone underneath the synthesizer checking connections; observe kids hooked up to the listening post obviously oblivious to the world while grooving to the latest pop music; and watch composers busy with pencil on staff paper. The music you hear presents a pastiche as culturally and artistically diverse as the group of kids. It resonates with what really matters in music education. You are in the company of musicians in "The Music Producers' Studio."

Just as you get close to the teacher, she raises her hand in the air and waits until the signal reaches the most focused, then silence erupts, and eyes turn her way. She smiles at you acknowledging your welcomed presence but then asks everyone to listen to a new bit "hot off the press" from a student composition recorded on the digital recorder and asks the classmates to reflect on what they like best about it, how it made them feel, or what it reminds them of...a composer's style, a piece they may have heard before, and then asks for any suggestions for the composers. The students settle in to listen and obviously care, clapping with enthusiasm after the short performance. Responses to the composition *are thoughtful, tactful, and productive. The composers take suggestions, ask for clarification and enlist one of the students who had a "great idea" to consult for a few minutes. Then, back to work.*

Nearing the end of the period, the timer set to protect that important time for celebration and goal setting, the students gather up their work and come together to talk about what they learned that day, how things went, what problems were most crucial at that moment, what next steps or assistance they need, and what they are planning on doing next. Things are noted on the planning board, particular questions are recorded by the teacher on her always handy clipboard, experts are enlisted to help particular students, recordings or scores are found to inspire, and time is scheduled to teach in response to robust questions. There is a workshop suggested that would help students working on a certain musical genre planned for next class. Announcements are made about ensembles currently practicing. A conducting workshop is offered by the teacher for all those interested in conducting ensembles and assisting at the elementary school. Invitations are given to students who might like to get something together to play, sing, or dance for the local seniors home, a committee is established to research and plan what repertoire would be appropriate and enjoyable for that. Another opportunity to do some music education for the primary division of the adjacent elementary school with volunteers enlisted to work that up with the teachers is presented with enthusiastic response. There are some kids who want to be teachers and this will give them great experience. Concerts and performances that are happening locally are described. The teacher invites students to a concert at which she is singing Carmina Burana by Carl Orff suggesting that they would find the repetitive melody and rhythm patterns interesting and that it might give them some composition ideas. She demonstrated the section that she is struggling with and talks about how she needs to warm up her voice for the performance. She offers to lend anyone the CD of the work which she says is bawdy and raucous not unlike contemporary rap songs. The teacher has arranged to have mentoring available by various 'experts' who are playing, performing, teaching, and doing music in the real world...these are listed on the bulletin board and the students are invited to sign up.

And then there is the CD they are working on as a class...their own compositions and performances getting polished and produced, published and marketed. The potential for music making is enormous and these kids have the power to make it happen. Music is real, meaningful and relevant!

The class ends by singing their personally composed class anthem (sounding more like the 'we will, we will rock you' you hear at games than the National anthem) and they are gone only to return after school for music club, rehearsals, jamming, working in the recording studio, listening to some 'cool' music on the good speakers and just hanging out together. Plans are made to meet in someone's garage to continue to practice and write some more. CD's are signed out and exchanged. Scores are borrowed. Guitars are slung over shoulders and away they go.

If you read the walls of the classroom you see music making invitations, student posters announcing their work, media announcements and current information, ideas, ideas, ideas...that keep music alive and irresistible.

The energy, enthusiasm and engagement that effectively provokes and evokes learning in Room 101 has its evolution in the teacher's commitment to music making and belief that music has transformative power for the maker and the listener. It is her dedication to her students and the belief that they all have musical potential that makes the difference. Music is a literacy the students are developing—a voice they are finding, ability to articulate musical ideas and to solve musical problems with ears they are able to really hear with, and a skill set they are mastering.

Behind the scenes we see a teacher who loves kids and loves music, someone who wants to bring them together so that they are one. She is a community builder, joining student with teacher, students with students, and students with the musicians and music of the world throughout time. "World music" includes the student's current and personal world of music which is accepted and validated through acknowledgement and options to compose, listen to, and start from.

Students love and respect their teacher—the musician, the woman, the teacher, the critic, the expert, and the "cultural engineer." In his book *Life in a Crowded Place*, Ralph Peterson (1992) talks about community building this way:

> "Teachers who make communities have a big order to fill. Students who show up at the classroom door when the school bell rings in the fall are not an all-of-a-kind family.... Teachers who make communities with their students are cultural engineers of sorts. The primary goal at the beginning of a new year or term is to lead students to come together, form a group, and be there for one another." (p.13)

There is much to understand from this vignette and glimpse into the *Music Producers' Studio*, Room 101. First, we understand what this music teacher finds important and what she values. Above all, she sees and respects her students as individuals. She believes students are entitled to have choice and encourages them to think about what, how, why, and when they learn. She obviously cares for her students, and they learn to care for each other.

The teacher views learning and creativity as a process. She provides support by continuously "being there" for her students. One way she provides structure is by protecting "that important time for celebration and goal setting" towards the end of each class. This important time encourages students to reflect on their present actions. Formative evaluation occurs regularly and in a comfortable and interactive environment where teacher and students give input, where technology is used to assist self-assessment. Students naturally take responsibility for their learning as they assess their current and future projects.

The plea for more creativity and ingenuity presents a tall order for music teachers. Innovation is rare. According to Marshall (2004), it is "because it relies on one of the great imponderables: imagination. We're talking about an extraordinary thought process—the dedicated, persistent application of free thinking, rule flouting, boundary crossing, convention busting mindset" (page 8). We witness this at work.

This teacher encourages growth by believing in her students' potential and caring about their interests. She helps them reach their potential by allowing flexibility within the curriculum. There is a healthy blend of what traditional music education would consider "extra-curricular" within the curriculum. This teacher allows students' personal musical interests; indeed, the ways they *prefer* to interact with music to guide learning. This vignette shows students playing instruments not associated with large ensembles, "grooving to the latest pop music" and planning musical routines that involve dance, as well as playing and singing. Such "extra-curricular" elements are ignored in traditional school music programs. As well, the teacher exposes her students to musical happenings in the community in a way that involves their interest and gives meaning to their endeavours. In this kind of environment, students have multiple opportunities to develop their widening range of musical interests.

How do students experience this kind of environment? They have the freedom to be themselves while developing a group identity. The restraints of traditional instruction are lifted and they may talk to each other, choose the nature of their music-making, and confidently express their creativity and musicality. They experience music-making as a *social* activity, where open interaction with other people is integral with interaction with sound. Their musical experiences are deep and engaging and full of social, emotional, and cognitive meaning.

What is the nature of micro interactions in this kind of environment? This vignette reveals an overwhelming feeling of consensus between music students and teacher. We know that "children value adults who value them" (Deiro, p.3) and it appears reciprocal in this context. They support each other in the creative process of where they have been, where they are at, and where they are going. The teacher-student relationship is a **partnership**.

There is ample evidence from educational theorists and researchers that nurturing the emotional as well as the academic needs of students is of paramount importance as a condition of learning (Martin, 1992; McLaughlin & Talbert, 1990; Diero, 1996; Noddings, 1992; Sergiovanni, 1993). These researchers are suggesting that if educators assume responsibility for caring for and nurturing the social and emotional needs of students that the desired academic success will inevitably follow. Noddings (1988) claims that "It is obvious that children will work harder and do things—even odd things like adding fractions—for people they love and trust" (p.10). Other research demonstrates that when students' emotional and social needs are met they learn more readily (Coleman, 1987; Earls, Beardslee, & Garrison, 1987; O'Donnell, Hawkins, Catalano, Abbott, & Day, 1995).

Teachers are responsible to develop positive personal relationships with students according to Goodlad (1990), Lieberman & Miller (1984), and Noddings (1988, 1992). Teacher-student bonding means "the teacher and student have developed a close and trusting personal relationship involving an emotional connection with a sensitivity about what the other thinks and feels." Diero, (1996) and Talbert (McLaughlin & Talbert, 1990) found that when students have bonded positively with teachers, those teachers have more capacity to both motivate and engage students academically. The development of positive teacher student relationships is academically more beneficial than the utilization of "more traditional methods of social controls that emphasize obedience to authority or conforming to rules" (Diero, 1996, p.11).

Diero (1996) describes the characteristics of and criteria for a healthy influential nurturing relationship by suggesting that "intentional promotion of growth and change, empowerment of student through internalization of learning, and respectful use of power" (p.14) –are what matters.

In addition to fostering good teacher student relationships, it is critical to build a sense of community among students. A teacher can facilitate and help to build community by being inclusive and encouraging students to share with one another, to risk take without fear of reprisals, to limit competition and foster cooperation and collaboration and by demonstrating care. What mitigates against community is showing favouritism, setting up a competitive environment, using power structures to reward and punish, to not allow for communication. Opportunities for students to get to know one another and to work collaboratively in small ensembles, on projects, to compose something together, to practice some part together ...allow community to develop. When a sense of relatedness and belonging is felt amongst students, they are much more likely to be able to function more effectively with a higher level of engagement, with stress minimized and self-consciousness limited. Imagine how much more likely it is that a student would want to be a part of the Music Producer's Studio. Time to talk is so important. Time to laugh together, time to help one another, to work hard together and of course time to make music together are all part of what makes learning together meaningful and productive. Treat students with dignity and respect!

In a safe and caring learning environment: students feel comfortable making mistakes or approximating; sharing ideas and feelings without fear of reprisal, criticism or ridicule; they can have differing opinions from the teacher. In a safe learning environment students perceive the teacher to care because of evidence of encouragement, support and affirmation rather than judgement, criticism or belittling. For minority students, a safe and caring classroom is also culturally relevant (Ladson-Billings, 1992).

In summary:

The "T's" of Transformative Music Pedagogy that considers:

Transformative Teaching
We need to consider what we are doing is contributing to the students lives...making music a significant part of it and making them feel a significant part of the music. Music education can be life changing!

Tone/thoughtfulness/tact
Thoughtfulness and tact are two fundamental conditions of positive micro interactions that create the tone of teaching that is productive, seductive, and reproductive. Mindfulness, or being fully present, creates a tenor of care as teachers attend to the individual's needs, interests, purpose, productivity and potential.

Trust
Trust develops and should not be assumed...it takes time and attention. The kind of trust that is beneficial as a condition for learning involves micro interactions that are predictable, dependable, respectable, wise, helpful, productive, and respectful. Trust is necessary to curtail stress, to foster exploration, to facilitate communication and to really teach and learn. It enables the individual to be him or herself and know that he or she matters.

Time
Time is a consumable that we never have enough of. It is one of the genuine "yes but's" of legitimate excuses for teacher control. It is a macro structure issue that really affects effective micro interactions. We do not have enough time ever to accomplish what we want or need to. However, what we can do is open up the time we have by recognizing what is real, meaningful, and relevant and allowing time for that. If kids are excited about and engaged in the music that they are learning, time will expand into their negotiable time...they will be working on their music night and day! Class will never end. ...music education will become a life-long learning opportunity.

Talk

Conversations are so important in the development of relationship...a fundamental tool for learning, for processing learning, and for building community. Opportunities to talk about ideas, to question, to express feelings, to reflect and respond, to do the work of forethought, to work through problem solving... is critical. We need to beware of one-way communication where the teacher just uses regulatory talk...instructing, demanding, and criticizing.

Teaching

Teaching effectively involves all kinds of professional knowledge and skill. It is an art and a science. Developing strategies, gathering resources, growing and learning about potential pedagogic possibilities, questioning your practice, all improve practice, keeping professionally current. Remembering that the essence of teaching is that you teach people....and the nature of your micro interactions is fundamental. We need to consider who our learners are, realizing that they are unique as individuals with different aptitudes, abilities, interests, histories, cultures, experiences, emotional states, physical conditions, socio-economic constraints...that require special strategies and responses. We need to use this knowledge wisely as we interact in the teaching/learning process. It is important to attend to what they know already and what student's goals are. Keeping students informed about what we expect and inviting them to inform our assessments helps the teaching learning process be effective. There is not one right way to teach every child or to teach a particular skill. Our teaching repertoire needs to be as wide as our musical one.

Team or community

Belonging to a warm and caring community is empowering, energizing and enabling. The socio-emotional climate of the community makes the difference. The care factors high in the effectiveness. Having voice, choice, and place matters in the community. Community building is high on the music educator's "to do" list. Seeing community as beyond the classroom is essential. Being active in the community as a musician yourself is important.

"Tah Dah!"

Celebration of learning is fundamental for fulfilment, "job" satisfaction, and re-energizing. It can be other than public performance or adjudication in a competition. It is not about pride...especially the pride of the teacher, parent, or funder. Acknowledgement of learning and feedback should be for the learner as part of the learning process. It should be ongoing. When goals are met the teacher and the learner should notice so that new goals can be determined. The arduous labour for long-delayed gratification is unpleasant. Celebration possibilities might be a production of a CD, a soiree for students after school, an informal presentation for a senior's home or another class, a karaoke party, a publication of students' compositions, just a special look and smile for that little triumph...the ideas are limitless. Celebration builds community, self concept, self efficacy, enthusiasm, ...and gives lots of positive energy. It just matters that you celebrate with the students their accomplishments, their learning, your learning, and if you add the meta-cognitive level and the students can reflect on and articulate what they have learned...all the better.

Leonardo Da Vinci: "Where the spirit does not work with the hand there is no art."

References:

Bartel, L. (2000). The Rehearsal Model. *Orbit*, 31 (1), 25.

Bartel, L. & Cameron, L. (2002a). "Pedagogical Dilemmas in Dance and Music: Balancing the Demands of the Art with the Needs of the Person." Unpublished paper presented at American Education Research Association, April 3, 2002, New Orleans, Arts and Learning SIG.

Bartel, L. & Cameron L. (2002b). Face the Music: Pedagogical Dilemmas and Binaries in Tension, *Proceedings of the RAIME Conference in Norway*. Edited by Harold Fiske. Pp. 115-129.

Cameron, L. & Bartel, L. (1999). Engage or disengage: A study of lasting response to music teaching. in *Music Education at the Edge: Needs, Identity and Advocacy. Proceedings of the 1998 International Seminar for Music in Schools and Teacher Education*, Kruger National Park, S. Africa. Editors: Sam Leong and Glenn Nierman.Publishers: Stord/Haugesund University College (Norway) and CIRCME

Cameron, L. & Bartel, L. (2000). Engage or disengage: A study of lasting response to music teaching. *Orbit*, 31(1) pp.22-25 (reprint).

Cambourne, B. (1988). *The Whole Story: Natural Learning and the Acquisition of Literacy in the Classroom*. Toronto: Scholastic.

Coleman, J.S. (1987). Social capital and the development of youth. *Momentum*, 18, 6-8.

Cummins, J. (1996). *Negotiating identities: Education for empowerment in a diverse society*. Los Angeles: California Association for Bilingual Education.

Deiro, J.A. (1996). *Teaching with heart: making healthy connections with students*. California: Corwin Press.

Earls, F., Beardslee, W., & Garrison, W. (1987). Correlates and predictors of competence in young children. In E.J. Anthony & B. Cohler (eds.) *The Invulnerable Child* (pp.70-83). New York: Guilford.

Friere, P. (1998). *Pedagogy of Hope: Reliving Pedagogy of the Oppressed*. New York: Continuum.

Gardner, H. (1983; 1993). *Frames of Mind: The theory of multiple intelligences*. New York: Basic Books.

Gatto, John Taylor. (2003). Against school: How public education cripples our kids, and why. *Harpers Magazine*, September, 2003.

Goleman, D. (1995). *Emotional Intelligence: Why can it matter more than IQ*. New York: Bantam.

Goodlad, J.I. (1990). *Teachers For Our Nation's Schools*. San Francisco: Jossey-Bass.

Kohn, A. (1999). *The Schools Our Children Deserve*. Boston: Houghton Mifflin

Ladson-Billings, G. (1992). Reading between the lines and beyond the pages: A culturally relevant approach to literacy teaching. *Theory Into Practice*, 31(4), 312-320.

Lieberman, A., & Miller, L. (1984). *Teachers, their world, and their work*. Alexandria, VA: Association for Supervision and Curriculum Development.

Mans, M. (2000) "Using Namibian Music/Dance Traditions as a Basis for Reforming Arts Education." *Journal of Education and the Arts*, vol.1, #3

Marshall, Robert. (2004). "Creative Juices—True innovation flows from a freethinking, rule flouting, convention-busting mindset" *Macleans magazine*, October, Special Commemorative Issue, Leaders and Dreamers, Canada's Greatest Innovators and How they Changed the World

Martin, J.R. (1992). *The schoolhome*. Cambridge, MA: Harvard University Press. pp. 87-100

McLaughlin, M.W., & Talbert, J. (1990). Constructing a personalized school environment. *Phi Delta Kappan*, 72 (3), 230-235.

Noddings, N. (1988). Schools face crisis in caring. *Education Week*, 8 (4), 1-32.

Noddings, N. (1992). *The challenge to care in schools*. New York: Teachers College Press.

O'Donnell, J., Hawkins, D, Catalano, R., Abbott, R.D., & Day, L.E. (1995). Preventing school failure, drug use, and delinquency among low-income children: Long-term prevention in elementary schools. *American Journal of Orthopsychiatry*, 65, 87-100.

O'Toole, Patricia (1993-94) I Sing in a Choir But I Have "No Voice." *Quarterly Journal of Music Teaching and Learning*, 4(4)-5(1) (Winter 1993-Spring 1994): 65-76.

Peterson, R. (1992). *Life in a Crowded Place: Making a Learning Community*. New Hampshire: Heinemann.

Salovey, P., & Sluyter, D. J. (1997). *Emotional development and emotional intelligence*. New York: Basic Books.

Sang, R.C. (1982). Modified path analysis of a skills based effectiveness model for beginning teachers in instrumental music education. Unpublished doctoral dissertation, University of Michigan, Ann Arbour.

Sergiovanni, T. (1993). *Building community in schools*. San Francisco: Jossey-Bass.

Sergiovanni, T. (1998). Leadership as Pedagogy, capital development and school effectiveness. *International Journal of Leadership in Education*, 1 (1), 44.

Small, C. (1998). *Musicking*. New England: Wesleyan University Press

Sternberg, R. J. (1997). *Successful Intelligence*. New York: Plume.

Van Manen, M. (1986). *The Tone of Teaching*. Toronto: Scholastic

Wiggins, J. (2000). *Teaching for Musical Understanding*. Toronto: McGraw Hill.

Yarbrough, Cornelia and Price, Harry E. (1989). "Sequential Patterns of Instruction in Music" *Journal of Research in Music Education*, 37/3 (Fall), 179-187.

CHAPTER THREE

From Dilemmas to Experience: Shaping the Conditions of Learning

LEE BARTEL & LINDA CAMERON

Abstract

Music is a demanding art. Learning, from the first attempts to elite performance levels, is fraught with musical, pedagogical, and motivational dilemmas and the needs of the person are often neglected. How can these needs be addressed while pursuing the ideals of the art? We propose the key is the protection and nurturing of the individual's engagement with the art. We propose that the choices teachers make related to the dilemmas set the conditions of learning and determine levels of engagement: choosing predominantly one way leads to engagement and an experience that will probably be a positive, enjoyable, motivating, and rewarding one that is likely to lead to a life-time of music participation. Choosing predominantly the other way may lead to disengagement and a music learning experience that, for the average student, will probably be a negative, de-motivating, psychologically damaging one, and in most cases lead to a cessation of music-making

INTRODUCTION

"...competition in one form or another is a pretty basic part of it... We try to keep it down a little bit here by rotating part assignments but, there is a merit base in part assignment. You're not going to put your worst player to play a first horn on the Bruckner fourth Symphony. You try not to put somebody on the part that will embarrass them and the school."

"I think a lot of people have a sort of a love- hate relationship. I mean, if you didn't have a fair component of love you couldn't make yourself do it forever but the resentment of all the time it takes and how much you miss in your life."

The study and pursuit of art is a fulfilling and delightful manifestation of a fundamental need of the human spirit. The engagement with new challenges of achievement is invigorating. The pursuit of ideals of excellence gives purpose and meaning to life. But, in the context of a consumer society, art is easily appropriated as cultural entertainment capital. Artistic concepts, aesthetic standards, and creative innovation can become idealizations of perfection forced on performers being exploited for societal pleasure. Individual achievement is mythologized as symbol for the corporate society. In this context emerge dilemmas of teachers' goals versus the students' needs, music's demands versus students' motivations and commitment, technical requirements of music versus its potential expressive import, and the digital age audience expectations of perfection versus the reality of the limits of human ability. In this context, how can the needs of the individual be balanced with the demands of the art?

A first, and very important step, is the admission that a problem exists – that the demands of the art in our time may not be aligned with the needs of the individual. It requires the recognition that pedagogic dilemmas exist and a conscious awareness of the values inherent in choices and behaviours. As researchers, it requires both a willingness to see beyond the "appropriate answer" of the discursive frame and to confront the "ugly" side of art but at the same time objectivity and responsibility toward time-honoured artistic values and practices.

Sociology of sports (Donnelly, 1997) now very openly admits there is a problem of verbal and emotional abuse of those considered talented as well as of many simply falling short of coaches and parents' expectation. A recent colloquium addressed the issue "head-on" (Talented Children in Sport, Music and Dance: How can we Nurture Talent without Exploiting or Abusing Children? – University of Toronto, Centre for Sport Policy Studies, Sept 28-29, 2001). In music education we have essentially no research looking at this issue and little if any acknowledgement it even exists. In dance there is acknowledgement that there is risk of physical injury and eating disorder, but less attention to emotional issues of pedagogy. In music education we have the further concern of "legitimised deprivation" of opportunity for children on the basis of "talent." Since music is a naturally occurring intelligence, education for the development of musical potential should be every child's right.

Social justice literature points to places where the "system" deprives a certain group of the opportunity to develop a natural potential. Epp & Watkinson (1997), in a book entitled "Systemic violence in education," state that they view as "violent" any practices and procedures that adversely impact individuals by "burdening them psychologically, mentally, culturally, spiritually, economically, or physically. It includes practices and procedures that prevent students from learning, thus harming them." Parker (2000) and Bartel (2000) have pointed out applications to music.

Whether emphasizing technique over expressivity, selecting the "talented" for inclusion and the "untalented" for exclusion, or selecting music that is culturally understood by children or is musically foreign to them, teachers daily face pedagogical dilemmas. In this chapter we argue that the choices teachers make related to the seemingly unavoidable dilemmas of music teaching establish the conditions of learning and determine the experience children have with music. These experiences can be motivating and positively transformative but just as surely debilitating and alienating. We argue that the traditional music education paradigm, both school music and private instruction, is positively motivating in the long run for only a small percentage of the population. The rest "face the music" that they are untalented, unwanted, and unnecessary. We propose that, by attending to a particular side of the dilemmas we identify, music education could be reshaped into a positively motivating, transforming, and engaging experience for a much larger percentage of the population.

THE FOUNDATION FOR OUR VIEW

This chapter is based on the findings of a series of research studies we and a number of graduate students have conducted since 1996. Our research has had three facets:

Conditions of Learning (Written Personal Narratives). In an article entitled, "What really matters in music class" (Cameron & Bartel, Fall, 1996), we invited students and educators to submit personal narrative accounts of memorable experiences with music learning - positive or negative. We also gathered accounts from students at the University of Toronto. We were looking for learning conditions facilitating engagement. Initial findings were reported at the Canadian University Music Society conference in 1997 (Bartel & Cameron, 1997). We have now acquired some 200 individual usable accounts. We conducted a thematic analysis of the narratives and compared our results to the conditions of learning model of Brian Cambourne (1988) and the student-centred philosophy of Max Van Manen (1986). We found that our findings matched these models but extended the significant categories to include aspects perhaps specific to music learning. We reported the findings at a commission of the International Society for Music Education (ISME) in South Africa in 1998 (Cameron & Bartel, 1999; Cameron & Bartel, 2000).

Self-Efficacy of Generalist and Specialist Teachers Teaching Music. In 1997 we began a questionnaire study on teachers' self-perception of confidence to teach music and perceptions of musical talent (Bartel & Cameron, 1998). The questionnaire asked teachers to describe in detail any critical incident or series of incidents that affected their self-perception of ability and confidence to teach music. In 2001-2002 we continued this research in a comparative education study focused on the "generalist" teacher required to teach music. This study, conducted with Jackie and Robert Wiggins, compared teachers in New Zealand and Canada in self-efficacy and related factors. Most recently we expanded this to include in-service and pre-service music specialists. Findings have been reported at the International Society for Music Education in South Africa in 1998 (Cameron & Bartel, 1999; Cameron & Bartel, 2000) at American Education Research Association (AERA) conference, 2002, and ISME conference in 2002 in Norway.

Face the Music (Interviews on Systemic Issues). During 2000-2001 we focused our research on broader systemic issues and began in-depth interviews. A graduate student working in our research program conducted a small pilot study with interviews stimulated by movie excerpts (Jacques, 2001a) that replicated our results in the Conditions of Learning but re-focused analysis and proposed several new themes in the data. Jacques (2001b) conducted further interviews to explore the effectiveness of various approaches to the use of video excerpts. We then began conducting semi-structured interviews with musicians (School music teachers and private studio music instructors teaching beginners, intermediate, advanced, and pre-professional students, n=31). Interviews used video clips from popular movies as thought stimulators and memory "joggers" and focused on the following themes: (1) Value of excellence, (2) importance of virtuosity, (3) role of teacher as conductor, (4) perceptions of human motivation and ability, (5) concept of talent, (6) and role of music in culture. We used qualitative theme analysis to examine data and identified factors in the perpetuation of the "talent-oriented" system. Partial results have been reported in papers at AERA 2001, AERA 2002, and at the Research Alliance of Institutes for Music Education in Oslo in 2001.

Since 2001 we have also interviewed dancers and dance teachers, done initial work on theatre, and are currently beginning with gymnasts. We believe that there are pedagogical and psychological commonalities in the teaching, learning, and practicing of artistic performance in time – temporal expressive performance. Here, however, we focus on what we have learned from music.

MUSIC EDUCATION DILEMMAS

The study and pursuit of music seems to be fraught with constant tensions and dilemmas: the student likes the positive teacher but feels something is being missed; the teacher emphasizes technique but then demands expressivity; to be an excellent performer a child must start very young but loses out on holistic development; all students deserve equal opportunity to participate but some students achieve a better performance; there is motivational benefit in competition but psychological cost in not winning; critical ability must be developed to be artistically responsible but the inner critic can ruin confidence and the love of the art. The decisions teachers make regarding these dilemmas determine to a great extent the quality of the experience of students. Setting the most productive conditions may vary from student to student, so possibilities for error are great. Because the decisions are not all "student-related," dilemmas become more complex. There are at least three categories: music-related dilemmas, pedagogy-related dilemmas, and student-related dilemmas. There is certainly interaction among these and some are not an "either-or" situation, but rather a matter of emphasis or balance.

Music-related dilemmas

There is a cluster of dilemmas related to the characteristics of music itself or the choice of music to be learned. Although they are music-related, it really is a matter of philosophical beliefs and musical values that influence a choice on these binaries or dilemmas. It is how music is viewed. It is what the teacher considers important, and what musical practice or tradition the teacher is perpetuating, that determines which side of the dilemma is emphasized. The most pervasive and evident is the binary of expressivity and technique.

Musical Expressivity — Technical Proficiency. Music experienced from the perspective of a listener is sound with structure and expressive import. Dance from the perspective of viewer is gesture with stylized technique and interpretive expressivity. So even from the perspective of audience, the technique-expressivity binary is evident as the listener/viewer may attend to the syntax, the form, the compositional elements, and the traditional movement elements but may respond primarily to the expressive elements. However, when you experience music as a performer, the technical aspects —the repetitively practiced motions of muscle and bone—are inescapable. When the music is performed is a replication of a composer's or choreographer's intent, "mistakes" become glaringly evident, and a first priority of the performer. An excellent performance is one "not only technically competent but also musically good" (study participant).

In the study of music this demand for technical competence seems to be the basic ingredient but it is meaningless without artistic expressivity. Technique is a prerequisite but expressivity is the justification.

> I want to be amazed but I also want to be moved and that is the dichotomy of the technical vs the artistic and the really amazing performances obviously combine the two.' D011

> Looking back in retrospect, sometimes you feel you're always being told a double theme from your teacher. You know you're told that musicality is important — you should feel this, feel that, or whatever — but it has to be perfect. I've always found that those two things shouldn't really, fundamentally be

put together. And yet, as a student you are always being bombarded with this idea that there is perfectionism that's absolutely required.

This is technical perfectionism?

That's right. So, the idea that he's fuming at him [Shine- movie] to have everything, all the notes there—"don't disappoint the composer, don't disappoint me" — that sort of thing, yet at the same time, "feel the beauty of the notes." It's a double message.

What do students usually opt for?

[laughs] well I find that at least today — I think there is at least in the top conservatories a real over-concern with perfectionism at the expense of real character and musicality.

If it is a dilemma for students, it is equally a dilemma for teachers. Expressivity is limited by technique. But an emphasis on technique may ignore the expressive. For teachers the question is whether you go through technique to expressivity, through expressivity to technique, or whether you go back and forth. For sensitive teachers, the dilemma seems more evident because, as in the experience of students, they seem to feel that insisting on technical matters is an expression of discipline, of rigidity, of the "tough" side of teaching and misses the motivation and "heart" of the art.

...if that trust is created between teacher and student, the teacher can later on go on and become just technical for a while, but actually you shift from this to that — you need to do both sides. You need both sides but you can start off by creating the trust and then you can become more rigid at certain moments....

Because artistic excellence is associated with technical perfection and the rigor and discipline of its development, students may feel a need for the "whip" of technical discipline.

there was one girl who asked me a couple weeks ago to help her. She wants to do her masters and she really needs work on technique, then I heard her sing in recital and I thought, she's got a wonderful singing spirit, and to really focus on technique would be detrimental to her because a lot of that is happening naturally—so I wondered what makes her think that she needs to do this, because she doesn't feel brutalized, perhaps?

The expectation of performative perfection, which always means note perfect, technical perfection, may come from teachers, may come from the students' internal competitiveness, but both may be fueled today by the image we set up as the ideal.

There is a higher premium on technical perfection and accuracy than there used to be and it's easy, and very possibly correct, to blame recordings. We hear so much perfect playing that you expect that live.

The cost of greater technical perfection may be the richness of individual expression.

...for some people it's a major accomplishment to let go of worrying about technical growth and focus on musical growth, and on your own personal character identity in you're playing. And, that's what we are missing, of course, these days.

The "Bar" is technique...but that is a circus trick...Get people to value excellence...of passion, vision, ...raising the bar so that there is more beauty or passion or thought or idea...and it isn't about better "technique"

But, the greatest cost of an emphasis on technical perfection is not just "these days" — it is a long-standing problem of instruction. Technical imperfections are blatantly evident, especially when they result in "mistakes." Consequently, teachers are often sticklers for technical development, intolerant to mistakes of any kind, and upset at a lack of similar values by students. A student's inability to achieve the desired perfection is most commonly attributed to a student's lack of ability or lack of sustained effort. Rarely is it considered a weakness of pedagogy. This translates easily into a sense by students that the teacher is justified in being upset, that being upset is attributed to such a strong passion for the demands of the art, and that is it is the insufficiency of the student that is ultimately at fault.

I had some classes with someone in Israel actually who was the sort of person who just badgered you over and over again until — that was more in a musical sense— you could tell he felt so strongly about phrases and this and that — even though it was difficult you felt he was doing it for a certain point.

We weren't allowed to learn any pieces at all—only scales and studies. [The Cleveland teacher] was a bit horrified that our wonderful quasi-Suzuki teacher had no interest in any of that, any of what you would call standard technique... so there was sort of a corrective summer. And probably really great in a sense because after that point there was always a sort of double teaching — [The Cleveland teacher] was very regimented in Galamian technique and the [London teacher] was always talking about sunshine and the soul and the spirit, and that sort of thing and it was a really good combination. So this sort of dual studying thing went on the right up until I was 14.

As is evident from these last quotes, the emphasis on technique seems associated with one kind of teacher, usually a demanding, picky teacher who may be considered necessary like bad tasting medicine, while expressivity is associated with a pleasant, inspirational teacher. However, since technique is so essential, the unpleasant teacher is sometimes considered more important and in fact more desirable.

Relative standards — Objective standards. The first response to music or dance by audience, performer, adjudicator, or clinician always seems to be critical judgment. In fact, we teach strongly for such a response stance. This critical judgment can be norm referenced – relative to the person's potential and progress, the age level of the performer, the size of the school, etc or it can be criterion referenced — with objective standards or criteria set by the ideals of the art. Most striking in the data from our participants was the tension experienced between these two bases for critical judgment. They might begin with avowing adherence to a relative, student-centered approach, but slip into an objective artistic standard.

"As a teacher I am nurturing, as a director I'm a bitch" D09

I think you can have an excellent performance by even a young ensemble which would necessarily be judged at a different level than a professional ensemble.

So is it then the personal best of the performer or the group in the moment? *Maybe, although some people may not be capable of a personal best which would rise to the level of any definition of excellence.*

So there is an objective definition of excellence in music to which we aspire, we rise toward, we work toward?

Well, in terms of musical phrasing and being together and obviously right notes and right rhythm— it's not going to be excellent in the way I would feel about it unless they meet the standards of the music.

A sub-category of this dichotomy between relative and objective standards is the dilemma for teachers of **personal best effort versus musical perfection**. When responding with relative musical standards, the teacher can give recognition to personal best effort and reward it with praise and encouragement and public celebration. However, if the teacher has strongly in mind objective standards of musical achievement which expects nothing less than musical perfection, it is very difficult to give unqualified praise and celebration. The high school teacher may want to encourage and praise a student's best effort but if the teacher knows the student will go and audition at a prominent music conservatory and the teacher's reputation will be associated with the student, the teacher may be much less ready to respond to the student in terms of the student's best effort, but rather "be realistic" about the student's potential. This problem can also be phrased as a **learner focused - art focused dilemma**. It is the very nature of the art.

I remember doing a lot of high school clinics, and a teacher would say oh I've got a great group they're playing really great, and I'd go in there, and they could hardly blow their nose, they could barely put their instruments together, and you don't want to say anything to the high school instructor that you've been deceived or something like this —you think, it's nice that the instructor is so enthusiastic about his students and thinks so well of them.

When you say, "that was an excellent performance" what do you mean?

I mean, for them where they are now. There was a student who sang today "that was really excellent" I said, those are the words I used. Was it as good as he could do? No, but for where he is at right now, those are the goals he set, and considering all that went on before, things he's got out of alignment, he did well. It's different for each student.

You don't hold up a fixed musical criteria?

No, no it's school.

How important is the pursuit of what you perceive as the standards, even though the student may be this far away, are you still gunning for those artistic standards?

Yeah, it depends, if the student really has it, then I really push them with lots of encouragement. I always let them know that they're good and I believe in them, but they really need to do the skill work, or the structured work. If I don't think that that is there, I don't tell them that. I get them to be the best that they can be.

Self-judgment is a powerful and constant element in learning and performing. The teacher may be fuelling this self-judgment by pointing to the standard, the ideal, or possibly the unattainable goal for the student's potential.

The musicians self-esteem is so highly based on how you actually play, and even without Kiwanis and competitions, almost everybody is constantly aware where the level is around them and, you know, even with students I have here we set up unattainable goals. Because, we say go to the Toronto Symphony and listen to the soloist. And they're playing the same piece but we know that they are never realistically going to play in that same vein, and yet that's what we set up for them as the pinnacle.

Culturally-familiar repertoire --- Artistic exemplars. One of the choices that must be made in music education is what music will be the focus of music-making and ability development. In the traditional music education paradigm, this choice is made by the teacher. Granted the teacher may give students some choice among a few options equally acceptable to the teacher, but, the "study repertoire" is controlled by the teacher. And, usually the teacher places great emphasis on "great music," "classics," on "artistic exemplars" of valued music. In a private study situation the "artistic exemplars" are probably determined by the "canon" of acceptable and approved literature. In the British – Canadian conservatory system, the "curriculum" is set out in grades with literature lists for each grade, controlled through required selection for the centrally administered examinations. In school music programs, teachers select music with the strong consciousness of the expectations at music competitions and peer assessments of public presentations. Along with this comes a societal assumption about the symbolic cultural value of art: to be an indicator of achievement and "getting somewhere" by being aligned with the dominant elitist values. So when students from an urban school in New York city play "classical" music on the most symbolic instrument of elitist European art, the violin, the hearts of an audience and a nation thrill at the "hope," the "elevation through art," the sign of cultural progress that they are witnessing. Like changing from regional dialect to dominant language, from local accent to mainstream pronunciation, learning "classical" music is a sign of becoming educated, cultured, and worthy of respect. Like learning Latin or Shakespeare the value of learning classical music within our culture has a utility apart from its inherent functionality and even personal enjoyment value for the person.

The alternative choice of repertoire is music selected for its cultural familiarity to students, perhaps even selected by students. In most contexts today that means popular music. As Senyshyn in his chapter in this book illustrates with personal narratives, considerable discontent among students can arise over repertoire. Music teachers may ignore it and over time establish programs where students not willing to work with the repertoire selected simply elect not to take music. But, where students do not have a choice regarding participation, repertoire can become a significant factor in motivation and enjoyment. For many students today "classical" music is like a second language. Some students have the motivation and ability to adopt and adapt. Others, the majority in our schools today, simply elect not to participate. And, the dominant music education paradigm that accepts that music is essentially for the talented and the motivated 10 percent, finds this reality acceptable.

Music teachers do recognize the dilemma and attempt to address the problem in places by using jazz or music theatre as possible options. In a way, jazz and music theatre have reached "classic" status and the "artistic exemplars" within those styles are acceptable school fare. But like "classical music" they are really not the musical language of children and youth today. They may feature more of the "groove" and sensuality of today's popular music and thus give them a greater sense of cultural relevance, but participation still requires a "second language" approach and commitment.

This dilemma is made difficult for teachers not only by cultural and societal forces but by their personal musical language ability. Music teachers tend to teach the way they were taught. Our present music education system selects classically trained musicians and inducts them into classically oriented programs. Most do not have the "chops" to deal with popular music even if they personally like the music. And, the culture of perfection has resulted in a culture of fear of mistakes and a desire to be able to know all the answers and control all eventualities before trying something in class. As a consequence, music teachers like to stay with band or choir playing and singing the "standards" and a few new "sanitized and concertized" arrangements of film or pop tunes to keep the less serious students happy. Only rare teachers have the ability and courage to add or change to steel pans, guitars, rock band, or other approaches strongly connected to many students' real culture.

Manipulable Elements --- Replicable Prescriptions. A choice of most music teachers, without even recognizing it as a choice, is to make the replication of existing music prescriptions the primary focus of music lessons. This is so because the traditional music education paradigm is premised on notated musical works created by the "specially gifted composer." These may be the great classics of the past centuries or songs and arrangements specially created for educational purposes. But regardless of type they are primarily notated. The music teacher then focuses on teaching children to decode these notations and to replicate the composers intentions as perfectly as possible.

The alternative choice teachers could make is to make the manipulation of musical materials a primary activity of music lessons. Young children learn through play. And the observation of young children reveals that the "play" with musical materials as well – they experiment with sound, with melody, with timbre, with rhythm. But when most adults and most teachers take control of children's learning by formalizing learning, play with sound is reduced and the teaching toward replication begins. We even reduce acceptable sounds to a small set of "domesticated sounds" (cp. Marsella in this book). The problem with replication is that you can get it wrong. And so teachers focus on mistake elimination, on precise tuning, precise rhythms, desirable timbres, and contrived performance disassociated from the real social community of children. In the process many children "get it wrong" and before fifth grade decide music lessons are not for them.

There are real possibilities for teachers to make musical material manipulation, music composition, and improvisation a mainstay of music lessons. Many music curricula give it a place, but many teachers give it little because they themselves are not comfortable with composition or improvisation. In our study of teacher self-efficacy we found that music teachers rated their confidence lowest in the area of teaching composition. In language learning research has informed practice to the point where most teacher now have children compose their own stories as they learn to read others' stories. The two processes synergistically support language learning. Imagine children in the first six years of schooling learning to read by reading fine literature, but never being given an opportunity to write their own ideas and stories. In most cases that essentially is what is done in the traditional music education paradigm. The music teacher may deal with the "phonics" of musical notation, may even have children do some musical "spelling," "copying," or "dictation" assignments, but never ask children to write a musical "story" or create their own "book."

Pedagogy-related Dilemmas

Regardless of what music or what dimension of music becomes the focus of instruction, teachers are faced with a cluster of dilemmas related to pedagogy itself. Of course, some types of musical contexts demand a certain general approach to pedagogy – the concert band requires a conductor, a program of chamber music groups requires a coaching style. However, there are many other choices to be made that reflect the teacher's motivations, philosophy, personality, learning style, and perhaps even psychological health.

Encouraging Teacher—Pushing Teacher. A clearly evident theme in our data was the experience with teachers considered difficult, demanding, harsh, and unpleasant and in contrast, teachers who were pleasant, supportive, encouraging, and inspirational. In some cases students quickly left the unpleasant teacher, but disturbing in our data was the evidence that students often do not leave harsh and demanding teachers, and may in fact consider them necessary to the difficult challenge of conquering the "monster" of the non-compliant body or instrument.

> *I had a range of teachers some of whom were very harsh and some were extremely nice, and the extremely nice teacher didn't produce the same results, in a sense. I got the impression that he was, like, very happy with his own playing, all of that, and that shined — that was always apparent, and so maybe in a sense that was a learning experience, because one did feel inspired, but one wasn't actually feeling like "oh my God if I don't prepare well for the next lesson he is going to skin me alive."*

> *He was not a mean man at all but he was very picky and inside of a couple of years I was so unsure about what to do that I'd pick up the horn and I'd almost freeze. ...and actually I started taking lessons on the sly with other teachers. In the summer in Boston there was this wonderful former bass trombonist of the Boston Symphony who had actually been a roommate of my Curtis trumpet teacher when they were both at Curtis but they couldn't have been more different — one was very fussy and this trombone player was very casual laid-back rather crude and had a very simple approach: " tongue and blow kid—play it louder faster"—and he'd take you through easy stuff, "play it out a kid — tongue and blow" —he got me going again. And then there was a Boston Symphony trumpet player, Armando Ghitala, who is a wonderful almost father figure and the combination of this got me playing again and I think the teacher at Curtis probably thought his lessons were finally kicking in.*

These study participants described what they recognized as harsh and demanding teachers. Yet, they found some value in these teachers and, in fact, felt that the more pleasant teachers had perhaps not served them as well. This phenomenon seems related to a belief in another dilemma: students may have the **desire to achieve** but they **lack the ability to self-motivate** adequately. This may be a belief absorbed from the teacher's impatience and "pushing" while being a student. There may in fact be a different basis for the "pushing" in teachers than is perceived by students. The teacher may be so "envious" of the perfection of the art that lack of attainment of this perfection is upsetting and angering, and to justify this anger a scapegoat is created – the student's lack of motivation and commitment (an application of Rene Girard's memetic theory, Jordan, 2000). The student comes to believe this is his or her personal short-coming and that the teacher's pushing is needed.

Further, the demand of the art is such that growth in technical and expressive excellence is "a forever thing" and therefore, the belief and feeling that one is "good" can be considered inappropriate. The feeling "I am really good at this" can be interpreted as being out of touch with professional artistic reality since this could only be held by the most elite performers of the art and if held by a student would probably serve to inflate expectations unrealistically and probably place a damper on motivation. The tough critical teacher is then viewed as being the voice of realism and honesty. Data from our interviews with dancers illustrates this, but we believe the same is true in music.

> they were very lenient ...I took advantage of that and I tried to run the class myself and I thought I was so much better than everyone else ...My dancing went downhill a lot...those four years...really factored on me progressing... when I left there I had a lot of catching up to do... when I went to the National...it was hard because I had to go back to what I did when I was younger...

The theory that students may have the **desire to achieve** but inevitably **lack the ability to self-motivate** adequately is not in fact true. Several participants in our study described their development as entirely lacking in teachers who had to push them. They admitted knowing about such teachers, hearing fellow students descriptions of such teachers, and even fearing the possibility with their own teachers. However, they counted themselves "lucky" in not having such teachers or in avoiding the teacher's displeasure through conscientious work and commitment.

> and then the guy at Eastman was the most humanistic beautiful person you can ever meet. He could have taught any instrument and you would've just loved what you were doing. One time I played something for him — and he was 80 years old — he taught most trombone players — he turned out a lot — he was legendary — and I played something for him and he goes "wheww!" and he brushed me on the shoulder. I didn't know what he was doing. He says "... you keep playing like that and you'll be in the Philadelphia Orchestra someday." I mean ...it was tough playing lessons for him because, he'd say "what's wrong?" — I'd make a mistake or something wouldn't sound right because I was smiling— and it's tough to play when your smiling. I was so happy to be studying with the guy and I'd break into a smile sometimes. I never had any experience like that [movie clip from Shine] at all thank goodness, because I think it would've turned me right off.

Some students recognize that "abuse" may not be about themselves as people or about the art:

> Sometimes it is not about the art, making the dancer better, its not about anything but making some one feel small..to hurt them so you feel better.

As well, difference in personality is involved in the perception of "pushing" and the response to it:

> Some people who are pushed, push back...I'll do that better than you can even imagine. It comes down to ego...some push back others leave...

Some student's who managed to avoid teachers who really pushed them, still felt somewhat guilty that they had not been pushed – and attributed some of their technical shortcomings to this lack, and therefore their own inadequacies or personality deficiencies.

> —she was the one I had after Mrs. Teacher, so I would have been 9 or 10 or 11 in there—I just didn't like her, her face was stern, and things weren't good. And then we moved to[another town]. I had [this new teacher]—I spoke to her this morning on the phone actually —lovely lady, and I liked it

49

because she didn't push me. So back then I could explore my own—I could do a watered down version of the Hungarian Rhapsody......I still got the joy of it. I'm still not great doing all the scales and chords and so on...

And why does it matter?

I don't know — maybe, it's the "I must work harder" mentality.

Is there such thing ... that without that moving catastrophe of being insulted or embarrassed and generally torn apart, that you might not have worked as hard and achieved as much. Is there justified abuse in the pursuit of excellence?

I would have to say yes. I don't think it needs to go to the degree that it sometimes goes to, but I think everybody, no matter what field they are in, needs somebody at a certain point to say "hey, make sure you're serious about this. If you are I'm going to kick your butt and try to realize your potential."

There is no doubt that participants in this study have experienced what must be called abuse – physical, verbal, and emotional. Many participants named it as such. But is it justified abuse as the quoted participant above seems to think? Other participants agreed:

I guess that [physical abuse] helped me a great deal, seeking for perfection.

In a way it [physical abuse] also made me stronger, 'cause I really want to prove to her that "you're wrong! I can do better— a lot better than you think!"

Maybe to some people because it pushes them to want to progress...but to some people it makes them give up...A couple of times I wanted to quit because I was so embarrassed but I think then my mom tells me not to worry about it. It does push me to want to do better...but it also makes me step back and look at it and think whether Do I really want to do this? Do I want to keep going at this...do I want to get embarrassed EVERY day I go to...class...You have to deal with this...if you do, then obviously you really want it bad and that passion... is there.

The teacher has the ability to affect your emotional state and can create an emotional environment that either leans more to the pleasure of the movement or can be a very uncomfortable environment... the great teachers are the ones who make the environment a positive place to be even when they are working on you and correcting you and letting you know that it isn't working. Change can hurt...but in the long run, I am glad that I got totally emotionally trashed by teachers-- in the long run it was necessary. That happens to everybody...that trashing...It can be a terrible thing...depending where the environment is that it is happening.

We recognized the effects of abuse in many expressions, beliefs, attitudes, reported and observed behaviours. The scope of this analysis and implications are, however, beyond this chapter.

Performance-focused feedback—Person-directed feedback. The data of our study and much of the foregoing discussion makes it clear that the teacher's "pushing" may be directed subjectively at the student and be perceived as a personal attack, or directed objectively at the requirement of the art and an insistence on artistic perfection. The later is not perceived as abusive, and when associated with expectation of the student's ability to master the challenge, may be productive and rewarding. However, if expectations of the teacher are unattainable or never satisfied, the student comes to the ultimate realization of inadequacy and develops a powerful inner critic.

> Well it is needed to drill you and needed to embarrass you somewhat but to an extent that they are telling you that you aren't any good and you can't do it anymore and you should leave...that shouldn't be a part of it....there is nothing wrong with telling you you need to work harder at this.

How to direct criticism is a pedagogical choice. This choice is partially related to the attribution the teacher makes regarding the imperfection addressed. If the problem is attributed to an inherent characteristic of the student -- inability, lack of talent, laziness, stubbornness, dimwittedness, lack of effort, lack of focus, etc. – then it is likely the teacher will "attack" the person, rather than insist on particular standards of achievement. If the teacher fundamentally believes in the students ability and effort, the teacher is more likely to make demands accompanied with expressions of positive expectations of the student. So, how to direct criticism is not really a pedagogical dilemma. Directing criticism as an attack on the person is rather simple mispedagogia. It may stem from many sources, not the least of which is the psychological state of the teacher which in itself stems from many sources. It may be mispedagogia conducted with good intentions. Teachers most often teach the way they were taught. They are trapped in a model of learning. They may honestly believe that they need to put this sort of pressure on students to get them to reach their potential, unaware of the long-term damage being done to the psychological make-up of the student.

Positive person-directed feedback on the other hand can be very motivating and inspiring. For the teacher to compliment the student's ability, effort, energy, intelligence expressive sensitivity, and so on may prove to be very important to the development of self confidence and motivation. The mistake too often made on this binary is to compliment the quality of the performance and criticize the inherent person, rather than criticizing the performance and complimenting the inherent person.

Optimistic expectation—Pessimistic expectation. One of the crucial factors in student engagement in music learning is expectation. If students expect to achieve they achieve; if they expect to fail they fail. The teacher's expectation of the student is particularly influential because it has a strong effect on the student's expectation of themselves.

> From the first note I made on the instrument, he [the teacher] knew that I had potential, and fuelled my desire to be a better player. By the time that a few months had passed, he had me playing solos at feeder schools...

But expectation has to be appropriate. Like the related concept of self-efficacy, people may believe they are competent when they are not, or may believe they are not competent when in fact they are (Cameron, Wiggins, et al 2004). Similarly a teacher may have an expectation of the student that is appropriate to the student's ability or not. Having too high an expectation for the skill level results in anxiety and worry on the part of the student and possible abusive demands and feedback from the teacher. Having expectations that are too low for the student's skill level results in boredom, apathy, and discouragement (Csikszentmihalyi, 1997). But here lies the dilemma. If the teacher is some-what pessimistic and believes that the pessimistic assessment is in fact "realistic," students without exceptional "talent" are easily regarded as not really worth that extra effort, that perhaps risky opportunity, because they might fail and that would look bad for the teacher and might result in an embarrassing experience for the student. A teacher's low expectations quickly communicates, " I don't think you are capable of doing this."

> She told me that I had an excellent touch and could feel and interpret music well but for the more technically difficult pieces she always gave me the easiest choices. Her attitude made me feel that I was not able to play these pieces. I was never challenged to try and when I wanted to play a particular piece that I loved she would not allow me to do it deeming it beyond what I was capable of doing.

Another student expressed it like this:

> When I went back to her saying that I actually succeeded in playing it at a certain speed, she didn't believe me because I was unable to do it again, with her being in the room.

If the teacher holds optimistic expectations, believing that the student is indeed capable of meeting challenges set, this can be very motivating to the student. If the teacher is right in those expectations and sets the challenge appropriately for the skill, the result can be optimum progress. The key is for the teacher to be able to determine what Vygotsky called the "zone of proximal development" (Wiggins, 2000) – the range of challenges that can be met with appropriate help from the teacher.

Challenge appropriate to the student – challenge stimulating to the teacher. Another pedagogical dilemma possibly contributing to the existence of harsh and abusive teachers is the difference between the level of challenge appropriate to the student, especially the beginning to intermediate student, and the level of challenge rewarding and stimulating to the teacher. This is a basic problem of music since the task of the student is determined by a "repertoire" of performance prescriptions in notation and often available in immaculate recordings. If the teacher is expecting to find his or her primary musical fulfillment, stimulation, and reward in the music-making of his or her students, and those students are not able to cope satisfactorily with the musical repertoire this requires, the teacher will experience considerable frustration. Data seemed to indicate that music teachers who find personal music-making opportunities appropriate for their own level (apart from teaching, perhaps in the community), have more understanding and patience for students. The teacher whose primary artistic self-expression is "through" students, either as a teacher or conductor, is likely to experience more frustration at imperfections and is more likely to express this frustration as anger directed at the students.

A Caution and Concern. We recognize that a teacher's self-report of pedagogy may not be completely accurate and neither might a student's version of that pedagogy. But, perhaps most troubling is the possibility that the social psychological theory (Helson, 1964) of adaptation-level operates here. Adaptation-level is a level of stimulation that becomes neutral through repeated exposure and serves as a reference point for judgments on that dimension. Music students may learn to expect and tolerate certain behaviours and accept them as normal, although these very behaviours may have adverse psychological effect. As well, teachers may teach in a certain way because that simply is the "model of learning" in which they themselves were trained and the model used by their peers. One teacher seems to recognize this possibility:

> I have been watching teachers...surrounded by teachers that are so strict like.. that it obviously feeds off to me...and I think when I teach that is exactly what I do... even though I say I don't like it.

Holistic approximation – Fine-grained perfection. Often associated with the encouraging teacher versus the demanding teacher, this dilemma really reflects a choice music teachers make constantly. Presumably, music teachers facilitating students' music-making can hear a myriad of "flaws" in every student attempt. However, does the teacher react to each flaw? Or does the teacher respond to the larger picture, the broad strokes of the attempt, and possibly find several things to compliment and select very carefully as to which flaws to address. This may well be a somewhat personality dependent aspect of pedagogy, but musicians are educated to listen for minute flaws, to make mistake elimination the first priority. So, all musicians face the choice of when and what to celebrate in students' attempts and what things to criticize. The choices teachers make ought to be informed by educational psychology. Psychology suggests that focusing on what children do well is more motivating and productive for achievement than focusing on what they do poorly. Further, observation and study of how children learn language shows that focusing on the positive attempts at speech and continually modeling the desired target is particularly productive. Pointing out incorrect attempts and scolding are not productive. Following the language learning model in music education, Suzuki advocates that an error made by the child is corrected by improving and increasing the modeling of the parents. These progressive attempts at approaching the ideal model is known as approximation. In the rehearsal model of music education that dominates the traditional music education paradigm, modeling and progressive approximation are often perceived as inefficient, and inefficiency in rehearsal is one of the greatest sins a music teacher can commit. The alternative is the identification of flaws and directive "fixing" of these imperfections. Pedagogically this is a dilemma, more acute in music education than in some other fields.

Equality of opportunity—Merit-based assignment. Another tension in the pedagogical/performance task of teachers exists between the benefits of providing equal opportunity for all students (especially for solos or chair placement) and the performance excellence advantage of merit-based assignment.

> Well, I think competition in one form or another is a pretty basic part of it. You know, it's what kickstarted me. Getting any job is a competition—an audition or an interview is a fact of life. We try to keep down a little bit here by rotating part assignments but, there is a merit base in part assignment. You're not going to put your worst player to play a first horn on the Bruckner fourth Symphony. You try not to put somebody on the part that will embarrass them and the school. I don't like competition particularly. I much prefer adjudicating or going to noncompetitive festivals or category festivals than ranked festivals, but it's all around — competition is all around and it is not something you can ignore because it's there. The trying out for parts, the auditioning to get into the faculty of music — some are accepted and some are rejected. You can't just say yes to everybody.

This is a pedagogical dilemma with considerable input as a music-related dilemma. The difficulty of music presents a challenge that not all students equally can meet. However, it is the level of excellence expected or required in the context of peers and community that often determines the choice rather then the learning possibilities inherent in a performance. One student might benefit from the challenge of a particular piece while another might offer a more predictable performance. So in a way this really is a dilemma of educational excellence versus musical performance excellence. The very attitudinal context created by the teacher may determine the choice.

Another aspect of this problem lies in the subjective assessment of ability that can well be influenced by personal "favourites."

> *...they have their pets, their students...they know who is going to have the solos...*

Teachers may profess equality and yet favour particular students, or may profess assignment on basis of merit but in fact act preferentially. This is a dilemma that requires both a philosophical stance as well as conscientious self-monitoring for either position.

Collaborative environment– Competitive environment. This is a dilemma of how to create the musical community and is strongly related to the dilemma of equality versus merit. It is quite blatantly a philosophical and political choice. Those who believe that the pursuit of excellence is the highest good, will likely be willing to acknowledge that if there are to be winners there must be losers, that the possibility of winning over fellow competitors is highly motivating and that this motivation leads to greater excellence, even if for only a few. Those who value collaboration, cooperation, and a community of equity will likely value the process over the product, the maintenance of equanimity, goodwill, caring, sharing, and the lack of "losers" over possible slight gain in achievement excellence by a few at the expense of the many. The competitive approach leads to the scenario in the movie *Shine* where one competitor says to the other, "It's a tough game isn't it Roger." And the other replies, "It's a blood sport." The music educator must weigh the educational costs and benefits of the social climate established. The teacher must attend carefully to the nature of the community created among learners. Principles of social justice and democracy must become decisive determinants of pedagogic practice in the music classroom.

Authentic music-making—Contrived performance. Music-making has a natural meaning and function in the rites and rituals of a society. Music made in a church worship context has a functionality apart from the very act of performing. Music at a football game, a party, a funeral, a parade, a political rally, a protest similarly serves a particular function and does not specifically draw attention to itself and the act of performing. These are all authentic music-making contexts. Presumably music at a concert serves the purpose of artistic fulfillment, aesthetic response, sensual enjoyment or something like that, although many members of the audience are focused on criticism – they judge the performing quality of the artist. However, the Chicago Symphony does not create a concert to demonstrate that they have learned a new piece, reached a new level, or can out-perform the Toronto Symphony Orchestra. But, students are frequently subjected to these contrived music-making experiences – to be patronized in their progress and achievement, to "make their parents and teachers proud," to compete against each other, to be judged for opportunities, to play simply to play what has been studied to develop technique, to perform to get used to performing, and so on. These are inauthentic music-making experiences, contrived for an "educative" purpose and usually associated with particular stress and terror, especially if "losing" is going to be taken as an indicator of personal worth and character. Music educators are constantly faced with choices about music-making context. They feel an obligation to have students perform, and feel that "education in performance" is needed. When music learning is not valued as a process, when the community of students itself is not seen as a fully worthwhile context for music-making, when there are few real community and cultural "rites and rituals" in the school context, teachers have few opportunities to involve students in authentic music-making experiences. The best they can do is create a public concert. And, of the possible performing experiences, concerts are the most tenuous and hazardous of authentic experiences because audiences find "moving artistic experiences" difficult to achieve and critical reaction easy to express.

Student-responsibility – Teacher-responsibility. The question of who is responsible for what is to be learned in music lessons is related to the dilemma of culturally-familiar repertoire versus artistic exemplars but is broader than merely repertoire. As in some previous dilemmas, this may not even seem like a dilemma to music educators—teachers simply select what is to be learned, what is to be rehearsed, what is to be performed. However, teachers exist that do encourage student responsibility and choice and evidence indicates that allowing and encouraging student responsibility increases engagement and motivation.

> *She had me choose my own repertoire and prepared me for my grade 10 and for my auditions. He also helped me start up my first brass quintet.*

> *He was limiting my musicality and making me play a piece the way he liked it. He then entered me in a music festival and forced me to play a piece that I did not like at all.*

Teachers may be ready to encourage student responsibility of r repertoire or interpretation at advanced levels in individual study contexts but hesitant to do so at lower levels or in group contexts. The traditional music education paradigm features large ensemble performance or at least whole class activity with the teacher firmly in control of all decisions. Consequently, few places seem to exist where student responsibility is possible (other than the way the term is often used, be responsible to show up on time, look after your instrument, etc). If a more project-oriented approach were used in music class, choice and responsibility would immediately become a greater possibility.

The real issue, and dilemma for a progressive music educator, is who is responsible for what goes on in a learning context. Does the student take responsibility for what is to be learned, when, and how? Does the student have responsibility for decisions about interpretation or expression? Or is this responsibility carefully guarded and exercised by the teacher? Music teachers have been educated in a tradition of control – we need to control every sound, every expression. We are loathe to take on any situation without adequate preparation and rehearsal because we are afraid to lose control. And so music teachers may believe they are "sharing responsibility" for interpretive decisions or are developing "critical thinking" in students through a process of Socratic questioning about performance decisions. In fact, the Socratic process is a very teacher controlled discourse. The teacher "leads" to the "right" answer. A process that gives students more choice and more responsibility shifts control to students. It trusts students to "get to a possible answer" even if it is different from the teacher's.

Dilemmas related to student motivation and personality

The dilemmas related to music and to pedagogy interact directly with the dilemmas related to student motivation and personality. There is no doubt that certain students respond positively to technical challenges, to competition, to the replication of pre-scribed musical works, or to a focus on fine-grained perfection. Some students may even be more resilient or tolerant to personal criticism and coercion. In fact, there may be a generational "vicious circle" in music related to who "survives" the system to be come the perpetuators of the system. The traditional music education paradigm has operated to a great extent with a conservative Darwinist approach: an assumption of survival of the fittest that finds ways to select the fittest without wasting time or resources on the ones not likely to survive anyway. We have heard this frequently in comments made by music teachers who say they have no patience for the students who do not practice or come prepared to lessons, who believe they have little role in motivating students but rather "turn on the heat" assuming that "if you can't stand the heat, get out of the kitchen" applies and prepares students for "the real world" of music. If the goal of music educa-tion of all types is to develop the potential of everyone, as we believe it should be, then greater attention to motivation and personality variables is required. The following dilemmas are not directly related to personality differences but reveal the effects of the interactions with the previous dilemmas.

Social play—Secluded practice. One dilemma faced by most parents of children taking music lessons is the desire of the child to engage in social play and the demands of music for secluded practice. This demand increases as the ability level of the child increases. It is probably one of the principal reasons for drop-outs from music lessons in childhood. One, of course, attributes the problem to the child's motivation, and perhaps indirectly to the motivational ability of the teacher. In fact some of that attribution is in place as is evident from our discussion of the previous dilemmas. However, the child may in fact experience some motivation to learn but greater need and motivation to play with friends. One must also worry about the type of person and personality that therefore succeeds in music in isolation from social play. For many children this is a minor problem since they are not required to practice many hours, but it becomes an especially serious problem in the peri-od heavily social oriented adolescence when "serious" musicians are expected to practice hours every day. It is also a very real problem of the gifted child as we discuss next.

Healthy childhood holism—Singular focus for peak achievement. One of the really serious dilemmas is the tension between the need to start a child very young and keep them consistently practicing for them to become peak performers, and the damage done by the removal of that time from the normal holistic pursuits of childhood.

> Because kids are brought up musically, that becomes their only way to be loved and appreciated, so it becomes this overwhelming search for appreciation... I think parents and teachers contribute to varying degrees. I don't have a solution. To be a successful violinist you need to create that facility and technique when you're younger, it's a sort of fact of violin playing. And so you have a real problem there.

Having been through what I consider perhaps a mildly abusive musical upbringing, it seems to me that there are some things to do that could enrich a child's education that would not be terribly difficult. I wouldn't really advocate dismantling the entire Kiwanis system, but at the same time the Kiwanis can be very detrimental— so much is up to the parents — and the parents are not aware of these kinds of issues. I don't really know how one would solve that besides having some kind of counseling to go along with every Kiwanis class which actually probably would not be a bad thing.

A related issue to this dilemma is the investment parents make in the achievement of their child. During the time the child is subject to parental influence, a great weight of obligation can be placed on a child.

they had put in a tremendous amount of money and emotional effort into me continuing...you can't quit...we have put too much money into it...you have to keep going until you make it ...we are not going to waste the money we have put in...Keep going!

Little thought or research has been given in music education to considerations of the ethical issues inherent in the development of gifted musicians. As stated in the introduction, sports sociologists and psychologists are beginning to recognize this problem and are raising alarms related to these ethical issues. Music educators urgently need to do so.

Musical–soulful reward—Ego–achievement reward. Artistic achievement can be pursued for several reasons. A person may in fact love and enjoy music and find great fulfillment in its study and performance. However, the act of achieving is in itself ego-rewarding. Achievement in a field where there is essentially little recognized challenge will not be particularly rewarding for someone who seeks recognition for the act of achievement. But, a field that presents great challenge and in addition, the meeting of that challenge is in public performance, presents great opportunity for ego-driven achievement. Music seems especially subject to such ego-driven effort.

Even if one professes love of music it's often, you know, still sort of a clever veil for one's ego.

You mean what one actually loves is achievement, the recognition of achievement rather than music itself?

I think it happens quite often.

Is it typical that the teacher starts to want the student to succeed for their own ego...

Oh sure

Rather than the student's goals?

Yes, I think it's a real danger all of the time, because the way you are seen as a teacher whether in the community or in the larger context, gives you access to better students who will then know your reputation. If you can start with better students you'll be producing even better — you know, it's sort of a chain. Because people often say that derogatorily about various very famous teachers who don't seem to actually teach at all but they always have terrific students.

Certainly everyone who is going to stand up or sit and perform for others, there has to be ego there.

How much varies considerably and I think it varies at different times of our own lives. I think ego is not really enough to sustain a career. It's sort of insatiable — you need constantly new conquests. I also think that the love of playing an instrument is not enough to sustain a career. I can think of trumpet players that I think love playing their instrument but they get bored with the music and I think that's sad. It's really the love of music that can sustain a career.

When can a musician stop struggling for greater excellence and enjoy competence?

Boy, that's a hard one... It's probably when your love of music becomes stronger than your ego that you can enjoy competence and if you're good enough to play well — competently at whatever level you're playing.

When you think of your own personal inner critic, what fuels it or where does it come from in your case?

Probably ego, that we always want to be the best, that typical American thing of being the best you can and working hard at it — no pain, no gain, kind of thing. Always perhaps wanting to be the best and that's unfortunate.

Factors other than a focus on the real meaning and experience of the art can also be a parental motivation. The ego of the parent may thrive on "showing off" a child.

Putting little girls on display to show off instead of a sharing of an art form....

This may be the motivation of parents from the "impromptu living room concerts" when guests appear, to the interest in monthly, quarterly or annual recitals at the teacher's house, to the kindergarten holiday concert or the recital hall debut concert. It is the very act of achievement that is the motivation and reward rather than an authentic love of music or the experience of the music itself. And, this thrives in a culture where fascination is with the new "child star" or the new talent on the concert stage, and a culture where the very atten- dance of the concert may be of greater value than the experience of the music at the concert.

Love the music — Hate the cost. Music is an art that is exceptionally demanding in terms of the time and effort involved in the development of the ability required to reach a professional level. But not only must the performer spend much time and effort during the formative years, this time must continually be spent if the ability is to be sustained. Even those who have an abundant love of the art and are not simply pursuing ego-driven achievement, the cost of maintaining ability is great but without the ability being main- tained near its peak, the enjoyment is lost.

I think a lot of people have a sort of a love-hate relationship. I mean, if you didn't have a fair component of love you couldn't make yourself do it forever but the resentment of all the time it takes and how much you miss in your life. Armando Ghitala, the principal in Boston and the man in the poster up there who is such a great artist said, he resented all of the time it took, all of the books he couldn't read etc.

Music has many similarities to dance in this regard. Musicians experience some of what this ballet dancer said in an interview:

Ballet is unforgiving, it's ruthless. It is an absolutely cruel and horrendous world, but it's beautiful!"

But, the cost is not only a personal one. We may, as a culture, so value something that we are willing to close our eyes to things we should not, or perpetrate things we might not except for the great value we place on a certain experience.

> Do we still allow things to happen or justify things because finally we have these elevating experiences with the arts and, therefore, almost anything is justified in the creation of this experience? The end justifies the means?

> *I think that happens. There's been books written about a certain conductor and his opera orchestra and yet everybody seems to be totally willing to overlook all his personal failures because of his great musical successes.*

Incredible art—Rotten profession. Related to the "love the art--hate the cost" dilemma is the conclusion that a number of the participants seem to reach, music is an incredible art but a rotten profession.

> *I feel really guilty about all of the students who are trying to become musicians — I think it's an incredible art and a rotten profession, because it's so poorly paid and the failure rate is so high. I worry about all the students here and other places that have such a hard road and are probably not going to make it in terms of traditional performing. I think the music schools are guilty, but on the other hand who do you tell "no."*

> *There's a difference between the music business and the business of music— one is great and the other is horrible, but you have to combine the two. Some people are just scraping by... But, they seem to enjoy what they're doing—maybe they're just unrealistically waiting for their break.*

CONDITIONS OF LEARNING

Music is a demanding art. Learning, from the first attempts to elite performance levels, is fraught with musical, pedagogical, and motivational dilemmas and the needs of the person are often neglected. How can these needs be addressed while pursuing the ideals of the art? We propose that the key is the protection and nurturing of the individual's engagement with the art. We propose that the choices teachers make related to the dilemmas set the conditions of learning and determine levels of engagement: choosing one way or another may lead to engagement or to disengagement. Further, the dilemma choices are inter-related: a choice on one dilemma may influence the effect of a choice on another.

The dilemmas we have discussed are the following:

Musical expressivity	—	Technical proficiency
Relative standards	—	Objective standards
Personal best effort	—	Musical perfection
Learner focused	—	Art focused
Culturally-familiar repertoire	—	Artistic exemplars
Manipulable elements	—	Replicable prescription
Encouraging teacher	—	Pushing teacher
Desire to achieve	—	Lack of ability to self-motivate

Performance-focused feedback	—	Person-directed feedback
Optimistic expectation	—	Pessimistic expectation
Student-appropriate challenge	—	Teacher-stimulating challenge
Holistic approximation	—	Fine-grained perfection
Equality of opportunity	—	Merit-based assignment
Collaborative environment	—	Competitive environment
Authentic music-making	—	Contrived performance
Student-responsibility	—	Teacher-responsibility
Social play	—	Secluded practice
Healthy childhood holism	—	Singular focus for peak achievement
Musical–soulful reward	—	Ego–achievement reward
Love the music	—	Hate the cost
Incredible art	—	Rotten profession

In a general way, if the conditions of learning are predominantly those from the left hand column, the music learning experience will probably be a positive, enjoyable, motivating, and rewarding one that is likely to lead to a life-time of music participation. If the conditions of learning are predominantly those from the right hand column, the music learning experience for the average student will probably be a negative, de-motivating, psychologically damaging one, and in most cases lead to a cessation of music-making. The "talented musicians" that endure and survive this approach to music-making are likely to have suffered some psychological damage that leads to a life-time of struggle in various forms of stress and anxiety, ego-gratification, and a tendency to perpetuation of the abuse on others.

The model of the conditions of learning (Cameron & Bartel, 2000) that we have been developing for the past few years has **engagement** at its core – primarily engagement of the student with learning music but also the engagement of the teacher with pedagogy. This model expands with the adaptation of these dilemmas and particularly needs to demonstrate the dynamic between the psycho-social and the socio-cultural dimensions of music education.

References:

Bartel, L. R. (2000). Today's systemic violence. *Orbit*, 31(1) 37.
Bartel, L. R. & Cameron, L. (1998, June). Lack of Talent or Miseducation: A Study of Teacher's Perceptions of Inability. *Canadian Society for Studies in Education*, Ottawa, Ontario. Unpublished Paper.
Bartel, L. R. & Cameron, L. (1997, June). Conditions of Music Learning. *Canadian University Music Society Conference*, St. John's, Newfoundland.
Cambourne, B.. (1988). *The Whole Story: Natural learning and the acquisition of literacy in the classroom*. Auckland, NZ: Ashton Scholastic.
Cameron, L. & Bartel, L. (1999). Engage or disengage: A study of lasting response to music teaching. in *Music Education at the Edge: Needs, Identity and Advocacy. Proceedings of the 1998 International Seminar for Music in Schools and Teacher Education*,Kruger National Park, S. Africa. Editors: Sam Leong and Glenn Nierman.Publishers: Stord/Haugesund University College (Norway) and CIRCME
Cameron, L. & Bartel, L. (2000). Engage or disengage: A study of lasting response to music teaching. Orbit, 31(1) pp.22-25 (reprint).
Cameron, L. & Bartel, L. R. (1996) "What really matters in music class," *Canadian Music Educator* 38(1).
Cameron, L, Wiggins, R., Wiggins J., and Bartel, L (2004) *Implications Of Generalist Teachers' Self-Efficacy Related To Music*. Paper presented at the Thirteenth International, Music In the Schools and Teacher Education Commission Seminar, Malmö, Sweden, August 2002. With Linda Cameron, Publication in the MISTEC Proceedings

Csikszentmihalyi, M. (1997). *Finding Flow: The psychology of engagement with everyday life.* New York, NY: Basic Books.

Donnelly, P. (1997). Child labour, sport labour: Applying child labour laws to sport. *International Review for the Sociology of Sport.* 32(4).389-406.

Epp, J. R. & Watkinson, A.M. (Eds.) (1997). *Systemic violence in education: Promise broken.* Albany, New York: State University of New York Press.

Helson H. (1964). *Adaptation-level theory: An experimental and systematic approach to behavior.* New York: Harper & Row.

Jacques, B. (2001a). Abuse and persistence: Why do they do it? *Canadian Music Educator,* 42(2), 8-13,

Jacques, B. (2001b). Learning from narrative: An examination of data-gathering techniques. Unpublished paper, University of Toronto.

Jordan, J. (2000). *The musician's soul.* Chicago: GIA Publications Inc.

Parker, M. A. (2000) A legacy of violence: The castratos. *Orbit,* 31(1) 37

Van Manen, M. (1986). *The Tone of Teaching.* Toronto: Scholastic Canada.

Wiggins, J. (2000). *Teaching for Musical Understanding.* Toronto: McGraw Hill.

Chapter Four

Put the "Play" Back in Music Education

Mary Kennedy

Abstract

This chapter addresses a pervasive belief in society, education in general, and music education in particular that one must learn and achieve more, earlier, and faster if one is to succeed. The "earlier is better" mantra, coupled with the over-emphasis on performing which characterizes most current secondary music programs, prompted the writer to propose a "new prescription" for music education. Following an examination of three important issues that affect positively (and negatively) the nature and scope of school music programs—the "earlier is better" mentality, the role of "play" in music, and students' views on music education—the writer weaves these themes into a tapestry that portrays a progressive conception of music education. Establishing a truly balanced curriculum, reducing performance expectations, building support through community connections, taking time to enjoy the ride, and preparing teachers for the "new prescription" classroom are key elements of this progressive conception.

Introduction

I am a choral and general music educator with over twenty-five years' experience in K-12 education. Now I am teaching at the university level. Throughout my teaching career, I have attempted to balance the development of musical skills and understanding with the nurturing of performing skills, most often with choirs. I count myself fortunate to have been left to my own devices (for the most part) as far as curriculum was concerned. So when I wished to develop units for secondary general music classes, no one interfered or complained. When I favored adjudicated/clinic festivals over competitive festivals, I received no negative feedback. I routinely planned choir trips with my students [1] as I knew that valuable musical, social, and educational lessons were to be learned through participation in such events. I also knew that they were fun!

From time to time I reflected on my success as a teacher, wondering if my students were receiving as valuable an education as the students of my more performance-oriented colleagues. The music my students sang was not as difficult, nor did they routinely soar to the dizzying heights of performance excellence. However, when they delighted in their research projects/presentations on great choral masterworks, worked overtime to complete their composition projects, or contributed thoughtful evaluations on their quartet singing and conducting videos, I banished such thoughts and carried on.

More recently, however, I have become alarmed at the extent to which the educational system, and indeed society as a whole, is being subjected to the belief that one must learn and achieve more, earlier, and faster if one is to succeed. The new focus on formal music education for pre-kindergarten children is but one manifestation of this trend. While I strongly support musical experiences from the cradle [2] to grave, I take exception to programs that stress performance and skill achievement over other outcomes, particularly for the young. The "earlier is better" mantra, coupled with the over-emphasis on performing that characterizes most of our current secondary music programs prompted me to respond with what I call a "new prescription" for music education.

Setting the Scene

Beethoven extended the possibilities of the double bass when he wrote the solo in his 9th symphony. Composers are always "pushing the envelop," exploring new techniques on the instruments for which they write. "A man's reach should exceed his grasp or what's a heaven for?" chimed the poet.[3] Czikszentmihalyi (1996) agreed, postulating his now famous concept of "flow" (the task must be a little above the skill level of the person's current capabilities in a domain to present the desired challenge and engender flow). They say "you can't stop progress" and they seem to have been proven right considering Western civilization's track record in the 150 or so years following the Industrial Revolution. The Industrial Age was followed by the Technological Age and now we are enjoying the fruits of the Digital Age and the Age of Virtual Realities. But, there is a world of difference, I argue, between progress that enriches the life of society as a whole and progress that threatens to fragment, marginalize, and take control. One type of progress carries artistic expression to a higher, loftier level while the other takes control of the pace of life, edging us all onto a dangerous though exhilarating speedway. This second type of progress has a cost: to ourselves, our humanity, and especially to our young. When American parents are worried about placing their as yet unconceived offspring into the "right" pre-schools and unload colossal amounts of money to secure places (National Public Radio, November, 2002), something is clearly amiss.

Let's now look at two high schools and their choral programs—two snapshots, two programs, two remarkably similar viewpoints. One school has a highly developed choral performance program. Three teachers share responsibility for numerous "leveled" choirs (there is only one unauditioned choir), and the performance stakes are high. It is not enough to maintain the program as it is—one has to keep the focus on growth. The township is behind the program financially, and there are expectations. Still, I detected a tiredness on the part of the lead teacher and a questioning attitude on the part of another. "Does there have to be so much emphasis on performing? What about creativity? I'd like to have time to develop more musicianship in my students." A second school reveals a young teacher in her fourth year who is battling destructive scheduling (among other things) in her attempt to build a singing culture in her school. On entering her classroom, I noticed immediately the evidence of nurture and care. She has prepared the soil well and these students are ready to "bloom where they have been planted." Yet she too is under pressure to perform at levels (and with music) that is sometimes beyond her students' current capabilities. The expectations of the district are getting in the way of what she knows to be appropriate for her students.

Demands on schools and teachers to cover more material earlier and pressure on graduating high school seniors to compete for the limited number of places at institutes of higher learning are omnipresent in our society. The pervasive view that "if I don't do it now, it's curtains" adds another layer of stress to an already overburdened and increasingly emotionally fragile student population. The mantras of "the earlier the better," "there is only a window of opportunity," and the "it has to be perfect" have wormed their way into the psyches of parents as well as students and educators, and the race is on.

While it may seem that I am a reactionary luddite who glories in extolling the virtues of "the good old days," I am actually a dedicated musician and educator who is concerned about the effect of this race on our children and indeed on our society as a whole. My position is as follows: *If we don't allow a child to be a child when it is age-appropriate, then most likely that person will revert to childish behaviors in mid-adulthood when it is not looked upon so favorably.* Yes, I have a huge argument with the western consumer model, but I am wise enough to know that I can't change the whole machine. I can say, however, that brave music educators can stem the tide of the tsunami performance rush and allow their students some time to blossom and grow in the music class. In what follows I first examine three important issues that affect positively (and negatively) the nature and scope of school music programs and subsequently proposes a progressive solution offering an alternative to the current paradigm of secondary music courses that place a heavy emphasis on performance.

Issues of Importance

The "Earlier is Better" Mentality. Elkind (1990) sketches the historical background of the "earlier is better" ideology. Juxtaposing literary examples (pp. 5-6) that demonstrate the importance of the early years for later development[4] with those that emphasize the special qualities of childhood as a unique period,[5] Elkind contends that the roots of this worldview go back many years. He contrasts "the nurture views of child nature [which view] childhood as a 'preparation for adulthood' [stressing] the importance of early education because of its long-term consequences" (p. 6) with the "nature views of children [which stress] the unique qualities of childhood and the valuing of these qualities" (p.7).

Elkind then relates these two views of childhood to two notions of human abilities. Implicit in the nurture view is the idea that ability is an individual matter. Every human has the potential to grow up "straight" or "crooked" and it is the environmental intervention that a person receives while still a child that shapes the character of the adult. There are "good" and "bad" interventions and what is "good" for one child will be good for another. The second notion, reflected in the nature view, sees ability as more of a group matter. Celebrating the unique qualities of the child's nature, ability is related more to age level than to the individual. While still conceding that there are "good" and "bad" interventions, this view of human ability correlates interventions to age rather than to a specific behavior. Thus, what might be "good" for a child at three is not "good" for a ten-year-old.

Elkind goes on to argue convincingly that the individual conception of mental ability has emerged as the dominant ideology in American society. He cites the American characteristics of individualism, egalitarianism, capitalism, and frontier mentality as contributing factors to this dominance. In addition, the changing place of women in society, the civil rights movement, and the restructuring of the American family have also played a part. The premise that any child, given the right environment at an early age, will grow up to be well-adjusted and successful has arisen from this individualistic view of human ability. Despite the fact that Elkind is writing from a uniquely American perspective, his words ring true far beyond the borders of the United States. Although Elkind's examples of a "Prenatal University" and a computer math program for six- month olds are drawn from his own milieu, many of us can attest to the existence of similar initiatives closer to home.

Fueling the fire of the "earlier is better" mentality is the rapidly growing body of brain research, in particular the effects of music on the brain. Flohr, Miller, and DeBeus (2000) report on several EEG studies with young children. They summarize as follows:

> The EEG studies described here point to the benefits of music training for children. The brain appears to be more plastic and malleable during the first decade of life than in adulthood ...The coherence studies lend support to the idea that music instruction for children at an early age will promote more profuse and efficient connections, as, as cited earlier, there is evidence that the brain of a novice learner is less efficient and "expends more energy" when confronted with a challenging task than does the brain of an expert learner (p. 30).

Flohr, Miller, and DeBeus (2000) and Gordon (1997) underline the "significant window of opportunity" for music learning in early childhood. They explain the distinction between "optimum" timing, a time in development when environment and instruction can produce an effect more easily than at any other, and "critical" timing, a time of development when the lack of stimulation or inappropriate stimulation affects the brain for life, stressing that "substantial evidence amassed by neuroscientists and child development experts over the last decade points to the wisdom and efficacy of early intervention. The findings indicate that all music educators and parents should be informed about the advantages of early music education" (Flohr, Miller, and DeBeus, 2000, p. 31).

Supporting the belief in the positive benefits of early music education are "a number of renowned pedagogues [who] base their philosophy on the premise that music education, like language acquisition, should begin as early as possible" (Szabo, 1999, p, 17). Kodaly, Suzuki, Orff, and Gordon all advocate for music instruction to begin at an early age. However, there is an important difference between the "immersion" of natural language development in a literacy-rich home and the contrived, scheduled, formal "music lessons" designed to "push" children to achieve.

And then there is the notion that early vocal and/or instrumental learning is the key to success. Jorgensen (2001) looked at the relationship between conservatory students' current level of vocal and instrumental performance and the age when they started formal lessons. Results indicated that for the whole student population, those with the highest grades started earlier, although there were large differences between students and some of the best players were the ones who started later. Offering a contrasting view, Mills (2003) reports on a 1985 study in which she questioned members of professional orchestras in England. Of the 46 respondents "almost half took up their main instrument on the strength of the advice of a secondary school teacher whom they did not meet until the age of at least 11, and two changed music instruments when they were at college" (p. 331). When one factors in the number of students who begin early formal vocal and/or instrumental tuition at parents' bidding or insistence and then subsequently discontinue the lessons, it would seem that an early start advantage is open to question.

At this point it is important to clarify the difference between early music immersion, exposure, and natural learning, and structured music "lessons" that often have a performance ladder as the primary focus. One type of instruction seeks to "create a rich music setting" (Upitis, 1992, p. 19) furnishing children with the materials to explore their musical environment in a spirit of independence, curiosity, and delight. The second type can exhibit these same qualities but more often tends to favour structure, discipline, and contrived musical materials, and repetitive "drill and practice."

Lest it appear that I am out to jettison the fragile hold that music education has on the public school curriculum and dash all the efforts of researchers and advocates to raise the profile of music in schools and society, let me make myself clear. I am not against early childhood music education. Nor am I against vocal and/or instrumental training for the young. What I am cautioning against is a misinterpretation of current research results which can have the unfortunate result of firing up a populus to believe that an early start to formal education (in any discipline) is essential and that if a child doesn't read by kindergarten entry or begin instrumental study in the pre-school years, she will be destined for failure (or at least for second place). Like Elkind (1981), I believe that we are doing a disservice to hurry our children. Like Guddemi, Jambor, and Moore (1998), I believe that "children learn best through play" (p. 521). Unfortunately daily informal, unstructured play is rapidly disappearing from the lives of children. It is to this topic that I turn next.

In defense of play. The importance of play in the healthy development of children is widely supported (Bergen, 1988; Fromberg & Bergen, 1998; Klugman & Smilansky, 1990; Lytle, 2003; Stone, 1995; Weininger, 1979). Further, musical exploration and play is crucial for the development of musical behaviors (Hargreaves, 1986; Papousek, 1996; Tarnowski, 1999). Children's modes of social play (Parten, 1932) move through the stages of *solitary play, onlooker play, parallel play, associative play*, and *cooperative play*. Cognitive play, first described by Piaget and later modified by Smilansky (1968), has four categories: *functional play, constructive play, dramatic or symbolic play*, and *games with rules*. Guddemi, Jambor, and Moore (1998) discuss the importance of three contemporary play forms: *informal, nonformal*, and *formal. Informal play* "which stimulates children's capacity to learn, and to develop basic skills and competencies through exploration and engagement of the world around them" (p. 519) is deemed to be not only the most important of the three for a child's healthy development but also the most endangered in today's society.

Given the wide support for the benefits of play in a child's development, one wonders at the ebbing of this activity from our children's lives. What is causing the disappearance? Guddemi, Jambor, and Moore (1998) suggest seven factors: 1) continuing poverty for over 20% of children in the US where older children often raise younger children and younger children are forced to take on household duties well before their time. In such an atmosphere, there is no time for frivolous matters such as play; 2) changing cultural values in which play is devalued by parents who want their children to "learn" at the earliest possible age; 3) inadequate time set aside for play in contemporary children's overly organized weekly itineraries; 4) inadequate space for play in our contemporary cities where the voices of commercial interests drown out those of more enlightened citizens calling for more parks and the preservation of green space; 5) changing school agendas where recess and lunch, formerly the times for unstructured play, are often filled with enrichment, remedial, or even musical activities; 6) decline of child fitness whereby an overindulgence in fatty foods and a lower level of physical activity are causing children to suffer health problems such as obesity, high cholesterol, and diabetes, conditions heretofore restricted to the adult population; and finally, 7) increased guidelines for playground safety which can lead to sanitized and thoroughly unimaginative playground materials which enhance child safety but spurn creative play. This final point can be extended today to a general fear in our society, a sense that the world is a very dangerous place for children, and so because children must be supervised every minute of the day because of the inherent risks and the ultimate parental responsibility for risk management, children's lives should be structured and supervised.

Despite the weight of forces that would eradicate play from the lives of today's children and youth, there are those who continue to advocate for the right of children to play. Speaking in defense of play in a child's pre-school years and beyond are knowledgeable music educators (Campbell, 1998; Campbell & Scott-Kassner, 1995; Scott-Kassner, 1999; Stone, 1995; Tarnowski, 1999) and child development experts (Klugman & Smilansky, 1990; Weininger, 1979). Adding a personal voice to those who know the value that play has in the healthy rearing of children, I reflect on my own years of teaching in the field from my early days as an elementary music specialist to my current post at the university level. Echoes of those years serve to illustrate the life-giving nature of play in children (and adults') lives. The first voice comes from a primary school class that always entered the music room in a singing line that formed a circle. Woe befell me if I forgot to include "Bee, bee bumble bee" or "I pass this shoe from me to you" or another of their favorite singing games in the music lesson! That was by far the favorite class activity. In another school, another grade level, and another time, I was teaching a grade 10 choral music class. We instituted a system of body warm-ups to music and each class member took a turn as leader. The imaginative exercises (and choices of music!) kept students and teacher both engaged and enthralled. A third echo comes from a recent university class. The topic was *Creativity in the Music Classroom* and students were third and fourth year vocal and instrumental music education students. As we moved through some limbering up exercises using ideas from R. Murray Schafer, a student exclaimed: "I haven't had this much *fun* in music since I came to university! Why can't all our classes be like this?"

In our efforts to compete with other academic disciplines for a finite amount of curricular time, music educators have often stressed the cognitive benefits of music, which are considerable, to the exclusion of the playful aspects—which are no less beneficial or integral to learning. A heavy emphasis on achieving music literacy or superior levels of performance, while valuable goals in themselves, can lead to a dearth of time for musical exploration and play. In addition, some students may even be turned off to music by such an approach. In conversations with children about the meaning of music in their lives, Campbell (1998) recorded the words of Jonathon, a well-groomed sixth grader who not only played the violin but also sang in the school choir. In response to Campbell's question about whether he had learned a particular piece by listening or by learning the notes, Jonathon replied: "A little of both." And then later he added, "Don't you music people ever decide that too many notes might get in the way of the music?" (p. 154).

While understanding the constraining influences on children's play in our current societal climate, we as music teachers can do much to restore the place of play in our own classrooms. We can integrate our efforts to teach music literacy and performance skills with playful *moments musicaux* creating more balanced music programs. More about that later. For now, it is time to hear from the students themselves as to what music means to them and what they value about their own music instruction. We might well glean valuable insights that can help to shape more holistic and well-conceived curricula.

Students' Views on Music Education. What do students value about music education and the place of music in their lives? Are their in-and-out of school experiences with music in harmony with each other? Can music educators learn anything important from their stories? Two recent publications yield helpful information. *Kid's Voices: Young People Talk about Music* (MENC, 1996) and Songs in their Heads (Campbell, 1998) address the meaning of music in children's lives. While children's responses span the gamut from the trite to the sublime, some examples are both pointed and poignant and serve to emphasize the need for a capable teacher with a balanced approach.

> I like having music in school, but I think you have to have the right music teacher to like it. My music teacher makes it fun for me. (4th grade girl; MENC, p. 42)

> To tell you the truth, I never liked music class. It was so boring. When I came to Pierrepont School, I began to enjoy it. My teacher is really funny and we play bingo sometimes. When my teacher teaches her best (with humor), her words jump into my head very quickly. This is actually the first time I have enjoyed music class. (8th grade boy; MENC, p.43)

> My favorite music activities are when we play the instruments because it shows me I'm learning something while having fun. If it is with a partner or group, then it shows me what teamwork can do—create beautiful music together. (5th grade boy; MENC, p. 39)

> My best friends Lisa and Joey—she's a girl—are in band with me. Lisa sings in the choir with me. At school, Lisa and I play clarinet together, and Joey plays flute. We usually share the same music stand, and watch Mr. Simmons wave his arms and beat the stand. Actually, I usually know the band songs by heart, we do them so many times, but I can read notes for new music anytime he gives it to us. Which isn't often. He can be boring. You're not going to tell him that, are you? (5th grade girl; Campbell, p. 142)

The foregoing examples highlight students' liking for participatory musical activities that are fun, as well as their need for teachers who challenge. A sense of humor seems to be a valued quality for a teacher. Students are well aware that "just anyone" won't do as a music teacher. A teacher has to be "right." And just what would the "right" teacher look like? As part of a study that investigated the experience of junior high school boys in choral music, Kennedy (2002) reported on choristers' views of their teacher. They liked her as a person, acknowledged her authoritative yet humorous teaching style, and appreciated the fact that "she makes it fun like with all the field trips that we get to do" (p. 30). So once again, humor and the light touch emerge as important qualities for a teacher that wishes to reach her students. In addition, a sense of authority and a personality that can relate to students is key.

Adderley, Kennedy, and Berz (2003) investigated the "world" of the high school music classroom. The meaning and value that performance ensembles engender for their participants was one of the themes of the study. Results indicated that students reaped both musical and non-musical benefits through their participation in the ensembles, with the non-musical benefits being further divided into academic, psychological, and social subcategories. Although students named "making music" and the "acquisition of musical skills and knowledge" as by-products of their ensemble membership, they placed a significant degree of importance on the social aspects of belonging. Relationships with their teachers, with the other members of their section, and with the group as a whole were deemed to have high currency. It is well known that adolescents identify with their peers in schools and in society (Cotterell, 1996; Cusiak, 1973). Perhaps less attention has been afforded to the notion that adolescents often form a connection with their teacher first and the discipline second (Gerber, 1989).

So what can we learn from these student views? Students certainly value an element of play in their learning while at the same time appreciating the musical skills and knowledge they are acquiring. They like to be active, engaged, and challenged in class. Music can be boring without a teacher that relates well to her students and/or possesses the ability to match curricular material to their abilities. Finally, music class is a place where students can get to know each other and their teacher in a different way than in more formal academic settings and students cherish the opportunity to form firm friendships through participation in their ensembles.

I have explored three crucial dimensions of the delivery of music education in our current society: (1) the "earlier is better" mentality, (2) the role of play in children's lives, and (3) students' views on music education. I will now explore the pragmatic implications of these for a progressive concept of music education.

A "New Prescription" for Music Education: Time to Enjoy the Ride

Establishing a truly balanced curriculum. It is time to heed the words of writers and theorists who have long called for a balanced music curriculum that includes at all levels age-appropriate opportunities for performing, listening, and creating. One need go no further than the National Standards for Arts Education (Music Educators National Conference, 1994) or the Achieving Musical Understanding Documents (Coalition for Music Education in Canada 2000, 2002) to find support for this idea.

Of the three strands of the curriculum, creating has been the most often neglected, particularly at the secondary level (Kennedy, 2000; Kennedy, 2001). Incorporating creative opportunities into music classes at all levels can do much to restore a playful atmosphere[6] and redress the balance between a heavy emphasis on the acquisition of music literacy and performance skills. Numerous authors have provided quality materials for the incorporation of creative activities into music classes (cf. Wiggins, 2001; Kaschub, 1997) and so teachers need not plead the lack thereof. While they may argue that time is the constraining factor, I counter that it is all a matter of priorities and it is time to get them straight. Performance is not the only "game in town."

Reducing Performance Expectations. Polished performance ensembles are most often the "heart and soul" of the secondary music program and highlighted features of elementary and middle school programs. These ensembles can do much to advance the musical education of their participants and may also be important avenues for their social, emotional, and psychological growth. Students note the importance of the social contacts made through membership in performance ensembles and these are valued outcomes which should be preserved. These ensembles do much to raise the public profile, and secure the position of, music programs in schools. So why am I concerned about performance expectations in school music programs? Because, despite the many positive outcomes—musical and social—these ensembles often stress performance expectations to the exclusion of other worthy musical goals such as musical understanding, general musicianship, and creativity. If I have heard it once, I have heard it countless times—"I *know* that I should be spending more time on musicianship training and creative activities, but the concert's so close... I wish I had more time!"

The only way to carve out a parcel of time for these activities is to reduce the performance expectations—one less piece on the concert, one less concert, an "informance" instead of a performance. Inserting some less challenging pieces into the repertoire will also lower the performance stress, and allow for greater emphasis on the expressive and affective dimensions of the experience. While I am a firm believer in quality literature for students at all levels, I do not subscribe to the idea that choral students, for instance, need to perform all the major choral works *before* they graduate from high school! Far better that they sing material that is vocally appropriate for their developing voices and then experience through guided listening, concert field trips, and research projects a sampling of the array of choral works that await them in their adult years.

Abandoning the competitive festival in favor of the adjudication-clinic model that is gaining ground in certain constituencies is another way to lessen the performance stress on both students and teacher. Having experienced this model as both a choral conductor and an adjudicator, I believe it is superior (to use a popular rating word!) and does much more for students' musical growth than the competitive model. It is an indisputable fact that those who aspire to the world of the professional musician will indeed encounter competition as they apply for orchestral and/or vocal positions. And yes, they need to be prepared to meet those challenges. But the responsibility for those preparations should rest firmly in the hands of the private studio teacher, not the public school music teacher. Nor should the public school music teacher have to fear for her job upon receiving the results of a competitive music contest.

A shift in focus of this magnitude will call for some adjustments to current advocacy efforts. It is to this topic that I turn next.

Building Support Through Community Connections. Music programs that base their support solely on the extent of their performance output will have to re-group and establish other means of advocacy. (I am not so naïve as to feel that music teachers will ever be able to abandon their advocacy efforts). There are, however, other avenues of approach. Establishing connections with community organizations is one way to both serve the humanistic needs of our students and our art and build support for music programs.

What music teacher has not taken a group of students to sing (or play) for a senior's residence or hospital? But how many schools have established a continuing relationship with a specific group of residents? In Kennedy (1999), I wrote of an organization called Interlink, a music and language program connecting seniors with elementary students. Students write letters to the seniors who become their pen pals. The music teacher holds weekly choral rehearsals with both groups individually, and after three months, the groups get together for a combined rehearsal and social. The program culminates in a public concert which is followed "with some outreach concerts in senior facilities, hospitals, and hospices, or at government-sponsored conventions" (Frego, 1995, p. 18). While this example profiles elementary choral students, the concept can easily be adapted to other levels and ensembles.

Another approach involves bringing the generations together to perform at regular school performances. While high school choirs might invite alumni to join them in a rendition of the school song or, (to my dismay!) the "Hallelujah Chorus" at the end of the winter concert, they less often invite parents, other staff members, and even Board members to be part of such an endeavor. In my experience, I have found both parents and staff members eager to participate and sing with my high school choir to the enrichment of all parties. More recently, I have been fortunate to direct two church and community musical productions that included choristers from eight to eighty! Working with multi-aged groups not only demonstrates that music is a life-long pursuit but also can go along way towards building a new constituency of support for music programs in schools to replace current advocacy treatises that stress the musical and societal values of a performance-based approach.

Taking the time to enjoy the ride. "If we don't allow a child to be a child when it is age appropriate, then most likely that person will revert to childish (not child-like) behaviors in mid-adulthood when it is not looked upon so favorably." Reflecting on this mantra expressed at the outset of the chapter, I feel that it is paramount that students have time to play, explore, imagine, create, and have fun as they progress through their music classes. I also believe that "if a thing's worth doing, it's worth doing well." Are the two ideas incompatible? I think not. I am not countenancing a lowering of performing standards, rather a lessening of performance expectations. I am not advocating a "carnivalesque" music room where entertainment is the main objective and musical bingo reigns supreme. Rather I am advocating a playful music room where teacher and students take time to try another approach, create a new ending, spontaneously walk down the hall in the middle of a lesson to sing/play for the principal. It's the classroom where teacher and students feel free to interject a new idea and try it out on the spot, the classroom where teacher and students are joint adventurers on the road, the classroom where teacher and students take time to enjoy the ride that will make the grade in the 21st century. Children and young people fortunate enough to experience such a classroom will carry their ability to be fun-loving and child-*like* into adulthood where it will be a valuable resource for living.

Preparing Teachers for the "New Prescription" Classroom. And what about the teachers in this "new prescription" classroom? They will have to be as well prepared musically as ever, but they would do well to have some training in improvisation and/or composition at the tertiary level. Such creative activities can easily be incorporated into existing methods courses or become the focus of an independent special topics course.[7] Pre-service teachers will need to experience models of teaching both at the university and in the field where the focus is on a balanced approach to musical instruction. Most important, however, student teachers will need an ongoing forum for open debate of issues that impinge on the teaching profession as a whole, i.e. what makes a good teacher, what is the purpose of music education, why do you want to be a music teacher? Questions such as these and more need to be raised and revisited throughout a music education student's university career. Shaping a teacher takes time and ingrained attitudes and beliefs need to be challenged before new thoughts and ideas can be grasped and incorporated.

It is my firm belief that teachers brave enough to try this approach will find it life-giving, self-motivating, and less stressful. I even contend that teacher burn-out will be reduced. Taking a cue from music students' views, teachers wishing to relate well to their students need to cultivate a sense of humor and rediscover, recapture, and retain the sense of fun that was first experienced in childhood.

References

Adderley, C., Kennedy, M, and Berz, W. (2003). "A home away from home": The world of the high school music classroom. *Journal of Research in Music Education*, 51(3), 190-205.

Bergen, D. (Ed.). (1988). *Play as a medium for learning and development*. Portsmouth, NH: Heinemann Educational Books, Inc.

Campbell, P. S. (1998). *Songs in their heads*. New York: Oxford University Press.

Campbell, P.S. & Scott-Kassner, C. (1995). *Music in childhood*. New York: Schirmer Books.

Coalition for Music Education in Canada & Canadian Music Educators Association. (2000). *Achieving musical understanding: Concepts and skills for Pre-kindergarten to Grade 8*. Toronto, ON: Coalition for Music Education in Canada.

Coalition for Music Education in Canada & Canadian Music Educators Association. (2002). *Achieving musical understanding: Concepts and skills for Grade 9 to Grade 12*. Toronto, ON: Coalition for Music Education in Canada.

Cotterell, J. (1996). *Social networks and social influences in adolescence*. London; Routledge.

Cusiak, P. A. (1973). *Inside high school: The student's world*. New York: Holt, Rinehart & Winston.

Csikszentmihalyi, M. (1996). *Creativity: Flow and the psychology of discovery and invention*. New York: HarperCollins Books.

Elkind, D. (1990). Academic pressures—too much too soon: The demise of play. In E. Klughman & S. Smilansky (Eds.), *Children's play and learning: Perspectives and policy implications*, pp. 3-17. New York: Teachers College Press.

Flohr, JW., Miller, D. C., and DeBeus, R. (2000). EEG studies with young children. *Music Educators Journal*, 87(2), 28-32.

Frego, R. J. D. (1995). Uniting the generations with music programs. *Music Educators Journal*, 81 (6), 17-19, 55.

Fromberg, D. P. & Bergeb, D. (Eds.). (1998). *Play from birth to twelve and beyond*. New York: Garland Publishing, Inc.

Gerber, T. (1989). Reaching all students: The ultimate challenge. *Music Educators Journal*, 75(7), 37-39.

Gordon, E. (1990). *A music learning theory for newborn and young children*. Chicago, IL: GIA Publications, Inc.

Guddemi, M., Jambor, T., and Moore, R. (1998). Advocacy for the child's right to play. In D. P. Fromberg & D. Bergen (Eds.), *Play from birth to twelve and beyond*, pp. 519-529. New York: Garland Publishing.

Hargreaves, D. J. (1986). *The developmental psychology of music*. Cambridge, UK: Cambridge University Press.

Jorgensen, H. (2001). Instrumental learning: Is an early start a key to success? *British Journal of Music Education*, 18(3), 227-239.

Kaschub, M. (1997). A comparison of two composer-guided large group composition projects. *Research Studies in Music Education*, 8, 15-28.

Kennedy, M. A. (1999). Where does the music come from? A comparison case study of the compositional processes of a high school and a collegiate composer. *British Journal of Music Education*, 16 (2), 157-177.

Kennedy, M. A. (1999). The music is the message: The "how" and "what" of communication. In B. Hanley (Ed.), *Leadership, advocacy, and communication: A vision for arts education in Canada* (p. 265-278). Canadian Music Educators Association.

Kennedy, M. A. (2000). Music for all Canadians: Dream or reality at the high school level. In B. Hanley & B. A. Roberts (Eds.), *Looking forward: Challenges to Canadian music education* (p. 139-156). Canadian Music Educators Association.

Kennedy, M. A. (2001). *Listening to the music: Case studies of high school composers*. Unpublished doctoral dissertation, University of Washington, Seattle.

Kennedy, M.A. (2002). 'It's cool because we like to sing:' Junior high school boys' experience of choral music as an elective. *Research Studies in Music Education*, 18, 24-34.

Kids' voices: Young people talk about music. (1996). Reston, VA: Music Educators National Conference.

Lytle, D. E. (Ed.). (2003). *Play and educational theory and practice.* Westposrt, CT: Praeger Publishers.

Mills, J. (2003). Musical performance: crux or curse of music education? *Psychology of Music*, 31(3), 324-339.

Music Educators National Conference. (1994). *National standards for arts education.* Reston, VA: MENC.

Papousek, H. (1996). Musicality in infancy research: biological and cultural origins of early musicality. In I. Deliege & J. Sloboda, Eds., *Musical beginnings*, pp. 37-55. New York: Oxford University Press.

Parten, M. B. (1932). Social participation among preschool children. *Journal of Abnormal Psychology*, 27, 243-69.

Peery, J. C., Peery, I. W., and Draper, T. W. (1987). *Music and child development.* New York: Springer-Verlag.

Stone, S. (1995). Wanted: Advocates for play in the primary grades. *Young Children*, 45.

Scott-Kassner, C. (1999). Developing teachers for early childhood programs. *Music Educators Journal*, 86(1), 19-25.

Smilansky, S. (1968). *The effects of socio-dramatic play on disadvantaged preschool children.* New York: John Wiley and Sons.

Szabo, M. (1999). Early music experience and musical development. *General Music Today*, ?, 17-19.

Tarnowski, S. M. (1999). Musical play and young children. *Music Educators Journal*, 86(1), 26-29.

Upitis, R. (1992). *Can I play you my song?* Portsmouth, NH: Heineman.

Weininger, O. (1979). *Play and education.* Springfield, IL: Charles C. Thomas Publisher.

Wiggins, J. (2001). *Teaching for musical understanding.* New York: McGraw-Hill.

[1] Every second year, I took my high school choir to a different place in Canada.

[2] I also support the notion that babes *in utero* can be affected by music.

[3] Robert Browning, *Andrea del Sarto*

[4] For example, 'Just as the twig is bent the tree's inclined' from Pope, *Moral Essays*, 'Epistle I, to Lord Cobham,' line 150.

[5] An example Elkind gives is the following quote taken from Orlenschalger, cited in Catercas & Edwards [1952], p. 76: 'The plays of natural lively children are the infancy of art. Children live in a world of imagination and feeling. They invest in the most insignificant objects with any form they please, and see in it whatever they wish to see.'

[6] Implicit in creative expression is the freedom to explore one's own sonic environment, be it an Orff instrument, a piano, a synthesizer or a full orchestral palette. Novice and experienced composers often refer to periods of exploration or playful 'doodling' (Kennedy, 1999; Kennedy, 2001) as precursors to the act of musical invention.

[7] Such is the case at Rutgers University where I teach.

CHAPTER FIVE

Music for Life: Contaminated by Peaceful Feelings

KATHARINE SMITHRIM & RENA UPITIS

Abstract

When our previous research showed clearly that Canadian children enjoy singing less and less as they progress through elementary school, it suggested to us that we are doing a poor job in music education in this country. As advocacy groups across the country work hard to try to save our music programs, we find ourselves asking what it is that's worth saving. We suggest that, as music educators, we have the dispositions and skills required to completely rethink musical goals and practices in Faculties of Education, in Faculties of Music, and in schools. In response to recent writings of Regelski, Sloboda, and Green, we suggest that a much wider variety of teacher roles, of paths towards arts engagement, and of arts activities will serve both students and the arts more effectively than standardization of curricula and proclamations of national standards.

Contaminated by Peaceful Feelings: The Power of Music

It was Christmas Eve, 1914, in the trenches of Belgium. The German and British lines were only 60 or 70 yards apart and stretched for hundreds of miles. A man could not stand up in No Man's Land between the enemy lines and remain alive. Then the German soldiers began to light candles on thousands of little evergreen trees that had been shipped to the front. As they lit the candles clamped to the fragile branches, they sang Stille Nacht, Heilige Nacht out into the dangerous darkness. The British soldiers did not shoot. They sang back Silent night, Holy night. And, as the story goes, they pulled themselves up out of the mud, both sides, and walked out onto No Man's Land, greeting each other, sharing food and smokes. On Christmas Day, after they had cleared away and buried the bodies of their fallen compatriots, spontaneous games of football broke out on the 60 yards between the enemy lines. In some places, the unofficial "Christmas Truce" lasted almost until the new year, when the outraged governments on both sides—who had already banned singing in the trenches—were finally able to restore the war with threats of court marshals and by rotating the troops that had participated in the truce back to the reserves. These singing soldiers were replaced with fresh troops that were "not contaminated by peaceful feelings" (Weintraub, 2001).

Such power in the singing and in the song. In countless choirs, ensembles, primary class-room circles and private studios all across this country, music is contaminating young people with peaceful feelings. Or enlivening their imaginations. Or giving them a reason to stay in school. Or awakening a sense of self.

And yet, we are gravely concerned that in countless more classrooms, music has become another subject to sit through, learn and regurgitate without thought, without passion, and without question. In recent research involving nearly 7,000 elementary school children across Canada, sobering statistics emerged (Upitis, Smithrim, Patteson, & Meban, 2001). In Grade 1, 60% of the students said that they were happy when they were singing. It will come as no surprise to most readers that more girls were happy singing (66%) than boys (54%)—a gender difference that appears to be entrenched and robust as early as Grade 1. It is disheartening to realize, that by the time children reach the age of six years, one in every two boys *already* does not enjoy singing. This is not the case across art forms or across school subjects. For example, 76% of Grade 1 children reported that they were happy when they play with puppets (81% girls, 72% boys), and 90% of Grade 1 children reported that they were happy when using a computer (same for both genders).

What happens to students' attitudes as they make their way through the early elementary grades? By Grade 4, the gender gap is even more pronounced, and overall pleasure associated with music and singing has declined even further. Relatively few children strongly agreed with the statement, "I am good at music" (27% overall; 33% girls, 20% boys) or "I am good at singing" (28% overall; 37% girls, 18% boys). In other words, by the end of Grade 4, only one boy in five believes that he is good at singing. The same pattern emerges for playing an instrument (23% overall; 26% girls, 20% boys). Ask them if they want more music in school, and 21% of the Grade 4 students will tell you that they want more music, as opposed to 56% who want more visual art. This could, of course, mean that the students were satisfied with their existing music programs and felt that they had sufficient time in music. It is more likely that most of the students don't like the music they have and don't want any more of the same. Because it's not as if students don't like *music*. Of all of the out-of-school activities (e.g., listening to music, watching television, playing sports, playing videogames, reading for pleasure), listening to music was the most favoured activity by boys and girls alike, with an overwhelming 83% of the Grade 4 students reporting that they like to listen to music in their spare time. It's *school* music that falls short of their expectations.

When children enjoy singing less and less as they progress through elementary school, it says to us that we are doing a poor job in music education in this country. When thousands of students who play in high school bands never play their instrument again once they've left high school, it says to us that we need to re-visit what music education is for.

It is no wonder that some music experiences leave students scarred. When we first started teaching music education courses to preservice teachers in the mid-1980s, we heard, in every class, that at least two or three of these young future teachers had not sung since they were told, as children in elementary school, to "mouth the words." We have now heard these stories for two decades—every year, it's the same thing. Franklin (2000) supports this observation and claims that many generalist teachers are "musi-phobic" because of negative experiences they have had with music teachers as children. Cameron and Bartel (2000) report research findings pointing to pervasive psychological and physical "abuses" in music studios and classrooms. These are not abusive practices of the past, these are abusive practices of the present perpetuated by both music specialists and classroom teachers.

One of the teachers we interviewed five years ago had this to say about the way that she taught music when she felt compelled to follow the curriculum:

I was the worst recorder teacher in the world. I remember one Grade 6 class; I was just like Hitler. They did learn to play, but it was painful, not joyful. I was so mean to them when they held the recorder the wrong way. Or played the wrong notes.

Of course there are pockets of exemplary practices—in classrooms of specialist and generalist teachers alike—but overall, we think that we're missing the boat. As advocacy groups across the country work hard to try to save our music programs, we find ourselves asking what it is that's worth saving. Where is the power of music in our lives? Is it ever in school? And when it is in school, what does it look like? Taste like? Feel like? Sound like?

In a satirical piece, in which aliens investigate musical practices in the United States, O'Toole (2000) gives voice to the aliens who have been led to "the cement structures" which earthlings call schools.

> First, outside the cement structures, music was available all the time and every where; inside, music only happens at designated times in designated areas. Unlike the world at large, music in schools is not as common as having a conversation. Further, school music seems to have little to do with the 'outside' musical lives of students. Music in schools sounds different and students interact with it differently... While we've observed music in everyday life to be continuously diversifying, music in schools appears static and restrictive... We often hear music teachers say they desire students to become creative, independent musicians [however] teachers rarely reward students for initiative that deviates from the teacher's educated musical interpretation (p. 34)

Roy McGregor, a columnist at the *Globe and Mail*, said on the CBC recently that he thought the only way to save professional sport in this country was to have a cataclysmic breakdown of the existing system and start from scratch with a new vision of what sport is for. We wonder if the whole system of music education needs a cataclysmic breakdown and a starting up from scratch. Indeed, we seem to be well on the way to the cataclysmic breakdown, at least in the province of Ontario. Some of the very best teachers are struggling. One of these teachers wrote a painful and compelling piece in which he reported a conversation he had with another fine veteran music teacher: "We laugh to share how deeply insecure we are, how confused we are about how we're supposed to make it work in our music programs" (Rush, 2002, p. 13). We know this teacher. We have worked with him. We have seen his dynamic teaching. Yet he is struggling. Later in his article, when talking of his Open Voices Community Choir, a stunning success on any terms, Rush says, "While it was difficult to follow my passion within my school teaching position, it has been extremely easy to do it outside school" (p.15). Music in schools is damaging teachers as well as students, while music outside schools continues to nourish and sustain people of all ages.

What is Music For?

Which of our various musical practices are worth preserving? Abandoning? Surely part of the answer lies in considering the broader goals of education and reinforcing how music can help achieve those goals. If the goals of education include the fostering of a peaceful, tolerant, fulfilled, and literate citizenry, then there is no question that an arts education is an essential route to those goals (Greene, 1995; O'Reilley, 1993; Pitman, 1998;

Whitehead, 1929). This means that whatever students learn in school about music ought to, somehow, help them be fulfilled and capable as adults. As Regelski (2002) recently argued, although high school graduates may have fond recollections of their ensemble experience, "any tangible *value-added* to graduates' musical lives or society is not evident" (p. 112). That is, few are touched by their ensemble experiences in ways that affect them directly in their adult lives. Regelski suggests that ethically accountable teaching empowers students by "increasing the scope of musical choices and capabilities by which they can musically self actualize independently of the teacher" (p. 113).

An example of this self-actualization is one direction the Newfoundland Symphony Youth Chorus is taking under the direction of Susan Knight. In performance in Toronto in June of 2002, Knight did not conduct for at least three quarters of the concert. These choristers were so aware and involved that they performed difficult polyphonic music while walking around and through long lines of dining tables covering the entire floor space of Hart House (the dining room at Hart House, at the University of Toronto, is the kind of very long and large, elegant, wood-paneled formal dining room you see in old universities). They were listening and watching each other and obviously living *in* the music. These young people *were musically self-actualizing*. Most of them would tell you that singing in this choir has transformed their lives.

It is true that recognizing what is worth preserving and celebrating, and recognizing what new innovations are worth embracing, is made more difficult by our current social and educational context. These are difficult times. As Shirley Thomson (1999), then Executive Director of the Canada Council for the Arts, noted,

> We are fighting a new barbarism, not of dark ignorance but of information glut and too many diversions... Arts education is essential to discernment and judgment, and in the broadest sense, arts advocacy is the fight for the return of the life of the spirit to the centre of our existence...people forget that art and artists render life bearable (1999, p. 139).

Do our music education practices develop the discernment and judgment referred to by Shirley Thompson? Do they teach the dispositions, skills and "ways of knowing" Elliott Eisner claims the arts teach? Eisner argues eloquently about the role of the arts in teaching students to savour ambiguity, to tolerate difference, to learn that nuance matters. The arts are also about experiencing the joy of creation, cultivating the ability to attend to detail, and about learning ways of expressing thoughts, knowledge, and feelings beyond words alone (Eisner, 2002; Greene, 1995). The arts are about developing capacities with which to make sense of the world, as well as developing technical skills for the production of creative work. The arts teach us how to make judgments in the absence of clear rules, that human purposes and goals are best held with flexibility, and that some activities are self-justifying (Eisner, 2002). We need to ask ourselves if the music education we offer teaches our students the forms of thinking Eisner and Greene describe. They provide a good set of criteria for discerning what is worth embracing.

Many teachers would rightly argue that, partly as a result of the information glut referred to by Thomson, the students we now teach are very different from those students that we taught only a decade ago (Tapscott, 1997). Technology is pervasive; television, the Internet, electronic games, and recorded music have altered the ways in which students think and learn (Upitis, 2001).

But some things remain unchanged. Scholars and philosophers all over the world have argued that music is part of what separates humans from other species. Some researchers have taken a bioevolutionary view and have claimed that music and other art forms serve a similar function to language in the development of the human species (Dissanayake, 1995). Dissanayake points to the importance of repetition, rule, and ritual associated with artistic activities and shows how these characteristics assist in the ordering and shaping of physical and social worlds. She claims that the arts evolved in order to make socially significant experiences memorable and pleasurable, and therefore, that the arts are essential to human survival. Keen observers of children's musical behaviour have also claimed that "all children, to a greater or lesser degree, are musical" (Campbell, 1998, p. 169). Do we teach music in ways that reflect children's natural musical explorations? Is the music that we teach in school memorable? Pleasurable? Powerful? Do students learn to shape their physical and social worlds through school music?

The argument has also been made that because of the presence of music specific neurons in the brain, music is a fundamental and essential aspect of being human (Nelson & Bloom, 1997; Weinberger & McKenna, 1988). Gardner lists musical intelligence as one of the ways that people solve problems and create products in context-rich and authentic environments (Gardner, 1983). As with the other intelligences identified by Gardner, music is considered as a separate intelligence not only because of the potential for isolation due to brain damage, but also because of the existence of exceptional individuals, an identifiable set of core operations, a developmental history, an evolutionary history, experimental and psychometric support, and an associated symbol system (Armstrong, 2000; Gardner, 1983). In examining the ways in which people with strong musical intelligence create music and solve problems, does school music reflect these context-rich and authentic activities?

Mixed Messages: School Music and Life Music

What is inherent in the cultural, bioevolutionary, and brain-related views described in the previous section is that music is central to human experience, and that musicality is expressed in many different ways. Yet, an examination of many school music practices and curriculum documents would lead to the false conclusion that there are only a few ways to experience music. In many cases, school music emphasizes performance (which is not always pleasurable) over other aspects of music, most notably those that involve creative expression or composition. In fact, scholars and practitioners claim that composition is a specific musical ability everyone possesses, and that the challenge for schooling is to make composition a central feature of music education rather than an add-on (Campbell, 1998; Hargreaves, 1986; Kratus, 1989, Tsisserev, 1997; Upitis, 1992).

It is no coincidence that powerful tools for composition have emerged in the popular culture in the form of computer supported software and hardware (Upitis, 2001). If schools don't embrace the importance of composition, and the technology that goes with it, students will *still* find ways to make music, because making music answers a call of the human condition. Put another way, garage bands will simply become more sophisticated, and move yet another step away from school experiences (Upitis, 2001).

Lucy Green (2001) interviewed fourteen popular musicians living in and around

London, England to see how they acquired their considerable skill and knowledge. She found that they

- immersed themselves in the music and musical practices of their surroundings
- copied recordings by ear (the main learning practice)
- played with peers who shared their knowledge and skills
- watched and imitated others during music making
- practiced five or six hours a day in the early stages, and
- used musical elements effectively without knowing the theoretical language.

Their learning strategies were vastly different from typical school music learning. Green concluded that school music could and should adapt some of these practices.

When we see teachers struggling with provincial curriculum documents that require them to teach standard notation to students for whom standard notation has no connection to their own out-of-school music interests (even though it should)—to students who would rather be doing *anything* but learning that "F" is the first space on the treble clef staff—it brings to mind some of the observations made by educator James Herndon over three decades ago (1971). Herndon reflects on why the so-called 'creative classroom projects' that he and his co-teacher, Frank, provided were simply not of interest when students were given the option of not participating. He noted that two of the irrefutable rules of school are that students have to go there and participate in the activities the teacher assigns, and that they will be marked on their efforts. When these conditions were removed and students had the option of not doing anything at all and leaving the classroom entirely, the teachers got what Herndon termed "a brief version of the truth." Students would prefer to do anything but what the teachers wished for them to do. He wrote:

> All the great notions we had, all the ideas for things to do, all our apparatus for insuring a creative, industrious, happy, meaningful class didn't seem to excite the kids all that much. ... On the edge of complete despair, Frank and I began to figure out what was wrong with the ideas that had worked so well in our regular classes. It was very simple. Why did the kids in regular class like to do all that inventive stuff? Why, only because it was better than the regular stuff. If you wrote a fake journal pretending to be Tutankhamen's favorite embalmer, it was better than reading the dull Text, answering Questions on ditto sheets ... or taking Tests. ... Why should we have assumed that the kids would want to do a lot of stuff that we didn't want to do, wouldn't ever do of our own free will? It sounds non-sensical, put that way. Yet that is the assumption under which I operated, Frank operated, for many a year, under which almost all teachers operate, and it is idiotic. Does the math teacher go home at night and do a few magic squares? Does the English teacher go home and analyze sentences? Does the reading teacher turn off the TV and drill herself on syllables and Reading Comprehension? Or do any of us do any of those things, even in the classroom? (pp. 29-31; 44-45).

What do teachers do when they go home? Most of them listen to music. Some sing in community or professional choirs. Some play guitar with a local band. Are these the things that they bring to school when they approach the teaching of music? What would happen if they did? Earlier, we talked about the teacher who described herself as a "Hitler recorder teacher." Here is the continuation of her story. At one point, this teacher told us that she had always wanted to play the guitar. We encouraged her, and provided some workshops and resources. Over a period of several years, by taking private lessons with a high school student, she became a competent guitarist. Early on in the process, she summoned up the courage to take her guitar into the classroom. Her students watched her struggle. They encouraged her. She showed them that making mistakes was part of the learning process. And over time, her teaching of music changed dramatically:

> It's so different now. I still teach recorder (when we're not playing guitar!), but I've
> found a play-along CD—a jazzy thing—that we use to accompany easy B-A-G
> tunes. Last week, a group of students started dancing spontaneously to the music.
> It was wonderful! And it was something that I would never have allowed before.
> And now I have eight kids taking lessons from [my guitar teacher]. You should see
> the change in these kids. It's changed their lives, I guess that's why I'm so jubilant
> about it.

And that's what it should be about. Music education should be about changing students' lives. Regelski (2002) raises concerns that music teachers often do not have a firm "ultimate goal" of music education to guide their practice. He believes that music education should have a lasting affect on life outside school and in the adult years ahead of the students. He speaks of the personal, social and musical *goods*, in other words, what in life music is *good for*, the musical benefits now and into the future life of each student.

Music for Life

What kinds of musical experiences in schools would have an effect on students' out-of-school lives? What kinds of musical experiences would have an effect on students' *in-school* lives? In a study of singing in the lives of women through the 20th century, Smithrim (1998) found that the most common singing practice of girls in the decade from age 10 to 20 was that girls sit on their beds, playing their guitars and singing. How many of those girls have learned to play guitar in school? Not many. And while we do not advocate that schooling should simply be a repetition of what students choose to do outside of school or simply a response to what students demand (no more than we would advocate feeding a 3-year-old child ice cream every day because she asked for it), unless we find ways to *link* out-of-school activities with schooling, we will fail to enrich students' musical lives to the degree that is possible—or as Regelski would say—ethically accountable. If the guitar is appealing, why don't we see more instruction of guitar in school?

The teacher we have referred to throughout this paper, five years after beginning to play the guitar herself, has now introduced the instrument to hundreds of children. One year, in her class of 25 students, 21 asked for guitars for Christmas—and received them. These are students who came from homes where there was little, if any, disposable income. Some of these students were, in her words, the "toughest around." After learning to sing and play the guitar, some who might otherwise have left school stayed—and learned many other things besides guitar playing. What would our students say if we asked them what they wanted to learn in school music classes? Have you ever asked that question? Do you think you could teach what they want to learn?

We know a fine folk musician who plays guitar and sings with children every Friday morning in his small local school. He takes his two young children and the family dog.

The whole school community looks forward to Friday mornings and everyone has learned to love singing. Some would say "Ah, that's all well and good, but you couldn't call it music education." We call it music education of the highest order. Is there any music education goal that could be more important than fostering the love and the practice of music-making in community?

Implications for Teacher Education

In Labrador, and probably all across the north, Inuit children used to carry and play with tea dolls as their families moved between hunting grounds. For weeks, families carried everything they needed with them on their komotiks (sleds). Efficiency of space was a critical factor in survival. Children needed to help carry things and needed to be able to entertain themselves. The tea dolls embodied perfection of function and form. The mother or grandmother would make a doll for each child and stuff it with tea. The children carried and played with the dolls day after day. When the tea was needed, someone picked open a seam, poured out the tea and refilled the doll with whatever was available, such as moss, fur or skin scraps. The function had changed, the form had adapted, and the tea dolls kept travelling. This perfection of function and form seems to be at the root of how we could proceed as teacher educators in order to challenge the troubled status quo of current music education practice.

What is the function of music education? John Sloboda (2001), the British music psychologist, maintains that the function or purpose of music education is no longer clear.

> Music education in schools cannot function effectively without an implicit agreement between stakeholders (e.g. teachers, students, parents, governments etc.) about what it is for. The meaning of music is a constantly shifting function of the discourses of these diverse groups, which may coalesce around a "dominant ideology" which gains enough inter-group consensus to generate a stable educational agenda. I would argue that such a stable agenda existed in mid-20th-Century music education, but its underpinning consensus collapsed as a result of major cultural shifts, most evident from the 1960s onwards. (p. 21)

Some of the cultural shifts Sloboda identified are multiculturalism, youth culture, electronic communication, feminism, secularism, niche cultures and postmodernism. He suggests that in England, a national curriculum for music "was probably introduced at the very moment in history when its sustainability has never been less certain" (p. 21).

We agree with Sloboda. In Canada, as in Great Britain, there are attempts to create national and provincial music education guidelines, models, curricula, and agendas, at a time when we maintain it would be impossible for stakeholders across the country or within provinces to agree even on the function or purpose of music education. Would they accept Regelski's (2002) assertion that music education should have a lasting affect on life outside school and in the adult years ahead? If there are no common goals or functions, then attempts at common practice and curriculum are not only inappropriate, but may in fact be working against, rather than toward, the viability of music education.

We would argue that many different kinds of music programs, many different kinds of music curricula, and many different kinds of teacher strengths and passions are needed.

Standardization of curricula and proclamations of national standards, although often defended as critical for "making music an academically important subject" may, in fact, be doing just the opposite. They often intimidate classroom teachers and destroy their confidence in their own ways of music-making in the classroom. They constrain music specialists to limited, and often conservative, notions of what music is and what music is for. They tend to result in an emphasis on *what* to teach, and in so doing, minimize the importance of *how* we teach, *why* we teach, and *who* will teach. In a study of engagement in musical learning Cameron and Bartel (2000) concluded that teachers

> need to develop attitudes and techniques to help all children experience engaged music-making in an environment that supports first attempts, that legitimizes musical expression, that expects passions and preferences to surface, that aims above all to open to students the joy, and release the energy of life through music (p. 22).

Unless musical activity engages the whole child and the whole teacher—intellectually, physically, and emotionally—little learning takes place.

Sloboda (2001) concluded that the key concept in a viable arts education for today's students is variety—variety in providers, in funding, in locations, in roles for educators, in trajectories, in activities, in accreditation, and in routes to teacher competence. His response, then, to the multiple ideas about the function of music education is to create multiple forms. Many of Sloboda's ideas fly in the face of current arts education practices and policies. We believe that those of us involved in teacher education in the arts have both the responsibility and the capacity to examine our assumptions, beliefs and practices. As Eisner (2002) proclaims, work in the arts gives people experience with situations in which there is no known answer, where there are multiple solutions, where nuance can be all important, where the tension of ambiguity is not only tolerated but appreciated as fertile ground, and where imagination is honoured over rote knowledge. We, as artists and arts educators, are well equipped to take up the challenge. Consider with us, three of Sloboda's suggestions.

First, teacher educators must consider adopting a wider range and variety of roles so that beginning teachers in turn might bring these roles to schools. In the case of music education, Sloboda suggests the following: teacher, animateur, coach, mentor, impresario, fund-raiser, programmer, composer, arranger, and studio manager (p. 22). In the case of elementary music education, we would add such roles as observer, explorer, dancer, campfire song leader, and actor. What roles do we assume in our university classrooms? If we are always at the front of the class, if we talk more than the students do, and if we are sure we already know what students should learn, then we are playing a singular "teacher" role which is possibly outdated and ineffective.

Second, today's students need a variety of paths towards arts engagement. Teacher education programs should include long-term courses for some, and short term projects for others, depending on the needs and parameters of both the students and the project, "rather than be subject to the tyranny of the school term or year" (p. 22). This suggestion may seem impossible because of the credit structures and schedules in our Faculties of Music and Education. There are, however, ways to provide a variety of paths within external structures. Providing a selection of modules for a certain portion of each course is one strategy to consider. Depending on our space and resources, we could offer some combination of longer and shorter modules. Topics are generated by students and by resources at hand and might include, for example, drum making, soundscapes, guitar, multi-media production, digital recording, Canadian singer/songwriters, and Klesmer. There are likely students in each class we teach with expertise in a particular subject area who could plan and present a module either individually or as part of a team. We find that students are always pleased to have their abilities recognized and utilized. They are happy to add peer teaching at the university level to their portfolio. Local teachers are another important resource. Many principals will support teachers taking a few quarter or half days to present workshops at a Faculty of Education. This module format is an example of the kind of strategies Sloboda refers to in his third suggestion.

Solboda's third suggestion is that a wider variety of activities will respect the wide range of teacher candidates' and students' musical and artistic experience: workshops, talks, program planning, the business of arts, assistance in new and varied art forms such as DJ-ing, performance art, and CD ROM production.

In order to truly respect teacher candidates' and students' musical and artistic experience, music and arts educators need to be willing to expand their own views of what constitutes art. In addition to the traditional trio of choir, band and orchestra, music education now includes computer assisted composition, steel band, guitar, fiddle, folk music, popular music, musics from many cultures, jazz band, jazz choir, Orff, Kodaly, Dalcroze Eurhythmics, synthesized music, technological enhancement of sound, and more. No one person can be expected to provide leadership in all the diverse disciplines and fields. Teachers can, however, develop the willingness to find alternate ways to support student learning in areas outside the teachers' competence. Strategies include peer teaching, inviting local artists to give workshops, becoming involved in teacher-artist programs at the school and community levels, and taking students to visit production houses and studios. As teacher educators we need to provide both beginning and experienced teachers with such diverse models.

One strategy we have used consistently to encourage teacher candidates and graduate students to expand their views of what constitutes art and to become learners in the arts is to make one assignment for our courses a personal project. In this assignment, each student learns a self-chosen new skill, often something the student has "always wanted to learn how to do" (e.g. twig furniture making, welding, Tai Chi, mime, watercolours). We also ask the students to document their learning process in some way. This assignment serves two important purposes, although students report many additional benefits. It provides experience in being a novice learner and it gives most students both new confidence in, and excitement about, learning new things. We find, to our continued amazement, that students take on this assignment with unusual seriousness and determination. Having read students' reflection papers about this assignment for many years, we can report some of the reasons for their commitment to this personal project. Many say they are willing to take the risk because their project will not be graded. Many mention how novel and exciting it is to be given total control over what they choose to learn, how they will go about learning it, and how they will present their project. Many also talk about an "aha" sensation at some stage along their process: when suddenly they make connections between theory and practice or realise that what they had considered givens are really assumptions. The following passage is from one student's reflection paper on her personal project.

To be honest, I was hesitant to take part in the "making art" project when it was announced at the beginning of the semester. As both a teenager and an adult I made a conscious effort to avoid participating in arts related activities. I think my fear of the arts stems from my inability to attain desired achievement levels as a child. I can clearly remember the stain the seemingly inevitable "C" in the area of the arts left on my report cards. By the time I left for high school I had sworn off the visual arts and limited myself almost exclusively to instrumental music because it was the one area where I was able to meet expectations . . . .Although the "making art" project was a course requirement, I think that I decided to genuinely pursue a study of digital photography because I knew that at the end of the day my work would not be for mally judged. . . . In conclusion, this small project transformed my perceptions of art and art-making. I now realize that I am capable of making art. This knowledge has had a profound impact upon my attitude towards the arts and I now look forward to pursuing other artistic endeavours. I also believe that the experience of art-making will make me a better teacher, as I now truly understand that arts is something much more than formalized curriculum objectives. Creating art provides one with intrinsic satisfaction and I want to ensure that my teaching practices do not inhibit or discourage creativity or art making.

This master's student's comments reveal that not only has she learned a new skill, but that her attitude towards the arts has undergone a profound transformation.

Sloboda's suggestions about both function and form bring us to ponder the relationship between the two. Form reflects function, but function also reflects form. We do not need to put function first. We do not even need to put curriculum first. In fact, working "backwards" from form can open the way for surprising learning.

We encourage preservice (and practicing teachers) to teach from their strengths. For example, if a teacher plays tin flute in a Celtic group, then that teacher can base the music program on tin flute and Celtic music at either the secondary or elementary levels. We suggest that only after the teacher plans the unit in his or her area of specialty, particularly in elementary, should he or she consult the mandated curriculum. At that stage, the teacher will usually find that many curricular strands will already be addressed in the teacher-planned program. With a little tweaking, several more related curricular strands, outcomes or items can be approached. When teachers approach music from an area of personal strength, they are likely to bring excitement, integrity and even passion to the class-room. When these same teachers, particularly elementary classroom teachers, approach music from the curriculum guidelines, they often bring frustration and feelings of incompetence.

The power of musical experience lies in engagement of the whole being. Teachers must them-selves be so engaged to allow music to attain its transforming power. In Franklin's (2000) report of an exploration into Toronto teachers' phobias about teaching music, he suggests that "If the child is to feel the art alive within [sic] themselves, so must the teacher" (p. 33). Teacher educa-tors themselves must be so engaged to allow the hard questions about their practices to emerge.

Hard Questions

Regelski suggests that for teachers to become critical and reflective about their prac-tices, they need to ask some of these questions:

MUSIC FOR LIFE

- How did I acquire my guiding beliefs and convictions and why do I hold them so strongly?
- What factors and influences in my own history have narrowed my thinking?
- How much of what and how I teach have I uncritically accepted on the basis of how I've been taught? (p. 112)

These are hard questions indeed. Many teachers know, somewhere deep in their minds and spirits, the answers to every tough question that we've asked in this paper. It takes courage to acknowledge what we know. But it is essential that we move forward with more honesty than we sometimes have in the past, particularly with the very well-intentioned notion of preserving music education. We know that some of the music classes we ourselves have taught over the years have been "endulling," a term coined by Shor (1992) to describe the process by which teaching dulls students' minds. Most of those classes were the result of feeling compelled to follow a curriculum that was not life-related. We also know when our classes have wings, when we try to live more by our instincts and less by the curriculum. We know there are others out there who are trying to do the same. And that our students are being contaminated by feelings of peace. Feelings of joy. Feelings of competency. Feelings of being fully awake to the world. They deserve nothing less.

The writing of this paper was supported, in part, by the Social Sciences and Humanities Research Council of Canada (Standard Research Grant 410-2000-0052). An earlier version of the paper appeared in Canadian Music Educator, 44(3), 12-17.

References

Armstrong, T. (2000). *Multiple intelligences in the classroom*. Alexandria, VA: Association for Supervision and Curriculum Development.

Cameron, L. and Bartel, L (2000). Engage or disengage: and inquiry onto lasting response to music teaching. *Orbit*, 31(2), 22-25.

Campbell, P.S. (1998). *Songs in their heads*. New York: Oxford.

Dissanayake, E. (1995). *Homo aestheticus: Where art comes from and why*. New York: Free Press.

Eisner, E. (2002). *The Arts and the creation of mind*. New Haven: Yale University Press.

Franklin, M. (2000). Overcoming music phobia. *Orbit*, 31(2), 32-33.

Gardner, H. (1983). *Frames of Mind: The Theory of Multiple Intelligences*. New York: Basic Books.

Green, L. (2001). *How popular musicians learn: A new way for music education*. Aldershot, England: Ashgate.

Greene, M. (1995). *Releasing the imagination: Essays on education, the arts, and social change*. New York: Teachers College Press.

Hargreaves, D.J. (1986). *The developmental psychology of music*. Cambridge, UK: Cambridge University Press.

Herndon, J. (1971). *How to survive in your native land*. New York: Simon and Schuster.

Kratus, J. (1989). A time study of the compositional processes used by children ages 7–11. *Journal of Research in Music Education*, 37(1), 5–20.

Nelson, C. & Bloom, F. (1997). Child development and neuroscience. *Child Development*, 68(5), 970–987.

O'Reilley, M.R. (1993). *The Peaceable classroom*. Portsmouth, NH: Boynton/Cook-Heinemann.

O'Toole, P. (2000). Field report on music in the schools. *Orbit*, 31(2), 34-36.

Pitman, W. (1998). *Learning the arts in an age of uncertainty*. Toronto: Arts Education Council of Ontario.

Regelski, T. (2002). On "methodolatry" and music teaching as critical and reflective praxis. *Philosophy of Music Education Review*, 10(2). 102-123.

Rush, A. (2002). There and back again. *Canadian Music Educator*, 44(1), 12-15.

Shor, I. (1992). *Empowering education: Critical teaching for social change*. Chicago: University of Chicago Press.

Sloboda, J. (2001, April). *Emotion, functionality, and the everyday experience of music: where does music education fit?* Paper presented at the International Research In Music Education Conference, Exeter University, England.

Smithrim, K. (1998). Still singing for our lives: Singing in the everyday lives of women through this century. In: B. Roberts, (Ed.). *Sharing the voices: The phenomenon of singing.* St. John's, NF: *Memorial University of Newfoundland,* pp. 217-232.

Tapscott, D. (1997). *Growing up digital: The Rise of the net-generation.* New York: McGraw-Hill Ryerson.

Thomson, S. (1999). Advocacy in the arts: A Canada Council perspective. In B. Roberts (Ed.) *Connect, combine, communicate: Revitalizing the arts in Canadian schools.* Sydney, N.S.: University College of Cape Breton Press, pp. 137-144.

Tsisserev, A. (1997). *An ethnography of secondary school student composition in music: A study of personal involvement within the compositional process.* Unpublished doctoral dissertation, Faculty of Education, University of British Columbia, Vancouver, British Columbia.

Upitis, R. (1992). *Can I play you my song? The Compositions and invented notations of children.* Portsmouth, NH: Heinemann.

Upitis, R. (2001). Spheres of influence: The Interplay between music research, technology, heritage, and music education. *International Journal of Music Education,* 37(1), 44-58.

Upitis, R., Smithrim, K., Patteson, A., & Meban, M. (2001). The Effects of an enriched elementary arts education program on teacher development, artist practices, and student achievement: Baseline student achievement and teacher data from six Canadian sites. *International Journal of Education and the Arts,* 2(8), http://ijea.asu.edu/v2n8/.

Weintraub, S. (December 22-28, 2001). Christmas on the battlefield, an interview with S. Weintraub about his book *Silent night: The Story of the World War I Christmas Truce* with Kathryn Jean Lopez, National Review Online. Retrieved January 26, 2004. http://www.nationalreview.com/weekend/history/history-weintraub122201.shtml

Weinberger, N. & McKenna, T. (1988). Sensitivity of single neurons in auditory cortex to contour: Toward a neurophysiology of music perception. *Music Perception,* 5, 355–390.

Whitehead, A.N. (1929). *The Aims of education.* New York: Macmillan.

SECTION 2:

QUESTIONING WHAT WE TEACH AND FOR WHAT WE TEACH

BENNETT REIMER
MERELY LISTENING

BETTY HANLEY
A "MIDDLE GROUND": THINKING ABOUT LISTENING TO MUSIC IN ELEMENTARY CLASSES

YAROSLAV SENYSHYN
POPULAR MUSIC AND THE INTOLERANT CLASSROOM

RENATE ZENKER
MUSIC AS A LIFELONG PURSUIT: EDUCATING FOR A MUSICAL LIFE

RICHARD MARSELLA
ON BEHALF OF THE UGLY IN MUSIC

BERNARD W. ANDREWS
CONCEPTUALIZING NEW MUSIC FOR YOUNG MUSICIANS

CHAPTER SIX

Merely Listening

BENNETT REIMER

Abstract

In this chapter I relate the sad tale of a sinner in need of salvation. My sin was that I loved too well. Loved to listen to music, that is. Despite attaining the virtue of being a performer, I continued my nefarious love affair with listening until enlightened by music educators who, in their wisdom, convinced me of the error of my passive ways.

The tale encompasses my sinking into despondence when realizing how pervasive were my iniquitous behaviors. I was in much of my life (this is hard to confess) a consumer. Forgive me. Yet through my vale of tears a beam of possible redemption began to shine through. My tale, I hope, has relevance for the music education profession, in its need to rescue itself from its unconscionably high level of irrelevancy to the vast majorities of the populations it purports to serve.

––––––––––

I never listen to music. Well, I should say I never *choose* to listen to music. These days it's all around, so sometimes you just can't avoid it. But when I'm somewhere music is playing I try not to pay attention.

I used to listen all the time. My large collection of LPs, cassettes, and CDs are evidence. I spent lots of money on those recordings, and on hi-fi equipment, tickets to concerts and recitals, operas and musicals, cover charges at jazz clubs, all because I wanted to listen. I got a lot of pleasure from it. It was an important part of my life, something I treasured. I read reviews about pieces and performances. I often planned social evenings around musical presentations, talked with family and friends and colleagues about music we enjoyed listening to, planned ahead to get to concerts in cities I was traveling to all over the world, read books about music. So you could say I was a devoted listener, a faithful audience member.

But I gave it all up. I got educated. I read what a lot of music educators had to say about listening and it wasn't a pretty picture. I began to realize what a musical clod I had been. All that energy, time, money, wasted on being a listener. That's not quite accurate. Being merely a listener, *passively* a listener, *only* and *just* a listener. Being (I can hardly bring myself to say this) a *consumer.* Kind of like being hooked on drugs. Something you thought was wonderful while you were doing it (listening, I mean) but that was frying your brain. And getting you regarded with contempt by those who know better, who are above all that. Those who are musically active not passive, creative not brain-dead, making music not taking it. Who are not interested in autonomous musical works as I had become. Not caught up in formal elements, auditory designs, sound patterns, in disinterested perception, in rarified and purposeless listening experiences separated from life.

That's what they said about people like me (You could look it up). I didn't recognize myself in all this but I knew it had to be me they were talking about because I usually was engrossed in what the sounds were doing when I listened and sometimes I indeed felt like I was in a different world when I was doing so. How could I have gotten so far off track? What possessed me? These people were heavy hitters in music education, who wrote books, articles, gave speeches. If you can't trust music educators in such matters whom can you trust? These people have the musical welfare of everyone at heart, don't they? So if merely listening is *verboten* among these experts surely I had better rethink what I was doing, who I was, what my musical values had been all those years when I loved to listen. Clearly I was a musical sinner in need of redemption. Who wants to be merely, after all? To be passive and just and only, a consumer rather than a creator? Immersed mindlessly in perceiving sounds and what they're doing, often in works I had regarded as monuments of achievement that I could return to over and over for their challenges and satisfactions. Works, it turned out, that separated me from real life, the life of actively performing them rather than passively only merely just consuming them. I had gone seriously astray.

Of course in the years when I was a performer (on clarinet, bass clarinet, alto, tenor, and baritone sax, oboe and English horn,) I was OK. Then I was active. That's because when I listened, not only to myself when I was playing but also to others, I had something to listen for. Listening for is good (You could look it up). It means you should focus on things musicians need to attend to, like all the things performers need to notice in music they're performing. That sure was what I did when I was a performer. I was so intent on being a good player that I listened avidly to music for my instruments so I could learn what other performers were doing and how they did it. I seldom listened to other music, and when I did I waited for the moments when my instruments could be heard so that I'd have something to listen for. The rest of the time I was bored. All the music that didn't use my instruments was a waste of time for me because it gave me nothing to listen for. So I know a lot about listening for.

I had a sneaking suspicion during those years I was a performer that I was missing something when I listened for, but I didn't know what it was. Sometimes I wondered what all the people in the audiences were getting from what we musicians were doing. Some, of course, had played or presently played an instrument, so I figured they were listening the same way I did. Those were the ones who came up after the performance and corralled the performers of their instrument so they could talk about all the "listening fors" of performance. But lots of others—most others, in fact—were not and had never been performers. They seemed to enjoy what we did also, even though it was clear they couldn't listen for as musicians did. That puzzled me. And my response was to kind of condescend to them. They clearly didn't know what was going on. They just loved it. But who cares? They were, I recognize now that I've become enlightened, the great unwashed, the ones still thinking there was music to be savored, even over and over, musical pleasures to be had unrelated to musicianship, musical experiences so deeply satisfying in their lives that they would go to great lengths to get them. Sad.

And eventually I had become one of them. Sad. I had to give up performing for health reasons. So as the years went by I found myself less caught up in listening for what was once so central to my musical being and more engaged in the sounds than in how they were made. I was gradually losing the musician perspective on music, becoming more a taker than a maker. Never entirely, of course. I still got caught up in listening in the old, correct way, especially when a really fine player on one of my instruments was doing her or his stuff. Then I regressed immediately. Did I say "regressed?" I mean, of course, I returned to really being a listener—to listening for. The rest of the time, more and more as the years passed, I sank into becoming the audience member I once knew enough to disrespect. I gave myself up, shamefully, to just listening, as I described at the beginning of this story. I developed a love for music beyond performing it, taking excellent performance for granted because it was so readily available, appreciating it, of course, but no longer tied to it when I listened. Sad.

I also don't read about music any more. Another thing I learned from the music education experts was that listening and verbal language were like oil and water. It's OK to use language to help learn the processes of music making—musicianship, that is. But when teachers and others use language as a way to enhance what is heard it reduces listening to a slavish memorization of verbal concepts (You could look it up).

All the sad years I was a listener I depended a lot on verbal concepts. They pointed out to me all sorts of things going on in the music that I would have missed otherwise. Much of the music I enjoyed listening to challenged me a great deal, from Boulez to Charlie Parker, and I appreciated all the help I could get in hearing what was going on. Each time I heard more there was more to enjoy. And when I read or was told about the backgrounds of the music, issues connected to it, its place in history and culture, I also was affected as a listener, broadening and situating what my ears heard. So I read up about pieces and performers before I went to hear music, studied program notes, even, sometimes, when I got really lucky, followed verbal descriptions of what was going on in the music as it was played and sung. That really helped. It was like a guide in a strange city pointing out all sorts of things I'd never notice by myself. Then when I heard that music again on my own, or visited the city again, I felt like it was part of me, not like I was a musical or geographical tourist. I was "in the know" and listened/traveled at an enhanced level of enjoyment.

Sad. I had been deceived again. Words I had depended on to disclose and explain had only led me further astray, making me even more merely only passively just, a musical nonentity. All those teachers, cultural scholars, historians, theorists, commentators, bent on despoiling my listening experience. So I stopped reading about music. An empty gesture, I know, since I no longer listened, but at least symbolic of my newly acquired enlightenment.

I wish everyone were like me, having become educated about the passivity of merely listening. Think of all the time it would save, the money, the effort. Not only for listeners, of course, but for everyone really actively involved in music. Everyone who is a musician, that is. Performers, conductors, improvisers, even, I suppose, composers (are they musicians?) would no longer have to labor to do what they do. *Because there would be no one to do it for.* Well, I guess they could do it for themselves, because they are the ones who know enough to listen for what they do. And they could do it for others like them, other performers, conductors, so forth. Not much of an audience, of course. Not enough to sustain all those musicians we now have, all of them trying everything they know how to do to entice lots of people to listen to them, go to their performances, buy their recordings. They are the ones most implicated in promoting mass consumership, persuading people to be passive with music by listening to what they do. That's got to stop. It may cause havoc if we lose the main audience for what musicians provide. It may well end our musical culture or reduce it to the tiniest fraction of what it is now. But at least we'll finally have what we need—a few musicians doing what they do for a few musicians. The enlightened reigning.

Recently I was watching TV in the evening before going to sleep, switching channels looking for something interesting. I came across Leonard Bernstein conducting the New York Philharmonic in the Beethoven Sixth. I immediately clicked to the next channel, of course. A perfect example of what I needed to avoid—passive listening to a work from the canon of dead white males, conducted by another. Whew! Close call. A little later (I guess this was just not my night) I came across a performance by the Three Mo' Tenors. I confess that I was so riveted by the excitement of their singing that I lingered for a while. I was struck by how much the audience was enjoying it, applauding, laughing, enthralled with these three singers' virtuosity in a great many styles of music and their savvy showmanship in addition to their sensitive musicianship. For a moment I, too, shared the sheer joy of their performance and of the music they were performing. I let myself go, I'm ashamed to say, fell into the old bad habit of just merely passively only. It lifted my heart. But soon reason prevailed, thank goodness. I clicked on.

Reflecting on that experience the next morning I was struck by a revelation. Not only does listening force one to be passive and uncreative, but listening on TV compounds the error. Watching TV is itself the archetypal example of couch potatoship, the depths of merely. It's not just listening to/watching music on TV that exemplifies this vice. It's watching TV in the first place! Few people who watch TV are actors, producers, scriptwriters, camera persons, news anchors, and so forth. Most people don't "do" TV—they just watch. So they can't possibly watch for, as those involved in the TV industry must do. Not being able to watch for, they can be only merely etc. Like me. All of us, millions, no, billions of us, all over the world, subjecting themselves to subservience, to only taking not making.

I shuddered. How could I have missed this obvious fact literally staring me in the face? How often had I read about the evils of watching the boob tube, never recognizing that I was the boob in question? My enjoyment of some favorite programs, of sports, newscasts, documentaries, yes, even musical presentations, had slipped under my watchful gaze, my now being enlightened.

TV had to go. For some things I had depended on TV for, such as sports events, there was a remedy. I could go to the games in which I was interested. Not often, of course, because I couldn't travel around the world to all the events I would have been able to watch easily on TV. And even where I lived I didn't have the time or money to attend often. Do you know what it costs for tickets to watch successful teams play? (Of course, living in Chicago this is seldom a problem.) And I could go to theater productions instead of watching dramas on the tube, go to the movies instead of watching them on TV, read the newspaper instead of watching the news, go to museums, dance productions, lectures, restaurants instead of watching the food channel. (Oh, dear God, can I please watch the food channel?)

Notice how I was deceiving myself, the depths of my blindness to the fallacy with which my life had become pervaded. Going to a sports event was no better than watching it on TV. Going to a concert or a club was no better than listening on TV or to a recording. Whether in person or once removed one was still a consumer, a taker not a maker. Still a merely. There was only one way out of the dilemma. I would have to become a football player, a basketball player, and many other athlete types I had so unknowingly enjoyed watching. I would have to become a movie actor or director or something. A theater actor or playwright, a dancer or choreographer, a museum curator, a lecturer, a chef, on and on with all the things I must now do instead of only *consume*. The revelation continued. Read a newspaper? Read fiction, poetry, scholarly books and journals, professional material? Cook food I had not grown or raised myself? Wear clothing I had not made? Drive a car I had not manufactured? Take medications I had not formulated? Where did it all end? Where did my obliviousness to my rabid consumerism reach bottom? I knew I was just scratching the surface. I was staggered by the depth of my unawareness of how dependent I had become on being merely only just a passive consumer.

The nail in the coffin came shortly thereafter. For many years I have been an enthusiastic, no, passionate, collector of contemporary art. I got hooked while a young professor, when I wandered into a student show at the Cleveland Institute of Art and was captivated by a ceramic vase so graceful, so sensitive, so heart-wrenchingly beautiful that I just had to have it. It was twenty dollars, an extravagance I could ill afford. But something inside me made me overcome my frugality and go for it. I still have it, and it continues to shape my inner life. I was changed forever by that purchase, learning that I could surround myself with objects I loved, that challenged and instructed me, that satisfied a deep need for spiritual satisfaction just as music did when I succumbed to being a listener. Over the years I have amassed a large collections of art works in a great variety of media, works reflecting my expanding, deepening tastes as my eye, mind, and body have become more discerning, more widely receptive, more knowledgeable, and more mature. Much of my history as a human being is captured in the works I have acquired, reflecting my journey of inner growth.

All this went through my mind when my awareness of my unfettered consumership had finally surfaced from its unexamined depths. This too, this collection of art, so close to my identity, revealed how contaminated my life had been by passive taking, how thoroughly I had succumbed to the siren call of uncreative merely. I was shaken by this epiphany, this suddenly revealed unworthiness.

I had tried to do the right thing, to make art rather than only take it. I had taken ceramics classes and drawing and painting. Hated it. It was just not me, not only because I was so pathetically bad at it but because it just didn't "feel me." Yet my discernment of what others could do was highly developed, my relationships within the art world very close, and my involvement in the art museum and gallery culture intense. I was, in deep and broad ways, an important player in the world of the visual arts, a world in which I dwelled with great satisfaction, a sense of being at home, and a role to play that I knew was essential. That is, the role of visual art partaker, a partner in the larger enterprise, in fact the end toward which the enterprise aimed—the enlightened, enthusiastic participant in and co-creator of the meanings artists make available. Just as I had become in music when making was no longer possible, and as I had long been in theater, dance, movies, literature, and poetry. I didn't "make" in any of the arts now, yet each of them filled my life with their special joys and challenges to my inner creativity. And, in turn, I and others like me gave those who made them the discriminative audience they depended on to do their best work. So was it possible that I was not entirely merely? That I actually played an active role, a needed role in the world of the arts which my culture provided me?

I felt myself slowly turning a corner, once faced with the enormity of what I would lose if I abandoned my role as a consumer of the arts. I had been headed down a lonely, dark path, in my zeal to follow the prescriptions of those for whom my life represented a fall from the grace of artistry. Those who preached the salvation of making while, perhaps with a sense of guilt but also, perhaps, with unawareness, were takers in much of their lives as all of us are. Had my acquiescence to their argument been unwarranted?

A great weight began slowly lifting from my shoulders, from my spirit. A glimmer of hope that my life, so full with the pleasures the arts had afforded me, my goings out into a world of fascinations, might, after all, be worth living. Perhaps there was another way to construe what taking meant, what it entailed, how essential it was and how it needed to be nurtured by education. Perhaps, in fact, by the profession of music education, not as an afterthought, not as secondary (if that) to what really mattered, not with disdain, but as a major reason for its being if it truly cared about nurturing universal musicality.

Musicality? Aren't we back to musicianship? Universal? Aren't we back to the notion that everyone, if they are to be involved with music genuinely, must be a musician? And to the widespread belief that the purpose of music education is to see to it that everyone plays that particular role? Further, that even if some (actually most) do not choose to play it, an education devoted to training musicianship is the only valid route for all? Those, in fact are pervasive beliefs in music education today. For a very long time, when the music in one's life had to be the music one made for oneself, musicianship training was fundamental. But for over a century the world of music, along with all else, has been radically transformed. We may bemoan the loss of a romantic idyll in which people produced all they needed and wanted. But who would choose to return to that condition, which was, in fact, one of paucity rather than plenty for the vast majority of people? The arts have flourished dramatically during the past century, not just for the few, as before, but for all who choose to become involved. Although opportunities to create art now exist to an extent never before known in history, most either cannot devote themselves to creating art or choose not do so. Instead, with gratitude and often with great zeal, they surround themselves with the arts they prefer, their partaking becoming a precious part of their lives.

As had occurred for me. In music I had the experience of starting with musicianship and then having to continue with listenership. So I too had bought in to the notion that being a musician was the one true path to being musical, as I described earlier. That made me vulnerable to the condemnations of those who decried and minimized the partaker role I had come to assume. But I have the advantage of knowing both the benefits and drawbacks of the musician perspective on music and am, therefore, able to view the role of the consumer with a more discerning eye. It is indeed life-enhancing to create in any of the arts. That is something I deeply know. However, I am able, from experience not from theory alone, to understand the benefits of partaking unfettered by musicianship concerns. There is a purity, an openness, a directness of mind and feeling when one confronts music as, unguardedly, a respondent, free from all the special details and issues to which musicians must attend. Dare I say it? Music has become more spiritual for me, not less, since my change of roles. Gradually, of course, and never entirely because I continue to be a musician in one part of my psyche. But I have tasted what devoted consumers taste, and, I admit, I find it sweet. I suspect that is why the other arts, the visual arts particularly, are so compelling and profoundly satisfying for me, in that my responses to them can be without pretense of professionalism. I can be, for them, wholeheartedly, even guilelessly, an amateur, one who loves an activity or enterprise for the sheer sake of the enjoyment it affords.

But not mindlessly. Not superficially. Not, in fact, passively but with passion and devotion. That is the main point this essay, a mixture of satirical fantasy and reality, leads me to propose. The musicianship roles are active, *but only when those pursuing them are being active when doing so. That is, the musicianship role being played can be active or passive depending on qualities supervenient upon the role itself.*

That applies equally to the consumership roles, or, if one prefers, the listenership roles. Those roles include listeners in all the multifarious ways and circumstances in which music listening takes place in our real lives, and all the roles supportive of our understandings of musical experience—music theorists, historians, critics, psychologists, philosophers, anthropologists, sociologists, and so forth—all the non-musician roles existent in a culture. Each calls upon a particular way to be intelligent and creative within the domain of music just as the musicianship roles do, and each can be pursued passively or actively depending on qualities of that pursuit, just as with musicianship. *Passive or active are not in themselves determined by the role being played, but on characteristics associated with the way it is being played.*

What are those characteristics? Being active in any musical role requires an investment of energy. All musical engagements are mental/emotional acts, *ipso facto* requiring the body's participation as well. The mind, in all musical experience whether creating, or sharing what has been created, or exploring and explaining what occurs in musical engagements, must be involved as it must for all other experience, in the case of music in the discernment of sounds and their interconnections as meaningful occurrences in the context of the ways various cultures provide for such meanings to come into existence. Musical discernments and interconnections are constructive, imaginative, individual acts of meaning-making, as fully as anything else among human endeavors. That is, they are acts of intelligence.

Musical meanings are diverse. They come from the sounds themselves as created and shared. They come from those sounds as situated in particular systems of belief about music. Those systems, being human creations, are saturated with many other beliefs related to musical ones, impinging on, qualifying, and coloring how musical meaning is construed. To put it differently, music both reflects and absorbs a host of relevant beliefs, assumptions, values, and practices, transforming them into sound-constructions that both incorporate them and subject them to a metamorphosis—a change in form and substance only sounds regarded to be musical are capable of accomplishing. All these dimensions of mindful operation are primally implicated in musical experiences. The degree of engagement is the degree of active energy being expended by a person playing a musical role, a degree ranging on a continuum from extreme passivity to extreme activation.

What demarcates the level of passivity or activity, then, is not the overt physicality of the engagement but the quality and fullness of a person's investment of energies in it. Reading a book, surely quiescent physically, can be more active—more fully engaged by one's selfness—than pounding rocks with a sledgehammer. Listening to music with absorption, imagination, discernment, understanding, feeling, and caring, is as active as reading a book when all those characteristics are being manifested energetically. Both can be passive, of course, when none of those qualities are present or are minimally present, as is true of any other activity such as performing. "Hands on," so often invoked as the essential criterion of being active, is in no respect such a criterion, because hands can be engaged with none of the other qualities being evidenced. Whatever the role, requiring actions of the body or not, the degree of the energies of selfness being expended is the degree of activeness attained.

Which brings us to the heart of the dilemma for music education. How do we encourage (unfortunately we cannot insure) optimum levels of active involvement when students are engaged in any musical role? It is unlikely, perhaps even undesirable, for peak activation to occur at all times: few can or should maintain the uppermost reaches of energy expenditure constantly. (In fact when some children do, we have to intervene to help them lower the temperature of their inner furnace.) But certainly we want to achieve high levels of activation during the very short periods of time available to us to actually teach, making the most of that precious opportunity in its impact on our students' quality of musical experience.

Perhaps the hardest of all roles in which to succeed in that goal, unfortunately, is in the teaching of listening. Unfortunate because it is the most pursued musical role of all, involving far more people than all the other roles put together. If we want to help all people become more musical, an aim we have embraced in theory but not in practice, we have to get real about how to do so. That is, we cannot go on assuming that everyone must adopt the performer's perspective. That perspective has guided us toward creating the school music program we now have and have had for well over half a century in its present form, and extending back from that to the origins of music education in American history. The good news is that we have been, in my opinion, remarkably successful in that endeavor, a success of which all of us can be very proud. It has been our great achievement.

The bad news is that it has been our only such achievement. In our present world, where performance is an option chosen by relatively few, we have massively neglected all the other ways to be musical in our culture. Which is why it is unfortunate that the teaching of listening, which should be the bedrock of our professional contribution, on which all others are based, is so infernally difficult to do well. Of course all music teaching is challenging, each role presenting its own complexities. But in the case of listening the availability of immediate, reliable, and accurate feedback is scarce or nonexistent. When a student's engagements occur entirely inwardly as they do in listening, with no reliable way to represent them so that teachers can help carry them forward, teaching can only be insecure and uncertain. In education, input without feedback is a recipe for futility.

Exactly how can feedback—demonstrations of what is being heard and with what scope, depth, and investment of energies—be obtained from those who listen? That question has bedeviled every music educator who has attempted to develop those qualities in the act of listening. Many approaches have been tried, including invented notations that indicate what has been heard and how it is being structured in the listener's mind; verbal reports both specifically descriptive (loud, slow, fugue, electric bass, Baroque, early Beatles, raga, etc.) and generally interpretive (sad, happy, like clouds, a storm, winter, "it reminded me of...," etc.); body movements indicating specific or general qualities; iconic, pictorial representations; brain scans of mental activity while listening, and any other attempts teachers and others have made to pin down the otherwise entirely elusive responses of those who listen.

All these attempts to acquire feedback are deeply problematical because of their inadequacy to capture the phenomenological uniqueness and complexity of the listening experience. The hapless teacher of listening operates in a haze of indeterminacy, relying on hunch, hope, and the bits of "data" the various feedback mechanisms might provide. The world of performance could not be more dissimilar, with its ongoing, tangible, exacting demonstrations of what is occurring, able to be addressed directly so as to refine and deepen the qualities of creative expression performance entails.

I do not mean to overstate the difficulties of teaching listening or to underestimate the complexities of teaching performance. Each, of course, has challenges aplenty, each in its own way as does the teaching of each other musical role. I do want to clarify why listening is peculiarly resistant to security in the teaching act. More so, I would suggest, than even those who teach listening regularly, and feel confident that they are doing it well, imagine. I simply am unconvinced that the distinctive nature of musical listening has allowed us to achieve anything like the expertise—the remarkable skills and insights—we have developed in teaching performance, and I have not seen or heard anything to persuade me differently (although I would be delighted—and amazed—to be proven mistaken.)

That reservation applies, I must add, to my own ongoing, dedicated attempts to devise useful and respectful mechanisms to help listeners get more from music than they would likely get on their own. I have long been fascinated by the musical/pedagogical interface of puzzles the teaching of listening presents, and am far from satisfied that my work in it has been any more than provisional. Given the many determinants of what goes on in the listening act, the attempt to be helpful, as teachers are supposed to be, is more than daunting.

Helpful how and for what? Each of the many dimensions of music and of our experiences of it can, indeed, be "helped" if we conceive that to mean enabling each learner to engage as fully as possible with music in both its contextual and "context made musical" dimensions and with the selfness of creative energies. But that in itself, while one construal (among others) of what "helping" might mean in the listening role, is a generalization. Translating such a generality into the practices called for in the actualities of real teachers dealing with real people in particular settings remains an unfinished, even largely unaddressed, agenda. It is not enough, not *nearly* enough, to posit a general goal and assume that is sufficient to achieve or even improve teaching effectiveness. Until we as a profession take seriously, with the help of coordinated, issue-focused research, our obligation to translate generalities into teaching practices genuinely related to them, we will continue to generate an abundance of "sound and fury signifying nothing."

All this and much more flooded into my mind when I began to see my way out of the despondency to which my acquiescence to the argument of listening as passive had led me. My energies, dampened by my avoidance of beloved activities, began to return, as did my joy in living. I felt the freedom of a liberated attitude—liberated to enjoy, openly and without guilt, the role of partaker to which my life had led me. I began to indulge in all my previous involvements, now with a refreshed perspective on their genuine value.

I even began to read again. I returned to a book I had recently read and found vivifying, Tia DeNora's tightly argued *Music in Everyday Life*.[1] For DeNora the role of the consumer of music is an energetic one in constructing meaning, feeling, and corporeality in musical engagements. "We are now a long way from any conception of music listening as passive," she asserts.[2] (And now my resolve to write an essay with not a single citation has gone down the tubes. Alas, the yoke of academic scholarship binds me tightly.)

Perhaps the actions of listening, as deeply an amalgam of thought, subjectivity, and embodiment as anything in human experience, can, after all, be rescued from the neglect or indifference in which it tends to exist in music education. Perhaps listening can be recognized, finally, as a genuine, precious role in and of itself, not only as a means to other ends. As with every other way to be musical, but more urgently given its primacy in our musical culture, the role of the listener deserves the full devotion of our energies and intelligences, to face its dilemmas, devise useful means to surmount them, and position ourselves thereby to make the fullness of contribution our culture deserves from us.

I plan my activities for the next month. Several musical events to attend, both on campus and in the city. A Saturday at the art galleries and the Art Institute. Two theater productions I'm dying to see. A couple of good movies in town, for a change. My favorite modern dance group in a new production. A novel I've got to finish. A lecture I want to hear on gender and post-postmodern thought. A friend got us tickets to a basketball game. The wine group has a tasting scheduled. Are there some originals of West Wing on TV rather than only reruns? A reservation at that new restaurant that got rave reviews. (Be still my heart.) And, by the way, there's work to be done, as always. Too busy. I've got to get better at scheduling in some time to be passive.

NOTES

[1] TIA DeNORA, *Music in Everyday Life* (CAMBRIDGE UNIVERSITY PRESS, 2000).
[2] DeNORA, "THE EVERYDAY AS EXTRAORDINARY: RESPONSE FROM TIA DeNORA. *Action, Criticism, and Theory for Music Education.* VOL. 1, #2 (DECEMBER, 2002), 6. HTTP://MAS.SIUE.EDU/ACT/V1/DeNORARESPONSE02.PDFChapter Seven

CHAPTER SEVEN

A "Middle Ground": Thinking about Listening to Music in Elementary Classes

BETTY HANLEY

Abstract

Music educators, while claiming that listening to music is an active, not passive experience, have typically adopted a pedagogical approach that privileges an understanding of music as an aesthetic object where the formal aspects of the work are the focus of student learning. Furthermore, teachers tell students what to listen for. An examination of the underlying assumptions of widely used elementary music textbook series and listening resources confirms this conclusion. The Integrated Listening Model (ILM) offers a solution in which both students and teachers are sources of knowledge; the students identify what they listen for while the teacher helps deepen the experience; both students and teachers shape the listening strategies; there are multiple ways to listen to the music, and the students are active in constructing their own meaning and understanding. The ILM offers a middle ground between approaches that are totally teacher-directed or entirely student-directed.

Introduction

> *The development of every student's listening intelligence...is a crucial obligation of music education.* (Reimer, 2003, p. 225)

Two paradigms have been used to explain how we view music. Modernists assume an industrialist, clockwork view of a world where progress and reason are primary. In this view, music is conceived of as a work, an object whose meaning transcends everyday living; as autonomous—disassociated from the listener; and as best understood by an analysis of its components. An aesthetic experience of music, the most desirable way of engaging in music, requires emotional distance from the object and a focus on its properties.

In postmodernist views, music is not considered an object but an action, something that people do. That is, music is a verb, not a noun (Elliott, 1995; Small, 1998). Music is part of everyday life, not something that belongs in a museum, concert hall, or score. Listening is considered "musicking." Furthermore, there is no single right way of experiencing music; there are multiple possibilities. Meaning is not in the music (or not only in the music) but constructed by the listener based on social conventions and biology. Both paradigms suggest very different approaches to music teaching and learning.

Davis, Sumara, and Luce-Kapler (2000) provide a useful connection between music and learning by identifying two ways of perceiving the world that produce very different theories of learning and teaching: complicated and complex theories. In complicated learning theories, knowledge is viewed as a thing, something external to the knower to be defined by the teacher/expert. Complicated systems are based on assumptions that value cause and effect, predictability, objectivity, and mechanical process. What is to be learned is broken down into smaller pieces that, when put together, will reproduce the whole, much like a clock that can be taken apart and reassembled. A close connection between complicated theory and modernism is evident.

In contrast, complex systems are unpredictable, living, changing, and adaptable. They are organic and holistic (like the weather). Knowledge is not something external to the learner but is a "potentiality" shaped by biological capacity, social and natural environments, and historical conditions (p. 53). In complex systems, knowledge is embodied: "The biological body is not a structure through which one learns, but a structure that learns" (p. 66). Learning is a creative act: "Learning is a process through which one becomes capable of more sophisticated, more flexible, more creative action" (p. 73). The assumptions underlying complex theory are shared by postmodernism. [1]

Reimer (2003) claims that developing students' listening intelligence is "a crucial obligation of music education" (p. 225). I agree. But how is this important aspect of music education addressed in classrooms? Are the underlying assumption about learning made by Canadian and American elementary music teachers when they present listening lessons based on complicated or complex learning theories? Observing teachers would provide the most reliable information but would be costly and time consuming. A survey of teachers would be the next best option (but would not necessarily provide accurate information). A third option is to examine the materials teachers use. While this evidence is indirect, as Koza (1994) explained, "In addition to having an impact on children's attitudes and behavior, curricular materials such as popular textbooks are cultural artifacts that can reflect and reinforce dominant cultural discourses" (pp. 145–146). Although Koza was writing about gender issues, her statement applies equally well to paradigms of learning. Additionally, despite attempts by some educators to eliminate basal series, existing evidence confirms the fairly widespread use of music textbook series by teachers (McLellan, 1996). Therefore, to answer my question, I will examine approaches to listening to music found in a sample of well established Canadian and American elementary music textbook series and listening resources from the past 25 years to uncover underlying assumptions about learning and music. Are they complex or complicated? Modern or postmodern? I will also revisit my Integrated Listening Model (Hanley, 1997), an attempt to address challenges emerging from complicated assumptions about listening to music. To make the task manageable, I have restricted my analysis to the following eight resources for elementary music teachers (teachers' editions):

- *Silver Burdett Music*, grade 4 (Silver Burdett, 1974)
- *The Music Book*, grade 3 (Boardman & Andress, 1981)
- *Musicanada: Resource Centre*, grade 6 (Brooks, Kovac, & Trotter, 1984)
- *Musicanada*, grade 6 (Brooks, Kovac, & Trotter, 1984)
- *Share the Music*, grade 3 (Macmillan/McGraw Hill, 1995)
- *Adventures in Music Listening*, level two (Burton, Hoffer, & Hughes, 1997)

- *Music Connection*, grade 4 (Silver Burdett Ginn, 2000)
- *Musicanada Encore: Listening and Appreciation*, grade 4 (Cobbold & Wamsley, 2000)

The following questions guide the analysis:

1. Who is the source of knowledge about music?
2. Who is responsible for identifying what students should listen for?
3. Who is responsible for identifying the strategies to be used for listening?
4. Is there a "correct" way of hearing the music?
5. What do the authors mean by "active" listening?

That is, are the assumptions in these resources for teachers predicated on complicated or complex theories of learning?

Music Series and Resources—An Analysis

Given the postmodern direction of our society (Harvey, 1990), in my analysis I have used a chronological approach, reasonably anticipating a change in the way listening lessons have been conceptualized by the turn of the century. That is, I would expect a move-ment from complicated to complex learning theories and greater evidence of the latter in the most recent publications. Although some of these series are no longer in use, I have chosen to use the present tense when discussing each one. [2]

Silver Burdett Music. *Silver Burdett Music* (1974) uses a concept-approach to teaching music based on the psychological and philosophical thinking in the 1970s. Bruner's ideas about the need to base curriculum on the structure of the disciplines results in a spiral curriculum that features all the elements and concepts of music in each grade. Reimer's absolute expressionism, where the aesthetic qualities of the music are the underlying reason for helping students perceive the musical concepts, forms the philosophical underpinning. Two important aids for listening in the series are "Call Charts," for guided listening, and "What Do You Hear?," to evaluate the learning. In one version of the listen-ing selections, a voice on the recording calls out numbers corresponding to numbers on the chart as the music plays so students can follow along. [3] Both teaching strategies use visual icons and word maps to help students more fully and accurately perceive the con-cept(s). The series goes beyond mere identification of concepts by linking these con-cepts to expressive purpose. Thus, while the lesson focuses on repetition and contrast in Kingsley's *Commissioned Piece 3* (p. 69) one of the objectives states that "[t]he ongoing experience of most pieces includes a recognition of what came before and its relation to what came after—a perception of structure, or form" (p. 63). That is, the authors attempt to help students link perception and response. [4]

Nevertheless, although the students are actively engaged in moving, tracing, and look-ing, the focus is on the concepts identified by the authors of the series as worthy of attention, and teachers presumably use the strategies set out for them. The presence of the voice on the recordings means that students do not have to use their ears to identify what is happening. While one cannot assume that students are not making their own meaning, regardless of how lessons are taught, the teaching method for listening lessons does not explicitly support or value meaning making on the part of students. There is a "correct" way of listening, as the "What Do You hear?" exercises indicate.

The Music Book. Based on a generative approach to teaching music, *The Music Book* (Boardman & Andress, 1981) directs students to focus on musical concepts outlined in a musical concepts bank and presented by the teacher. Boardman and Andress, however, also invite the children to participate more constructively in the music experience. One example will illustrate the point. In a lesson featuring Rameau's "Tambourin," the instructions in the student's text read as follows:

> Listen to the music.
> Follow the boy or girl's dance movements.
> *[The image shows people dressed in period costumes moving in a circle formation.]*
> Can you tell when they pause to greet each other?
> Can you tell when they come to a stop at the end of the phrase?
> How many times could they repeat this pattern?
>
> Plan your own dance to follow the phrases.
> Move with the same feeling.
> When will you want to move in different directions? (p. 20)

While students' attention is focused on phrase, pattern, and cadence, they are clearly invited to hear for themselves and use their imaginations in response to the music.

In this series, although the focus is on the development of "essential musical concepts" and sometimes the "correct" answer is given, the manual suggests ways for teachers to allow students to take responsibility for their own learning and develop musical independence (p. viii). For example, on page 55, students are asked to determine when the tonal centre changes in Sherman and Sherman's "Scales and Arpeggios," not told when it happens (for example, with a voice-over). The way is open for students to develop musical understanding rather than a compendium of facts about music.

Musicanada and Musicanada: Resources Centre. *Musicanada* (Brooks, Kovac, & Trotter, 1984) focuses on concepts, usually with a loose connection to expressive purpose. For example, in the Grade 6 *Resource Centre* (1984), the students are told the kind of feeling the music will elicit (rest and unrest in Weait's "The Jolly Raftsman," p. 4) and are to provide a word for the mood of Bizet's "Farandole," (p. 5). In *Musicanada,* active listening:

> Develops auditory skills
> Provides a challenge
> Tests previously learned concepts
> Stimulates imagination
> Provides a variety of musical experiences
> Aids enjoyment. (p. 8)

Active listening is explicitly acknowledged to be desirable by Brooks, Kovac, and Trotter.

An examination of the series shows that students do read maps, move to music, and draw. These are all worthy activities. If active listening means doing, then this series promotes active learning. If active means constructing one's own understanding, then the students are not being encouraged to be active learners. Decisions concerning what is to be learned and how it will be learned are being made by the teacher. There are generally correct answers, as is evident in the worksheets for students.

Share the Music. A more recent addition to music textbooks, *Share the Music* (Macmillan/McGraw Hill, 1995) focuses the musical learning on concepts. On page 172, children learn minimal information about the violin then are told that the violins play the melody in Tchaikovsky's "Waltz of the Flower." A set of transparencies accompanies the program. These are colourful maps for a variety of music selections. In each map, the focus is on a musical concept, and the icons often present images suggested by the title. For example, the "Overture" to Mozart's *Marriage of Figaro* uses characters from the opera to show form. William's "Three Rides at the Park" uses a Ferris wheel, merry-go-round, and rollercoaster to illustrate the form of the work, drawing students' attention to programmatic factors.

Although the students are involved in the, by now familiar, listening activities, there is little overt connection made to personal responses. One exception is found on page 11 when students are asked to explore the difference between "historical and musical facts about 'Sabre Dance' and individual opinions about the piece." On this occasion, the children are asked about their feelings, and there is an implied connection between what is heard and what is felt. Once again, in this series the teacher is the sole source of knowledge and the decision maker.

Adventures in Music. The authors of this three-level Bowmar series (Burton, Hoffer, & Hughes, 1997) use a highly teacher-directed approach to listening for music concepts, learning about the composition and the composer, and making connections across the curriculum. [5] There are attempts to engage the learner by asking them to offer their "general impressions about what they heard," but the suggested answers deal with musical concepts such as style and performance medium. The typical approach is to direct the students to listen for specific elements in the music. There are "correct" answers provided by the authors. Here are some examples of the teacher-directed approach presented in this resource. The students are told that Grieg's "In the Hall of the Mountain King" suggests "fright" (p. 37). That is, the mood of the music is identified for students. Similarly, on page 92, the students are told that the "Prelude" to Act III of Wagner's *Lohengrin* is joyous then asked for their impressions. Students are to choose from among three suggestions for the kind of dance Copland's "Hoe-Down" from Rodeo suggests, rather than being allowed to use their imaginations and experience to make suggestions (p. 33). When the imagination is invoked, students are guided to the correct answer (see Villa-Lobos' "Little Train of the Caipira," p. 87).

This resource is teacher-directed when it comes to music learning: teachers are the source of knowledge; they identify what will be learned and how it will be learned. Interestingly, suggested activities occasionally involve students in music making. Students' imaginations and initiative are more typically invoked in the extended learning and curriculum connections rather than in the listening experience.

Music Connection. The approach used in the *Music Connection* (Silver Burdett Ginn,

2000) is strongly concept-based in the section called Concepts, with little connection to expressiveness or personal response. For example, students are asked to listen to the "Gavotte" from Prokofiev's *Classical Symphony* for the "movement of tones" (steps, skips, and leaps, p. 42). That's it. [6] In the Themes section of the series, the listening selections relate, as the title suggests, to themes such as "how people work and play" and "moving people and goods." Here, the learning is focused more on curriculum connections and less on music learning. Across the program there are colourful transparencies that, like *Share the Music*, guide the listeners to hear designated aspects of the music through the use of icons and content-related images.

The content is teacher-directed, with little personal construction of meaning on the part of students. The use of "What Do You Hear?" strategies for evaluation indicate the presence of right answers to student listening.

Musicanada Encore. This listening and appreciation resource (Cobbold & Wamsley, 2000) complements the earlier *Musicanada* series. The overall approach remains conceptual, as is evident in the sample assessment checklist, which lists such skills as identifying high and low sounds, maintaining a steady beat, identifying specific instruments, identifying changes in form, and identifying meter in twos and threes (p. 7). But there are also signs of emerging differences with the earlier series. A chart on page 16 asks students to identify what they heard ("ear shots"), how they felt, and why. This request is not evident in every lesson, but it does appear. Later, students are asked to discuss the context of different musical styles. Under "Music Classroom Management Ideas" teachers are offered the following advice, advice that is not, however, interwoven throughout the resource book:

> Allow time for students to share their thoughts and interpretations of the music. Music is a very personal thing and influences people in many different ways. In the area of interpretation (*What did it make you think of?*), no answer is wrong and every answer should be given equal respect. (p. 39) [7]

While this resource is teacher-directed and conceptually-based, there is some allowance made for students' contribution to the learning process.

Summary of the Analysis. With a few notable exceptions (especially *The Music Book* and a few examples in *Musicanada Encore*), the authors of Canadian and American elementary music series textbooks and resources, while claiming that listening to music is an active, not passive experience, have typically adopted a pedagogical approach that privileges an understanding of music as an aesthetic object, where the formal aspects of the work are the focus for student learning. [8] In this approach, the teacher is the dispenser of knowledge about the music, is responsible for identifying what students should listen for, and helps students hear it by focusing the listening experience on targeted concepts. A "correct" way of hearing the music is assumed. In such classrooms, students may be active in the sense that they are moving to the music or lifting a shape to show the form, but are they really being active in the sense of constructing their own understanding? Listening lessons, if they follow the guidelines provided in widely used basal series are based on modernist assumptions about music and complicated learning theories. The conclusion must be that in the resources developed by publishers, written by master teachers, and used by classroom and music teachers across Canada and the United States, there has been only small movement towards addressing complex learning theories.

An account of informal research only reinforces my conclusion. In a workshop to a group of elementary, secondary, and private music teachers, I asked them to identify the strategies they used in listening to music lessons. Five of the twenty-one respondents interpreted the request to refer to the development of aural skills and ear training or to listening during performances. For the remainder, the preferred approach was that of guided listening, where the teacher asked students to listen for some specific music fea-ture such as the form, style, or melodic shape, or to look at maps representing the music. A few teachers asked students to discuss their emotional response to the music. A few asked students to move to the music or draw an image of the music. While I certainly cannot generalize from this informal sample, the results mirror what has been happen-ing in the music textbooks and resources.

I now proceed to an examination of the underlying assumptions of the Integrated Listening Model (ILM) I have been developing since 1993 (Hanley 1997). Is the model built upon complicated or complex learning theories?

The Integrated Listening Model (ILM)

As an elementary music teacher and music teacher educator I experimented with vari-ous kinds of approaches to listening to music for many years. I worked with icons and maps, movement, charts, drawing to music, singing the themes, and so on. Students seemed to learn and enjoy the lessons so I merely engaged in improving and expanding my teaching strategies. My focus was on helping students perceive the musical concepts and acknowledge and value (but not explore) their unique responses to the music, as conceptualized in *Silver Burdett Music* (1974 and later editions). But the concepts came first, and I was the expert. Then, I noticed that models for looking at visual art began with the students' response to the work itself and then proceeded to description, analy-sis, and interpretation (Feldman, 1970, 1987; Geahigan, 1993). What would happen if this approach were used in music?

It was at this time that I developed the ILM in which students listened to music and in pairs or as a class shared what they heard, saw, thought, or felt (Hanley, 1997). Through the ques-tions "What do you think, see, or feel?" "What do you hear?" and "So what?" the Integrated Listening Model encouraged students' personal responses to music by asking them:

- to express their feeling response,
- to identify what *they* heard in the music, and
- to explore how the way the music sounds contributes to their feeling response (the so what? part).

I have been using this model with children and adult learners, adapted for the develop-mental level, with what I have found to be exciting results (Hanley 2003; Hanley & King, 1995). The model is deceptively simple [9] but works best over time with teachers who are knowledgeable about music and who can, through questions and observations that connect student responses, probe and deepen the listening experience. Over the years I have been surprised at the insights grade 3 to graduate students bring to their listening experiences; more often than not, they provide "outside the box" observations that expand everyone's understanding.

When I developed the ILM, I was working towards a constructivist view of learning. Although at the time I didn't realize it, my emerging assumptions matched those of constructivism, one of the four complex learning theories outlined by Davis, Sumara, and Luce-Kapler (2000) that range from cognitive to ecological. [10] Constructivism is a complex learning theory where the focus is on the individual's cognitive growth: "Cognition is understood as a process of maintaining an adequate fit with one's ever-changing circumstances, as opposed to assembling an internal mental model of an external world" (p. 65).

How we construct our understanding of the world around us is discussed by Damasio (2003) in a book investigating the feeling brain, a topic of particular relevance to music educators:

> When you and I look at an external object, we form comparable images in our respective brains, and we can describe the object in very similar ways. That does not mean, however, that the image we see is a replica of the object. The image we see is based on changes that occurred in our organisms, in the body and in the brain, as the physical structure of that particular object interacts with the body (p. 199)

Note that Damasio's explanation accounts for both construction of meaning by the individual and similarities in how we experience the world that allow us to communicate. With the rapidly expanding understanding of how the brain works, researchers and educators are increasingly realizing the broader implications of what is meant by active learning.

A Middle Ground

> *The path of learning can never* be determined *by* the teacher. *However, the path of learning is* dependent *on the teacher.* (Davis, Sumara, and Luce-Kapler, 2000, p. 66)

On one occasion, I was demonstrating the ILM to a class of graduate students. The graduate students provided rich responses to the selection, both in terms of what they heard and what they felt. I am constantly amazed at the depth of the perception of "untutored" listeners, at least as a group. One participant's response, however, was revealing. He did not want to write anything down for fear of getting the wrong answer. It seems that he believed there was a right way to listen to music and express the experience, presumably using correct music terminology. Perhaps he thought he should be able to identify the form or the mode? I found this fearful response disturbing but acknowledged it as an honest reaction to past experiences.

In our eagerness to teach formal music education (how we as trained musicians have learned to construct music), have we overlooked and even denigrated what students bring to the music experience and classroom? Does this single-minded approach result in adults who do not trust their own experience? Gardner (1990) provides a helpful insight into what students bring to learning and what is expected of them in schools:

> When young children are first encountering music, they amass considerable intuitive knowledge simply by listening to and singing music. For instance, they acquire a

sense of how a work begins and ends, how various moods are expressed, how
rhythm groups are organized and accentuated. These forms of knowledge, which
are entirely serviceable for enjoying and making music, prove to be of a different
order than that form acquired by the mastery of formal music notation. (p. 30)

Surely we should be building on the perceptions that students have of music and their
constructions of its meaning, not denying them.

Davidson (1994) agrees with Feldman that we need "to redefine a domain in terms of its
psychological reality, not its logical analysis" (p. 104). That is, we need to find ways to
bridge the gap between novices and experts. We need to honour what learners bring
while providing them with pathways into the disciplines. We need to find a middle
ground. Given their assumptions about learning, teachers with complicated views have
not been taking into account new findings about how we learn and have, therefore, too
often been discounting the learner's role in learning and students' prior
experience/knowledge. The ILM is one way of addressing the disjunction between intuitive and formal learning because it both honours what learners bring and helps them
navigate a better understanding of the discipline (developing from a novice to an
expert). In this approach, students still learn the concepts of the discipline of music as
these are understood by experts. There is, however, one caveat. Expertise evolves. Our
growing awareness that our (Western) way is not the only way could lead to a re-think-
ing of musical concepts. Given our global, postmodern world, if we attend to how students perceive music (their psychological reality), it is entirely conceivable that new
ways of conceptualizing music education will emerge.

Expanding the ILM — Complex Learning Theories in Listening Lessons

There have been two main criticisms of the Integrated Listening Model: the first is that it does-
n't acknowledge the role of the body in musicking; [11] the second has to do with the verbalization of an experience that goes beyond words. Both criticisms merit attention. My response to
the first criticism is to agree that movement is an important response to music, both in the
sense that the experience can, and often does, involve physical moment but also in the sense
that the brain is part of the body, and learning is embodied. As Damasio (2003) wrote, "[a] feeling is the perception of a certain state of the body along with the perception of a certain mode
of thinking and of thoughts with certain themes" (p. 86). The ILM certainly does not preclude
using physical movement responses in addition to writing/drawing/discussing.

The verbalization criticism is an old one that challenges the necessity for the analysis of
music. Swanwick (1994) addressed this issue to my satisfaction in *Musical Knowledge:
Intuition, Analysis and Music Education*:

Propositional knowledge enters the dynamic process of musical knowing when it
provides a vocabulary and a framework for secondary analysis.... Unnecessary in our
private dealings with music, it lies at the heart of music education, an endeavour
which presupposes an exchange of ideas. (pp. 43–44)

Language is an important part of how we communicate and clarify our ideas, so its use
is important in music education.

I would add what, in my view, is a more important criticism of the ILM: even though it allows individuals to make their own meaning (with guidance from the teacher), non-musical meanings and social contexts do not play a big role. In *Music in Everyday Life*, DeNora (2000) convincingly examines the many purposes of music. That is, she does not limit the uses of music to aesthetic purposes:

> She [DeNora] portrays the reception of music not as an unpacking of a sound text but rather as a dialectical merging of the musical and non-musical meanings over time, a connecting of sound and the constantly changing ideologies, associations, circumstances, and situations, which themselves "constitute" the very perception of sound in the first place. (Cavicchi, 2002, p. 5)

The ILM would be improved by acknowledging the social context in which music lives. Barrett, McCoy, and Veblen (1997) have developed a Facets Model that looks at both the social context and the music, allowing students to examine both musical and non-musical meanings. The model uses a diamond-shaped organizer. Listeners are asked to consider the following questions regarding the work:

> Who created it?
> When and where was it created?
> Why and for whom was it created?
> What does it sound or look like?
> What kind of structure or form does it have?
> What is its subject?
> What is being expressed?
> What techniques did its creator use to help us understand what is being expressed? (p. 77)

Questions two and three can be too easily neglected in the ILM, but the other questions are addressed. Barrett, McCoy, and Veblen, however, go beyond the ILM with their expanded set questions, questions that are not explicitly addressed in the ILM:

> Who performs, dances, listens to, and values it?
> How and to whom is it transmitted?
> What are its functions for individuals and groups?
> What does it mean to individuals and groups?
> How does it change through different interpretations or versions?
> How do differences in performance or interpretation change its meaning?
> What does it mean within historical/cultural contexts? (p. 145)

While these questions could become teacher-directed and used in a didactic fashion, there is considerable opportunity for learners to think about the answers to these questions and address the "so what" question used in the ILM. There is also opportunity for teachers to use the Facets Model in conjunction with the ILM in creative ways that encourages and inspire students to experience music in increasingly deeper ways. Expanding the model in this way would move the ILM closer to but not totally congruent with Davis, Sumara, and Luce-Kapler's second example of complex learning theory: social constructionism, where collective cognition is collective and social.

The Integrated Listening Model shares the assumptions of complex theories of learning:

both students and teachers are sources of knowledge; the students identify what they listen for while the teacher helps deepen the experience; both students and teachers shape the listening strategies; there are multiple ways to listen to the music, and the students are active in constructing their own meaning and understanding. The ILM accommodates both biological and social considerations. It offers a middle ground between approaches that are totally teacher-directed or entirely student-directed.

The ILM, expanded or not, is not, of course, the only approach to listening to music based on complex learning theory. A growing number of music educators have been questioning the assumptions of modernism (see especially the MayDay group, http://www.nyu.edu/education/music/mayday/maydaygroup/index.htm), and some have been exploring approaches that accept complex learning assumptions (Barrett, McCoy, & Veblen, 1997; Wiggins, 2001; Richardson, 2002), but these are not yet the norm.

Our society is changing. Our knowledge of learning is growing at an amazing pace. Brain research is revealing fascinating data about how we learn. At the same time, our knowledge and understanding of ourselves and others is rapidly expanding as we work and live with people from many cultural backgrounds. Even though complex theory better accounts for how we learn, many music series and resources continue to model a complicated view of what and how children listen to music and to influence classroom learning in ways that promote a traditional, complicated way of listening to music. If we persist in using traditional approaches, will we be serving our students, the listeners of the future, in a way that will provide them with a lifetime of musical enjoyment that goes beyond the top forty and media manipulation? Will our graduates be mute if they think they don't have the "correct" answer? We need to find a middle ground between totally teacher-directed listening and laissez-faire classes. The expanded Integrated Listening Model offers one solution to this important challenge to music education.

References

Barrett, J. R., McCoy, C. W., & Veblen, K. K. (1997). *Sound ways of knowing: Music in the interdisciplinary curriculum.* New York: Schirmer Books.

Boardman, E., & Andress, B. (1981). *The Music Book* (Grade 3, Teacher's edition). New York: Holt, Rinehart and Winston.

Brooks, P. L., Kovac, B. A., & Trotter, M. M. (1984). *Musicanada* (Grade 6, Teacher's edition). Toronto, ON: Holt, Rinehart and Winston.

Brooks, P. L., Kovac, B. A., & Trotter, M. M. (1984). *Musicanada: Resource Centre* (Grade 6). Toronto, ON: Holt, Rinehart and Winston.

Burton, L., Hoffer, C., & Hughes,W. (1997). *Adventures in Music Listening* (Level two). Miami, FL: Warner Bros. Publications.

Cavicchi, D. (2002). From the bottom up: Thinking about Tia DeNora's *Music in everyday life.* Action, Criticism & Theory for Music Education, 1 (2). Retrieved from http://mas.siue.edu/ACT/v1/Cavicchi02.pdf

Cobbold, J., & Wamsley, J. (2000). *Musicanada Encore: Listening and Appreciation* (Grade 4, Teacher's edition). Toronto, ON: Harcourt Canada.

Damasio, A. (2003). *Looking for Spinoza: Joy, sorrow, and the feeling brain.* Orlando, FL: Harcourt.

Davidson, L. (1994). Songsinging by young and old: A developmental approach to music. In R. Aiello & J. A. Sloboda (Eds.), *Musical perceptions* (pp. 99–130). Oxford, UK: Oxford University Press.

Davis, B., Sumara, D., & Luce-Kapler, R. (2000). *Engaging minds: Learning and teaching in a complex world.* Mahwah, NJ: Lawrence Erlbaum Associates.

DeNora, T. (2000). *Music in everyday life.* Cambridge, UK: Cambridge University Press.

Elliott, D. (1995). *Music matters: A new philosophy of music education.* New York: Oxford University Press.

Elliott, D. (2001). Modernity, postmodernity and music education philosophy, *Research Studies in Music Education*, 17, 32–41.

Fehr, D. E. (1997). Clutching the lectern, or shouting from the back of the hall: A comparison of modern and postmodern arts education. *Arts Education Policy Review*, 96 (2), 2–15.

Feldman, E. B. (1970). *Becoming human through art*. Englewood Cliffs, NJ: Prentice Hall.

Feldman, E. B. (1987). *Varieties of visual experience* (3rd ed.). Englewood Cliffs, NJ: Prentice Hall.

Gardner, H. (1990). *Art education and human development*. Los Angeles, CA: The Getty Centre for Education in the Arts.

Geahigan, G. (1993). *Reconceiving art criticism for effective practice*. Paper presented at the International Society for Education Through Art, Montréal, QC.

Hanley, B. (1989). Educators' attitudes to philosophies of music education. *Canadian Music Educator Research Edition*, 31 (1), 100–123.

Hanley, B. (1997). An integrated listening model. *Canadian Music Educator*, 38 (3), 37–41.

Hanley, B. (2003). Navigating unpredictable possibilities in postmodern music education. *Journal of the Canadian Association for Curriculum Studies*, 1 (2), 93–116. Retrieved from http://www.csse.ca.CACS/JCACS/curr_pedagogies.html

Hanley, B., & King, G. (1995). Peeling the onion: Arts PROPEL in the university classroom. *Journal of Music Teacher Education*, 5 (1), 15–29.

Harvey, B. (1990). *The condition of postmodernity*. Cambridge, MA: Blackwell.

Koza, J. E. (1994). Females in 1988 middle school music textbooks: An analysis of illustrations. *Journal of Research in Music Education*, 42 (2), 145–171.

McLellan, N. D. (1996). *Music teachers' opinions regarding the use and effectiveness of elementary music series books in Missouri public schools*. Unpublished doctoral dissertation, University of Missouri, Kansas City.

Macmillan/McGraw Hill. (1995). *Share the music* (Grade 3, Teacher's edition). New York: Author.

Reimer, B. (2003). *A philosophy of music education: Advancing the vision* (3rd ed.). Upper Saddle River, NJ: Prentice Hall.

Richardson, C. (2002). Eastern ears in Western classrooms. In B. Hanley & T. W. Goolsby (Eds.), *Musical understanding* (pp. 185–199). Victoria, BC: Canadian Music Educators Association.

Silver Burdett Ginn. (2000). *Music Connection* (Grade 4, Teacher's edition). Glenview, IL: Scott Foresman.

Silver Burdett. (1974). *Silver Burdett Music* (Grade 4, Teacher's edition). Morristown, NJ: General Learning Corporation.

Small, C. (1998). *Musicking: The meanings of performing and listening*. Hanover, NH: Wesleyan University Press.

Swanwick, K. (1994). *Musical knowledge: Intuition, analysis and music education*. London, UK: Routledge.

Wiggins, J. (2001). *Teaching for musical understanding*. New York: McGraw-Hill.

---

[1] See Elliott's (2001) 'Modernity, Postmodernity and Music Education Philosophy' and Fehr's (1997) 'Clutching the Lectern, or Shouting from the Back of the Hall: A Comparison of Modern and Postmodern Arts Education' for a more comprehensive discussion of modernism and postmodernism.

[2] One earlier textbook series, *Musicanada*, is still used in some Canadian schools.

[3] A second version without the numbers is also provided.

[4] Given my research on attitudes to philosophies of music education and how teachers actually implemented absolute expressionism (Hanley, 1989), I wonder how many teachers actually read these connecting objectives and acted on them.

[5] Information about the composer, composition, and statements of outcomes, extensions to the lesson, and curriculum connections certainly go far beyond the 1967 Bowmar Orchestral Library, which provided a guided tour of selected Western classical works.

[6] There are no suggestions about how teachers would know whether or not students were actually hearing the intervals.

[7] While I sympathize with the intention of empowering students, I think it misleading to say that no answers are wrong. That attitude suggests that anyone could make up any answer, unrelated to the music, and it would be acceptable. Some answers could be out in left field. I do agree with the need to respect all responses (which is not the same thing) and to inquire about the reasons for answers.

[8] One aspect of modernism that I have not addressed, a privileging of the Western canon, is only evident in the listening selections in *Musicanada* and its resources materials. The other series and resource offer a broader spectrum of music.

[9] The simplicity of the model would allow teachers with no knowledge to accept student responses as the end of the learning rather than as a beginning.

[10] The four theories discussed by Davis, Sumara, and Luce-Kapler are constructivism, social constructionism, cultural and critical discourses, and ecological theories.

[11] Eleanor Stubley raised this concern at a presentation I made at McGill University (November, 2000).

SENYSHYN

CHAPTER EIGHT

Popular Music and the Intolerant Classroom

YAROSLAV SENYSHYN

Abstract

Without espousing an 'anything goes' philosophy the author believes nevertheless that there is a prevalent prejudice among music educators that discourages popular music as a mode of proper music instruction, either in performance or other modes of music education. This active form of elitism which discriminates against popular music can be traced back at least 2500 years in western culture and is motivated by a belief in the superiority of one's own musical tastes, an intolerance of other people's predilection for popular music, and an ignorance of its historical evolution. Ultimately the active suppression of popular music is a form of tyranny which victimizes its adherents and practitioners into a position of inferiority and helplessness. Patronizing it without an authentic understanding of its potential in music education can be just as damaging to its followers as the active suppression of it. This chapter will demystify the notions of elitism and tyranny of popular music and reveal a strategy of teaching that allows for its authentic inclusion in all curriculums of music education.

Introduction

Although I do not believe there is a teacher anywhere who would knowingly conduct an intolerant classroom, there is the possibility of unconsciously doing so. Unfortunately this is especially true of music classrooms. One is less likely to find "content intolerance" in a physics, mathematics, history, or geography class than in an arts class. General racist intolerance can, unfortunately, be found anywhere. Racist intolerance is not the intent here, although it may be an unconscious dimension in musical style intolerance and appears to be so in my second narrative in the next part of this chapter. I use the word "intolerance" in relation to the "musical taste" of teachers and students. Intolerance is rampant in music education. One is considerably less likely to find aesthetic intolerance in other arts, such as the visual and dramatic arts. This is probably so because music, as a social and artistic activity, permeates all strata of society as no other art can or does. It sets the fashion for our clothes, etiquette, general behaviour, and even our use of language. Not only is music 'there' to be heard and appropriated into these various functions, but it is there to be 'seen' as well. Music is ubiquitously constant and visible in all activities.

Given that there are many ways to define 'intolerance,' what do we mean by intolerance in music? This problem of definition is exacerbated by the addition of the education context to music. Distinctions that are seemingly possible in a musical aesthetic sense become blurred in an educational setting. My purpose in this chapter will be to delineate those distinctions so that our understanding of popular music vis-à-vis education will lead to a philosophy of music that will benefit both the teacher and student in the music classroom in all sectors of education.

First Narrative

It has been said that the best example by which we can learn is to provide one that is personal and thus obvious to most people. I will hazard the truth of this possibility by providing my reader with two such personal, narrative examples from my own teaching past. My narratives, which will stand on their own to make my point about the complexity of intolerance, are derived from two time periods in my high school teaching days.

When I was a neophyte music teacher in the mid-seventies in a small town in Ontario, I found myself teaching vocal music in a secondary school that could not, despite its best efforts, sustain such a program. I was hired for the job because the principal felt that I might overcome this obstacle and build a successful vocal program in his school. According to the principal the vocal program never lasted longer than a semester (the band managed much better) and, after many attempts to get it off the ground with various teachers, he had given up on the project until he met me. Ironically I was applying for a job that was predominantly history with some possibility of music teaching (I was certified a specialist in both music and history). Yet something about me led him to believe that I could succeed where no one else could. As I was anxious to land a job I naively assured him that I would succeed with the vocal music while still predominantly teaching history.

When September came I too found myself readily enough on the losing end of any chance of sustaining a successful vocal music program. I couldn't understand why my students didn't want to 'do' Monteverdi or a 'simple' arrangement of Mozart's "*Ave Verum.*" Of course I didn't listen to their complaints. They had been trying to tell me that none of their teachers in the past taught them the music they wanted to learn and perform. I wouldn't tolerate such talk because, in my arrogance and conceit, I was convinced that I knew better: I was the classical musician, the expert, and all they had to do was trust *my* musical taste. But it became more and more obvious that I too would fail and 'bite the dust' as so many others had done before me. About a month into the semester I had fully experienced my wake-up call: the night before my next class I decided on, what to me was then, a very drastic step. The next day after a sleepless night I announced the following to my vocal class:

"No doubt many of you will not be taking vocal music next year?" (They confirmed that readily enough). And no doubt you believe that this course 'sucks' (They gleefully confirmed that as well). Well, I would very much like to change your mind about this course (more derisive laughter). I have given it much thought and I wish to present you with a music contract that may change your mind about the possibility of taking music in the future. I hope you will take it again next year even though it has 'sucked' very badly till now." (That certainly caught their attention).

"What's this contract all about sir?"

I answered timorously: "I would like to spend a good part of this semester learning all your favorite songs of the Beatles. In return, after every two weeks of intensive Beatles music you will have to learn some of my favorite music as well. The idea is that we will spend most of the time on the Beatles and a little time on my stuff."

Now this did capture their attention. Like bees in a beehive they turned towards each other and swarmed and buzzed about this possibility in apprehensive and curious tones of both delight and consternation. They were basically in a state of utter disbelief. How could such a constipated 'classical' musician as myself possibly mean this or even carry it off? It was then that their latent musical intolerance in addition to my own previous history in this regard became all too obvious.

"How would you know enough, sir, to teach the Beatles music? You don't understand that kind of music."

"Well it so happens that I do! As a matter of fact I probably know more about it than you do. I was in my mid-teens when the Beatles became famous and I knew all of their songs." (This was not easy for them to grasp. But they swallowed it whole when I started to sing some of the more esoteric Beatles songs for them. They thought my performance was passable.)

"Why does it have to be the Beatles?" others retorted. "The Beatles suck. We like country music best."

Other students parried: "Give us a break! Country music sucks! What are you saying here? Are you going to force 'hurtin' songs on us?"

"Yeah, stuff like 'my heart is breaking baby and I don't know what to do' shit," mimicked another. It went on like this for quite some time and I was astounded by the wide variety of their musical taste and their boundless prejudice.

Despite this amazing intolerance, they finally agreed that the Beatles would be a step in the right direction. I offered a further measure of appeasement to accommodate the wide divergence of musical taste in the classroom. I suggested that every Friday would be our performance class. By this I meant that the students were to be free to perform any of their favourite songs to each other. This was to be done on a voluntary basis only. The only rule was that we would all listen to each other respectfully regardless of our musical predilections. This class also provided the students with an opportunity to experience all the positive and negative manifestations of performance anxiety (see Senyshyn & O'Neill, 2001).

After three years of this kind of activity in my vocal music classes the program took off and became exceedingly successful. We still did Monteverdi and Mozart and many others in the 'classical' stream and managed to turn out some prominent music teachers and composers from these efforts. Even the football players signed up for vocal music. And some students learned to weep over the 'Ave Verum.' And more to the point they became critically aware of 'good' and perhaps 'not-so-good' music in both 'popular' and 'classical' genres (for lack of better terms). And finally, the combined music program, both band and vocal, became a great success and even developed into a full department in about ten year's time. The school even won all those dubious distinctions and awards that so many unthinking teachers covet in music programs at the expense of more aesthetic and passionate aims in music education.

Second Narrative

In my second narrative a far more serious breach of tolerance in music teaching is in evidence. After more than thirteen years I became very tired of teaching music in the town high school. More to the point I felt that I was dangerously close to burnout and wanted to avoid this unwanted stigma in the teaching profession. Thus teaching history full-time in a Toronto inner-city high school seemed a great relief. And, even though I missed teaching music, it was the right thing to do at that time. As is well known music teachers burn out quickly and it is thus very important to get out in time.

My narrative begins when my good principal asked me to his office one day after school. (Again, I will not mention any names and alter some details in order to protect the anonymity of all my protagonists in this dark anecdote). One is always a little apprehensive when the principal summons a teacher to his or her office. My feelings of negative anxiety were not unfounded either, although I unsuccessfully groped for some dose of positive anxiety as well to cope with my apprehension of this interview (see Senyshyn, 1999). But this was not to be a day for prevalent positive anxiety. He did not waste any time and asked me right after we both sat down if it was considered 'normal' for a music teacher to refuse to teach or hire someone else to teach the steel drum, in a secondary music program on the basis that such an instrument was inferior to other western instruments and its associated musical literature. I was dumfounded by the question. My response was that any instrument as such, regardless of its origin or culture, was as difficult to master as most other instruments as long as it was highly valued in the culture that produced or invented that instrument. Yes, I did point out that some people within any particular culture such as our own argued that a French horn or oboe was considered to be more difficult then let's say a clarinet or saxophone etc. and that the viola or cello was easier to master than the violin, but I pointed out, according to my thinking, that this was all nonsense as no human being can be a virtuoso of more than one or two instruments at the very most (and that latter possibility is indeed very rare) to have the authority to make such a proclamation. Any instrument of value to its concomitant culture that is intended to be played at the bravura-virtuoso level demands a great deal of time, energy, sacrifice, and utter dedication on the part of its practitioner and is, therefore, worthy of serious study. I told him that it was very sad that fine musicians have been victims of a music education that all too frequently implied its own superiority, usually unconsciously, to its students in indirect and tacit communication. Thank heavens this is not as frequent today as it once was. New courses in popular music, jazz, ethnomusicology, and subtler insights into Western music and its history and philosophy of music have altered this extreme sense of musical cultural superiority in most of our students today. Many of them, if not most, favour an enlightened and tolerant attitude about other non-western instruments and musics, and both local and international popular music with its concomitant instruments in all their many and multifaceted possibilities of experience and expression.

The principal also told me that this teacher had also pointed out his particular view that the repertoire for steel pan instruments was of a 'popular' nature and thus deemed by him to be unsuitable and inadequate for music educational purposes. A few days after this strange and frightful interview with the principal, I was even more dumbfounded to be unofficially approached by very similar questions and concerns as those posed by my principal, by other members of the higher echelons of our school board. I too answered these concerns in the same way as outlined above.

In this secondary school where I taught history there was a sizeable number of students from the Caribbean who very much wanted to play music related to their traditional culture. It was not that the principal or the students wanted to supplant or usurp the music program in the school as it was. They merely wanted to have the option of learning the steel drum and its concomitant music along with the traditional program. Even after the students formed a committee and respectfully approached the music teacher to ask for such a course in their school, the teacher refused them with the very same arguments as I have already described in my interview with our principal and others. The students were understandably deeply hurt by this attitude from the music teacher. The principal finally 'solved' the problem by asking a parent who lived in the local area, and had the well-earned reputation of being a virtuoso steel drum player, to coach these students on the steel drums and its literature as an extracurricular activity. This became a very successful activity and led these students to participate in a famous world class competition in the Caribbean for steel drums in which they won a coveted first prize.

The hurt students wanted the opportunity to change the attitude of the 'traditional' music teacher of their school. With the help of their steel drum teacher they arranged, adapted and learned a very famous and difficult nineteenth century Russian score for their steel drum orchestra. They even played it for a school assembly in front of this teacher to make their point. It was a tremendous success and became the basis of a successful commercial recording. But, the teacher refused to change his mind... Such is the insidious nature of intolerance. The indignation grew in this school and unfortunately the traditional music program gradually came to a halt and the unyielding music teacher left his job for other opportunities in education.

With this backdrop for intolerance in music education I can now proceed to a fuller discussion of the roots of such obvious prejudice. In doing this my narratives will speak for themselves as they will be further informed by the following theoretical-philosophical notions which makes such intolerant practice possible, be it consciously perceived or not by its teachers and students as an active problem in their respective music classes.

Philosophical Roots of Intolerance of Popular Music

How are we to understand the roots of this strange anomaly and syndrome in music education that is characterized by what may be referred to as the 'popular' versus 'classical' debate or even that of 'popular' instruments against 'traditional' ones? I am often surprised by my students at our university who seemingly do not know that this dichotomy in music has existed as long as music itself. To put it more bluntly, there has always been a 'popular' music, or 'music of the people' if you will, and a 'classical, longhair, serious, historical' music in western culture. How unfortunate it is that these terms remain unexamined and unanalyzed and yet not one of them accurately represents the complexity of the issue at hand. Neither should we allow stylistic descriptions, historical categorizations, modal, melodic, contrapuntal, and harmonic aspects of any western music of the past to muddy the waters of this issue. Take the medieval-renaissance period as a case in point. One could rewrite the musical history of this period in terms of our contemporary dichotomy of 'popular' versus 'classical' music. Of course the church's disdain at the time for what it considered to be the vulgar, sinful, and ultimately 'unsuitable' music of the people was in fact an attack on the popular music of its time. But the essence of what music historians refer to as 'secular' music truly was 'popular' music, as we understand our own contemporary popular music, in every way that we designate the term 'popular' except in the actual use of harmony and modality which was obviously different in any of the past historical periods. But many if not all the other ingredients that characterize popular music are there: the use of any existing instruments of the time, a rigorous and hard-driving rhythmic pulse in the music, the use of percussion to accentuate the latter, lewd and lascivious texts pertaining to sexual provocation and imagery, or texts of more exalted social mores and values, and even anti-authoritarian strains and the use of a sneaky 'lewd' and 'vulgar' cantus firmus in the unsuspected church masses. The latter was taken from these very same popular or secular musics, but vastly slowed down in tempo to avoid detection by the priests— i.e., so that the religious authorities would not detect the private 'musical' joke, as it were, in the actual performance of the mass. Thus the cantus firmus could be derived from the 'melodies' taken from the popular music of its time which would not have been knowingly permitted by authorities representing the church. (Although one wonders if the more astute and tolerant ones may have chuckled under their breath as well).

And yes, it is now very respectable to listen to and admire (secular) popular music of the past, but this was certainly not always the case. The dichotomous notion of popular (vulgar or secular) music as opposed to religious, sacred music was very much in evidence. (One can even see parallels to 'rap' music in the ancient Greek chorus and the use of the 'recitative' in baroque music not to mention Schonberg's 'sprechtstimme' as well). As time went on and people lost these unnecessary associations and stylistic categorizations, and music was no longer guilty, as it were, of its popular and populist associations, the music simply became 'good' music and moved from the popular category to the 'serious' or 'classical' category. We can see this sort of 'evolution' of music, from popular dance music to the 'classical' in more recent examples, such as found in the aesthetic 'apotheosis' of the Viennese, Strauss waltzes. Instead of dancing to them, although that too is done more readily in Vienna, people are more inclined to sit at dining tables or concert seats during their performances, as demonstrated by the popular Boston Pops Orchestra concerts. And more recently the rather odd phenomenon of the 'three tenors' and their proclivity to popularize the opera and popular songs.

It is not difficult to visualize adolescent students in class groaning five hundred years from now because their teacher may have decided to introduce the 'classic,' 'We all Live in a Yellow Submarine' simply because the music somehow made it into that century and acquired a respectability among the elite not attained in its own time. It is useful to point out that it was not all that long ago that English critics despised Shakespeare's tragedies and celebrated the comedies as the highest form of dramatic art. That could happen again...who knows, even the popular Harlequin romance of today may evolve into some form of literary respectability, although I rather doubt that! How 'popular' or 'serious' are the novels of Sir Walter Scott today?

Let's start at the beginning of formal musical thought supporting the ever present *perception* of a dichotomy of 'popular' music against the 'classical.' We shall have to begin with Plato and Aristotle. This is not my unconscious eurocentrism at play but merely the historical evidence for such an argument. Perhaps some day scholars will find this dispute in earlier, as yet undiscovered, philosophies as well. Until such a time we must start with the Socratic and pre-Socratic thinkers. Ironically the latter knew more about the nature of 'external' music (of the spheres) and thus were unrestricted as such by cultural or historical designations and bias, than did the conservative Plato and Aristotle in this regard (Senyshyn, 2003, p.113). Some of these conceptual limitations of music have resulted in prejudices about popular music among those of us trained in eurocentrist notions of western music even though we have lost the semiotic associations with the ancient Greek modes. What was not lost was a prevalent belief in their semiotic potentiation for their contemporaries.

Plato had a very deep aesthetic feeling for music: "education in poetry and music...sink deep into the recesses of the soul and take the strongest hold there, bringing that grace of body and mind which is only to be found in one who is brought up in the right way" (Plato & Cornford, 1972, p. 90). However, he was not lenient on any notion of popular music or instruments (see Barker, 1984) and everyone knows that Plato believed that the modes employed in music predetermined the music's ethical value. Thus the particular modes that were used in the popular music of his time were seen by Plato to encouraged laziness, cowardice, sloth, and lewd and lascivious sexual behaviour in their listeners.

Aristotle's attitude was somewhat less strict and milder about popular music in his time and its concomitant modes than was Plato. Aristotle wrote that, when listening to music for educational purposes, "we ought not only to gain from it the common sort of pleasure, which everyone has the capacity to perceive (since music dispenses pleasure of a natural kind, so that the use of it is beloved by all ages and characters), but ought also to see whether it has a tendency to improve the character and the soul" (Barker, 1984, p.174).

He also differentiated rhythms in music. Some instances of popular music were associated with rhythms that were "of a more degenerate source" while traditional, conservative music was more likely to be associated with "stability" and rhythms "fitting for free men" (Barker, 1984, p. 174). As well he disapproved of the popular aulos (flute or recorder to be exact). He wrote that "the *aulos* is not a moral instrument but rather one that excites the emotions, so that it should be used in the kinds of circumstances where the spectacle offers more potential for *katharsis* than for learning" (Barker, 1984, p. 177).

In contemporary thought on this subject, it is useful to make certain philosophical distinctions. The problem today, I believe, is still perceived as an ethical and moral one, much in the same way as it was for Plato and Aristotle. It is no accident that many music teachers who have been trained in the conservatory tradition feel that there is something unethical about popular music and thus should not be tolerated in a school curriculum. Others are willing to pay some sort of lip service to it and then sweep it under the proverbial carpet as soon as possible. It is useful to understand the roots of such a negative anxiety over a moral, aesthetic issue. It is always helpful to remember Wittgenstein's great pronouncement that "aesthetics and ethics are one and the same" (Wittgenstein, 1974, p. 71).

It is useful to begin with an important foundational assertion: music without a text is amoral. Any music, whatever it is, cannot be guilty of immorality unless it has a verbal text. This is evident to a modern philosophical mind but, as we have seen, this was not the case for thinkers such as Plato and Aristotle. Ultimately there is no way one can ascribe a definite or even indefinite moral or immoral dimension to music without a text. Any such moral designations are purely subjective in nature. This is a ruthless statement but necessarily true. It is for this reason that we have musical dramas or the opera (see Senyshyn & Vézina, 2002). But having said this does not take away the fact that we can attempt to find moral or immoral dimensions to music and codify these in some kind of musical semiotics as is done today by various semioticians of music (see Senyshyn, 2003, p. 114, and see Nattiez, 1990). But that is another issue altogether. Music as itself and without the benefit of any text is, strictly speaking, neutral unless we "colour" it as it were with our particular categorizations of meaning that happen to subjectively-culturally agree with other people living in the same musical environment (a musical social contract of sorts). Thus, we can use music for worship and derive moral elevation from it in that context, but the music itself, remaining always neutral in morality, is still quite oblivious to its own moral worth in that specific context. Only with a text, and when the text is considered an integral part of the "music," does music take on a definite moral dimension or meaning, delineating that expression through language. We shall return to this latter point as I believe it is a very important one for music education. The teacher, who avoids or does not permit popular music in the classroom, is undoubtedly involved in a moral loop of his or her own (as was the teacher in my second narrative). Concomitant with this sense of morality is the erroneous belief that "good" music does more than entertain whereas popular music is nothing more than a vehicle of entertainment.

"The hidden and erroneous motive behind, and often attributed to, so-called popular music is mere entertainment and economic interests belonging to the masses. If this is not the case then the music may be referred to erroneously (again) as art music. The hidden and erroneous motive behind art music is religious, ethical, moral, emotional, and intellectual edification, and yes, even economic interests (one need only think of the 'three tenors' phenomenon and the 'popular classics' syndrome). These statements are an attempt to state the case for what is and is not an attempt to erode the value of entertainment or that of morally perceived exigencies relating to spiritual and intellectual edification... A non-entertainment value in music is just as ephemeral as an imposed ethical component to the music. Such a designation is the way a society imposes value on its music. But the music per se evades this in spite of our efforts to categorize music in this way" (Senyshyn, 2003. pp. 122-123).

Conclusion: Are there boundaries in Music Education?

Am I espousing an 'anything goes' philosophy? It would be a serious mistake to make that assumption. Let us go back to the concept that music as such is not guilty of any offence. Here I am referring to music per se and not any other non-musical associations such as the use of a text, visual images, or whatever. Music expresses music, (a necessary tautology) and what we choose to attribute to it. The fact that some of these attributes are also in accordance with the attributes of others is its great mystery. "What we cannot speak about we must pass over in silence" (Wittgenstein, 1974). But, when we add the text or lyrics to the music it takes on a different potentiality altogether. There are good lyrics (text) and bad. All too often popular music is accompanied by inappropriate texts—at least by classroom standards. No teacher should have to, or would want to, teach popular music that consists of a text that goes against the tenets of better judgment. Thus songs condoning violence, criminal acts, and untoward sexuality are out of order in the classroom. If the students insist on performing inappropriate texts in the name of freedom of expression then I would have them write out new lyrics for the songs in question. This, as all music teachers know, is quite an education in itself and can only benefit the students.

The old complaint that popular songs are out of the range of young voices is not an invalid objection. Even in classical music only a very uninformed and downright dangerous teacher would teach the *Queen of the Night* aria from Mozart's *The Magic Flute* to a young and inexperienced soprano. There is always the possibility of rewriting these songs or merely transposing them to more suitable keys with the necessary adaptations. Although current performance practice disallows this with classical music, the great strength of popular music is its very flexibility and, what could be referred to as, its freedom from performance practices that define what it is. That is the nature of popular music. Once upon a time classical music too had this freedom before it was fossilized into a museum culture. How many 'classical' pianists today, for example, extemporize their own cadenza in a Mozart piano concerto or take dynamic, melodic, or harmonic freedoms in the music they perform? They do not do this even though the very composers they perform often took these liberties with their own work and even with the compositions of other composers. Classical performers today are terrified to make even the slightest changes to the designated dynamics. What may be referred to as the constipated approach is now the rule in the performance of 'classical' music unless you happen to be the late Vladimir Horowitz—and he too clashed with the critics of his time (see Senyshyn, 1996).

Of course there are popular songs that could and do harm students' voices. I have spoken to teachers with these legitimate complaints about popular music who in their very next breath brag about how well their students are doing with an upcoming performance of their annual musical, a performance of Bernstein's *West Side Story*. Yes, this is by most peoples' reckoning an example of 'good' music but is it appropriate for young voices regardless of its category as a 'classic' or 'popular' music drama, musical, or opera? These categorizations are remarkably inadequate in their implied complexity!

I know of a secondary school teacher who ruined the voice of a very promising young soprano student. She tragically developed nodes in her vocal chords while straining out, in the name of 'projection,' difficult 'arias' in popular 'musicals.' And what about those five rehearsals in a row just before show time, and then the five performances in a row after the killing rehearsals—guaranteed to wreck any young and promising voice—the truest and deadliest sign of amateurism and ignorance in our schools throughout the continent. Surely, as responsible and accountable educators, we must beware of the ethos that avoids the popular music syndrome by retreating into killer musicals as an 'antidote' to the popular-classical issue. This is hardly a viable solution.

Having stated these practical objections to the performance of popular music or any music for that matter, I will now summarize the implications derived from my two anecdotes and the philosophical discussion of the origins of popular music. The greatest danger to an authentic music classroom are teachers who practice musical intolerance in their classrooms. We have seen from my anecdotes how severe this prejudice can be. By understanding the roots of such intolerance thoroughly we can prevent this kind of psychological damage and lack of authenticity in our classrooms. We have seen that even great minds such as Plato can fall into the loop of a moral argument. Music without the text or other recognized attributes is innocent of any wrongdoing. This must be thoroughly understood and emotionally appropriated by all educators. Not doing this leads to a false and insidiously negative elitism which can only result in aesthetic failure in the classroom regardless of all the possible trappings in the name of good educational practice.

It is also very important to understand that popular music has always been around and with it its concomitant prejudice by "educated" musicians who have mislead themselves into a sense of false aesthetic morality. Ultimately the active suppression of popular music is a form of tyranny which victimizes its adherents and practitioners into a position of inferiority and helplessness. Patronizing it without an authentic understanding of its potential in music education can be just as damaging to its followers as the active suppression of it.

Just as Foucault was concerned with the control and incarceration of the human body as a form of abusive power in the excusive and highly arbitrary notions of madness and sexuality, (see Foucault, 1967, 1990) we too can see popular music as this potentially abused 'body' in the name of some aesthetic moral authority. Educators should not fall into the trap of becoming 'control freaks' in their music classrooms in the name of a misguided and incorrect moral argument about the merit or demerit of popular music and its relation to madness and sexuality. To do this can only lead to diminishing returns in our music classrooms.

Although it is not my intention to deny the power of music in our everyday lives, it is an error to let a false and misleading elitism, resulting from our secret wants and wishes, distort the power of music. We do this at the expense of students' identities and values which are passionately based on the very music that is, at times, suppressed in one way or another. More precisely, a sense of social justice, love, art, nostalgia, and many other human attributes and values are located in what is referred to as 'popular' music and its collaborative texts. It would be no less than a tragedy on the part of teachers to assume that all texts and music from "popular music" are negative in import. And when we, as educators, impose this one-sided negativity blindly on our students we do them and ourselves a great disservice. Ultimately, in doing this, we strip our students of their humanity and dignity. Students are their music regardless of our aesthetic and moral positioning.

We must not forget that one of our most important purposes, whether with music or any other discipline, is to educate our students to cope with a difficult and complex world, and we must do so in a way that does not infringe on their legitimate rights and the rights of others. Tolerant teaching is perhaps the best way in which we can foster tolerance in our students and the love of an authentic musical experience.

SENYSHYN

References

Barker, A. (1984). *Greek musical writings: The musician and his art* (Vol. 1). Cambridge; New York: Cambridge University Press.

Foucault, M. (1967). *Madness and civilization : a history of insanity in the age of reason.* London; Sydney: Tavistock Publications.

Foucault, M. (1990). *The history of sexuality.* New York: Vintage.

Nattiez, J. J. (1990). *Music and discourse: toward a semiology of music.* Princeton, N.J: Princeton University Press.

Plato, & Cornford, F. M. (1972). *The republic of Plato.* London: Oxford University Press.

Senyshyn, Y. (1996). *Horowitz and the enigma of art.* Interchange, 27(1), 79-84.

Senyshyn, Y. (1999). *Perspectives on performance and anxiety and their implications for creative teaching.* The Canadian Journal of Education, 24(1), 30-41.

Senyshyn, Y., & O'Neill, S. A. (2001). *Subjective experience of anxiety and musical performance: a relational perspective.* Philosophy of Music Education Review, 9(1), 42-53.

Senyshyn, Y., & Vézina, D. (2002). *Wittgenstein, Collingwood and the aesthetic and ethical conundrum of the opera.* Philosophy of Music Education Review, 10(1).

Senyshyn, Y. (2003). *Musical aphorisms and common aesthetic quandaries.* Philosophy of Music Education Review, Vol. 11(Fall), 112-129.

Wittgenstein, L. (1974). *Tractatus logico-philosphicus.* London: Routledge.

CHAPTER NINE

Music as a Lifelong Pursuit: Educating for a Musical Life

RENATE ZENKER

Abstract

This chapter examines the educational disconnects between traditional music studies and music as a lifelong pursuit. It suggests how we, as music educators, can alter our current music education paradigm to educate students for a musical life. The first half of the chapter, "what are we doing now?" is a critical examination of the formal context of music education; a critique which moves beyond the traditional group performance-based music education paradigm. It looks at what we mean by music education in terms of its wider contexts and purposes. It also examines the notions of talent, giftedness, genius, and music as a frill and their detrimental effects on the lifelong pursuit of music. The second half of the chapter, "what might we be doing" addresses the particular conceptual and educational goals of educating for a musical life necessary in order to widen the context of music education beyond the traditional school classroom. The chapter concludes with the curricular and educational policy changes that would have to occur to make possible a shift to a "music as a lifelong pursuit" music education paradigm

Introduction

This chapter is a critical examination of an increasingly important aspect of the music education of our society: "music as a lifelong pursuit." It is important because of what can be clearly seen as several educational disconnects. At the same time as music education is being cut in many school budgets, the baby boom generation is returning to private music lessons. Many students are not being given the opportunity to study music in school, especially at the higher grade levels unless they are proficient at playing a band or string instruments and can join the band or strings programs. In many cases students choose not to pursue music in school and instead take guitar, piano, or drums privately because these instruments are not offered in school. Presumably due to public interest, continuing education centers and public music organizations, such as the symphony and the opera, are reaching out to the general public through continuing education programs, which the Vancouver Opera, for example, calls "lifelong learning." Yet in school we are mostly failing to provide students with a music education that can last throughout their lives by simply not providing them with any music education at all due to budget cuts, or by not providing them with a music education that appeals to their interests.

As the central part of the music education paradigm, our emphasis in both school music and in private lessons has been on perfection in performance, especially for those students who are "talented" or "gifted." Yet how does the musical experience of playing third trombone for years in the high school band realistically prepare a student for continuing musical engagement and enrichment throughout her life? Similarly, how does a private piano student's completion of the grade eight Toronto Royal Conservatory of Music piano examination reflect on her inability to harmonize "Happy Birthday" or play any Christmas carols by ear at a family gathering?

The question of what concepts, values, critical abilities, and music making skills would be involved in a music education that fosters music as a lifelong pursuit is of central importance to the music education profession. Music has perhaps become a frill because it is only concerned with those students who can perform as part of an ensemble rather than fostering individual music potential and general musical and cultural education. We need to question why we continue to educate "musicians" in the highly practised perfectionist sense and how this value and focus of music education realistically relates to the important role of music as a lifelong cultural phenomenon.

The first half of the chapter, "what are we doing now?" is a critical examination of music education, a critique which moves beyond the traditional group performance based music education paradigm. It looks at what we mean by music education in terms of its contexts and purposes and also looks at talent, giftedness, genius, and the notion of music as a frill.

The second half, "what might we be doing" discusses what might be involved in a music education that made music a lifelong pursuit rather than just a school subject. It looks at what we mean by "knowing" music and how important it is to be involved with music that we recognize. It considers how music education would change if we focussed on educating for a musical life and the continuing musical and personal/societal benefits of a lifelong study of music. It addresses the particular conceptual and educational goals of educating for a musical life and the curricular and educational policy changes that would have to occur to make it possible.

WHAT ARE WE DOING NOW?

The purpose of this paper is to examine how well the current music education system prepares a student for a musical life and what type of education, we as educators, could be providing students to reach this goal. In considering the question of educating for a musical life should we abandon "music education" as we know it or can we make important changes? One thing is certain: we need to realistically rethink how music functions in our culture and how we might respond to that as educators. In this section I will outline some of the complex issues involved in an assessment of the current state of music education.

What do we mean by music education?

When we examine the current state of music education, we need to consider the contexts in which music learning takes places, as well as the purposes and value of learning in those contexts.

When we think of music education we tend to think first of traditional "school music" programs. However there are many contexts for music education, both "formal" and "informal." Different formal contexts for music education include traditional school classroom music, arts organization educational programs, community bands, community and church choirs, private piano lessons, and private lessons on other instruments.

Different informal contexts for music education are very prevalent in our North America culture. The "players" in this implicit music education are many and have come into being mostly due to changes in technology. These informal contexts include learning from the media, (television, radio movies) musical toys, music on computer, and video games as well as many others.

Generally speaking, the interaction between the formal and informal contexts is very limited. The most likely scenario is that a music student taking private lessons learns to play a song from a Disney Movie or some such movie. Formal contexts tend to have a set music literature based on folk and classical repertoire.

Along with differing music contexts there are many possible purposes for music education as Bowman (1994) so aptly outlines in his description of the "why" of music education:

> Do we mean instruction of the musically talented, or something relevant and important for everyone, or both? Do we have in mind the refinement of skilled performing ability, or of perceptual skills, or of creativity, or of conceptual capacity, or of literacy? Is its scope confined to music's internal, intrinsic, or does it extend beyond them? If so, how far? If by music education we mean education *within* music, that points us in one direction; education *about* music, another; and education *through* music in yet another still. Which do you mean when you speak of music education? How would you distinguish between music education and, say, training or indoctrination? And when you speak of music education, what (or whose) musics do you have in mind? (p. 28)

To this list of the "why" of music education we can add a large amount of research commonly quoted in the media, which suggests that the study of music increases spatial ability, memory, mathematical ability, SAT scores, and slows down the progression of Alzheimer's disease. Or we can add to the list a litany of non-musical benefits such as learning discipline, social skills, perseverance, and a roster of mental physical, emotional, and social benefits.

But of all these great ideas of the "why" of music education, what is really driving the public system? According to Bartel (2001) music education has not changed much in the past 100 years. We have relied on what Bartel calls the "rehearsal model" which he describes as the teacher trying to get all the kids to make music together with as few mistakes as possible. According to Bartel, this model can include a grade three class playing Orff instruments, a grade five class singing with Kodaly handsigns, the grade 6 recorder class, a grade 8 band class, a grade 9 guitar class, a high school choir, orchestra, or band.

And Fiske (2000) suggests that the elementary curriculum as we know it has been carried out largely incorrectly for the past 30 years with a focus on group performance rather than on other aspects of music education:

The (Kodaly) approach is particularly effective when carried out correctly in that it amalgamates ear training, listening, performance (singing), creativity (such as melodic improvisation), movement (through games), and rudimentary music theory concepts (melodic continuity, interval direction, and so forth). When carried out improperly, however, where the mechanics of the approach (e.g., hand signs) out weigh more desirable musical ends, the approach becomes abstract, irrelevant, and unmusical. (p. 291)

McPherson (1997) describes music education as "often overspecialized, emphasizing technique and a re-creation of a body of existing literature rather than a range of abilities needed to develop as an all-around musician"(p. 71). By these range of abilities McPherson means being able to play by ear and compose.

In consideration of the various formal and informal contexts for music learning as well as the many possible purposes or "whys" of music education, we have created a very narrow perspective on what constitutes music education in the school system. Namely, that traditional school music learning should take place within the formal context of the school, ignoring any other formal or informal contexts and that the purpose of music education is the refinement of skilled group performing ability. We believe that the rehearsal model is "the way." But the type of music education we are providing does not promote music as a school-long pursuit, let alone as a lifelong pursuit.

How do we continue to justify this "production" model of perfection in performance? One way we justify it is through our societal values generally and specifically concerning music. We live in an instant society. There is a tension between activities producing instant results versus discipline, time, and hard work. So when we create an elementary school band, the expectation placed on music teachers is that the students will "produce" a concert in a very short time. This puts the teacher and the students in the position of learning to play a few simple songs as fast as possible.

Students and educators also justify music education through socialization. In other words, through playing music in the band students learn cooperation, how to listen to others, how to be a "team player." While these are all laudable goals, they seem to be more about the development of personal skills and less about the study of music itself.

There is also a problem with continuing to justify the current music education paradigm through what I call "curriculum babble." These are the worn-out meaningless phrases of which nobody really knows the meaning. I asked a Vancouver school board representative what we might do to increase the likelihood that students will participate in music after high school, besides the usual goals of playing, listening, and composing. When I pressed for a more creative answer, the answer I was received was "dramatizing feelings in music." My question is, does anybody really know what this phrase means? As Bowman (1994) describes it, "the gap between our claims for music education and our musical instructional practices, between what we say and do, between our actions and promises, has become a yawning gulf" (p. 28).

Playing, listening, composing, dramatizing and other standard responses to how we interact with music are really based on the "classical" model of music instruction, which despite enormous changes and developments in the world of music, continues to persist.

Talent, giftedness, genius, and the notion of music as a frill

By far the most destructive value of music education that is perhaps not only responsible for the continuation of the rehearsal model, but the reason behind it in the first place, is the notion of talent. In this section I will delve more into the notion of talent with regard to music, and its effects on music education.

We tend to talk about talent, giftedness and genius in music as if we all know what they mean. The Collins English dictionary (1986) defines talent as an "innate ability aptitude or faculty, especially one unspecified; above average ability: *a talent for cooking; a child with talent*" (p.1553). The same dictionary defines gifted as a person "having or showing natural talent or aptitude: *a gifted musician; a gifted performance*" (p.640). These definitions seem to make it clear that a gifted person is a person who has talent(s).

McPherson (1997) examines the differences between giftedness and talent in music and comes to a different conclusion about their relationship. According to McPherson, musically gifted children can be assessed in terms of "musical potential." That is they can be given a series of tests to measure their general music abilities such as performing a steady beat, improvising ostinatos, and moving in appropriate ways to music. If a student is assessed to be musically gifted, s/he has the ability to develop a musical talent: that is s/he is able to demonstrate musical giftedness on a particular instrument or by composing a song (p.70-71). According to McPherson a child may be gifted without displaying any specific talent but not the reverse (p. 69).

According to Roberts (1990) Canadian University music education students see talent as a potential or possibility of musical success which can be accomplished through work but this "talent" is not uniformly given to the general public and, therefore, do not expect to find it in their own future classrooms.

Bartel (2000) bridges the gap between the commonly accepted notion that musical talent is innate, and that students may still possess musical potential:

> One of our culture's most devastating misconceptions about people's music learning potential is that music is a talent possessed by only a few. Those who are not deemed talented are systematically impeded in learning because the system is created with value and practices that work against the students with less inherent ability (but still great potential). Further our culture finds it quite acceptable and justifiable for many people to say, "I have no musical ability, I can't sing. I am hopeless at music. I quit music." (p. 37)

The trouble in our culture and in the music education climate is that we assume that "this talent possessed by a few" can only be demonstrated through perfect performance. This is assuming many things about the notion of talent with regard to music:

> 1) A performance is the only way we can assess musical talent. McPherson (1977, p. 71) argues that all too often musical talents discussed in terms of the narrow range of abilities with the performance of music seen as important above all else.

2) We assume that when people demonstrate a "performance talent" that it some how requires no work.

3) Talent is a "before the fact " concept. It is complete and obvious at any point in a child's development.

Perhaps we should instead consider:

1) There are ways other than through performance to assess musical talent.

2) A displayed "performance" talent still requires an incredible amount of work. If one is musically capable one can improve upon these capabilities with work and training.

3) Talent is a dynamic concept relevant to age. It seems to make no sense that talent would be a be-all and end-all concept meaning that either one is talented completely or has no talent at. It seems to make more sense that "talentness" is a matter of degree.

How different our music curriculum would be if we made these our musical maxims:

1) To musically succeed requires work and dedication, in addition to talent.

2) Anybody can attain a certain level of musical skill through dedication and practice.

3) Talent can only "appear" once a person has had musical experiences and has been trained.

There are also two other notions that weigh in heavily on our focus on talent and gifted-ness in music: genius and perfection.

There is a characteristic of the notion of genius, which leads us to believe that especially children should display musical genius and, therefore, music perfection. The Collins English dictionary (1986) defines a genius as "a person with exceptional ability especial-ly of a highly original kind" and "such ability or capacity: *Mozart's musical genius*" (p. 633). Kivy (1993) describes Mozart as the supreme child prodigy, the "child man and man-child," which particularly causes us to associate the notion of genius in music, through the idea of a child prodigy, with children. There is also a culture of perfection in classical music. A classical performance is measured as being "perfect" firstly through all the cor-rect notes, as if a person can play like a robot with perfect precision every time.

Summary

The formal context we have chosen for the study of school music, our "why" of music education being the rehearsal or production model and the associated concepts of talent, giftedness and genius, in strong combination have been very detrimental to the study of music. Our focus on perfection in group performance context as well as our focus on the reproduction of existing literature and the quick division of students into the talented/untalented causes most students to cut short their musical studies in school.

Beyond the "proven" academic benefits of studying music, and by this I mean that music is important insofar as it sharpens the mind to study "real" subjects, the study of music is viewed as a "waste of time" in the real world. There is some philosophical discussion that music is somehow "important" or psychically good, but this type of discussion is not taken very seriously in practice.

Music education is perceived as a frill because the study of music can only be accomplished by the students who have perceived talent. Music education is easily "cut" as an educational program because it is only for the "talented." Our music philosophy, goals, and values in music education are for the musically talented only (which in turn means only those who can demonstrate a certain level of musical skill). Added to this is the notion that music supposedly comes so easily to those who are talented in it. Roberts (1991) describes the view of music by non-musicians that it is "somehow frivolous and easy, i.e. confined to the fun playing of various instruments" (p.45).

The point is that since musical talent, as we currently conceive of it, either "is or isn't," that there is no point in trying to study music unless we have talent. However, in the school system we are expected to study many subjects, although we may not be talented or gifted in them. Bartel (2000b, p.37) points out that although some people believe they do not have mathematical ability the school system requires that they study it well into high school. He writes, "But if you were to look at the role of music versus math in most people's life following school, music is vastly more important as a cultural phenomenon." We are expected to receive a mathematical education throughout high school whether we are mathematically talented or not. And yet for the majority of the population we have music as part of our lives more than math. Why is music the first subject to be removed from the curriculum because of budget cuts and yet we are immersed in it for the majority of our waking hours the rest of our lives? Below I will address this question through considering music as a lifelong endeavor

WHAT MIGHT WE BE DOING?

Introduction to a musical life

This second half of the chapter considers what would be involved in lifelong pursuit of music and educating for a musical life rather than the current music education paradigm of the rehearsal model, the focus on talent, as well as the re-creation of existing literature.

At the time of writing, I had a parent of one of my private students make a statement pertinent to this paper. The father said, in reference to his fourth child, the only one in the family who has been taking private piano lessons from me, "All my kids have taken music but it hasn't become a part of their teenage young adult lives. They don't want to play in a recital, they want to play in a (rock) band." and we proceeded to discuss how his son could learn to compose and create his own rock/jazz music.

In public and in private music instruction, we have long accepted that, in the main, there is a certain body of existing music literature as well as methods to teach it "correctly" and we continue to use these materials and practices. In the case of private music instruction the unending hours spent practicing to learn sophisticated classical material is revered by parents and teachers as "discipline" and dreaded by the students. I have so often heard adults tell me that, yes, they know how to play the piano, up to Royal Conservatory Grade 8 and now they hate it so much that they never play. And while I in no way mean to denigrate the beauty of classical music played well, in my studio I include all types of music and modes of playing it such that a student recognizes her ability to connect with the world around her through the instrument. If she goes to a movie or watches a television show or hears a piece of music anywhere she can learn to play it.

Knowing music

We often find ourselves saying that we "know" a song when, for example, we suddenly hear a song on the radio that we have not heard for a long time. We also say that when people are learning an instrument that they like to play songs that they "know" and again we mean songs that a person has heard before.

However the meaning of "knowing" a song is different for young children. Many times in my studio I have played "Mary had a little lamb" for a young child on the piano and asked them if they know the song. The answer is repeatedly negative. Then I insist that of course they know the song, and again a negative response. However when I then rephrase the question and ask them if they have heard it before, then they say, "Yes."

This concept of knowing a song is a very interesting and relevant point, because young children obviously think that "knowing a tune," means being able to play it on the instrument sitting in front of them. It seems odd, but true, that prior to playing a song that they have heard before on an instrument many children do not realize that one instrument can reproduce a tune which they may have sung or heard before. They are empowered and excited when they can play what they have heard before.[1]

How is it that music instruction has become so far removed from what we "know" and why do we cling to the classical model and "sanctioned" music? Why are we so afraid to make the connection to other musics and abandon largely unsuccessful methods such as Kodaly, and Orff, as well as unsuccessful musical contexts such as band and strings? Why don't we, fashion music education after Bowman's comments above, so that we would teach and learn "within," "about," and "through" a wider variety of musics and contexts

DeNora (2000) provides what I believe to be a simple but plausible explanation:

> Western music has been encumbered with the paraphernalia of "high art"; "good" music has become, and has been designed as, an object upon which to reflect, an object for rapt contemplation. This ideology has also been projected backward on music that was originally designed to be heard within social contexts: Telemann's *Tafelmusik* is perhaps the most famous example, but even Mozart was often heard amidst cries from the sausage sellers. (p. 157)

With this limited view of what music is, it naturally follows that the type of training to produce this music would be limited. This is the situation that I am attempting to remedy here. The point is if music is something that is so "compartmentalized" into school music or rigorous private lessons that we are left for no taste for it in our everyday lives, how can it be said that we are leading a musical life? And this being the situation it is no mystery that the average person's musical endeavors cease when they play that one last band concert as third trombone or complete that one last Royal Conservatory of Music Examination.

What if we were to reevaluate how music functions in our culture including informal learning from the media, musical toys, music on computer, videos and how we might respond to that as educators. What if we were to reconsider what music really is around us and how we include music in our lives, rather that considering it in some "abstracted" form. Again DeNora explains this quite eloquently.

> The abstraction of music from the flux of daily existence, and its excision of the body—both in terms of bodily rhythms in compositions and in terms of the motionlessness stipulated as appropriate listening conduct—have served to obliterate the none-the-less vital tradition of other music and its role in social life outside the concert hall, its role as it is woven into the tapestry of social life through the informal singing of songs, the pop concert, the car radio, the jukebox, ambient music, organizational music, amateur music production, singing, whistling and humming, and the playing of records, tapes and CDs. It is it all of these locations— from the gilded concert hall to the mega-mall, from bus terminal to bedroom—that music makes available ways of feeling, being, moving and thinking, that it animates us, that it keeps us 'awake.' (p. 157)

The how: education

Of course there is a strong tension between the traditional ways of teaching music and the type of music education suggested by DeNora's description of music in everyday life. As well there are cultural restraints on how the average person behaves musically. Unlike people in other parts of the world, we in North America simply do not burst into song at any moment and we would think somebody quite strange if she were walking down the street singing at the top of her lungs. Our interaction with music seems to be culturally distinctively personal because we think nothing of someone wearing a Discman every free moment or constantly having music play in the car. Of course this acceptable musical behavior is no doubt a result of the education system and thus we are stuck in an endless loop of trying to make small changes.

Considering that it is music *education* which we are discussing we can see how we can include music in everyday life by returning to some basic definitions and ideas. The Collins dictionary (1986) defines the verb "to educate" as (1) to impart knowledge by formal instruction to a pupil; teach. (2) to provide schooling for children (3) to improve or develop a person, judgment, taste, skills, etc.(4) to train for some particular purpose or occupation. And it defines education as "knowledge or training acquired by this process" (p.487).

What has happened in music education is that the "training" is occurring for those whom we deem capable but are we are not imparting knowledge or improving and developing a person, their judgments and tastes for those deemed to be untalented. Bartel (2000a) describes this distinction as the difference between music being a sport or recreation.

Is music a sport? Is it a sport or recreation? In school physical education and athletics there seems to be a fairly clear distinction between the education of students for life-long fitness and recreation and development of skill and training for competitive sport. The recreation orientated approach includes all students— and hopes all students will develop abilities, attitudes, and motivations that will see them continuing recreational activity as a lifelong pursuit because of a psychic dividend it yields and the physical health benefits. (p.18)

Bowman (1994) makes this same point "To the extent it warrants its claim to being educational, music education must somehow intervene, cultivate, refine. It must help people become broader and more discriminating than they might otherwise be" (p. 29).

In other words, by focusing on teaching musically capable students to be technically proficient in music, we are making music into a sport rather than part of a person's general education. It is well known that music is one of the oldest subjects in the curriculum. In the middle ages it was one of the Seven Liberal Arts that formed a person's basic education, along with grammar, logic, rhetoric, mathematics, astronomy, and geometry. At the time a balance of these subjects was necessary for a comprehensive basic education that then allowed one to specialize in a particular field of inquiry. To a certain extent these subjects were concerned with ways about finding out about the world as different types or modes of inquiry. Yet music somehow developed into a discipline concerned with training rather than with educating.

And while there is no doubt that being able to play music certainly is the best way (and some would argue the only way) to "know" it, somewhere in the process of playing we need to be able to sort the good from the bad in whatever type of music a student is playing. Here we come up against the problems of including every type of music we hear around us, as described by De Nora, as part of music education. Perhaps it is fine to include them but to teach, as Bowman suggests, students to be discriminating regarding music.

Further to this point, Gatto (2003) in his interesting and radical article in Harper's Magazine, *Against School*, urges us as members of society, to help kids engage in serious material: grown-up material in life such as: history, literature, philosophy, music, art, economics, and theology. He makes the important point that some of the media in which we engage is empty entertainment for empty minds. I extend that argument to mean that one of the goals of music education, and this is a very important point, should be to teach children to be able to discriminate between what is worthwhile and what is empty music to make their lives more meaningful, as Gatto suggests:

> Well-schooled people are conditioned to dread being alone, and they seek constant companionship through TV, the computer, the cell phone, and the shallow friendships quickly acquired and quickly abandoned. Your children should have a more meaningful life and they can. (p. 38)

Continuing musical and personal/societal benefits of a lifelong study of music

When we consider Bartel's description of how music education might be, as quoted above as "recreational activity as a lifelong pursuit because of a psychic dividend it yields and the physical health benefits" and Gatto's focus on a "meaningful life" we can see that these two views are compatible.

What we want is music to be part of lifelong learning through continued musical involvement throughout the lifespan. Music as a lifelong experience is not a stagnant experience, something we do only once, such as taking a cruise to Alaska, nor a repetitive experience such as brushing one's teeth every morning. It is continuing, evolving and changing: it is dynamic. Our understanding of music changes, as we are more musically involved and have more musical and personal experiences to bring to the music.

A lifelong learning of music deepens our understanding of it as well as providing mental, physical, social, emotional, and personal benefits. There is a strong interrelationship between the nature of lifelong learning and musical understanding. As with many other subject areas, music education is far from complete when a student graduates from high school. Many necessary musical experiences that contribute to making people more musically knowledgeable and intelligent continue to occur throughout the lifespan. We musically change and grow, not only in school, but afterwards. The more we study, the better we understand the music, but the better it is for us as individuals and as a society. People can develop a more sophisticated and complex understanding of music through time. As well as a laudable educational and personal goal, continuing education in music is an important societal goal. The question of continuing education in music gets at the root of the epistemological question of what it is to educate. Through developing a more sophisticated understanding of music people can better appreciate it and can make more educated judgments about the music they hear around them as both they and the music change throughout time Educationally speaking our experiences add to our understanding of music, but personally speaking musical experiences contribute to our quality of life.

Conceptual and educational goals of music for life

How different would the conceptual and educational goals of music education be if we focused on making the study of music a lifelong pursuit rather than something, which swiftly ends when a student leaves high school?

Musical acquisition and development would certainly have to begin differently starting in Kindergarten. Rather than beginning with songs from the "classroom repertoire" we would begin with what the students know. For example, rather than teaching students to keep a steady beat on Orff instruments, by repetitively playing the same song, students could learn to keep time to clapping along to the theme from their favorite television show or computer game.

Beyond a variety of western music (classical, pop, rock,) non-western music, and a mix of both, high school students could also involve their "own" music in the curriculum as a learning source and tool. For example, they could bring in the latest rap song, one of which in 1997 had Coolio rapping to samples of Pachabel's "Canon in D." As well as an opportunity to teach how "samples" are used in rap music, students could learn about Pachabel and his music. This endeavor could turn into an entire research project and presentation on the uses of Canon in D in the media, about which there are several sites on the internet. The project could culminate with a students' performances of the canon in the style of music of their choice, or in several styles and on different instruments such as live on piano or guitar, sung in a variety of styles, computer generated, or used as background to their own commercial. This comes closer to DeNora's notion of how music function in our society and we want to develop this concept in students so that they continue to pursuit the study of music throughout their lives.

Culturally speaking we would have to readjust our thinking concerning Western art music. While this music is certainly the basis of Western music over a long history, it grew up alongside church music as well as folk music in later years. We tend to forget that it was Church music coupled with the soulful singing of African slaves in America that led to the development of jazz and blues and eventually the "White man's" version of it, Rock and Roll. While Western classical music or "high art" music is not music for the average person living in North America, Top 10, Rock, Rap and Hip Hop are. We can no longer continue to operate under the assumption that these musics are not worth studying or including in the curriculum.

In terms of student's ability to play music we would have to discontinue our discrimination against the untalented and our "group production" of music education paradigm. Students should be given the opportunity to learn to play on a basic level on a solo instrument, such as guitar or keyboard, or compose on computer. This type of individualized instrumentalization allows a person to have skills to continue to play music on his or her own as well as the possibility of playing with others.[2]

We need to reconsider the notion of the entire focus of music education being on the production of music in the sense that not all students can play to the same level of complexity nor play all genres of music. However, students can learn to hear to a level of complexity that they themselves cannot play. In the process of listening to the types of music they do play, they can extend their listening to other types of music. And in this instance it is the responsibility of the education system to expose students to music they may only hear in passing in popular media. While some students may experience peak experiences by playing, others may experience them by listening.

Although learning to play an instrument requires practice, we need to change our attitude towards music being a discipline that is *entirely* composed of training and hard work. We forget that music is part of life. We dance around to our favorite fast song when we are happy, we sing along in the car, we hear the start of our favorite television program in the distance, we sing in church and we cry at the sad part of the movie when the violins are playing. We need to view music as an activity that gives meaning to life, comfort, and joy rather than boredom and discontent.

Also we need to realize that students have a lot to offer musically. While we can *tell* them what a particular piece of music "means" or what it may be depicting, in my experience students have fantastic imagination and create their own images when they are playing or listening to music. The problem is that they are often too intimidated to offer their opinions freely since in traditional music teaching we tend to teach "from the top down." We should consider non-standard ways of interacting with music, such as including true student imagination, personal experiences, and student opinion. Part of the solution is in revisiting the relationship between musical and nonmusical outcomes, not in the education sense of improving test scores or improving spatial reasoning, but in the sense of what music brings to our lives. As DeNora says, music keeps us "awake" and brings joy and meaning to our lives in a real way. These personal and societal outcomes of studying music are often superceded by the practical and intellectual benefits of studying music.

Curriculum and policy changes

In reality the possibility exists that not all the different types of music or musical experiences that could contribute to making music a lifelong pursuit can be carried out in school and made part of the curriculum. As well, if every students is given the opportunity to play a solo instrument to his or her level of ability, the higher level performance curriculum would perhaps need to moved out of school. As Roberts (1995) asserts, performance-based music education must be moved out of the schools if it is to reach its full potential.

However, there is a great possibility for cooperation between public, community, and private sector music education so that schools can access musical experts in the community and students can benefits from their expertise. One possible solution in that students would create a music portfolio fashioned after British Columbia Ministry of Education (2003) graduation portfolio. The graduation portfolio is a record of student achievement in six areas: information technology, community involvement and responsibility, personal health, employability skills, educational and career panning, and art and design. Students demonstrate their knowledge and competence in each of the six areas through presenting projects they have completed, a memo from a teacher or letter from a community organization attesting to the student's participation, a video or photographs of the students demonstration a skill, a document of certificate for completing a course or project, a verified record of hours of fitness activity outside of school, an oral report recorded on tape, a demonstration of a product or computer program developed by the student, or a website designed by the student.

If we were to apply this model to a "music portfolio," the methods of demonstration of achievement would be the same, but the elements, which made up the portfolio, would naturally be different. The elements may include:

- Programs taught by musical experts out-sourced from the community who bring "modules" of music experience to the schools providing the student with an element of their portfolio[3]

- Continuing certification of participation in classical study through the Royal Conservatory of Music or the Western Ontario Conservatory.

- Participation and/or volunteering in arts organization educational programs

- Community bands, rock groups, drumming circles

- Community based recitals such as the one in Vancouver "Young Artists Performing" Club

- Concert rehearsal and formal concert attendance

- Making a music video, cutting a CD

- Performances of musical compositions, either live or computer generated

- Private lessons on any instrument

- "Shadowing" all types of professionals in all fields of music (from concert conductors to jingle writers for commercials) to explore careers in music

However in order for the music portfolio to be successful there would have to be a change in educational policy to include the recognition of musical experts and groups in the community. Roberts (1995) makes this important point:

> Non-school based educators, with a secure public system in place, have no ability to replace, let alone influence the allocative function of our schools. Whatever achieve ments we make with children will be lost to them unless there is a way to amalgamate our superior out-of-school educational possibilities with the recognized authority of the school system to exercise its allocative role in society (p.74-75).

It is possible to amalgamate the private instruction /public school system if students can study and participate in music outside of school and receive credit from school so that their work is "captured."

Conclusion

In the first half of this chapter, I have examined what we are currently doing in the music curriculum to discourage music as a lifelong pursuit through our current music education paradigm that focuses on perfection in group performance, and on individuals within the group who are talented or gifted. If we mean by music education one and only one thing, that is perfection in music performance within an ensemble, then we are perhaps achieving that goal in some high school bands, choirs and orchestras. However, if by music education we mean that individuals can simply play music on their own, in a way that is meaningful to them, have a more sophisticated understanding of music, and can make choices about the music that they hear around, then we are failing.

In the second half of the chapter, I have outlined changes that would need to be made to the music education paradigm in terms of what concepts, values, critical abilities, and music making skills would be involved in a music education that fosters music as a life-long pursuit. I have suggested curriculum and policy changes that would be required to allow for cooperation between the school music education system and private, commu-nity, and public musical opportunities.

It is clear that we should we make changes to broaden the traditional school classroom. In making the types of changes I have outlined, we are neither entirely abandoning music education as we know it, in that it would still be school based, nor are we "de-schooling" school music education; we are extending the context of music education beyond that traditional school classroom

If we adopt the music education paradigm of educating for a musical life, we harness student imagination, personal experiences, and opinion to assist them in developing the motivation to continue to explore, throughout their lifespan, the variety of music to which they have been introduced. Our goal then is to prepare students for continuing musical engagement and enrichment throughout their lives and make them more discriminating re music, not more musically discriminated against because they are not musically "talented."

References

Bartel, Lee (2000a). Is music a sport? *Orbit: Lessons from Music*, 31 (1), 18.

Bartel, Lee (2000b). Today's systematic violence. *Orbit: Lessons from Music*, 31 (1), 37.

Bartel, Lee (2001). Music education's pedagogic model. *Canadian Music Educator*, 43 (1).

British Columbia Ministry of Education. (2003, May). Graduation portfolio assessment for 2004. *The graduation program.*

Bowman, W. (1994). Justifying music education: contingency and solidarity. *Canadian Music Educator*. 35 (6), 27-32.

Collins dictionary of the English language. (1986). London: Collins.

DeNora, Tia (2000). *Music in everyday life.* Cambridge UK: Cambridge University Press.

Fiske, Harold. (2000). A 2020 vision of music education. In B.A. Roberts and B. Hanley (Eds.),. *Looking forward: challenges to music education.* CMEA, Friesens, Canada.

Gatto, John Taylor. (2003, September). Against school: how public education cripple their kids, and why. *Harper's magazine*, pp. 33-38.

Kivy, Peter (1993). *The fine art of repetition: essays in the philosophy of music.* Cambridge; Cambridge University Press.

McPherson, Gary E. (1997). Giftedness and talent in music. *Journal of Aesthetic Education*, 31 (4), 65-77.

Roberts, B.A. (1995). Perspective on Music Education: Reconsidering the de-schooling of school music education. *Research Studies in Music Education*, (5), 66-77.

Roberts, B.A. (1991). *A place to play: The social world of university schools of music.* St.John's, NF: Memorial University of Newfoundland.

Roberts, B.A. (1990) social construction of talent by CanadianUniversity music education majors. *Canadian Journal of research in music education*, 32 (2).

---

[1] It is interesting that later in life "knowing" a tune becomes recognizing it being performed for the vast majority of people, rather than being able to play it themselves.

[2] This desire in students is demonstrated by the proliferation of students who discontinue band in High School and learn to play guitar outside of school instead. These same students will spend time researching their favorite bands on the internet looking for tabbed music to play.

[3] An example of this is the Vancouver artist in residence program whereby masters in their particular musical discipline travel from school to school a week at a time and provide students with a musical "module."

CHAPTER TEN

On Behalf of the Ugly in Music

RICHARD MARSELLA

Behold the new orchestra: the sonic universe! And the musicians: anyone or anything that sounds

R. Murray Schafer, 1977.

Abstract

Music education has been limited in its appeal to children by the predominant focus on the pursuit of "beautiful" music. This chapter contends that the inclusion of "wild sounds," sounds that we might consider noise, into the palette of music education would make it more appealing to many children. Also, this chapter advocates for the development of a keen awareness of the sounds around us everywhere, and encourages the exploration and use of these sounds in "compositions." The chapter ends with a series of "project" suggestions that employ wild sounds, that champion what we have designated the ugly in music.

Introduction

Humans should think without limitation and not suffocate their imaginations by only dwelling on the *beautiful*. We must acknowledge both the flower and the manure that helps it grow. This chapter is in defense of ugliness in music and calls for an expansion of the palette of sounds we use to compose it.

Composer Frank Zappa (1989) says that "music can be anything, but it doesn't become music until someone wills it to be music, and the audience listening to it decides to perceive it as music" (p. 141). The factors involved in why an individual accepts or neglects certain kinds of music are intangible. For all we know, one's musical taste could be related to the blood pressure of our parents, the tempo of our mother's walk, or our economic environments (Van Eijck, 2001). One thing we cannot deny is that musical taste is certainly related to musical upbringing, and the socially-bred concepts of harmony versus dissonance.

The Zoo of Sounds

Even before birth, a child's sonic vocabulary begins to develop from womb sounds. Almost immediately after birth, a child's definition of music begins to take shape. They might not consider certain sounds to be music, unless they are encouraged to hear them as music.

When I work with younger students, we have no trouble exploring humanly conceived concepts such as ugliness and beauty in music. When I first meet with a class, I sometimes pull out a fork and scrape it on a dish to make an interesting sound. This sound usually makes teachers and students cringe in fear, quickly plugging their ears. Yet many students have also screamed for an encore performance! It is at this time when I usually invite a few brave students to scrape their nails on the blackboard while I accompany them on classical guitar.

These annoying sounds can be classified as a *wild* sounds. A wild sound, like a wild animal, is usually observed from afar, but not generally accepted in a musical context. I am confident that as a sophisticated species, our ears can accept so much more from the sound spectrum. We tend to cling to a concrete definition of what our music *should* sound like, and do not care to expand this repertoire of sounds. More usage of wild sounds would be a first step in changing the future of music.

Some other wild sounds that I think deserve musical domestication are:

- feedback
- engines
- screaming
- whoopee cushions
- door-stoppers
- jackhammers, and other machine sounds
- barfing, burping etc...
- breaking glass
- a horse eating
- a dentist's drill

Beauty versus Ugliness

I deeply respect the history of music and its evolution throughout the ages. I recognize the somewhat natural gravitation towards a consonant musical end, and do not condone musical barbarianism. But all music whether it be tonal or atonal works from the basic notion of tension and release. How we achieve this tension and release is the point in question.

The purpose of music is to mimic the ongoing plight of humans to find peace in their lives. I am not calling for the destruction of traditional instruments or the abolishment of proven musical techniques. For example, I will always love Rimsky Korsakov's *Scheherazade*, and the sound of a traditional symphony orchestra. I just think we have enough of it. Let's face it, Rimsky Korsakov didn't have the technology to sample an actual swarm of bumblebees, or his *Flight* would have sounded significantly different.

It is necessary to stretch our musical boundaries by educating children using alternative methods, some of which I will outline later. With an understanding of music theory, we can apply the proven techniques of form, harmony, and rhythm in a completely new way. If classical structure were applied to a newly invented junkyard orchestra, then music would open the imagination of its listener in a new way.

Why am I attracted to the darker, uglier side of art? There is obviously a darker side to myself which I am trying more and more to understand by pursuing this work. We need not be cynical or miserable people in order to explore the darker sides of art. I have recently noticed that my work seems to be highly effective with misfit students, those who simply do not resonate with traditional teaching methods.

My musical deviance has grown because I find much more validity in exploring the lesser-known sea of sounds. Sounds are the precious ingredients of music and, unfortunately, music seems stuck in a TV dinner routine. Carl E. Seashore's (1947) *In Search of Beauty in Music* refers to this routine as the "horse and buggy stage of musical instruments" (p. 368). Seashore (1947) and Russolo (1986) call for a new set of musical instruments to help re-examine our notions of music. "The only emotion that they [traditional instruments/repertoire] can still produce is that of widening the mouth—into an inevitable yawn! And the yawn is not exactly the newest of emotions" (Russolo, 1986, p. 82). Russolo goes on to say:

> One of the reasons that spurred me to enlarge the field of orchestral timbres by borrowing them from noises was precisely the *boredom that our ear feels* in hearing the now commonplace timbres of the orchestra and the virtual impossibilities (encountered in even the most advanced modern orchestrators) of creating *new* combinations from the paltry and outworn timbres that ordinary orchestras offer." (p. 82)

With music, as with food, a little bitterness can be a healthy option. It has been important for me to approach music from every angle, from the recording of incredibly angry and sometimes destructive music, to the calming side of my solo classical guitar playing. I love these extremes in my musical personality, and embrace each side as viable communicative forms.

I have spent the last six months constructing a small 20-note barrel organ in my studio. During construction, I had a problem with my bellows "belching" and my pipes not speaking properly. A friend asked me: "Why do you have a problem with the way your barrel organ sounds, I thought you condoned *ugly* music?" That question made me think of how and why I appreciate ugliness in music. Surely, I appreciate the natural acoustic flukes in nature, like the Doppler Effect, or when a cicada buzzes in the August sun. But with music, I treat ugliness seriously, as seriously as one might strive for *perfection*. I learned classical guitar for over 15 years before I became enthralled with the beauty in playing deliberately poorly and slightly out of tune. With my barrel organ, I would like to master how to make it sound consonant, before I inject my ugly slant. This is similar to a painter first mastering realism before developing a surreal side.

Young children embrace chaos in music as an equally fulfilling avenue to explore. They accept this outlook quite easily, because they seem less programmed. No matter what the age, we can successfully squeeze music out of a set of brake drums, a kitchen sink, a blackboard, and a set of drawers I turned into a dulcimer. Although I enjoy seeing structure prevail, I try not to curb the chaos. Why is there such a fear of chaos in music? Does it somehow question our effectiveness as educators and musicians? I enjoy giving students the option to play with music, and permission to go a little crazy. I consider myself to be a role model for how to remain functionally crazy while working within a system that does not allow for much experimentation.

Noise Music

Everybody has a personal threshold that separates how they would classify noise and music. Noise is any unwanted sound in your life, the sounds that have no significance, and that merely annoy us. "Noise has been linked to every known bi-product of stress. It deafens us, aurally and – there is strong evidence to suggest – morally as well" (Keizer, 2001).

Yet some music exists on the borderline between noise and music, acting as an alarm clock for a society drenched in boredom. Noise musicians such as the Nihilist Spasm Band from London, Ontario have helped shape my musical outlook. Their structure-free music, performed on homemade noise instruments forces the listener to think. I love the rebellious ideal that they portray with their work, using anti-music (ie. noise) to make music!

For over 35 years, The Nihilist Spasm Band has represented a side of our culture with which I am very proud to affiliate. Their music deliberately lacks form and organization. Their treatment of music is similar to real life conversation, based heavily on the art of improvisation and chaos. These men pride themselves on the fact that they do not stem from any formal music training. They are doctors, librarians, visual artists, Latinists, and printers. Yet when the Nihilist Spasm Band gathers to make noise music, it is such a unique statement that it makes us question the true purpose of music education. For 35 years, these men continue to genuinely love music, when many of our young students will never pick up their clarinets again after high school.

When the Nihilist Spasm Band performs in North America, the audience's reactions are sometimes negative, due to our cultural prejudices. Whereas in Japan and France, since noise music is an actual genre and is more culturally accepted, the Nihilist Spasm Band are duly embraced as a pioneering group.

How to Play Your Bathroom

Some adults who observe my work question the validity of my recent scores, *How to Play Your Bathroom* and *How to Play Your Classroom*, where mundane bathrooms and classrooms become complex musical instruments.

How to Play Your Bathroom includes specific instructions, much like in any other musical score, for anybody who enjoys bathroom exploration. The piece arranges the sounds of blow dryers, nose blowing, toilet flushes, rubber ducks, gargling the national anthem, and a lot more. Most students love this approach to music, and I find that even conservative children are open-minded enough to try it.

Inevitably, a colleague asked: "At the end of the day, would you actually listen to somebody 'playing their bathroom' and call it *music*?" I feel that over time, if we approach music with thirsty ears for new sounds, perhaps a kitchen sink, mixed into a piece with many other layers would not seem so strange. When a pop musician such as Beck can creatively use the sound of a Squeegee cleaning glass in a palatable way, I see hope for freeing more sounds from the zoo. After all, good composition is still the underlying factor in what makes music *resonate* on its listeners. A good composer should be able to effectively organize *any* group of sounds, and a good musician should be able to draw music from any given object.

Musical Taste

The term *musical taste* confuses me. We do not discuss the smell of a Mozart Symphony, but we constantly hear people flaunting their high "tastes" in music. To look at taste in a literal sense, I have noticed more daringness in the palettes of restaurant-goers over the past 10 years. People seem to have embraced the multi-cultural fabric of our society and are excited to explore different foods. Music listeners should be as hungry for new sounds and ideas as they are for different culinary experiences.

If one were to blend a cheese slice with prunes, garlic, ginger and pineapple, would it taste good? Probably not, but mistakes and fearless experimentation have always lead to gourmet results. As composers, sound should be approached with the same courage. I think that through constant mixing and matching of sounds, we can create a gourmet menu for the ears of tomorrow, and not simply accept a fast-food musical diet. We need a new music theory that acknowledges the past, but that does not exclude the majority of our creative children.

A conservative musical attitude is in line with prejudiced thought patterns, for new sounds are just as interesting as new cultures. To return to the odd garlic-pineapple blend above: if it does not taste good, I am not suggesting training yourself to like it. I am suggesting that we continue to invent new instruments, new sounds, and new music that we can *genuinely* love. We can turn perceived ugly sounds into a new form of beauty by taming our wild sounds into music.

Musique Concrète

My musical ideologies are inspired by many sub-cultures of music. Take for example, the *musique concrète* approach of electronic composers like Matmos, whose album *A Chance to Cut is a Chance to Cure* uses sampled sounds recorded from various surgeries, from liposuction to eye surgery. I have always been inspired by the sound palette of the German experimentalists, Einsturzende Neubauten, whose music uses everything from razor blades on mirrors to shopping carts, air compressors and electronic pianos set on fire.

I think music education must always delve deeper into the music of its time, and should mirror the trends of its society, whether they be social, or political.

Composer Karlheinz Stockhausen went as far as calling the September 11th tragedy "the greatest possible work of art in the entire cosmos" (website: http://www.andante.com/article/article.cfm?id=14377). He was referring to the mere sonic and visual experience offered as a bi-product of this terrible act. Stockhausen's uncommon attitude is similar to the futurist composer Luigi Russolo, and his fascination with the noises of war:

> Marvellous and tragic symphony of the noises of war! The strangest and the most powerful noises are gathered together there! A man who comes from a noisy modern city, who knows all the noises of the street, of the railway stations, and of the vastly different factories will still find something up there at the front to amaze him. He will still find noises in which he can feel a new and unexpected emotion. (Russolo, 1986 p. 39)

Many modern music educators claims to be very interested in world music, and I feel that my suggested approach to music should be embraced with exactly the same openness. If a student's sound vocabulary were extended to include vacuum cleaners, forks screeching on plates, and a gander of Canada Geese, how can that hurt? I would much rather associate the sounds of Canada Geese with our culture than that of a violin or Céline Dion. Canada Geese act as excellent exporters of our funny Canadian soundscape every time they fly to Florida.

I think it is a good way to expand the minds of young children by first introducing them to the non-traditional sounds of our society. By beginning with these raw or wild sounds, students can perceive music to be much less confined than it has become. It also allows music educators an opportunity to discuss foreign sounds, and how to keep an open mind to other cultures. I am always surprised when a crowd of adults begins to laugh at a foreign sound in a concert setting. For example, I recently heard a concert by the great Viennese instrument inventor Hans Tschiritsch, who played classical repertoire on such instruments as a sewing-machine hurdy gurdy and the musical saw. There was also a bass clarinetist on stage, who likewise played classical repertoire on her flatulent instrument. The audience of adults could not stop laughing out loud at the foreign sounds emanating from the hurdy gurdy, yet they seemed dull and uninterested by the wonderfully humourous sounds of the bass clarinet. I found it strange that we tend to laugh at things that are new to our brains. I wonder if we once laughed at other races similarly?

Beware of the Media

As a music educator, it is important to know your enemy. Since mass media more or less controls the trends of our audio-visual world, our society is dangerously at the mercy of commercialism, and not particularly in caring hands. MuchMusic or MTV has more impact on students than all of the country's music educators combined. Subsequently, the musical aesthetic is distinctly molded by this trend developer, and the minds of young thinkers often become numbed into compliance. We must try harder to not ingest the aural fast-food that we are force-fed daily by radio and television.

The negligence of a child's aural diet usually leads them to buy or steal music that is easily accessible and merely allows them to fit in, providing a false sense of identity. Instead of appreciating the journey to knowledge, children seem almost encouraged to stay on the sofa and let the music find them. Sadly, music becomes merely a way of categorizing humans by genre, as our society somehow defines us by our aesthetic *tastes*. The pursuit of acceptance is not logical, yet most humans chase it for a lifetime. Humans tend to focus more on the visual problems that stem from an unbalanced diet, for example obesity, but the effects of the fast-food listeners are equally detrimental to the inactive mind. I cannot trust the trends of modern culture, or the music of that culture. In a homogenized retail world, with only a few giant stores to choose from, perhaps the same thing is occurring in music. In an age of seeming chaos, we should strongly consider injecting some in our music.

Alternative Education Projects

Here are some suggestions that might help remedy the mess, or rather for making a constructive mess:

Installations and "The Musical Forest" Our current educational model prepares the finest musicians for a stale "life" in the orchestra. There are not too many creative options for the aspiring musician in Western culture. We must allow for a multi-dimensional music education, and expose children to more musical models than just the standard orchestra and the oxymoronic pop-punk band. Futurist composer Luigi Russolo suggests building an entirely new set of noise instruments in his influential treatise, *The Art of Noises* (Russolo, p. 82). We should encourage children to build musical installations, and to invent new instruments rather than simply treating students as future prophets of Bach. To quote The Residents, "Bach is dead."

I am more impressed by artists like Tim Hawkinson, whose giant Uberorgan can be walked through, with musical events happening as one walks through it. Another interesting approach is from composer Tod Machover and his Toy Symphony, as he has developed new musical toys for children of all ages, such as his electronic *Beatbugs* and *Shapers*.

This approach to music excites my imagination. I would like to eventually build a musical forest with a group of young students, where each student will design, compose, and plant their own musical tree, which plays spontaneously as the wind blows through it, perhaps like an Aeolian harp. Each student can grow old and nurture their "trees" in this mechanical music forest, grafting or pruning them as they wish over time.

Mechanical Music. One of my mentors is the Dutch organ builder Henk De Graauw, who thankfully introduced me to the history of mechanical music. Mr. De Graauw is the only man in Canada to have built his own orchestrion, which is a mechanical organ once used to make the music for large carrousels. Henk's childhood dream was to build a symphony orchestra using automaton monkeys. Composers such as Conlon Nancarrow wrote exclusively for the player piano. With mechanical music, I see a lifetime of opportunity and uncharted territory, where the concert halls of the future might better resemble a chocolate factory.

Music Roots and The Parade of Noises. Music Roots is a project that I began in 2003 which involves musical instrument construction, composition, CD production, and a performance in the annual *Parade of Noises*. The *Parade of Noises* is a wonderful celebration of sound, with fire engines, ice cream trucks, over 700 grade four students, a 40-person Theremin ensemble, an orchestrion, a concert band, and just about any other sound imaginable, held outside in Brampton's Chinguacousy Park in June. I am always happy to involve children in an unconventional performance, where an element of chaos is embraced by teachers, parents, and the general public.

R. Murray Schafer's recent spectacle in Coimbra, Portugal involved over 2500 musicians from all proficiency levels in an outdoor concert called Coimbra Vibra, where the entire city was played or *vibrated* like a musical instrument. In a performance like this, the lines between the traditional and non-traditional instruments are blurred from the distraction of an engaging, meaningful musical experience.

I agree with John Cage's opinion, that instruments like the Theremin have been misunderstood and improperly implemented in a musical context. To use such a technology to merely perform highly technical Italian arias, and not explore its greater potential is wrong (Beckstead, 2001). The Theremin is a logical answer to eliminate the need for refined technique and focusing on a more-inclusive musical approach. I am happy to be using Theremins in the Music Roots program, as students are genuinely fascinated by its diversity.

Overall, I feel that technology and popular culture have developed so rapidly that music education has not been able to adequately adapt. This lack of balance puts music education in a potential danger of becoming extinct. If music educators are not all yet comfortable teaching the five volumes of Carl Orff's *Schulwerk*, how can they possibly be concerned with new technologies?

Sound Pals. Video game technology is also developing at a rapid pace, as children in Canada are able to connect with others around the world using headsets and Internet technology. They usually apply this technology to sports and war games, but I also think this untapped region would be especially interesting for collaborative music projects with children around the world.

Borrowing from the idea of pen-pals, I am currently developing a project entitled "Sound-Pals" which will use technology to bring students from across the world closer together. Using the Internet to communicate and computers as sound manipulators, grade six classes in Canada will be paired up with participating grade six classes in different countries. In this sound exchange program, students will become field anthropologists, recording sounds from their own environments and exchanging them via email with their partner class from another culture.

After the students have gathered all of the desired sounds from their sound pals, such as the sounds of their police sirens, dial tones, restaurants, language, and school bells, the students will have a chance to manipulate these sounds and compose them into a new piece of music. This project is another method of using music as an international language, and treats raw sounds as building blocks for composition. Instead of making music with traditional sound sources like violins and pianos, the students will begin with sound waves from a different culture and use these ingredients to create something new, and hopefully a friendship in the process.

The International Moment of Noise. Sole ugliness in music is not what I am directly requesting, but every sound must be accepted in music-making, and not so frowned upon. John Cage says, "I keep my mind alive and alert...As a result, everything dissonant, I hear as consonant" (*For the Birds*, p. 78). I have heard that it is healthy for a growing child's immune system to periodically swallow dirt. I consider the ingestion of foreign sounds and dissonance to be a necessity for the growing mind. I recently imagined the benefits of having an "International Moment of Noise," where every human across the planet honoured the dead and acknowledged the stupidity of war with one minute of pure noise rather than silence. In this context, noise could act as a glue to connect the communities of the world.

Perfecting Mistakes. Music education needs to allow traditional piano instruction and prepared piano instruction to co-exist in harmony. We must spend years with children treating sound like clay, free to sculpt, without fear of consequence. The term *polish* is neurotically used to describe the refinement of music. In schools, the majority of time is spent *polishing* music so that adults can understand it in a sterile concert setting, forgetting about any other musical options. The standards are set high for our children, to perform music, and not to play music. Even smiles are fraudulent when a student is perfectly performing music, because raw emotion becomes pre-packaged and not sincerely improvised. Why not spend a good portion of time decomposing a piece, even destroying it into something completely different?

Perhaps we should honour the mistakes in music, as Miles Davis suggests. In the summer 2004, I had the pleasure of working with an energetic group of students at the University of Toronto on a project where we deliberately butchered the Canadian national anthem. We inserted wrong notes, cell phone rings, and mistake-making conventions such as repeating a wrong melody until it was correct. We performed the remixed National anthem in Toronto's Queen's Park, the home of the provincial legislative building, and never informed our audience that we were performing it *deliberately wrong*. The students performed the anthem so rightly wrong, that the audience was left confused, and giving false accolades in order to console us. That is a blatantly transgressive musical act. That is a musical mental challenge. That is the sign of a great performance!

The purpose of this exercise was to directly engage the students in a fun confrontation with aesthetics and question what the final purpose of music should be. Looking at the traditional wrong way of doing something is an important step to knowledge. In music, we are not often granted the opportunity to explore personal rights and wrongs. With this in mind, I am not sabotaging without reason: I think that students should be given the opportunity to explore music from different angles, and from the wrong perspective, a lot of learning can be done. It is not my duty to teach children how to make perfect music. With perfect music comes social dissonance and an entirely different set of psychological issues. The choice of the national anthem was to commemorate the freedom of speech we have as Canadians, as an exercise similar to this might be considered illegal in some other countries.

Today's music should acknowledge its participants more than the music of our past. Composers like John Zorn, and his improvisatory game pieces should be introduced in schools, where musicians of all skill levels can partake in the raw act of making music. We should learn from composers such as R. Murray Schafer, who include children and "professional" musicians simultaneously in their work. The more we rid ourselves of the notion that great music and technical proficiency are correlated, the healthier our culture can become. When the technique of a performer is in the foreground of a musical experience, then something is usually wrong with the music. Some might consider this to be a 'lowering of the standards of musicianship in Canada.' By no means am I condoning poor musicianship, but rather I suggest we pursue healthier musical goals.

It Never Ends

I do not want to seem like a prophet merely on behalf of ugly music, somebody who deliberately only writes ugly music, and chases a flaccid ideal. I recently saw the importance in making incredibly beautiful music using foreign sounds and new techniques. This to me is the greater challenge, to make something truly monumental with all of the current options at our disposal.

It is too difficult and pointless to draw a distinct line between an ugly and beautiful sound. I like the fact that for every ten students that hate the sound of nails scraping on a blackboard, there is always one who appreciates its uniqueness. It is said that the garbage of one man is the treasure of another, and that one's perceived noise will ring comfortably on the soul of another. *The Rite of Spring* caused veritable riots after its debut performance in France in 1913, and today we hail it as high art. I will not stop *polishing* my musical ideologies, and look forward to exploring the limitless musical avenues found in my lifetime. My musical life includes the ongoing journey with the classical guitar; but also includes walking through a mechanical music forest, the annual Parade of Noises, and playing my Whoopee cushion organ in the International Moment of Noise.

References

Beckstead, David. (2001) *Music Educator's Journal*. 87 (6); pp.44-50.
Cage John. (1976). *For the Birds*. London: Marion Boyers Inc.
Hand, Dr. Ferdinand. (1880) *Aesthetics of Musical Art or The Beautiful in Music*. Toronto.
Hanslick, Edward. (1974). *The Beautiful in Music*, New York: Da Capo Press.
Helmholtz, Hermann. (1885). *On the Sensations of Tone as a Physiological Basis for the Theory of Music*. London: Longmans, Green and Co.
Keizer, Garret. (2001). Sound and Fury; The politics of noise in a loud society. *Harper's Magazine*, March.
Nietzsche, Friedrich. (1967). *The Birth of Tragedy*. New York: Random House.
Seashore, Carl. (1947). *In Search of Beauty in Music*, New York: The Ronald Press Company.
Schafer, R. Murray. (1977). *The Tuning of the World*. Toronto: McClelland and Stewart.
Stockhausen, Karlheinz. Website: (website: http://www.andante.com/article/article.cfm?id=14377)
Russolo, Luigi. (1986). *The Art of Noises*, New York: Pendragon Press.
Van Eijk, Koen. (2001). Social Differentiation in Musical Taste Patterns. *Social Forces* (US). 79(3) March, pp. 1163-1186.
Zappa, Frank. (1989). *The Real Frank Zappa Book*. Toronto: Poseidon Press.

CHAPTER ELEVEN

Conceptualizing New Music For Young Musicians

BERNARD W. ANDREWS,

Abstract

Contemporary composers have adapted to the changing musical landscape of the twen-
tieth-first century by employing both acoustic and electronic modes of composition, and
by integrating a broad range of compositional techniques – tonal, atonal, serial, environmental and electronic – into their works. Few composers, however, have successfully
written major works for young musicians. This chapter recounts the experience of
twenty-four Canadian composers who were commissioned to compose new music for
young musicians. The composers identified a diverse range of *stylistic features* in their
works, often merging cultural and historical influences with personal style and imagery.
They described a *conceptual approach* to writing that balanced pedagogical ambition with
sensitivity to the limited experience of the musicians. The majority of participants indicated that *prior experiences* with young people were invaluable in helping them to accurately gauge students' technical abilities and developmental levels. They identified a
range of important *compositional parameters*, notably melody, harmony, rhythm and texture, and integrated them within the musical structure to provide a challenge and reinforce learning. The composers also agreed that the *adjustments* to their compositions were
explicitly technical rather than stylistic, and that writing for young performers *did not
affect their personal style*. They expressed discomfort with the notion of pedagogical music
and preferred to see music for young musicians as "artistically valid" works equal to
those intended for people of all ages.

INTRODUCTION

Composers are one of our greatest natural resources. Unfortunately, the music of many
contemporary composers is inaccessible to young musicians, and consequently has virtually no impact on their musical education. The fundamental problem is that composers in conservatories and universities learn highly developed compositional techniques playable only by professional performers for specialized audiences. Music has
become, as Sir Harrison Birtwistle of the UK comments, "a mysterious thing and slightly
holy in a way, something you don't tamper with" (from Ross, 1998, p. 255). Juraj Hatrik
of Slovakia (2002) notes that many composers do not know how to write using musical
language that is comprehensible to young people and need to learn how to do so.
Michael Colgrass (2005), a Canadian composer, expresses the problem quite succinctly
when he reflects on his experience writing for a school band:

I was stymied ... After all, they're children. What can you expect when they can hardly even play in tune? But I knew that was an excuse. The truth was, I could write complex, highly demanding pieces, but I simply didn't know how to write interestingly for amateur musicians, let alone 12 year-olds. I was the one out of tune. (in press)

Music theorists in America (Adorno, 1980), Europe (Viera de Carvalho, 1999) and Australia (Walker, 1997) attribute the complexity of contemporary music to the dynamic changes in music during the twentieth century. The introduction of atonality and serialism represented a logical extension of the historical evolution of Western-European music beyond tonality. The rise of mass media fostered access to world musics and introduced the intricate nuances of alternate modalities, vocalizations and tuning systems on a much broader scale. As a consequence of these developments, music became more complicated, difficult to understand, and more challenging to perform. The German scholar Rudolf Frisius (1981) notes that an alternative method of composing emerged with the advent of the electronic field; that is, electro-acoustic music with its own theory and practice. Initially, this approach involved musique concrète,[1] electronic sounds and taped music. With the rapid advances in technology, electro-acoustic composing now involves analog and digital synthesis, the use of multi-media computers, and the development of alternate forms of representation, such as graphic notation. As the British composer Edward Williams (2001) points out, it also engenders innovative ways of manipulating and conceptualizing sound, and offers new possibilities for integrating music with other art forms through the use of multi-media.

Contemporary composers have adapted to the changing musical landscape, and they use both acoustic and electronic modes of composition. Many of them integrate a broad range of compositional techniques – tonal, atonal, serial, environmental and electronic – into their works. Few twentieth-century composers, however, have successfully written major works for young musicians with the notable exceptions of Bela Bartok, Paul Hindemith, Zoltan Kodaly and Carl Orff. Others have introduced alternative approaches to music composition in classrooms through the use of environmental sounds, peer assistance and group compositions, notably John Paynter (1982) in England and Murray Schafer (1977) in Canada. However, these approaches have not been integrated into mainstream music education programs in any systematic way (Andrews, 2004a; Carruthers, 2000). Researchers in Germany (Kim, 1995) and Australia (Gillies, 1990) have undertaken analyses of Hindemith's and Bartok's educational compositions, respectively, to obtain insights into their success. Their studies provide useful information on the nature of the musical works, such as the appropriate sequencing of rhythmic patterns and suitable ranges for young musicians. Unfortunately, we do not learn about the compositional process; that is, how the composers conceptualized and composed music for young musicians.

The different ways that young musicians interpret sound and the varied levels of technical ability among them produce unique challenges for composers creating new music for students enrolled in private studio instruction, and in elementary and secondary school music programs. These challenges cannot be resolved by conventional methods alone, that is, through textbooks, score study and listening activities, but require problem-solving and contact with young musicians. This chapter outlines the creative solutions that composers associated with the Canadian Music Centre (CMC) developed and applied in generating new music for young performers. It is a story told through the eyes and ears of the composers themselves, and it is based on the assertion that the development of high calibre works appropriate for young people is contingent on effective practice; that is, on successful engagement between composers and students in the creative process within classrooms, studios and rehearsal halls. By systematically examining their own compositional process, composers provided valuable insights and deepened our understanding of the parameters for composing new music for young musicians.

EXPOSITION

The Canadian Music Centre (CMC) is a national non-profit organization dedicated to promoting and preserving Canadian Music. The CMC prints and disseminates scores, produces and distributes recordings, undertakes educational initiatives, and collaborates in research projects (Carruthers, 2000).[2] Within the CMC, there are five regional centres - Atlantic, Quebec, Ontario, Prairies and British Columbia. Each region is administered by a regional director and administrative staff, and they report to a regional council comprised of composers, music educators and community members. There is also a national office with an executive director and a board comprised of the chairs and vice-chairs of each of the regional councils (Keiser, 1990). In recent years, members of the Ontario Regional Council, most notably John Weinzweig and Louis Applebaum,[3] expressed concern about the *lack of new music* in the Canadian Music Centre libraries across the country appropriate for young people in schools, and of the need for the CMC to become more proactive and connect more effectively with the educational community (Andrews, 2005a; Carruthers, 2000). In discussions on this matter, composers on the Council noted that, in general, many of them are not familiar with the *parameters for writing music for young musicians*. Most composers derive their income from writing film and television scores, or undertaking commissions from professional and/or community groups, and many lack experience in composing explicitly for young people. In order to fill this knowledge gap and develop guidelines for effective practice, councillors agreed that it would be worthwhile to pursue a commissioning project and examine the compositional process employed in writing new music for young musicians.

As a member of the Ontario Regional Council of the CMC and also its vice-chair, I was intrigued by the notion of developing an understanding of the parameters of pedagogical composition by working with professional composers. "The most difficult problem for the composer is to create a continuous, unfolding succession of musical events which is varied yet unified, constantly changing its character and quality, yet coherent" (Rochberg, p. 186). Those researchers who have investigated composers' improvisational and compositional processes predominantly focused their studies on the analysis of recordings, scores and sketchbooks. They developed complex schemas, including computational and linguistic models (cited in Lerdahl, 1988 and Krumhasl, 1991) to explain a musical work. Other researchers speculated on the compositional processes of well-known creative individuals (e.g., Gardner, 1993) but few studies examine the compositional processes employed by the composers themselves.

The Ontario regional director at the time, David Parsons (also a composer), was equally convinced that composers could not only could write effectively for young performers but, if given the opportunity to reflect on the compositional process, could contribute to the development of useful guidelines for practice. Subsequently, the New Music for Young Musicians Project [4] was developed under the aegis of the Canadian Music Centre "in order to begin addressing the problem of a lack of contemporary music repertoire for young musicians" (Steenhuisen, 2000, p. 1). Through a concerted effort by the CMC and its regions, the Canada Council approved a Millennium grant in 2000 to commission professional composers to compose new music for students who were undertaking instruction in schools and private studios. Ninety-five composers from across Canada were commissioned by the CMC in consort with provincial arts councils: three from the Atlantic region; fifteen from Quebec; twenty-seven from Ontario; fifteen from the Prairies; and thirty-five from British Columbia. It was anticipated that the commissioning of new works would "add a wide variety of music to the repertoire introduced to students by music teachers throughout the country, and make recent Canadian music more prominent in the musical lives of young performers" (Steenhuisen, 2000, p. 1). Within the parameters of the New Music Project, an evaluation study was undertaken to examine how composers compose new music for young musicians.[5]

As a *composer*, I experienced the challenge of writing for young musicians and the frustration of obtaining adequate renditions of these works. In the role of a *music educator*, teaching and administering music programs in schools, I was aware of the major initiatives of the CMC to promote Canadian music in classrooms across a vast country (Shand, 2004).[6] The John Adaskin Project is a multi-year initiative that involves cataloguing, grading and producing guidelists of Canadian music for young musicians (e.g., MacInnis, 1991; Shand, 1993; Stubley, 1990; Walter, 1994). The ComPoster music education kit is comprised of cassette recordings with an accompanying teacher's manual (Canadian Music Centre, 1992). Creating Music in the Classroom involves composers composing new music with students in schools; and Composers in Electronic Residence has composers critiquing student compositions via the internet (Barwin, 1998). And now as a researcher in a faculty of education teaching music certification and curriculum courses, I know that despite these efforts there is very little Canadian music, new or otherwise, performed and studied in schools (Bartel, Dolloff & Shand, 1999; Newman, 1988; Shand & Bartel, 1998) and in post-secondary institutions (Andrews & Carruthers, 2004; Canadian Composer, 1965, 1966a, b, c, d; Caruthers, 2000), or broadcast in the media (Beckwith, 1997). Indeed, our knowledge is limited concerning how composers compose for young musicians, or indeed how they write new music per se for that matter (Gardner, 1993; Lerdahl, 1988; Reynolds, 2002; Sloboda, 1988). As the composer, Roger Reynolds (2002) explains: "A musical work is achieved gradually over time in a manner that doubtless varies for each composer: part discovery, part construction, even admittedly, part contrivance and ... also part sheer undirected bumbling" (p. 4). Ironically, we have achieved a more comprehensive understanding of young children's compositional processes when they improvise and create simple melodies using pencil and paper (Davidson & Scripp, 1988; Kratus, 1989; Macpherson, 1998), computer software (Phillips & Pierson, 1997; Upitis, 1997), peer assistance (Claire, 1994; Miell & MacDonald, 2000), and cross-curricular integration (Cornet & Smithrim, 2001; Upitis, 1992).

Composers have an increased auditory acuity and hypersensitivity to sound and rhythm that appears to originate in the infant-mother sensory motor relationship. It is a preference for sound during childhood that establishes hearing as the chief sensory modality in organizing a composer's cognitive functions, object relations, and perception of the world (Nass, 1990). Compositional thinking is both operational and syncretic, and motivation is a key factor (Kulka, 1979). It is a high level cognitive activity (Petsche, Richter, Stein, & Etlinger, 1993) that involves alternating between a deep, focused involvement in creation, and talking about and reflecting on the compositional process (Whitaker, 1994).

Early creativity research acknowledges the challenges involved in studying and understanding the internal processes involved in creative expression. In 1926, Graham Wallas emphasized the importance of studying the creative processes. He noted "that unless we can recognize a psychological event and distinguish it from other events, we cannot bring conscious effort to bear directly upon it," and that this can be achieved if one explores the making of a creative object and asks "how it was brought about" (Wallas, 1926, p.40). Wallas identified four key stages in the creative process - *Preparation, Incubation, Illumination and Verification.* He remarked that the Preparation stage "includes the whole process of "intellectual education [that] men have known for thousands of years" (Wallas, 1926, p.42). Wallas distinguished this form of accumulated and regulated knowledge from what Hobbes describes as the "'wild raging of the mind" in which the thought process is undirected (Wallas, 1926, p.42). Further, he found that most often people move from Problem Identification to Verification without much thought. When no conventional solution can be found, however, individuals engage in the Incubation stage where they allow the problem to "sit" with them. Incubation can bring about Illumination, which Wallas noted is the stage where unconscious and less controllable processes begin to manifest. Rather than a "flash of inspiration," he saw this stage as the "culmination of a successful train of associations" (Wallas, 1926, p.51). Further, he noted that "setting aside a problem for a period of time (Incubation) seems to increase the chances of a later insight (Illumination)" (Wallas, 1926, p.16).

Subsequent to the work of Graham Wallas, John Bahle (1934) suggested that there are essentially two types of composers: a working type (craft approach) and an inspirational type (Bahle, 1934). Max Graf (1947) found that composers engage in four basic stages when composing music: productive mood (preparation), musical conception (incubation), sketching (illumination), and composition (verification). Stan Bennett (1976) undertook a comprehensive account of the composing process by undertaking in-depth interviews with eight composers. His study elaborated on previous findings by Wallas (1926), Bahle (1934) and Graf (1947). Essentially, he shifted the focus from feelings (productive moods) and thoughts (musical conception) as categories to the writing process itself (i.e., sketches and drafts). He suggested that composing involves more specifically a process of discovering a germinal idea (preparation), a brief sketch (incubation), elaborating and refining a first draft (illumination), and revising the final copy through rehearsals and performances (verification). This process has also been discussed and elaborated on in the writings and interviews of major twentieth-century composers, such as Igor Stravinsky (1947), Roger Sessions (1970), Pierre Boulez (1975), Morton Feldman (1984) and Elliot Carter (1946/1994). Pierre Boulez (1975) described the composing process quite succinctly when he stated:

> For me a musical idea is like a seed which you plant in compost and suddenly it begins to proliferate like a weed. Then you have to thin it out ... to reduce, to thin out the possibilities ... to create an evolution in time and not a superposition that would have been too compact. (p. 15)

Composers may not necessarily follow the set stages in sequence that Bennet identified but rather oscillate between (Hung, 1998). Others use a variety of strategies to compose in conjunction with these stages (Fulmer, 1995 cited in Bolden, 2004). Bennett also found that compositional activity seems to occur most frequently in association with feelings of tranquility, security and relaxation; composers tend to work in blocks of two or three hours and sometimes longer; and it is not uncommon for a work to be written in chunks of fifty, one hundred or three hundred bars or more. As Morton Feldman (1984) explains: "I work everyday more in terms of feeling that I have done a day's work. Now, it could be two days going into each other without sleep" (p. 146).

In addition to the research findings, there are a substantive number of textbooks available in university music departments and conservatories for the teaching of composition. Such works analyze the compositions of well-known composers and synthesize highly technical rules for writing music. This applies to both traditional serious music (e.g., Markland, 1990; Ottman, 1992; Sulzer & Schachter, 1989; Warburton, 1982), and those in the more popular idioms (e.g., Cacavas, 1975; Coker, 1980; Dobbins, 1986; Sorenson & Pearson, 1998). The rules for writing music, however, are not based on direct contact with composers themselves, nor do they identify the personal and contextual considerations that go into composing a piece. Rather the rules reflect highly structured conventions developed by theorists through the analysis of musical works (Roberts, 1991). Such a formalistic approach to teaching composition does not lend itself to understanding the creative processes involved in reconciling old forms with new understandings and generating music appropriate for specific contexts, such as new music appropriate for young musicians.

DEVELOPMENT

Twenty-four composers from the Ontario and Atlantic regions of Canada, commissioned through the New Music Project, completed an in-depth questionnaire in which they described the stylistic features of their compositions, and how they conceptually approached the writing of new music for young musicians. [7] They also commented on how prior experiences with young musicians impacted on their approach, identified the most important compositional parameters, described the adjustments that were made to accommodate young musicians, and explained how their own training impacted on these decisions. Finally, participants were asked to comment on how writing new music for young musicians affected their personal writing style, and to describe their views on the nature of educational music (refer to Table I). The in-depth questionnaire was developed by this writer from the literature (Andrews, 2004b) and refined in collaboration with composers, educators and community representatives on the Ontario Regional Council (after Cousins & Earl, 1992, 1995). Its design is based on the assumption that "there is a necessary (though by no means uniform) *staging* involved in the process of completing a musical composition. We can thus inquire into the process recognizing it as a multileveled search for ultimate integration rather than the unrolling of a scroll upon which has been inscribed an already, mystical complete continuity that one needs only to receive" (Reynolds, 2002, p.4). Consequently, the research questions are broad-ranging rather than focusing solely on compositional strategies and techniques. [8]

The composers identified a diverse range of *stylistic features* in their works, often merging cultural and historical influences with personal style and imagery. Taken together, the key feature of their compositions appears to be this very diversity; that is, the practice of drawing on and bringing together varied cultural influences. For example, one piece merges a Gregorian chant melody with some jazz rhythms which, in the words of the composer, "bridge[s] the time gap to the present." Another piece, written in a neo-baroque style, is interspersed with Latin-American musical influences. Other selections employ traditional forms and integrate them with modern techniques. For example, one piece outlines the parameters of ternary form through the use of tone clusters. Another composer referenced a work to the early 20th century by building upon the sonorities of Bartok, Ravel and Debussy, and still another draws on folk influences and adds brass accents to give the piece a more modern feel. Regardless of cultural and historical influences, compositions are most often infused with personal style. One work introduces a dark moody atmosphere (represented by loud dissonant chords) reflecting a composer's angst, and another selection highlights a composer's playfulness (characterized by changing time signatures, large interval leaps, syncopated rhythms). Still others employ visual imagery (e.g., flute themes weaving around each other) and associations with external objects (e.g., instrumental timbres used to describe insects and their movements).

Table I

Questionnaire - Conceptualizing New Music for Young Musicians

1. What are the *stylistic features* of your composition for young musicians?

2. How did you *conceptually approach* the writing of new music for young people?

3. In what ways did *prior experiences* with young musicians impact on your approach?

4. What are the important *compositional parameters* of the piece, and how are they used?

5. What *adjustments* did you make to those parameters to accommodate young musicians?

6. How did your *compositional training* impact on making these adjustments?

7. In what ways did writing new music for young musicians affect your *personal writing style*?

8. Have your own views on the *nature of educational music* been changed by the writing experience? Please explain.

The composers were keenly aware of the unique needs of student musicians. Most of them described a *conceptual approach* to writing that balanced pedagogical ambition with sensitivity to the limited experience of the musicians. Indeed, almost every participant noted the importance of creating a "simple," "easy to comprehend," composition that, while developmentally useful and musically exciting, was "not so difficult that [it could not] be performed with satisfaction." Each viewed his or her piece as an opportunity for student learning and experimentation, but strove to make the work accessible and appealing. One composer described his ambition to create a piece that students would "enjoy working on," and another explained his intent to create music that "would appeal to [students], stimulate their interest, and be both challenging and satisfying but not so difficult that they would be turned off!" This conceptual approach appeared not only as an afterthought but as a major focus in the formative stages of development of the piece. Indeed, composers made specific mention of the student learning they set out to facilitate. One participant noted: "I began with a set of objectives or outcomes based on what I hoped young people will learn form my composition." Another composer showed an appreciation for the opportunity to foster student experimentation: "I would give the young musician an opportunity to experiment not only as performers but also as active participants in the creation of the composition."

In those cases where the primary focus was to stimulate interest and enjoyment, there still appeared to be a strong concern to enhance student learning. For example:

> I wanted to have a sense of fun and enjoyment for the young musicians playing the piece. Because of its imitative quality the young performers are participating in a kind of tag or dialogue ... Inadvertently the young musicians will learn to listen and balance each other's parts while technically improving their abilities to play arpeggios and their variants.

As evidenced by the number of composer responses, the "learning focus" is the most important aspect of the compositions. Again to re-iterate, a composer noted:

> The music in the A sections is an identical canon that is played two bars apart ... This is a great learning tool as the two players can practice by playing their parts together which will help to improve their intonation and match articulations.

Further, the composers demonstrated confidence in the students' ability to perform when provided with a challenge. In one participant's words: "Children are capable of achieving far more than we realize they can do, given the right material and good teaching." Another composer summarized the sentiment of many of his colleagues when he stated: "By giving the students a challenge, they will certainly rise to it!"

When asked how *prior experiences* with young musicians impacted on their approaches to composing new music for young musicians, the majority of composers indicated that their experience in working with young people was invaluable in helping them to accurately gauge students' technical abilities and developmental levels. One individual wrote that based on her experience working with young people, she could not only identify differences in development relative to adult students and adjust her work accordingly, but also she could see differences between young musicians and adults. She commented:

"They [young musicians] easily conjure up images in their minds from verbal cues which can then be interpreted into music." Being aware of this aspect of development in young musicians, she was inclined to bring visual imagery to her piece. Another composer noted that personal experience led him to see young musicians as more flexible and open to new influences, noting:

> A young musician can adapt...sometimes with more ease than an older musician because they are not so overly trained in one approach...this applies to all parameters. I have also found that if they are inspired by the piece, they are likely to work harder at it.

A composer-educator reflected the thinking of many of the participants when he remarked that not only was professional experience important to his understanding of composing for young musicians, but personal engagement with young performers was essential also. This individual noted that despite twelve years of experience adjudicating community music festivals, it was teaching his two young boys piano that most strongly influenced his approach to composing for young musicians. As he noted: "Having to work daily with the same child helps to bring you a keen awareness of what works with children and what motivates them." In many instances, composers emphasized the need to be "in tune" with the technical skills of students in order to strike a balance between the level of difficulty of the piece and student ability. They attempted to compose music with sufficient challenge to "peak interest" and "maintain appeal" while still ensuring the piece was not so difficult that students would become "turned off" or "overwhelmed." Finding this balance required composers to be in touch with young musicians, to "put oneself in the student's position," and to "remember how students think and learn in rehearsal."

Composers found that direct contact with young performers was the most effective way to understand their skills and abilities and to know what material would suit them best. Even those composers without experience working with young musicians saw engagement with them as a critical component in the development of appropriate material. In these cases, composers harkened back to their younger years in an attempt to write music sensitive to young peoples' needs. For example, when asked how prior experience influenced personal approaches to composing, one composer wrote: "I did draw upon my own experiences as a cello student to gain insight into what some of the fundamental technical difficulties are which young string players face." In several instances, when composers had questions about the skill and developmental level of young people (and could not draw this information from previous experience), they consulted directly with the classroom music teacher. Composers emphasized that sensitivity to students' abilities facilitated a level of comfort that helped to foster learning. In the words of one composer: "Given a positive and nurturing environment, students will often take on the challenge to understand and learn music that is both new and difficult for them."

The composers identified a range of important *compositional parameters*, notably melody, harmony, rhythm and texture, and these were used in quite distinct ways. It is important to note also that compositional techniques were regularly employed (e.g., motivic repetition at different pitches) to provide a musical challenge and facilitate learning for the young players. In other words, opportunities for student learning and experimentation were embedded within the structure of the composition. One composer stated this most succinctly when he noted: "Melody, harmony and texture - [are] all used in what I consider an innovative and beneficial way for the young musicians." No matter what each composer saw to be the most distinct compositional parameter of the piece, the learning dimension remained constant. One composer who identified texture to be the most important aspect of the piece, wrote that he was "encouraging each musician to become totally involved in its performance by following all the other parts...and in many cases to act as conductor in the cueing of other players... [the piece] is designed to lend itself to a multitude of educational applications for student musicians." Some composers identified rhythm as a significant compositional element and noted the educational features of its use: "The rhythm is quite prominent in many sections, requiring substantial counting and sub-dividing mentally on the part of young players"; and "I wanted to challenge students rhythmically by writing a piece with irregular rhythms switching between 5, 6 or 7 beats per bar."

Other composers identified melody as a significant parameter of their pieces, commenting that long lines were used "in order to teach proper breathing techniques and flow." One individual referred to "a few small motivic devices that are repeated throughout the piece," noting that they were designed "to help make the violin parts easier to learn and master." In another case, imitation took on some significance, and the composer remarked: "The vocal writing in these duets uses a lot of imitative, contrapuntal lines which encourage the singers to be independent but to listen carefully to each other." Harmonic structures were also organized to foster learning, for example: "I used both flatted 7th chord structures along with diatonic 7th structures so the students can hear and understand the difference." Overall, student learning was facilitated through the internal structure of the compositions; that is, technical challenges were integrated into the music in ways that stretched and developed the young performers.

When asked what *adjustments were required in their compositional practice*, composers unanimously stated that all adaptations to their compositions were explicitly technical rather than stylistic. In the majority of cases, composers noted that because they had experience working directly with students, they could accurately gauge the technical abilities of young musicians. Consequently, few changes were needed, and those adjustments required were fairly minor. One participant summed up the kind of adaptations that were mentioned by colleagues: "I decided to use a narrow range on all instruments, repetition and modified repetition, [and] interchange of slow and fast – but "packaged" – melodic spurts." In general, the pieces were shorter, the range of skills required was narrower, and the melodies were more compact than music for professional musicians. One composer wrote that it was particularly important for him not to become carried away with the technical aspect of the piece "so that [his] little moments of bliss [would] not stand in the way of playability of the piece." Composers had to carefully consider the technical obstacles that young musicians could potentially encounter. As one individual remarked:

> I wrote in my usual style...I also considered some of the basic difficulties encountered when studying a strong instrument, and to a certain degree, I tried to minimize some of these difficulties so that the players would be able to be more in touch with the elements specific to my piece.

The majority of composers noted explicitly that while they were sensitive to the technical abilities of the performers, writing for young performers *did not affect their personal their* style. Composers almost unanimously resisted the tendency to "write down" to young performers. They found that composing new music for young musicians neither compromised the artistic integrity of the piece nor adversely affected their writing style. One individual summarized this by stating: "[Young people] don't like being written down to any more than they like being talked down to." Another explained: "I have decided not to "write down" to them, but rather to create an enjoyable and technically manageable valid work of chamber music." In one composer's words: "Limited skill should not limit a student's ability to evoke a truly musical response," noting that music for young musicians should be "uncomplicated, but musically meaningful." Another composer summarized this approach when he stated: "[I] wrote for them as I write for older musicians, only more carefully."

When asked about their *views on the nature of educational music*, many composers expressed discomfort with the notion of pedagogical music, and they preferred to see music for young musicians as "artistically valid" works equal to those intended for people of all ages. One composer grappling with his question said outright: "I am very uncomfortable with the term 'educational music'...In the past, this term had a definite stigma and some composers felt it beneath them to write for students." Another composer wrote: "Frankly, I have never thought of 'educational music' as any different than any other music...Just because a young musician may have limited skill, this does not mean that they are incapable of evoking a truly musical response given appropriate material." Most composers indicated that their involvement in the New Music Project did more to reinforce their convictions about 'educational music' than to change their minds. As one composer commented:

> My experience...has lead me to believe that children are often capable of achieving far more than we realize they can do, given the right material and good teaching. This project, while not changing my views, has reinforced my belief in the importance of worthwhile music for students.

RECAPITULATION

While no pedagogical model can encapsulate the composers writing new music for young musicians, almost all shared a common focus; that is, to stimulate student interest in contemporary music while simultaneously challenging young musicians to stretch their skills and abilities. The composers attempted to maintain stylistic depth while balancing the technical requirements of the piece with the skill level of the musicians. The central challenge composers faced in writing for young performers was respecting the musical abilities of the young musicians. For them, this meant keeping the work from being overly complex. They were careful to indicate, however, that 'level of difficulty' should not compromise the style of the piece. Most composers were sensitive to the skill level of the students, and they strove to reach their performers "in the exact place ... on the skill challenging curve."

The composers commented that their experience working on this project reminded them of the importance of providing young people with opportunities for learning. Several composers noted the shortcomings in the current educational system. One composer stated: "My feelings have developed over the years to lead me to wish that more students had more opportunities for performance and creativity in every school."

Another wrote: "I do not like what is out there, and have decided to continue writing some more of my own!" Still another participant commented: "I have learned that teachers at a high school level leave students really to fend for themselves when it comes to finding new or interesting repertoire or to extend students' capabilities and techniques." Perhaps more optimistically, some composers saw this project as an opportunity to address shortcomings in the system. One composer wrote: "My views have not changed but simply been reaffirmed. It is important to provide new music for young musicians so that they realize that music is still being written in this day and age." Another stated: "Because of my background in education, I feel the opportunity [to work on this project]...has reinforced the importance of introducing contemporary Canadian music to young musicians. I feel the repertoire created by this project will become an invaluable resource for teachers and their students."

In general, the composers emphasized the need for more quality contemporary music in schools; that is, music which is directed specifically towards the needs and interests of young people. Participation in the study reinforced this position for the majority of the composers. Some expressed dissatisfaction with the standard of music currently found in the school curricula. Others noted that the compositions created through the New Music Project will make a significant contribution to the repertoire for music teachers and their students. The Project also highlighted that the partnership between composer and student is mutually enriching. Composers working with young people enjoyed the personal contact and found the experience brought clarity and simplicity to their work. They also felt that this exposure will help to remind students that quality music is still being written and hopefully encourage young people to perform contemporary music.

CODA

In conclusion, composing new music for young musicians poses specific challenges for composers and requires "creative solutions." This chapter outlined those challenges and explored how they were addressed during conceptualization. As a majority of composers had prior experience composing for young people, they refined their works against their knowledge of young musicians' needs. Moreover, they also had the opportunity to work with students in classrooms and studios, and to test and refine their compositions through rehearsals and performances. Consequently, their understanding and advice are invaluable as the foundational basis for understanding how composers can effectively compose new music for young musicians in studios, and elementary and secondary music programs.

References

Adorno, T. W. (1980). Music and the new music. *Telos*, 43, 124-138.

Andrews, B. W. (2004a). Composing music in the classroom: The missing link in music instruction. *The Recorder*, 46 (3), 12-19.

Andrews, B. W. (2004b). How composers compose: In search of the questions. *Research and Issues in Music Education*, 2 (1), www.stthomas.edu/rimeonline.

Andrews, B. W. (2005a). Policy development for Canadian music in post-secondary settings. *Music Education Research*, 7 (1), 103-119.

Andrews, B. W. (2005b, forthcoming). Composing new music for young musicians: Emerging questions. *The Recorder*.

Andrews, B. W. (2005c, in press). How composers compose new music for young musicians: Refining the process. In M. Mans & B. H. Leung (Eds.), *Proceedings of the 14th Music in Schools and Teacher Education (MISTEC)*

Seminar, Granada, Spain. Nedlands, Western Australia: International Society for Music Education.

Andrews, B. W., & Carruthers, G. (2004). Needle in a haystack: Canadian music in post-secondary curricula. In P. M. Shand (Ed.), *Music education entering the 21st century* (pp. 75-83). Proceedings of the 13th Music in Schools and Teacher Education Commission (MISTEC) Seminar, Malmö, Sweden. Nedlands, Western Australia: International Society for Music Education.

Bahle, J. (1934). Gestalt as applied to vocal compositions of contemporary composers. *Archive furt die Gesamte Psychologie,* 91, 444-451.

Bartel, L. R., Dolloff, L. A., & Shand, P. M. (1999). Canadian content in school music curricula: A research update. *Canadian Journal of Research in Music Education,* 40 (4), 13-20.

Barwin, G. (1998). Composers in electronic residence. *Canadian Music Educator,* 40 (1), 23-25.

Beckwith, J. (1997). *Music papers: Articles and talks by a Canadian composer, 1961-1994.* Ottawa, ON: The Golden Dog Press.

Bennett, S. (1976). The process of creation: Interviews with eight composers. *Journal of Research in Music Education,* 24 (1), 3-13.

Bolden, B. (2004). Students composing: Examining the experience. *Journal of Research in Music Education,* 24 (1), 3-13.

Boulez, P. (1975). *Pierre Boulez: Conversations with Céstin Deliège.* London, UK: Eulenburn Books.

Cacavas, J. (1975). *Music arranging and orchestration.* Melville, NY: Belwin.

Canadian Composer (1965). Courses in composition and Canadian composers: Part I of a survey of Canadian schools of music. *Canadian Composer,* December, pp. 20, 42.

Canadian Composer (1966a). Courses in composition and Canadian composers: Part II of a survey of Canadian schools of music. Canadian Composer, January, p. 20.

Canadian Composer (1966b). Courses in composition and Canadian composers: Part III of a survey of Canadian schools of music. *Canadian Composer,* February, p. 38.

Canadian Composer (1966c). Courses in composition and Canadian composers: Part IV of a survey of Canadian schools of music. *Canadian Composer,* March, pp. 6, 41.

Canadian Composer (1966d). Courses in composition and Canadian composers: Part V of a survey of Canadian schools of music. *Canadian Composer,* April, p. 6.

Canadian Music Centre. (1992). *ComPoster music education package.* Toronto, ON: Canadian Music Centre.

Carruthers, G. A. (2000). A status report on music education in Canada. In S. T. Maloney (Ed.), *Musicanada 2000: A celebration of Canadian composers.* Toronto, ON: Canadian Music Centre.

Carter, E. (1946/1994). Surveying the compositional scene (collected essays and lectures). In J. W. Bernard (Ed.) (1997), *Elliot Carter: Collected essays and lectures, 1937-1994* (pp. 3-43). Rochester, NY: University of Rochester Press.

Claire, L. (1994). The social psychology of creativity: The importance of peer social processes for students' academic and artistic creative activity in classroom contexts. *The Bulletin of the Council for Research in Music Education,* 119, 21-28.

Coker, J. (1980). *The complete method of improvisation.* Lebanon, IN: Studio.

Colgrass, M. (2005, in press). *Music Educators Journal.*

Cornett, C. E., & Smithrim, K. L. (2001). *The arts as meaning makers: Integrating literature and the arts throughout the curriculum.* Toronto, ON: Prentice-Hall.

Cousins, J. B., & Earl, L. M. (1992). The case for participatory evaluation. *Educational Evaluation and Policy Analysis,* 14 (4), 397-418.

Cousins, J.B., & Earl, L.M. (Eds.). (1995). *Participatory evaluation in education: Studies in educational use and organizational learning.* London, UK: Falmer Press.

Davidson, L., & Scripp, L. (1988). Young children's musical representations: Windows on music cognition. In J. A. Sloboda (Ed.), *Generative processes in music: The psychology of performance, improvisation and composition* (pp. 195-230). Oxford, UK: Clarendon.

Dobbins, B. (1986). *Jazz arranging and improvisation: A linear approach.* Rottenburg, Germany: Advance Music.

Feldman, M. (1984). Lectures 1984. In W. Zimmermann (Ed.), *Morton Feldman Essays* (pp. 143-180). Wasserburn, Kerpen: Beginner Press.

Frisius, R. (1981). *Musikpädagogische Forschung.* Karlsruhe, Germany.

Gardner, H. (1993). *Creating minds: An anatomy of creativity seen through the lives of Freud, Einstein, Picasso, Stravinsky, Eliot, Graham and Gandhi.* New York, NY: Basic Books.

Gillies, M. G. (1990). Bartok as pedagogue. *Studies in Music,* 24, 64-86.

Graf, M. (1947). *From Beethoven to Shostakovich: The psychology of the composing process.* New York, NY: Philosophical Library.

Hatrik, J. (2002). Priestor medzi komposiciou a hudobnou vychovou. [The space between composition and music education.] *Slovenská hudba: Revue pre hudobn_ kult_,* 28 (2), 189-199.

Hung, Y. C. (1998). An exploration of the musical composition background/experience, processes, and pedagogy of selected composers in Taiwan. Ph.D. thesis, Teacher's College, Columbia University.

Keiser, K. (1990). The Canadian Music Centre: A history/Centre de musique canadienne. In C. Morey (Ed.), *Celebration* (pp. 7-49). Toronto, ON: Canadian Music Centre.

Kim, K. (1995). *Studien zum musikpädagogischen Werk Paul Hindemiths.* [Studies on Paul Hindemth's work as a teacher.] Ph.D. dissertation, Ludwig-Maximilians-U., München, Germany.

Kratus, J. (1989). A time analysis of the compositional processes used by children ages 7 to 11. *Journal of Research in Music Education,* 37 (1), 5-20.

Krumhansl, C. L. (1991). Music psychology: Tonal structures in perception and memory. *Annual Review of Psychology,* 42 , 277-303.

Kulka, J. (1979). Psychological analysis of thinking in composing music. *Ceskoslovenska Psychologie,* 23 (2), 119-125.

Lerdahl, F. (1988). Cognitive constraints on compositional systems. In J. A. Sloboda (Ed.), *Generative processes in music: The psychology of performance, improvisation and composition* (pp. 231-259). Oxford, UK: Clarendon.

MacInnis, P. (1991). *Guidelist of Canadian solo free bass accordion music suitable for student performers.* Toronto, ON: Canadian Music Centre.

Macpherson, G. E. (1998). Creativity and music education. In B. Sudin, G. E. Macpherson, & L. Folkestat (Eds.), *Children composing: Research in music education.* Lund, Sweden: Lund University.

Markland, T. (1990). *Counterpoint: Fundamentals of music making.* New Haven, CT: Yale University Press.

Miell, D., & MacDonald, D. (2000). Children's creative collaborations: The importance of friendship when working together on a musical composition. *Social Development,* 9 (3), 348-369.

Nass, M. L. (1990). On hearing and inspiration in the composition of music. In S. Feder & R. L. Karmel (Eds.), *Psychoanalytic explorations in music* (pp. 179-193). Applied psychoanalyses series. Monograph No. 3. New York, NY: Routledge.

Newman, E. M. (1988). *An analysis of Canadian content in vocal music textbooks authorised by the Ontario Ministry of Education, 1846-1988.* M.A. thesis, Carleton University, Ottawa, Ontario, Canada.

Ottman, R. (1992). *Advanced harmony: Theory and practice.* (4th ed.). Englewood Cliffs, NJ: Prentice-Hall.

Paynter, J. (1982). *Music in the secondary school curriculum.* London, UK: Cambridge University Press.

Petsche, H., Richter, P., von Stein, A., & Etlinger, S. C. (1994). EEG coherence and musical thinking. *Music Perception,* 11 (2), 117-151.

Phillips, R. J., & Pierson, A. J. (1997). Cognitive loads and the empowering effect of music composition software. *Journal of Computer-Assisted Learning,* 13 (2), 74-94.

Reynolds, R. (2002). *Form and method: Composing music.* The Rothschild essays, edited by S. McAdams. New York, NY: Routledge.

Roberts, B. A. (1991). *Musician: A question of labelling.* St. John's, NF: Binder's Press.

Rochberg, G. (1988). *The aesthetics of survival: A composer's view of twentieth-century music.* Ann Arbour, MI: University of Michigan Press.

Ross, M. (1995). What's wrong with school music? *British Journal of Music Education,* 15 (3), 255-262.

Schafer, R. M. (1977). *The tuning of the world.* Toronto, ON: McClelland & Stewart.

Sessions, R. (1970). *Questions about music.* Cambridge, MA: Harvard University Press.

Shand, P. M. (1993). *A guide to published Canadian violin music suitable for student performers.* Toronto, ON: Canadian Music Centre.

Shand, P. M. (2004). Support for teaching Canadian music. *Canadian Music Educator,* 46 (2), 9.

Shand, P. M., & Bartel, L. R. (1998). Canadian content in music curriculum: Policy and practice. In B. A. Roberts (Ed.), *Connect, combine, communicate* (pp. 89-107). Sydney, NS: University College of Cape Breton.

Sloboda, J. A. (Ed.), *Generative processes in music: The psychology of performance, improvisation and composition.* Oxford, UK: Clarendon.

Sorenson, D., & Pearson, B. (1998). *Jazz ensemble method for group and individual instruction.* San Diego, CA: Neil A. Kjos.

Stravinski, I. (1947). *The poetics of music.* Toronto, ON: Random House.

Steenhuissen, P. (2000). *New Music for Young Musicians Project Report.* Toronto, ON: Canadian Music Centre.

Stubley, E. (1990). *A guide to solo French horn music by Canadian composers.* Toronto, ON: Canadian Music Centre.

Sulzer, F., & Schachter, C. (1989). *Counterpoint in composition: The study of voice leading.* New York, NY: Columbia University Press.

Upitis, R. (1992). *This too is music.* Portsmouth, NH: Heinemann.

Upitis, R. (1997). The craft of composition: Helping children create music with computer tools. *Psychomusicology,* 8 (2), 151-162.

Viera de Carvalho, M. (1999). New music between search for identity and autopoiesis: Or, the tragedy of listening. *Theory, Culture and Society,* 16 (4), 127-135.

Wallas, G. (1926). *The Art of Thought.* London, UK: C.A. Watts & Co.

Walker, R. (1997). Visual metaphors as music notation for sung vowel spectra in different cultures. *Journal of Music Research,* 26 (4), 315-345.

Walter, C. (1994). *A guide to unpublished Canadian jazz ensemble music suitable for student performers.* Toronto, ON: Canadian Music Centre.

Warburton, A. O. (1982). *Melody writing and analysis.* Essex, UK: Longman

Whitaker, N. L. (1994). The process of understanding: Protocol analysis and musical composition. ERIC ED370970.

Williams, E. (2001). Obsolescence and renewal: Musical heritage, electronic technology, education and the future. *International Journal of Music Education, 37,* 13-31.

Endnotes

[1] Composers writing musique concrète utilize environmental sounds in their compositions.

[2] There are 622 composers associated with the Centre (505 living and 117 deceased), and 16,075 musical scores housed in CMC libraries across Canada, of which 3,775 are published. There are 23 associate composers of the CMC in the Atlantic Region, 150 in Quebec, 183 in Ontario, 61 in the Prairies, and 88 in British Columbia. Details provided in an e-mail correspondence with Jason Van Eyk, Ontario Regional Director, August, 25, 2004.

[3] John Weinzweig and Louis Applebaum are among Canada's most senior composers. In 2003, Weinzweig celebrated his 90th birthday with a performance of his works at the National Arts Centre in Ottawa. Sadly, Louis Applebaum passed away in 2000 at the age of 82 at the outset of the New Music for Young Musicians Project.

[4] Throughout the text, the shortened version of the title – New Music Project – is employed as it was throughout the duration of the project.

[5] The evaluation component of the New Music for Young Musicians Project involved a different emphasis in each of the CMC regions. This chapter focuses on an evaluation study funded by the Ontario Region (with monies allocated from the Canada Council Millennium grant and the Ontario Arts Council) and the University of Ottawa. The first phase focused on a description of the problem and development of the research instruments (Andrews, 2004b). This chapter discusses the findings of the second phase of the research which focuses on the conceptualizing of new music for young musicians by employing an in-depth questionnaire. The third phase recounts the composers' responses to emerging questions (refer to Andrews, 2005b, forthcoming), and the fourth phase reviews the refinements to compositions undertaken in rehearsals and performances (refer to Andrews, 2005c, in press).

[6] Canada is the second largest country (land mass) in the world after Russia. It consists of ten provinces and three territories. Ontario is located in central Canada, and it is the country's most populous province. Within Canada, 11 million of 31 million Canadians live in Ontario, 2.6 million children attend elementary and secondary schools, and they are taught by 130,000 teachers. The nation's largest city, Toronto, and its capital, Ottawa, are located in the province.

[7] Due to the small number of commissioned composers engaged in the New Music Project from the Atlantic region, the three composers from this region were invited to join the Ontario contingent. Twenty-four commissioned composers from the Ontario (21 of 27) and Atlantic regions (3 of 3) completed the in-depth questionnaire (16 males/8 females).

[8] Many thanks to Michelle Pajot and Laurie Graves, both graduate students, who assisted me with the project. The findings of the questionnaire were initially reported by the author at the Florida Music Educators Association (FMEA) Conference in Tampa, Florida in January, 2001.

SECTION 3:

QUESTIONING WHAT IS EXPECTED OF TEACHERS AND HOW WE TEACH THEM

Eric Shieh & Colleen Conway
Professional Induction: Programs And Policies For Beginning Music Teachers

Joseph Shively
In The Face Of Tradition: Questioning The Roles Of Conductors And Ensemble Members In School Bands, Choirs, And Orchestras

Susan Dill Bruenger
Teaching The Masses Or Coaching The Elite: A Comparison Of The Challenges Facing High School Music And Sports Educators

CHAPTER TWELVE

Professional Induction: Programs and Policies for Beginning Music Teachers

ERIC SHIEH & COLLEEN CONWAY

Abstract

A number of music educators and researchers have pointed to an apparent lack of change in approaches to music education over the course of the profession's history, despite large shifts in pedagogical approaches elsewhere. "Professional Induction" interrogates the degree to which the programs created to support beginning music teachers and the experiences common to these teachers restrict the degree to which a new teacher can engage in reflection and effect such change. The failure of many beginning music teacher support systems to promote critical reflection, we contend, directly affects the profession's ability to respond to concerns raised by the teaching profession at large, especially with regards to multicultural and critical practice. While we identify possible solutions centering on greater opportunities for dialogue both within in-service and mentoring programs, as well as among beginning teachers and students, most of our proposals are geared toward the development of teacher self-identities in and a greater awareness of educational contexts during pre-service teacher education.

Introduction

In the past several years beginning teacher mentoring and induction have become common topics for research and scholarship in American education (American Federation of Teachers, 2001; Darling-Hammond, 2003; Feiman-Nemser, 2003; Ingersoll & Smith, 2003; and National Commission on Teaching and America's Future, 2003). Many recent studies from around the world suggest that solid induction programs and strong mentor relationships contribute to the retention and success of beginning teachers (Bubb, Totterdell, & Earley, 2003; Conway, 2002; Feiman-Nemser, Schwille, Carver, & Yusko, 1999; Gold, 1996; Kester & Marockie, 1987; Paine, 2000; and Watt & Richardson, 2003). In the United States, England, and Australia the interest in the treatment of beginning teachers is a result of recent policies that require school districts to provide an induction and/or mentor program for beginning teachers. Several researchers have begun to examine the music education implications of beginning teacher programs and policies (Conway, Krueger, Robinson, Haack, and Smith, 2002).

Roughly parallel to the growth of interest in beginning teacher mentoring and induction has been a growth of interest in multicultural education and, in strong connection to it, critical pedagogy (Apple, 2000; Giroux, 1997; hooks 1994, 2003; Kanpol & McLaren, 1995; McLaren 1997, 1998, 1999; *Multicultural Education* Journal, begun in 1993). Central to both is the claim that education is not politically neutral, but instead tied to the agendas of certain groups of people, perhaps a particular race or class, or a group with a particular vision of society. Since the 1970s, but especially in the last decade for music education, an increasing number of educators and theorists have, with increasing urgency, called for a kind of education conscious of the politics hidden not only in what is explicitly taught, but also in how it is taught. Multicultural education and critical pedagogy, with their commitment to social change, require that an educator possess the ability to reflect critically upon the consequences of current practices and perhaps generate new practices which, for example, may prove more liberatory where others have been oppressive.

At the juncture between these two movements, the call for reflective practice and the desire to build stronger programs for beginning teachers, stands the word "induction." Used explicitly to refer to the varied support programs for a beginning teacher or simply the time of transition when teachers are moving from teacher preparation to teaching practice, the word "induction" also carries with it a sense of initiating someone or something into a practice already in existence. In other words, the idea of induction into the teaching profession presumes that the teaching profession exists as something to be uncovered rather than created. This reified idea of the profession at best encompasses the current practices of whoever is doing the inducting or, worse, encompasses all the stereotypes of what a "teacher" is. In both cases, the capacity of the beginning teacher to generate new practices or reflect upon current practices has been preempted. In most induction programs for music educators, this is exactly what happens, and we will suggest here, along with possible solutions, that in the profession's effort to support beginning music teachers it often robs them of the opportunity to make change both inside the profession as well as society at large.

Induction and Mentor Programs and Policies

Although there are many studies of beginning teachers (not necessarily of music), not all of these studies attend to issues of reflective practice when describing beginning teacher experiences. In fact, some of the information provided to policy-makers comes from studies funded and designed by educational corporations whose primary interest in beginning teachers is retention (i.e. Salzman, 2000; Henderson-Sparks, Tracz, & Quisenberry, 2003). These designs rarely consider teaching context or attempt to capture the "voice" of the beginning teacher; much of the research is conducted with an eye towards creating "how-to" suggestions for teachers working in mentor and induction programs (Gordon & Maxey, 2000; MacDonald & Healy, 1999; Moffatt & Moffatt, 2003; Wilke, 2003; Wong & Wong, 1998).

Some of the beginning teacher scholarship however has been carefully approached with attention to teacher voice (Bullough, 1989, 1997; Kowalski, Weaver, & Henson, 1994), development of teacher identity (Britzman, 2003; Bullough, Knowles, & Crow, 1989; Danielewitz, 2001; Kuzmic, 1994; and Vinz 2001), and reflective practice (Clift, Houston, & Pugach, 1990; Feiman-Nemser, 1983, 2000; and Schon, 1983, 1987). Several of these authors express concern regarding the role of induction policy in creating an environment for the reflective growth of the teacher. Feiman-Nemser, Schwille, Carver and

Yusko (1999) suggest: "When induction is narrowly defined as short-term support to help teachers survive their first year on the job, its role in fostering quality teaching and learning is diminished. What happens to beginning teachers during their early years on the job determines not only whether they will stay in teaching but also what kind of teacher they will become (p. 6). If the induction process only helps novices fit into schools as they are, then it serves as a force for continuity rather than change, a way of maintaining the status quo rather than a means of changing it (p. 20).

Both retention-driven studies and reflective practice inquires have led to induction program policies and designs in various part of the United States. Of concern to music education is that few of the general induction reports discuss the experiences of beginning music teachers. It has not been clear from general induction studies whether music teachers are served by any of the types of induction programs.

Induction and Mentor Programs in Music Education

In reaction to this concern that experiences of music teachers have not been examined in general induction research, there have been several studies of induction and mentor programs in music education. The Music Educators National Conference publication *Great Beginnings for Music Teachers: Mentoring and Supporting New Music Teachers* (Conway, 2003a) provides an overview of all of the published studies of mentoring and induction in music education in the United States. While many of these studies used such techniques as narrative inquiry (Conway & Garlock, 2002; Conway and Zerman, 2004, ethnography (Krueger, 1996, 1999, 2000, 2001), case study design (Montague, 2000; Smith, 1994) or phenomenological approaches (Conway, 2001, 2003) to capture the voice of the beginning teacher, none approached the study of beginning music teachers critically—that is, none sought to uncover the biases, assumptions, and social consequences implicit in the programs and policies constructed for these teachers. These concerns, as well as a concern over the degree to which the so-called "induction phase" may restrict the beginning music teacher from making change within a potentially oppressive teaching paradigm, are central to this examination.

The First Years: Pointed In the Same Direction

Irrespective of induction and mentoring programs, the music education profession is marked by a number of characteristics that restrict the degree to which a beginning music teacher can even begin to engage in reflective or critical practice. Most immediately, these teachers find the first few years of teaching to be overwhelming, and respond by engaging in a "survival mode" mentality. Conway and Zerman (2004) report from their interviews with beginning teachers: "Is overwhelmedness a word? It is now 6:00 and I just got home" (8-27-00) and "I swear I am on an emotional roller coaster with this job. Yesterday I was in tears thinking I just want out now and never teach again. Today, I just don't know" (9-11-00), or "I hate being like this. I normally can find the positive in my life no matter what is going on, but that's getting more difficult. Especially on Sunday nights. . . . I absolutely dread going back" (10-22-00).

This sense of being overwhelmed typically stems from a perception of the permanence or inevitability of current music structures, which the beginning teacher works to accommodate himself or herself too. In the case of the teacher above, when asked what she believed to be the reasons for her frustrations, she responded: "My evaluations are very public; I have to deal with larger sums of money coming from more sources than a classroom teacher; and I have so many outside of school requirements (festivals, trips, fundraisers, etc)" (Conway & Zerman, 2004). Likewise, many beginning music teachers cite performance pressure, community expectations for high festival scores, and student and parent expectations of extensive travel as causes of stress:

> I hate teaching to a concert. Got to look for a new job (first year teaching interview, 2000)

> Band festival is one of the more stressful times of the school year for me. Stressors include parent and community expectations, differing philosophies on festival, past festival experiences, future reputation of the program and, most importantly the emotional state of the students. The stress can also be connected to the various ways that people view festival and its purposes. Is it a competition? In the eyes of many parents, students, and administrators, and teachers, the answer is yes. (beginning teacher in Conway, 2003, p. 183)

Notice in each of the cases, the teacher speaks of the "job" as something unchangeable. Indeed, one teacher goes so far as to declare she must either teach "to a concert" or "look for a new job." Changing the values and practices of the status quo or recreating the expectations of the students, parents, and school are options lost to the pressures of the first few years. These constructs of the profession are further reified by a lack of time and difficulties with time management. The "traditions underpinning education and music education are often seen as immutable," writes Andrea Rose (1998, p. 26), "because music teachers and interns are seldom prepared, encouraged, or given the time and space to be analytical or reflective." Indeed, teachers in their early years often suggest that the time required for such duties as the administration of travel or the paperwork associated with high-stakes performances make it difficult to plan for teaching or to reflect on the teaching and learning process (Conway, 2001).

Nor does more experience in the job necessarily lead to an ability to alter the status quo. Looking over Colleen's interviews with music teachers into their fifth year of teaching, we are concerned that some of the teachers appear to have "survived" the initial stage, but settled into a groove of teaching their second year for the rest of their career. For example, "last year I was just getting everything figured out," notes one second-year teacher in Conway (2001). "Now I am ready to start teaching." Or, more recently, several of these teachers have expressed contentment with their situation, having been reconciled to issues that had previously been of primary concern:

> I feel pretty much like I know what I'm doing now. The concerts are going well and people seem happy. (elementary music teacher, phone interview, Spring 2003)

> I feel like I have been very successful here. We got a "I" at state festival last year so I'm starting to think – OK – I'm set. (middle school band teacher, phone interview, Spring 2003)

An essential component to teacher growth that seems to have been obstructed by the pressures of the first few years is dialogue. In his *A Pedagogy for Liberation* (1987), Paulo Freire argues that "through dialogue, reflecting together on what we know and don't know, we can then act critically to transform reality" (p. 99). Where the beginning music teacher might recreate teaching practices by engaging in mutual dialogue with the students, parents, or school administration, this rarely happens. Instead, most often the classroom is marked by what Freire calls "narrative" or "banking" education, wherein the teacher conflates his or her professional authority with authority to all knowledge in the classroom, positioning the students as empty vessels to be filled by his or her mono-logue (2000, p. 71-73). Perhaps Roberta Lamb (1995) articulates this most clearly for the performance-based music classroom when she writes that "[musical] performance is about control by a master, a conductor, usually male, usually white" (p. 126). So long as the beginning teacher takes this stance, sanctioned by tradition, dialogue with the students becomes impossible and the effects of his or her teaching are lost in silence. Yet if the beginning teacher rejects this model of education, he or she stands the risk of being considered ignorant of his or her subject matter.

Likewise, engaging in dialogue with others outside of the classroom, such as parents or school administrators, is also difficult. In her book *Practice Makes Practice* (2003), Britzman uncovers a number of myths that plague beginning teachers in their quests for legitimate, non-beginning "teacher" identities, among them the myths that "teachers are self-made" (p. 230) or "experience is the best teacher" (p. 30). Dialogue, then, becomes perceived by beginning teachers as a sign of weakness—an action that real teachers do not engage in. Thus, in her study of music education students, Beynon (1998) finds a number of students articulating that "they would learn to become teachers by *doing* it . . . that they would just know what to do by instinct when the time came" (p. 93, italics mine). The act of teaching becomes positioned from the outset as a reactive, almost passive act, and concerns of making change or envisioning new possibilities fade into the background.

A final, perhaps less apparent kind of dialogue largely inaccessible to beginning music teachers is the dialogue between music teachers and teachers of other subjects, as well as music education researchers and researchers of education in general. The marginalization of music as a subject in places of teaching and learning has created a culture of music educators and researchers who by and large view their profession as unique and separate from other teaching professions, guarding their autonomy and traditions not without some degree of resentment. Earlier we noted the lack of research in music teacher training informed by critical theory, despite its clear relevance to our field and its prevalence in general education research over the past few decades. Likewise, O'Toole's (2000) assertion that despite recent work in feminism and cultural studies "only music education hesitates to recognize them as crucial sites of inquiry" (p. 29), or Norman's (1999) seeming puzzlement over the "virtual lack of similar debate [over multiculturalism] within music education" (p. 37), and Bowman's (1998) statement that "in light of this interpretive turn toward plurality, diversity, and relativity [in contemporary philosophy], it is interesting to note the extent to which music education's philosophical and professional literature continues to embrace assumptions of absoluteness, universality, and uniformity" (p.136). Bresler (2002), indeed, notes that even in highly collaborative environments, music teachers seem to take the attitude that "unlike other disciplines, music could not or should not be integrated into the rest of the curriculum" (p. 17). So long as music education remains isolated from the teaching profession and research community at large, it seems change will happen slowly, if at all.

Additionally, the marginalization of music as a subject restricts the range of a music teacher's practices in another important way. In his essay "Educating Musically" (2002), Wayne Bowman argues that the advocacy efforts to persuade others of music education's worth tend to privilege what he calls "intrinsic," or "properly music" values over extrinsic, or extramusical ones (p. 65). In this scheme, the "music" in music education is highlighted in the search for uniqueness, and educational aims such as multiculturalism or democracy, or indeed any educational aims in general, become extra-musical and exiled from the classroom. One only needs to look at the *Music Educators Journal's* declaration of the "Objectives of Music Education" in 1997, or the National Standards for Music Education, all of which are intrinsically musical, to get a sense of what Bowman speaks of. Indeed, in Austin's (1999) study of pre-service music teachers' beliefs regarding the value of music education, such things as "helps student find meaning in world" or "develops good citizenship habits" scored lowest in the questionnaire, while "provides for well-rounded education" or "means of self-expression" stood at the top of the list (p. 24). But if a beginning music teacher is restricted to teaching only that which is intrinsically musical as a means of affirming his or her profession, then only the traditional performance-based classroom and a handful of other models must suffice. "This is an undervalued profession," notes a first-year teacher "We are constantly reminded that we are not as important as those subject areas which appear on the state tests." (Conway, 2004).

It becomes clear through this examination of the competing pressures and politics assaulting beginning music teachers that some sort of intervention is needed in order to enable beginning teachers to engage in reflective practice and create change in the profession.

In-Service and Mentoring Programs: Irrelevant or Impotent?

Professional support for the beginning music teacher comes largely from two sources: in-service programs sponsored by either the school district or state, and mentoring programs. Both suffer from many of the same concerns noted earlier: a lack of dialogue and a tendency to further the isolation of the beginning music teacher—characteristics which will again make reflective practice and change difficult. Over the course of the discussion on these induction programs, we will also use the concerns of multicultural education as a further lens through which to problematize these programs.

Colleen has written elsewhere that "many beginning music teacher induction workshops are set up like mini-music education conferences. Several experienced teachers are brought in to tell beginning teachers how to be good teachers" (2003, p. 59). Most in-service programs are, indeed, a kind of schooling for teachers, frequently with workshops focused on such topics as classroom management, assessment, or instructional strategies (Conway 2003, p. 35). A number of beginning music teachers have spoken of their frustrations with the "stand and deliver" format of these workshops when they have not been content-specific. For example, one beginning teacher noted that when he would ask questions relevant to the music classroom, such as "How do you manage a class of one hundred beginning instrumentalists who do not have any skills and yet are meeting all together for 'band'?" the typical reply would be "I really don't know anything about music" (Conway 2003, p. 37). Notice that the reply does not attempt to answer the question or even engage the beginning teacher in dialogue; the workshop typically brings in "experts" to speak about predetermined topics. In the case above, the lack of dialogue raises a concern about relevance.

However, even in cases where the workshops are specific to music educators, relevance is not guaranteed. In a number of her interviews with beginning teachers, Colleen noticed concerns with gender, sexuality, race, and religion that she found difficult to find a place for in mainstream music education journals. For example:

> "I have had to learn how to play the "female high school band director role." Most of the old guys are harmless, but I do get a lot of comments like 'she's such an energetic, pretty young thing.' Yuk." (high school band director in her third year)

> I saw my first pride sticker on a car today when driving to the mentor training session. It comforted me a great deal. I was afraid that there were not any visible gays in this town who were not student-age. Regardless, I'm pretty scared about being gay, alone, and without professional support—it's occupying my mind a great deal. (first year teacher)

> I have been getting a lot of heat from the parents regarding going to the Catholic Church. Everyone in this town is Catholic and one parent even told me if I thought I was going to get support from the town for the band I better convert to Catholicism. Yikes. (band director in his first year)

These concerns may not have to do with classroom management or instructional strategies, but they are clearly meaningful and relevant. Yet without dialogue, there is no place for beginning teachers to articulate these kinds of problems. Relevance, however, is not the only concern that arises from the lack of dialogue in beginning music teacher support systems.

In her book *Teaching Selves* (2001), Jane Danielewicz argues for the need of dialogue in the construction of individual teacher identities, stating that "dialogue creates the self ('what I think'), generates knowledge or understanding (the content, ideas, shared meaning), and constitutes the other ('what she thinks')" (p. 145). By creating a hierarchy between the experienced teachers who speak and the beginning teachers who listen, regardless of the relevance of the information transferred, the in-service workshops suppress the "teacher" identity of a beginning teacher. The teaching profession becomes reified, positioned as a pre-existing construction beginning teachers must adapt to in order to acquire their teaching identities. Rather than working with experienced teachers in solidarity, with the goal of constructing meaningful teaching practices, beginning teachers are restricted from making change. This becomes even more problematic for music teachers in a general education induction workshop for whom the instructional strategies may not be particularly useful. In this instance, the disconnect serves to estrange the music teacher further from the rest of the established teaching profession, adding to the sense of isolation discussed earlier.

In reviewing numerous comments from beginning teachers regarding these workshops, we also find concern in the apparent focus of these workshops on "best practice": "there was a lot of emphasis on 'best practices' procedures," notes one beginning teacher, "some of which are not applicable to all aspects of music learning" (Conway and Zerman, 2004). But not only are so-called "best practices" not applicable to the diverse aspects of music learning, they may also not be applicable to certain students, teachers, geographical locations, or even periods of history. And yet, as Bowman (1998) has noted, this kind of thinking—that there are universal, established methods to teaching certain things—continues to predominate the music education profession and often keeps the profession from changing.

Doubtless such an attitude is responsible for the continued assumption in most music education research and among music educators that multicultural education in the music classroom is somehow equivalent to the teaching of world music (Legette, 2003; Norman, 1999), or at best the teaching of such music in its socio-cultural contexts (Campbell, 2002; Walker, 2000). However, in this version of multicultural education, as a kind of glorified aesthetic education, differences between cultures are held as absolute and depoliticized, as if all world music coexisted peaceably—cultural artifacts to be studied independently from the realities of oppression and racism, concerns of tolerance and diversity, or experiences of the students and teacher. "Diversity that somehow constitutes itself as a harmonious ensemble of benign cultural spheres," argues McLaren (1995), "subscribe[s] to a form of social amnesia in which we forget that all knowledge is forged in histories that are played out in the field of social antagonisms" (in Steinberg, p. 141). In this sense, multiculturalism as it is commonly understood in the music classroom is not multicultural education at all in so far as it ignores its goals or intent, but instead is a reduction of multicultural education into a teaching method that can be transferred via an in-service workshop.

In contrast, leading writers on multicultural education outside of the field of music education such as Peter McLaren, Henry Giroux, or bell hooks, have continually argued that multicultural education begins where "best practice" approaches end. "Many teachers are disturbed by the political implications of a multicultural education," writes hooks (1994), "because they fear losing control in a classroom where there is no one way to approach a subject—only multiple ways and multiple references" (p. 35-6). A true multicultural education must be prepared to respond to the context of the classroom situation, to interrogate students' perspectives upon questions of race and class, gender and sexuality, and respond to them and work through them. Likewise, Giroux (1997) argues that teachers need "to explore zones of cultural difference by moving in and out of the resources, histories, and narratives that provide different students with a sense of identity, place, and possibility" (p. 252). However, in this kind of education, the problems that will arise in the classroom cannot easily be foreseen and "taught" in a workshop. Instead, dialogue is needed, wherein beginning teachers can bring in their concerns and talk over and through them.

Given the absence of this kind of space, it is probably not coincidental that in Glenda Moss's study (2001) of beginning teachers' responses to a course in multicultural education, the one music teacher in the study stands out in his rejection of a critical stance towards multiculturalism. "I was taught how to teach band," she quotes him as saying. "I approach a band the same way I approached it when I first stepped in front of a band. I teach it the same way" (p. 10). If the in-service programs continually focus on what can be taught, rather than what can happen in the process of teaching, such goals as multicultural education or reflective practice will be lost.

In contrast to in-service programs, one might expect mentoring programs, which pair a beginning music teacher with an experienced teacher (music or not), to generate dialogue and promote reflective practice. Unfortunately, in our examination of the interactions between mentors and mentees, this has not been the case. Instead, in most cases the information is one-way: the experienced mentor provides information to the inexperienced mentee so that the mentee can be successful in the short term. For example:

> Would you be able to come over some time this week and we can have a meeting with the agenda of checking to make sure I haven't over programmed for band festival? (email from first-year teacher to her mentor, 1-21-01) (Conway & Zerman, 2004)

> The interview with Tavia's mentor highlighted many of the issues which seem to make beginning teaching hard for music teachers. . . . He suggested that one of the most difficult things he has observed is that beginning music teachers cannot have all they need to know "in their head." He shared that "I still carry around my fingering charts that I bought for methods class in 1973." (Conway & Zerman, 2004)

Both these quotes suggest that mentees tend to restrict their relationship with their mentors to strictly factual questions—questions seemingly independent from context that can be asked without much information from the beginning teacher. Administrative duties, classroom management, parent interactions, or building and district policies head the list of topics discussed with mentors, while "very few of the beginning teachers said that they spoke to mentors about curricular issues" (Conway 2003, p. 77). Robinson (2003) suggests a reason for this which is reminiscent of Britzman's idea of the myth that teachers are self-made: "Many teachers are reluctant to share their problems or admit self-perceived weaknesses, believing them to be signs of weakness or incompetence and that 'good teachers' work these problems out on their own" (p. 133). If this is the case, then even though conversation is taking place, dialogue is not. Indeed, Colleen's examination of beginning music teachers and their mentors reveals that the mentees with non-music mentors found their mentors less valuable than those with music mentors (2003, p. 74), indicating that larger teaching issues outside of the content area are probably not being discussed.

Again, the implicit hierarchy between "beginning teacher" and "experienced teacher" come into play here as well, as they do in in-service workshops.

> I am hesitant to ask one of the Michigan School Band and Orchestra Association mentor teachers to come watch me teach. I mean, those guys are pretty much the same retired teachers who will then judge my groups in solo and ensemble and large ensemble festival at the end of the year. I just don't want to show my weaknesses months before they will judge me. (first year band director, Conway, 2004)

Where the mentee-mentor relationship could serve as a place for discussion, it often becomes a testing ground where beginning teachers feel they must prove their worth. There are, however, exceptions to this, and Robinson (2003), based on his experience as the music coordinator of the well-funded and elaborate Beginning Educator Support and Training (BEST) program in Connecticut, argues that "mentoring can be a powerful means for passing on the traditions and techniques of a profession or can be used as a forum for critical reflection on one's practice" (p. 133). However, currently mentoring programs are by and large so inconsistent and their expectations so ill-defined as to make the latter a rarity (Conway 2003, p. 69).

Proposals

From this examination of the programs and policies that await the beginning music teacher, it becomes clear that without significant preparation in pre-service, as well as changes in the support systems for beginning teachers in their first few years, it would be difficult for any beginning teacher to survive the onslaught of status-quo programs and policies that await them in the profession. Below we outline a number of proposals geared towards the development of critical reflection in beginning teachers.

Pre-service

In its current focus toward providing students with the music teaching skills a beginning teacher would need to survive the status quo, preservice teacher education has effectively silenced the students' abilities to combat the onslaught of status-quo programs and policies that await them in the profession. Where most college professors would state that they believe in the concept of the "reflective practitioner" (Schon, 1987), few currently utilize approaches to teacher education that might foster growth in this direction. The challenge for music teacher education and teacher educators, then, is to supply these necessary skills while simultaneously providing students with the means to develop their own teacher self-identities and engage in reflective practice.

An initial solution that has been explored to a limited degree in the past has been the use of alternatives to the traditional lecture-discussion approach to teaching and its variants (Apfelstadt, 1996; Barry, 1996; Conway, 1997a; and Wing, 1993, 1994). Such approaches, many of which have been documented by research in general teacher education though not music teacher education, might include the use of case studies (Atterbury 1994; Conway, 1997b, 1999a, 1999b; Lind, 2001; Robbins, 1993), teaching metaphors (Thomspon and Campbell, 2003), reflexive journals (Atterbury, 1994; Gromko, 1995; Robbins, 1993), professional development schools (Conklin & Henry, 1999, 2002; Henry, 2001; and Townsend, 2000), portfolios (Berg & Lind, 2003); and cultural immersion (Emmanuel, 2003).

As the lack of research of these alternatives in music teacher education might suggest, we have observed that often the students who pursue studies outside music are also those that take an interest in critical pedagogy and come to realize their individual teacher self-identities most fully. In Eric's case, mirrored in the experiences of a number of his colleagues, he was introduced first to critical theory in his pursuit of an English degree, and subsequently applied his work in materialist and multicultural literary theory to music and music education. Because of music education's insistence on its uniqueness, often this kind of work becomes near impossible for most students, and the critical "outside" perspective a student might gain from work across disciplines—or simply access to multiple perspectives—is lost.

In encouraging interdisciplinary pursuits, not to mention independent projects, the teacher education classroom becomes less a space marked by the transfer of status quo knowledge from teacher to students, but a space marked by the intersection of distinct individuals who overlap in their interest of music education. In downplaying the uniqueness of music education, general educational concerns as well as individual stu-

dent ideas can be given voice. Again, Paulo Freire's conception of dialogue as foundational to change surfaces: in this situation, allowing and encouraging multiple perspectives provides an interaction through which assumptions in the profession can be
uncovered and new ideas tested. Likewise, Danielewicz (2001) has argued that this kind
of exchange is fundamental to the construction of individual teacher identity (p. 145).

Similarly, much can be gained through a more scholarly approach to the undergraduate
music program. While the study of critical theory or education philosophy has proved
invaluable to the handful of students mentioned earlier who have stumbled upon these
fields, most programs in music education focus heavily on developing musicianship
(lessons, ensembles, conducting, theory, history, secondary instruments) and music
teacher skills (elementary and secondary methods, instrumental and choral methods). A
number of researchers have suggested that undergraduate students would benefit from
additional emphasis on music education philosophy as well as more opportunities for
study outside of music (Kahrs, 1992; Palmer, 1995; and Parr, 1996).

Other means of promoting reflective practice might take place through changes in the
practicum component of the music teacher education program. Based on the Holmes
Group recommendations in the early 90's (Holmes Group, 1986, 1990), many College of
Education programs in the United States now require a five-year undergraduate or a five-
year with masters degree teacher certification model. These programs typically allow for
an extended fieldwork (one year) experience in place of the 14-week student teaching
component that is most common in music education programs. Some of these models
require a four-year undergraduate degree in a content area before the formal teacher education begins (more like a Canadian model). Although few music programs in the United
States embrace the extended fieldwork model, we believe that this model may better
facilitate reflective growth. The vast majority of the states in the U.S. support a K-12
music certification model, and in the effort alone to ensure the skills needed to support
such broad range of instruction are developed, time for reflective growth suffers.

Of course, given the difficulty many teacher educators have in finding appropriate sites
for a 14-week student teaching (appropriate meaning that the teacher in the field models
reflective teaching practices), finding sites for an entire year would be even more challenging. However, researchers in general teacher education who support the extended
fieldwork model (Holmes Group, 1995) suggest that in a year-long student teaching
experience the beginning teacher is forced to grapple with many of the issues that he/she
often faces in the first years (i.e. the program is overly focused on performance, colleagues are not interested in anything beyond the status quo). When this struggle
occurs while the student is still connected to the University, a student is able to work
through the struggle more successfully than is possible during the "survival mode" of the
first years of teaching.

We also suggest in relation to the practicum component of a teacher education that the
possibility of field work in places outside of the traditional public school arena, such as
prisons, hospitals, homeless shelters, inner-city schools, open schools, or schools in other
countries, be explored. Most four-year colleges have programs that connect students
with such institutions, but by and large music students and music-related initiatives
have not played a large role in them, in part due, no doubt, to the mentality of music

education's uniqueness and its potential inapplicability to such work. On the contrary, the handful of examples of this work, such as Music and Social Change initiative at the University of Michigan, which works with the Prison Creative Arts Project to place music students into prisons to teach, appear to be successful in promoting critical reflection. One such student reflects:

> It's funny—I had been trying so hard to make sure there wasn't a dull moment . . . I had kind of been talking over the silences and leading the generation of the piece. I realized when Sally and I finally shut up that much of the workshop had been a guessing game of where Sally and I were "going" – and thus some people were confused about what had been going on. In a sense we had been silencing the workshop participants. How easy it was to fall back on and get forced into this kind of work! But once we stood back and showed we had no more idea than they, well, they took charge. 'I feel you've been trying to orchestrate this thing' said one of the guys to me in the middle of the discussion. 'We should be doing it.' How embarrassing. And how right. . . . In a way, learning begins where the teaching ends.

For the student involved in such work, the context for music education is highlighted and the student is often forced to grapple with questions related not only to approaches to teaching, but also to music's worth and relevance in each situation. Indeed, experience with alternative models of education and work in comparative education allow students to recognize and re-evaluate the politics and hidden assumptions in all educational situations, an important component to reflective practice. Instead of the traditional public school arena for education serving as a model for all education, it becomes another context with its own kinds of people and practices to consider.

A final proposal centers on the concept of action research or teacher research. Rideout and Feldman (2002) suggest:

> Action research can be thought of as an extension of the reflective practitioner movement. It, too, has become a common part of teacher education programs. For the purposes of this discussion, we define action research as systematic inquiry by practitioners to improve teaching and learning... Clearly, action research has had little impact on research in music education and music student teaching even though its potential contributions were expounded 30 years ago. (p. 881)

Preservice and inservice programs that introduce teachers to the possibilities of action research may help foster an environment of inquiry necessary for reflective teaching (Conway, 2000; Conway & Jeffers, in press; Leglar & Collay, 2002; Regelski, 1994; and Robbins, 1993). If teachers view themselves as the "doers" of research, the hierarchy between public schools and higher education can begin to soften.

In-service and mentoring

Where most of the relationships forged in the induction stage are inherently hierarchical—relationships between beginning teachers and experienced mentors or administrators, we would argue that beginning teachers are also in need of dialogical relationships which would allow them to construct their identity as a teacher and foster their sense of agency. Only when they can claim this identity of "teacher" instead of teachers-to-be or uninitiated teachers (only when "teacher" rather than "beginning" is emphasized in "beginning teacher"), can beginning teachers begin to make change within the profession. In this sense, interactions among beginning teachers, and especially beginning music teachers must be fostered. Where most induction programs currently pass on status-quo knowledge and skills, these same programs might also be used to create a space where beginning teachers can discuss concerns not only with respect to their position in the classroom, but their position in relation to the rest of the school.

Of course, in many schools, beginning teachers often network without the need for established programs. However, in a situation where the school system has constructed a claim as to who can be identified as a teacher (as opposed to a beginning teacher), it can prove tremendously difficult for any beginning teacher to usurp that claim without recognition on the part of the school of their presence in the profession. Though conversation between beginning teachers is no guarantee that they will constitute themselves within the profession and empower each other to make change, it is certainly a step in that direction.

Along these same lines, dialogue between teachers and students over educational issues can only serve to strengthen teacher identity and build a foundation for reflective practice. While we certainly acknowledge that many teachers have already made a commitment to critical pedagogy, we stress that the relationship is dialogic, and the active participation of students in their education also furthers reflective practice on the part of the teacher. When students are given a voice, the educational context is emphasized and the teacher is called upon to reflect and re-evaluate the content and methods of his or her teaching in a way productive to both students and teachers. A handful of music educators and music education philosophers have suggested models for music classrooms in which this kind of dialogue can take place, to varying degrees of complexity (Bowman, 2002; DeLorenzo, 2003; O'Toole, 2002).

Beginning music teachers who wish to explore these models for their music classrooms will need a forum for discussing this work. It would be rare for a beginning teacher to have experienced such democratic music classrooms in their own school music experience, their university performance classes, or their student teaching. Current mentor programs rarely provide an opportunity for a beginning music teacher to dialogue regarding processes of music teaching and learning since most of them set-up a "novice" and "expert" hierarchy where the expect feels pressure to tell the novice what to do.

Most of our suggested solutions focus on the pre-service experiences of music teachers. If young teachers do not enter into their beginning years of teaching with some awareness and curiosity regarding issues of critical pedagogy and reflective practice it may be difficult for them to acquire this interest in the early years of teaching. Of course, professional development of music teachers throughout their careers should be a concern of the profession and the need for attention to critical pedagogy in this phase should not be overlooked.

Conclusion

In her novel *China Men*, Maxine Hong Kingston writes of one teacher's experience in a classroom: "They boys were forcing him to turn literature into a weapon against them"

(p. 37). As she recreates the myth and memory of Chinese immigration to the United States, in both its triumph and injustice, Kingston returns continuously to education as a place both for change or, here, oppression. The distinction, as many educators, theorists, and writers such as Kingston have argued, lies in the teacher's capacity to reflect on and change his or her practice in order to ensure that the classroom becomes a space for possibility rather than inevitability.

Throughout this examination, we have suggested that so-called induction programs, in their desire to support beginning teachers, often take part in a larger professional and social paradigm that curbs reflective practice and change. It is important, however, that we emphasize here that our goal is not the termination of these programs, or to propose an end to all the "tried and true" practices currently being employed within the music education profession. Instead, we call for a recontextualization of these programs into a larger picture, one that recognizes the need for dialogue, for solidarity, and for the acknowledgment of multiplicity in the voices of beginning teachers and students. Thus, current practices will still hold weight in the sense that they have been "tried," but their truth will be reinvented for new students, new teachers, and better times.

References

Apple, Michael W. (2000). *Official knowledge: Democratic education in a conservative age, 2nd edition.* New York: Routledge.
American Federation of Teachers (2001). Beginning teacher induction: The essential bridge. *Educational Issues Policy Brief,* No. 13.
Austin, James R. and Deborah Reinhardt (1999). Philosophy and advocacy: An examination of preservice music teachers' beliefs. *Journal of research in music education,* 47(1), 18-30.
Apfelstadt, Hilary. (1996). Keys to successful teacher education. *Journal of Music Teacher Education,* 5 (2), 4-5.
Atterbury, Betty. W. (1994). Developing reflective music educators. *Journal of Music Teacher Education,* 4 (1), 6-12.
Barry, Nancy. (1996). Promoting reflective practice in an elementary music methods course. *Journal of Music Teacher Education,* 5 (2), 6-13.
Beynon, Carol (1998). From music student to music teacher: Negotiating an identity. *Studies in music from the University of Western Ontario,* 17, 83-105.
Berg, Margaret. H., & Lind, Vicki. R. (2003). Preservice music teacher electronic portfolios: Integrating reflection and technology. *Journal of Music Teacher Education,* 12 (2), 18-28.
Bowman, Wayne (1998). Universals, relativism, and music education. *Bulletin of the council for research in music education, 1998,* 1-20.
Bowman, Wayne (2002). Educating musically. In Richard Colwell and Carol Richardson (Eds.), *The New Handbook of Research on Music Teaching and Learning: A Project of the Music Educators National Conference* (pp. 63-84). Oxford: Oxford University Press, 2002.
Bresler, Liora (2002). Out of the trenches: The joys (and risks) of cross-disciplinary collaborations. *Bulletin of the council for research in music education,* 152, 17-39.
Britzman, Deborah P. (2003). *Practice makes practice: A critical study of learning to teach, revised edition.* Albany: State University of New York.
Bubb, Sara A., Totterdell, M., & Earley, P. (Institute of Education, University of London) (2003).Accountability and control: "Rogue" principals and schools' responsibilities to new teachers. Presentation for the Research on Teacher Induction Special Interest Group of the American Educational Research Association, Chicago, IL.
Bullough, Robert V. (1997). *'First year teacher' eight years later: An inquiry into teacher development.* New York: Teachers College Press.
Bullough, Robert. V. (1989). *First year teacher: A case study.* New York: Teachers College Press.
Bullough, Robert V., Jr., Knowles, J. G., & Crow, N. A. (1989). Teacher self-concept and student culture in the first year of teaching. *Teachers College Record,* 91 (2), 209-233.
Campbell, Patricia S. (2002). Music education in a time of cultural transformation. *Music educators journal,* 89(1), 27-32.
Clift, Renee T., Houston, W. Robert, & Pugach, Marleen C. (1990). *Encouraging reflective practice in education.* New York: Teachers College Press.
Conklin, Susan W., & Henry, Warren (1999). Professional development partnerships: A new model of music

teacher preparation. *Arts Education Policy Review*, 100 (4), 19-23.

Conklin, Susan W., & Henry, Warren (2002). The impact of professional development partnerships: Our part of the story. *Journal of Music Teacher Education*, 11 (2), 7-13.

Conway, Colleen M. (1997a) Reflection and the music methods course. *Southeastern Journal of Music Education*, 10.

Conway, Colleen M. (1997b). The development of a casebook for instrumental music education methods courses. Unpublished doctoral dissertation, Teachers College, Columbia University.

Conway, Colleen M. (1999a). The case method and music teacher education. Update: *Applications of Research in Music Education*, 17 (2), 20-26.

Conway, Colleen M. (1999). The development of teaching cases for use in instrumental music methods courses. *Journal of Research in Music Education*, 47 (4), 343-356.

Conway, Colleen M. (2000) The preparation of teacher-researchers in preservice music education. *Journal of Music Teacher Education*, 9 (2), 22-30.

Conway, Colleen M. (2001). Beginning music teacher perceptions of district-sponsored induction programs. *Bulletin of the Council for Research in Music Education*, 151, 51-62.

Conway, Colleen M. (2002). Mentoring and induction of the beginning music teacher. *Presentation at the Music in Schools and Teacher Education Commission of the International Society of Music Education*, Malmo, Sweden.

Conway, Colleen M. (Ed.). (2003a). *Great beginnings for music teachers: Mentoring and supporting new teachers*. Reston, VA: Music Educators National Conference.

Conway, Colleen M. (2003b). An examination of district-sponsored beginning music teacher mentor practices. *Journal of Research in Music Education*, 51 (1), 6-23.

Conway, Colleen M. (2004). The career cycle of the music teacher. Unpublished manuscript. University of Michigan, Ann Arbor, MI.

Conway, Colleen M., & Jeffers. Thomas (in press). The teacher as researcher in beginning instrumental music. *Update: Applications of Research in Music Education*.

Conway, Colleen M., & Garlock, Mandi. (2002). The first year of teaching K-3 general music: A case study of Mandi. *Contributions to Music Education*, 29 (2).

Conway, Colleen M., Krueger, Patti J., Robinson, Mitchell, Haack, Paul, & Smith, Michael V. (2002).Beginning music teacher induction and mentoring: A cross-state perspective. *Arts Education Policy Review*, 104 (2), 9-18.

Conway, Colleen M., & Zerman, Tavia E. H. (2004). Perceptions of a beginning music teacher on mentoring, induction, and the first year of teaching. *Research Studies in Music Education*. In press.

Danieliwicz, Jane (2001). *Teaching selves: Identity, pedagogy, and teacher education*. State University of New York Press.

Darling-Hammond, Linda (2003). Keeping good teachers: Why it matters, What leaders can do. *Educational Leadership*, 60 (8), 6-13.

DeLorenzo, Lisa C. (2003). Teaching music as democratic practice. *Music Educators Journal*, 90 (2), 35-40.

Emmanuel, Donna T. (2003). An immersion field experience: An undergraduate music education course in intercultural competence. *Journal of Music Teacher Education* (13), 1, 33-41.

Feiman-Nemser, Sharon (1983). Learning to teach. In L. Shulman & G. Sykes (Eds.). *Handbook of teaching and policy* (pp. 150-170). New York: Longman.

Feiman-Nemser, Sharon (2000). Creating strong contexts for novices' learning to teach: New roles for university and school-based teacher education. Paper presented at the annual meeting of the American Educational Research Association. New Orleans.

Feiman-Nemser, Sharon (2003). What new teachers need to learn. *Educational Leadership*, 60 (8), 25-29.

Feiman-Nemser, Sharon Schwille, Sharon., Carver, Cindy., & Yusko, Brain (1999). *A conceptual review of literature on new teacher induction*. E. Lansing, Michigan: National Partnership of Excellence and Accountability in Teaching.

Freire, Paulo (2000). *Pedagogy of the oppressed, 30th anniversary edition*. Trans. Myra Bergman Ramos. New York: Continuum.

Freire, Paulo with Ira Shor (1987). *A pedagogy for liberation: Dialogues on transforming education*. South Hadley: Bergin & Garvey Publishers, Inc.

Giroux, Henry (1997). *Pedagogy and the politics of hope: Theory, culture, and schooling*. Boulder: Westview Press.

Gold, Yvonne. (1996). Beginning teacher support: Attrition, mentoring and induction. In J. Sikula (Ed.) *Handbook of research on teacher education* (2nd ed.). New York: Macmillan.

Gordon, Steven, & Maxey, Susan (2000). How to help the beginning teacher succeed. Alexandria, VA: Association for Supervision and Curriculum Development.

Gromko, Joyce E. (1995). Educating the reflective teacher. *Journal of Music Teacher Education*, 4 (2), 8-13.

Henderson-Sparks, Joan, Tracz, Susan, & Quisenberry, Janine(2003). *Survival, challenges and retention: Four years of induction experiences of beginning teachers and their mentors*. Paper presented at the American Educational Research Association meeting, Chicago, IL.

Henry, Warren (2001). Music teacher education and the professional development school. *Journal of Music Teacher Education*, 10 (2), 23-28.

Holmes Group. (1986). *Tomorrow's teachers.* East Lansing, MI: Author.

Holmes Group. (1990). *Tomorrow's schools.* East Lansing, MI: Author.

Holmes Group. (1995). *Tomorrow's schools of education.* East Lansing, MI: Author.

Hooks, bell (2004). *Teaching community: A pedagogy of hope.* New York: Routledge.

Hooks, bell (1994). *Teaching to transgress: Education as the practice of freedom.* New York: Routledge.

Ingersoll, R. & Smith, T. M. (2003). The wrong solution to the teacher shortage. *Educational Leadership*, 60 (8), 30-33.

Kahrs, S. (1992). The aesthetic dimension in the preparation of music education majors at the undergraduate level. *Dissertation Abstracts International*, 50 (04A), 0825. (UMI No.AAG8910137).

Kanpol, Barry and Peter McLaren (Eds.) (1995). *Critical multiculturalism: Uncommon voices in a common struggle.* Westport: Bergin & Garvey.

Kester, R., & Marockie, M. (1987). Local induction programs. In D. M. Brooks (Ed.) *Teacher induction - A new beginning.* Reston, VA: Association of Teacher Educators.

Kingston, Maxine Hong (1989/1977). *China men.* New York: Vintage.

Kowalski, T. J., Weaver, R. A., & Henson, K. T. (1994). *Case studies of beginning teachers.* Addison-Wesley Publishers.

Krueger, Patti J. (1996). Problems-faced by beginning music teachers. *Dialogue in Instrumental Music Education.*

Krueger, Patti J. (1999). New music teachers speak out on mentoring. *Journal of Music Teacher Education*, 8 (2), 7-13.

Krueger, Patti J. (2000). Beginning music teachers: Will they leave the profession? *Update: Applications of Research in Music Education*, 19 (1), 22-26.

Krueger, Patti J. (2001). Reflections of beginning music teachers. *Music Educators Journal*, 88 (3), 51 - 54.

Kuzmic, J. (1994). A beginning teacher's search for meaning: Teacher socialization, organizational literacy, and empowerment. *Teaching and Teacher Education*, 10, 15-27.

Lamb, Roberta (1995). Tone deaf/symphonies singing: Sketches for a musicale. In Jane Gaskell & John Willinsky (Eds.), *Gender in/forms curriculum: From enrichment to transformation* (pp. 109-135). New York: Teachers College Press.

Legette, Roy M. (2003). Multicultural music education: Attitudes, values, and practices of public school music teachers. *Journal of music teacher education*, 13(1), 51-9.

Leglar, Mary & Collay, Michelle(2002). Research by teachers on teacher education. In Richard Colwell and Carol P. Richardson (Eds.). *The New Handbook of Research on Music Teaching and Learning* (pp. 855-873). New York: Oxford.

Lind, Vicki (2001). Designing case studies for use in teacher education. *Journal of Music Teacher Education*, 10 (2), 7-13.

MacDonald, Robert E., & Healy, Sean D. (1999). *A handbook for beginning teachers.* New York: Longman.

McLaren, Peter (1999). Challenges and hopes: Multiculturalism as revolutionary praxis. *Multicultural education*, 6(4), 32-4.

McLaren, Peter (1998). *Life in schools: An introduction to critical pedagogy in the foundations of education.* New York: Longman.

McLaren, Peter (1997). *Revolutionary multiculturalism: pedagogies of dissent for the new millennium.* Boulder: Westview Press.

Moffatt, Courtney W., & Moffatt, Thomas L. (2003). *Handbook for the beginning teacher.* Boston: Allyn & Bacon.

Moss, Glenda (2001). Critical pedagogy: Translation for education that is multicultural. *Multicultural education*, 9(2), 2-11.

Montague, Matthew G. (2000). *Processes and situatedness: A collective case study of selected mentored music teachers.* Unpublished doctoral dissertation, University of Oregon.

Music educators national conference (1997). Where we stand. *Music educators journal*, 84, 41-44.

National Commission on Teaching and America's Future (NCTAF). (2003). *No dream denied: A pledge to America's children.* New York: author.

Norman, Katherine (1999). Music faculty perceptions of multicultural music education. *Bulletin of the council for research in music education*, 139, 37-49.

O'Toole, Patricia (2002). Threatening behaviors: transgressive acts in music education. *Philosophy of music education review*, 10(1), 3-17.

O'Toole, Patricia (2000). Music matters: Why I don't feel included in these musics or matters. *Bulletin of the council for research in music education*, 144, 28-39.

Paine, Lyn (2000). Policies to support novice teacher learning: Lessons from abroad? Presentation at the American Educational Research Association, New Orleans, LA.

Palmer, A. J. (1995). Music education and spirituality: A philosophical exploration. *Philosophy of Music Education Review*, 3 (2), 91-106.

Parr, Carlotta N. (1996). Towards a philosophy of music teacher education: Applications of the ideas of Jerome Bruner, Maxine Greene, and Vernon A. Howard. *Dissertation Abstracts International*, 57-09A, 3867 (UMI No. AAG9701030).

Regelski, Thomas A. (1994). Action research and critical theory: empowering music teachers to professionalize

S<small>HIEH</small> & C<small>ONWAY</small>

praxis. *Bulletin of the Council for Research in Music Education*, 123, 63-89.

Rideout, Roger & Feldman, Allen (2002). Research in music student teaching. In Richard Colwell and Carol P. Richardson (Eds.). *The New Handbook of Research on Music Teaching and Learning* (pp. 874-886). New York: Oxford.

Robbins, Janet (1993). Preparing students to think like teachers: relocating our teacher education perspective. *The Quarterly Journal of Music Teaching and Learning*, IV (1), 45-51.

Robinson, Mitchell (2003). The mentor-mentee match: Preserving tradition or driving the profession? In Colleen Conway (Ed.), *Great beginnings for music teachers: Mentoring and supporting new teachers*. Reston: The National Association for Music Education.

Rose, Andrea M. (1998). Exploring music teacher thinking: A reflective and critical model. *Studies in music from the University of Western Ontario*, 17, 23-44.

Salzman, J. A. (2000). Talking the same language: Training mentors to use the pathwise performance assessment with induction-year colleagues. Paper presented at the American Education Research Association Conference, New Orleans, LA.

Schon, Donald (1983). *The reflective practitioner: How professionals think in action*. New York: Basic Books.

Schon, Donald (1987). *Educating the reflective practitioner: Toward a new design for teaching and learning in the professions*. Jossey-Bass: San Francisco.

Smith, Michael V. (1994). *The mentoring and professional development of new music educators: A descriptive study of a pilot program*. Unpublished doctoral dissertation. University of Minnesota.

Steinberg, Shirley (1995). Critical multiculturalism and democratic schooling: An interview with Peter L. McLaren and Joe Kincheloe. In C. Sleeter and P. McLaren (Eds.), *Multicultural education, critical pedagogy, and the politics of difference* (p. 129-154). Albany: Albany State University of New York Press.

Thompson, Linda K., & Campbell, Mark R. (2003). Preservice music educators images of teaching: A continuation. Presentation for the Music Special Interest Group at the American Educational Research Association, Chicago.

Townsend, Rick D. (2000). The Holmes Group: A private college plausibility study. *Journal of Music Teacher Education*, 10 (1), 24-31.

Vinz, Ruth (1996). *Composing a teaching life*. Boynton, Cook.

Walker, Robert (2002). Multiculturalism and music re-attached to music education. *Philosophy of music education review*, 8(1), 31-39.

Watt, M. (University of Sydney), & Richardson, P. W. (Monash University) (2003). *Motivational factors leading to teaching as a career choice*. Presentation for the Research on Teacher Induction Special Interest Group of the American Educational Research Association, Chicago, IL.

Wilke, Rebecca L. (2003). *The first days of class: A practical guide for the beginning teacher*. Thousand Oaks, CA: Corwin Press.

Wing, Lizabeth (1993). The question: What changes in arts teacher education are needed and feasible? *Bulletin of the Council for Research in Music Education*, 117, 51-65.

Wing, Lizabeth (1994). Beyond the how-to-manual in music teacher education. *Southeastern Journal of Music Education*, 6, 1-16.

Wong, Harry & Wong, (1998). *The first days of school*. Mountain View, CA: Wong Publications.

CHAPTER THIRTEEN

In the Face of Tradition: Questioning the Roles of Conductors and Ensemble Members in School Bands, Choirs, and Orchestras

JOSEPH SHIVELY

Abstract

An examination of the traditions in the profession and more contemporary notions about how teachers and learners might interact more meaningfully and, frankly, more humanely, leads to many questions about the roles of conductors and ensemble members that are perpetuated in school band, choir, and orchestra classrooms. Sustaining the traditional conductor/ensemble member dynamic will make it difficult to move ensemble based classes beyond what is often the singular focus of preparing performances toward a more comprehensive approach to music education. The focal points of this essay are how this structure might serve to provide experiences where the emphasis is placed on learning music rather than learning performance and how we might move these programs beyond traditional conceptions of the conductor/ensemble member dynamic to empower learners with greater responsibilities for learning within the classroom. All of this will require a willingness on the part of both teachers and ensemble members to discard traditional roles and adopt new ones, with the band director, choral conductor, or orchestra conductor "stepping down from the podium," both literally and figuratively.

Introduction

When I walk into almost any empty ensemble classroom in a school, I am faced with one recurring image. In these classrooms, I see the conductor's podium as the focal point of the room and the ensemble members' chairs and stands radiating from this focal point. While I will grant that this physical arrangement within the room is largely one of logistical necessity, the meaning that this arrangement takes on once the conductor and ensemble members come to occupy their places has become of increasing concern for me as a music educator. The inherent roles that conductors and ensemble members play in this setting generates an approach that remains teacher-centered and does not serve to support the musical development of the individual students in that ensemble. While my background as a middle school and high school band director continues to guide my thinking about the importance of performance in music education, I find myself rethinking the nature of the experiences provided students in bands, choirs, and orchestra in school settings. To this end, I have come to question the intended goals of these ensemble experiences and the means to these goals.

I wish to state upfront that this essay is not anti-performance. To the contrary, I find myself more dedicated than ever to the notion of the rehearsal room as a potentially fertile learning environment and performance as a potentially powerful means to develop musical understanding. However, as we rethink our educational goals in these settings, we must rethink the roles that teachers and learners play toward the fulfillment of these goals.

Tradition serves to frame much of our practice in band, choir, and orchestra teaching in school settings. The nature of band, choir, and orchestra classes is reflected in what I will refer to in this essay as performance-based music education. An examination of these traditions, as well as contemporary notions about how teachers and learners might interact more meaningfully and, frankly, more humanely, leads to many questions about the roles of teacher-conductors and ensemble members that are perpetuated in school band, choir, and orchestra classrooms. While conductors such as Reiner and Revelli led phenomenal performances by highly trained ensembles, their use as role models has created a number of teacher-conductors who lack a vision of what music education might, and should, be. Looking to these conductors of professional and high level amateur ensembles as the ideal for music teachers who teach performance-based classes in the schools greatly impairs the mission of music education. Sustaining this conductor/ensemble member dynamic will make it difficult to move ensemble classes beyond what is often the singular focus of preparing performances based on the musical decisions made by teacher-conductors toward a more comprehensive approach to music education that leads to performances that reflect musical understanding on the part of individual students and the ensembles as a whole.

Because of the predominance of ensemble classes in school settings, the traditional large ensemble will frame much of the discussion in this essay. I am not prepared at this moment to completely disassemble the large ensemble tradition in this essay, but rather I would like to discuss how the present structure is often ineffective and sometimes inappropriate. I have come to believe that the use of large ensemble as the organizational structure comes too early in performance-based music education, and in this essay, I will discuss the need to focus on structuring learning based on the needs of individual students until they have reached a level of musical development that will allow them to function effectively in the traditional large ensemble. Even then, we will need to think about how large ensemble experiences might serve better the needs of the individual students within that large ensemble. This will require consideration of shifting our focus away from the podium as the source of musical decision-making. In examining the large ensemble tradition, I will discuss: (1) how this structure might serve to provide experiences where the emphasis is placed on learning music rather than learning performance, and (2) how we might move these programs beyond traditional conceptions of the conductor/ensemble member dynamic to empower learners with greater responsibilities for learning within the classroom. Constructivist learning theories provide fertile ground for this very classroom environment. All of this will require a willingness on the part of both teachers and students to discard their traditional roles and adopt new ones, with the band director, choral conductor, or orchestra conductor "stepping down from the podium," both literally and metaphorically. Moving away from the traditions of our profession will not come easily. It will require music educators to reconsider their roles as teacher-conductors as they shift from transmitters of musical knowledge from the podium to teachers who facilitate the musical development of individual students within the performance-based music class. This might be particularly challenging for those teacher-conductors who are ego-driven in their approach to teaching in the ensemble setting.

The performance program in the schools is very much one of tradition. While there are certain aspects of this tradition to be valued, we should strive to look beyond the familiarity of this tradition and ask serious questions about the nature of performance-based music education. We must approach this with imagination because imagination "allows us to break with the taken for granted, to set aside familiar distinctions and definitions" (Greene, 1995, p.3). It is necessary that we call on our imaginations to help us bridge the present with the possible, for it is far to easy to cling to the status-quo and to reject new ideas as too radical without the courage that comes when we stretch our ideas from what we know to what might be.

In the face of tradition, our goal should be to create ensemble classrooms that allow for a more highly democratized learning environment. The belief system that is reflected in both the approach that teacher-conductors take with their ensembles and the kinds of activities in which they engage the learners in their classrooms is an incredibly powerful force toward the development of potentially richer learning environments. Toward this goal, we need to consider the sustaining purpose of our efforts in these classrooms. Performance will remain the foundational experience in these classrooms, yet we must move toward a reconstituted notion of the goals of performance-based music education and the actions in which teachers and students engage themselves toward the fulfillment of these goals.

This focus on performance should lead to exploration and experimentation with music rather than mere replication. Of further concern is replication based on musical decisions that are transmitted from the teacher-conductor to the students in the ensemble. The ensemble classroom should be thought of as a musical laboratory rather than a musical factory. The ensemble classroom should be a place where we are all engaged in working with musical ideas; where our examination of the music itself frames our efforts. We need to imagine rehearsal rooms where teachers and learners work together to develop greater levels of musical understanding. In this setting, performance itself is not sufficient, but enlightened performance becomes the goal. This enlightened level of performance must emerge from and reflect the musical development of students in the classroom and the responsibility of the teacher is to facilitate these experiences.

The Nature of the Ensemble Experience

One question that must be raised is whether our approach in performance-based music classes is dictated to some extent by the need to be efficient. Elliot Eisner (2002) believes that arts education should serve in contrast to the need for educational efficiency that underlies much of schooling. The manner is which students are grouped for ensemble classes is largely one that is based on the need to be efficient. All of the students in the same grade are placed in the same class regardless of the number of students or the range of ability levels. Restructuring ensemble classes in consideration of the needs of individual students would require more teachers, space, and equipment and subsequently, more money.

Another issue with regard to efficiency is the manner in which rehearsals are conducted. With the teacher-conductor transmitting musical decisions to the ensemble members and each ensemble member playing a specific role such as 3rd Clarinet or Alto II, the purpose becomes recreating the teacher's musical ideas as quickly as possible without any real attention to individual musical growth beyond each individual's contribution to that ensemble's performance. This teaching approach is based on the ability to correct performance problems as quickly as possible and to dictate specific ideas of musical expression. Almost right away, we place students into roles that are in service to the needs of the ensemble and students are immersed into what amounts to little more than pre-professional training with the profession being years as a 2nd violinist or 3rd trumpet. This is carried out to the point that your instrument and part becomes who you are and the name by which you are known. The simple action of moving students to different parts for different pieces would do a great deal to counter this mind set. The traditional environment of the ensemble classroom also creates certain perceptions of the teacher-conductor's means to success. In some cases, fear is the primary motivational technique employed by teacher-conductors; a technique based on the practices of certain renowned maestros.

The nature of the literature used with these ensembles must also be examined. In spite of every effort to design curricula for performance-based music education, the repertoire of bands, choirs and orchestras serves in many cases as a *de facto* curriculum. Any other curricular effort typically reflects little more than a skill-development sequence, and one that is often delivered in a manner that is not related at all to the literature being performed. It is critical that teacher-conductors accept that the repertoire is the foundation of the curriculum, and develop strategies for identifying the repertoire that serves best to support the musical development of learners in the ensemble classroom.

Further, literature is often selected to feature strong players and hide weak players. In the ensemble classroom, the growth of individual musicians is often sacrificed in service to the assumed good of the group. This is particularly the case when a performance will be adjudicated. Most ensemble literature, especially the literature written for instrumental ensembles, is orchestrated so that certain instruments usually play certain roles, with certain instruments typically responsible for melody, counter-melody, harmony, and bass line. While this literature might potentially provide an authentic experience for the ensemble members, the limitations created by the roles that the different instruments play would present barriers to individual musical growth unless certain teaching approaches are considered. The literature should be chosen for its musical quality and not merely the belief that it is a good teaching piece. Good compositions are by their very nature good teaching pieces. Many of the so-called teaching pieces are identified as such because certain musical ideas are found at the surface and these composition lack musical depth. This depth is not dependent on difficulty and there are compositions written for young ensembles that are of a meaningful level of depth for those students. The level of study and preparation that good music requires creates much higher expectations for the teacher.

Attached to this efficiency model is a highly developed pedagogical routine where teachers develop a familiar and secure approach to teaching. This pedagogical routine is comprised of rehearsal techniques that are based on preparing the best possible performance as efficiently as possible. The challenge comes in relinquishing our pedagogical routines when the nature of the subject matter or our approach to that subject matter is altered

(Eisner, 1998). Any discussion of rehearsal techniques quickly turns to the amount of time playing versus that amount of time talking. To consider merely the quantity of time is too limiting because the quality of the interaction is what is critical. If the teacher uses discussion to elicit student thinking about musical experiences, then time spent talking provides another way of constructing music knowledge.

Teaching the performance-based music class in a way that facilitates the musical growth of each individual requires a great deal of musical and pedagogical artistry on the part of the teacher. It is not a matter of lowering performance expectations. Rather it is a matter of raising them, as it requires much more in the way of musical understanding and engagement from each individual student in the ensemble. This approach also demands a much higher level of preparation and much greater musicianship on the part of the teacher. Above all else, this approach requires that we set aside our beliefs about performance-based music education and imagine how we might shift our focus from performance for the sake of performance to performance as a means to the development of musical understanding.

Rethinking Performance-Based Music Education

Performance-based music education should be based on more contemporary notions of how we learn, and subsequently how we teach. Because constructivist approaches to learning offer a range of possibilities for guiding learning and teaching in ensemble classroom, I will use them to frame my effort to rethink the nature of performance-based music education and consider the implications for teacher-conductors and students. Constructivist approaches in music have received increasing consideration (Shively 2002a 2002b; Wiggins 2000). Constructivism is an epistemological view which holds that there is a real world we experience, but that we impose meaning on that world, rather than a meaning in the world which exists independently of us; that there are many ways to structure the world, and that there are many meanings or perspectives for any event or concept (Duffy & Jonassen, 1992). This vision of constructivism is reflected in the following ideas about the nature of the learning process:

- Learning is the active process of making meaning out of one's experiences
- Learning is enhanced by exposing learners to experiences reflecting practitioner culture
- Learning is enhanced by involving learners in experiences that involve individual and group knowledge construction
- Learning is enhanced by engaging learners in experiences reflecting multiple perspectives
- Learning is enhanced by offering learners multiple means of representing knowledge
- Learning is enhanced by individuals who distribute the process of knowledge construction among other individuals and artifacts
- Learning is enhanced by experiences encouraging the reflective use of a learner's knowledge base (Shively, 2002a, p.171)

If the desire is to shift away from the traditional pre-professional training, away solely from the development of skill sets as the ends, then what might the classroom look like and sound like. The need to differentiate learning in our classrooms is critical. In many ways, ensemble classes reflect the last vestige of the one-room schoolhouse. We have learners at a variety of ability levels participating in the same learning tasks. The primary focus should be on the development of the individual musician within the classroom environment. It is certainly the case that focusing on the individual within the social setting that is the ensemble is a potentially powerful environment for learning.

The goals of performance-based music education should be altered to reflect the needs of the individual learner. Furthermore, the goal should be teaching for musical understanding and using the instrument or voice as the conduit for this experience. Within the performance-based classroom setting, the teacher must bring strategies to bear that provide opportunities for greater ownership in the learning process and students must take on new roles such as conducting rehearsals, making decisions about literature, rehearsal plans, critical reflection on the learning/rehearsal process, and writing program notes, This approach has significant ramifications for the nature of teaching and learning in the ensemble classroom.

Constructivist Learning and Teaching

While this essay is concerned with both teaching and learning, the process of learning serves to guide our teaching practices. The focus in constructivism is on how students learn not how we should teach. Nonetheless, they must be considered in concert and the teacher must act in a manner that will create the appropriate learning environment. As much as any classroom, the traditional conductor/ensemble member structure creates an environment where the teacher as knowledge transmitter and student as knowledge receiver are prevalent. "Constructivism leads to new beliefs about excellence in teaching and learning and about the roles of both teachers and students in the process. In constructivist classrooms, students are active rather then passive; teachers are facilitators of learning rather than transmitters of knowledge"(Stein et al., 1994, p. 26). This change to teacher as facilitator marks a significant shift in the nature of the teacher's role in the performance. Constructivist teaching is guided by five basic elements; (1) activating prior knowledge, (2) acquiring knowledge, (3) understanding knowledge, (4) using knowledge, and (5) reflecting on knowledge (Tolman & Hardy, 1995). Each of these elements serves to provide the teacher with guidance in creating a constructivist classroom environment. Brooks and Brooks (1993, (pp. 103-116)) listed the characteristics of a constructivist teacher. These characteristics, which continue to guide thinking in this area, largely reflect an emphasis on attitude and activity. Teachers set the tone for learning in a constructivist classroom and must constantly emphasize an attitude that values the learner. This list of general teacher characteristics and my own discussion of their applicability to performance-based music teachers follows:

1. Constructivist teachers encourage and accept student autonomy and initiative.

While each of these teacher characteristics is crucial to the development of a different kind of performance-based classroom, this has the most significant implications because of the manner in which it challenges the traditional dynamic between teacher-conductor and the ensemble members. This critical step reflects the notion of stepping down, literally and figuratively, from the podium. To this end, students must be placed in roles that allow for the development of autonomy and initiative. These roles might include those of conductor or coach, as well as being given opportunities to plan rehearsals or select literature.

2. Constructivist teachers use raw data and primary sources, along with manipulative, interactive, and physical materials.

The most important source material in the performance-based music classroom is the actual music. Regardless of whether it is music that has been composed by someone outside or inside this classroom, regardless of whether the music is itself composed or improvised, and regardless of whether this music is performed by the students in the class or has been recorded by other performers, the music must be of musical value. Assumptions should not be made about the types of music that can be of the highest possible quality, as it is necessary that the music used in the classroom reflect multiple perspectives. These multiple perspectives come in the way of styles and genres of music, as well as the ensembles or soloists for which these pieces have been composed. From the beginning, this music must be just that—music. The use of technical studies and scales should grow out of the need to develop certain musical skills in service to the performance of quality music. The most important characteristic of the music is that it reflect authenticity and musical integrity.

3. When framing tasks, constructivist teachers use cognitive terminology such as "classify," "analyze," "predict," and "create."

The cognitive nature of the musical experience is reflected in a range of music knowledge representations that grow out of the activities and related roles, such as performing, composing, improvising, writing about and discussing music, conducting, and coaching (Shively, 2002a; 2002b) that might be present in performance-based classrooms. Focusing on the music itself rather than the development of the requisite skills as the stepping-off point in the ensemble classroom will generate an environment where students and teacher will have the opportunity to examine and discuss the music in away that informs performance rather than merely detached theoretical study.

4. Constructivist teachers allow student responses to drive lessons, shift instructional strategies, and alter content.

The structure that underlies the learning and teaching should not be a traditional lesson plan, but rather should be based on significant musical preparation on the part of the teacher. This will enable the teacher to better facilitate the exploration of the music to be performed. Students should also be allowed at times to make decisions about literature to be performed, for certainly these decisions will tell us a great deal about the musical growth of the students in the ensemble. The rehearsal plan itself should be a product of student input. This is not to say that every class should end with a 60 person free-for-all about what and how to rehearse the next, but rather students should be given opportunities to discuss and write about individual, section, and ensemble performance with these reflections leading to the formulation of rehearsal plans.

5. Constructivist teachers inquire about students' understandings of concepts before sharing their own understandings of those concepts.

In the ensemble class, this occurs in the sense that the teacher elicits the understanding of the learners via performance. However, what typically occurs is immediate and specific corrective feedback on the part of the teacher. Discussion of the musical decision making process, even when the teacher models this process, should serve to frame the work in the classroom. While this might seem inefficient, providing students opportunities to develop a greater depth of understanding will lead to more easily obtained performances in the long run. In other words, the teacher will spend less time repeatedly re-teaching the same ideas.

6. Constructivist teachers encourage students to engage in dialogue, both with the teacher and with one another.

The dialogue in the ensemble classroom should occur in multiple forms, including dialogues of performance such as among ensemble members or between an ensemble member and a conductor, as well as more traditional verbal dialogue. Most importantly, this will make public the musical decision making process of students and the teacher. Most critical are opportunities for students to dialogue with one another in large and small ensembles, as well as in roles such a composer, conductor, or coach.

7. Constructivist teachers encourage student inquiry by asking thoughtful, open-ended questions and encouraging students to ask questions of each other.

This is a critical step in moving the rehearsal focus beyond the teacher making all of the musical decisions, as well as the decisions about rehearsal structure. As mentioned earlier in this essay it not that we do or do not talk in rehearsal, but rather it is the meaningfulness of what we say and ask that will lead the individual students and the ensemble toward much greater depths of musical understanding. The questions that we ask in the ensemble class also have the potential to lead to a much greater level of focus in the classroom. The underlying approach should be one where the focus is on developing, in the truest sense, a community of learners in the performance-based music class.

8. Constructivist teachers seek elaboration of students' initial responses.

Teachers and students must be willing to take rehearsal time to develop and try out ideas. This will require students to accept an approach where the teacher does not immediately provide the correct answer. Because musical knowledge representation is a the center of the performance-based classroom, students and teachers must be willing to accept ideas will have to be translated from non-verbal to verbal, and vice versa.

9. Constructivist teachers engage students in experiences that might engender contradictions to their initial hypotheses and then encourage discussion.

The teacher must be willing to model musical decision making processes and to place that model into a very public setting. In doing so the teacher will have the opportunity to demonstrate how our musical decisions are the product of a continuous process of examining music within a certain framework and subsequently testing our musical ideas through personal practice, conducting an ensemble, or composing. It should be noted that this approach requires a willingness on the part of the teacher to show that they do not necessarily have the "correct answer" and that they have the courage to place their thinking into the public arena. Of course, this should have powerful implications for the students' willingness to do the same.

10. Constructivist teachers allow wait time after posing questions.

Wait time is a basic questioning technique that is in the repertoire of all teachers. Nonetheless it mark two important themes in our performance-based music class: (1) the willingness to engage students in a discussion of the music being studied, and (2) an effort on the part of the teacher to resist the need to always jump in with an answer that seems pre-determined without any consideration of the student's ideas.

11. Constructivist teachers provide time for students to construct relationships and create metaphors.

Students in performance-based music classes need time to gain ownership of the music they study. In this setting, there is much to be said for valuing depth over breadth. The selection of literature will be critical to this process as it must have the musical depth to allow for meaningful examination and it must not always present so many technical challenges that the teacher and students are unable to move past surface level work.

12. Constructivist teachers nurture students' natural curiosity through frequent use of the learning cycle model.

There are learning cycle models that reflect, through a number of stages, the need to engage, explore, explain, extend, and evaluate the matter at hand. This requires a willingness on everyone's part to take the time to get to know the music and to invite everyone in the ensemble class to become deeply involved in the process of music learning.

The underlying focus of the performance-based classroom should be on making explicit the musical decision process. In this setting, teachers elicit student thinking and share their own thought processes. It is critical that teachers share the uncertainties of approach regarding music decisions, that the teacher model a working through of musical problems, evaluating and re-evaluating their decisions. In the constructivist classroom, learners need opportunities to make meaning, but what we typically do as teachers is to tell the meaning we possess—play it this way, phrase it like this, no this is the correct rhythm. However, what passes as efficient rehearsal all too often sets up a scenario where the teacher will eventually find himself or herself asking the question, "Why do I keep having to teach that?" The traditional teacher-centered rehearsal model does not encourage depth of understanding and it does not encourage student ownership of the learning process. The time invested in more thoughtful and thought-provoking rehearsal will lead the students in the ensemble class to more meaningful musical knowledge. These characteristics of a constructivist teacher demonstrate that they must allow learners to take an active role, but that the teacher does not become passive. The constructivist teacher must make every effort to create a classroom environment where learners are comfortable in the social roles that are crucial to the constructive process. There are certain characteristics of constructivist classrooms that make the notion less daunting. One of these is the focus on working in groups rather that alone. However, it requires that the teacher release some of the decision making within the group. The teacher should work to facilitate learning, to serve as a model of the musical decision making process, to think out loud how he or she approaches making a musical decision or goes about practicing.

There is one school ensemble in the United States where the teacher-conductor has shifted a great deal of responsibilities to the ensemble members. This ensemble is the much-maligned marching band. The educational value of the marching band remains a source of discussion for music educators. One reason I believe that it is as popular as it is with students is the level of activity and responsibility afforded to many of the students through leadership systems. Further, the marching aspect of the band places equivalent demands on all of the participants and it is a very public performance due to its visual nature. The weakest player in the band might struggle playing his or her part and few would know it, but anyone who had trouble marching in time and in step would be obvious to almost anyone. The members of a marching band enjoy a great deal of ownership in both the process and product. Granted the motivation may be logistical, but nonetheless. We need to consider how to increase the investment that individual learners make into the classroom community.

While constructivist approaches to learning and teaching provide significant guidance in shaping this approach to performance-based music education, work in constructivist leadership also provides the dispositions that are necessary for the teacher to be successful. Constructivist leaders need to develop a personal identity that allows for courage, risk-taking, low ego needs, and a sense of possibilities (Lambert et al, 2002). The expectations about the ensembles in schools provide a significant barrier to developing this leadership perspective. Preparing ensembles for public performance, especially public performance that is adjudicated by peers for festival rating or contest placement, places significant pressure on teachers to prepare an ensemble to perform at the highest level. Teaching in the manner that is discussed in this essay requires many teachers to buy into an approach that flies in the face of so much of our practice.

Any discussion about the possibilities for performance-based music education requires that imagination guide a sense of the possibilities. It is far too easy to accept the status quo in our field, but we must imagine an approach to performance-based music education where the individual musician is more highly valued than the ensemble itself. These ensemble classrooms will be places where there great expectations for performance and for musical understanding. These will be classroom where so much is expected of teachers and students.

Conclusions

Professional practice in performance-based music education is grounded in tradition and teacher-conductors have stood firm in the face most trends within music education and education itself. The role in schools of large ensembles and their directors, and the performances of these ensembles have long been at the center of instrumental music education. Constructivist notions of learning emphasize classrooms where teachers shift the focus toward the learner. In these classrooms, the focus is on engaging learners in practitioner culture, involving learners in group and individual experiences, providing learners with multiple means of knowledge representation, and immersing learners in experiences that reflect multiple perspectives.

Because learners should be engaged in the activities of practitioner culture, it seems natural that performance-based music education should maintain an emphasis on performance. However, there should be a distinction drawn between the role of performance for professional and advanced amateur musicians, and that of music students in elementary and secondary schools. In many cases, the nature of performance-based music education in the schools is that of pre-professional training. The focus, however, at this level should be a shift from instrument education to music education where the instrument serves as a tool to be used in the study of music. Further, the need for experiences providing for multiple means of knowledge representation requires immersing learners in other practitioner cultures, such as conductor, composer and teacher. While performance should remain at the center of these experiences, the nature of this performance and the balance of performance to other musical experience should be questioned.

Certainly there is a significant tradition of large ensembles within the schools. However, the shift of the responsibility for learning from the podium to the students in the class requires a rethinking of the role of the large ensemble within the school setting. Placing learners in individual and chamber ensemble setting would certainly offer a much richer context in which learning could take place. In addition, this would offer learners more opportunities to functions as practitioners in other domains, such as teacher or composer.

The need for learners to have experiences that reflect multiple perspectives should encourage moving beyond the traditional ensembles of instrumental music education toward the inclusion of more ethnic and electronic ensembles and individual experiences with those instruments. Even within the traditional ensemble structure, it is necessary to recognize that percussion ensemble has replaced band and orchestra as the appropriate large ensemble for percussionists.

Bands, choirs, and orchestras have traditionally played a central role in music education. My view is that they should continue to play a role, but only after students have reached the point where these experiences are an extension of individual musical development. Even then, the nature of the experiences in the school should be on the rehearsal room as laboratory. In these settings, teachers must relinquish the dominant role of the traditional conductor, and serve to facilitate the learning through guiding and modeling musical thinking. Students in these classrooms should be provided with opportunities represent music in a variety of ways. While performance should remain the cornerstone of these classes, students need opportunities to make meaning of music through composition, improvisation, conducting, and writing. These experiences will lead students toward a more enlightened performance

Performance-based music education must be structured in such a way that the focus of the educational enterprises is on teaching individual learners for musical understanding. The musical education of these individual learners should be the primary focus. The development of performance skills is important to the extent that these skills provide the necessary equipment to work in these musical laboratories, these rehearsal rooms. Imagine the possibilities for individual learners; imagine the possibilities for music education.

References

Brooks, J. G., & Brooks, M. G. (1993). *In search of understanding: The case for constructivist classrooms.* Alexandria, VA: Association for Supervision and Curriculum Development.

Duffy, T. M., & Jonassen, D. H. (1992). Constructivism: New implications for instructional technology. In T. M. Duffy & D. H. Jonassen (Eds.), *Constructivism and the Technology of Instruction: A Conversation* (pp. 1-16). Hillsdale, NJ: Lawerence Erlbaum.

Eisner, E. W. (2002). *The arts and the creation of mind.* New Haven: Yale University.

Eisner, E. W. (1998). *The kind of schools we need.* Portsmouth, NH: Heinemann.

Greene, M (1995). *Releasing the imagination: essays on education, the arts, and social change.* New York: Teachers College Press.

Lambart, L., Walker, D., Zimmerman, D.P., Cooper, J. E., Lambert, M.D., Gardner, M.E., & Szabo, M. (2002). *The constructivist leader.* 2nd ed New York: Teachers College Press.

Shively, J L. (2002a). Learning and teaching in the beginning instrumental classroom. In E. Boardman (Ed.), *Dimensions of musical learning and teaching: A different kind of classroom.* Reston, VA: MENC: The National Association for Music Education.

Shively, J. L. (2002b). Constructing musical understanding. In B. Hanley and T. Goolsby (Eds.). *Musical understanding.* Edmonton, AB: Canadian Music Educators Association.

Stein, M., Edwards, T., Norman, J., Roberts, S., Sales, J., Alec, R., & Chambers, J. (1994). *A constructivist vision for teaching, learning and staff development.* Unpublished manuscript, Wayne State University Detroit, MI.

Tolman, M. N., & Hardy, G. R. (1995). *Discovering elementary science: Method, content, and problem-solving activities.* Needham Heights, MA: Allyn & Bacon.

Wiggins, J. (2000). *Teaching for musical understanding.* New York: McGraw Hill.

CHAPTER FOURTEEN

Teaching the Masses or Coaching the Elite: A Comparison of the Challenges Facing High School Music and Sports Educators

SUSAN DILL BRUENGER

Abstract

Pressure to succeed at rating festivals and competitions has turned many US high school music programs into "musical sport," encouraging ensemble directors to concentrate on elite performing students. Since music is not a required core subject, ensemble directors are rarely required to go against this preference and teach the general student. Physical education teachers who coach elite athletes commonly teach the general student in required physical education classes. The socialization, role conflict, and personal needs of coaches examined in physical education/sport research could illuminate the issues that high school music educators would face were they required to provide "music for every child."

The importance of performance is a deeply ingrained value in both music and sport. Rather than attempting to alter a traditional system that produces exceptional performers, this paper suggests adding a new certification track for those with an interest in the diverse musical needs of the general high student. Such a program could attract future teachers with traditional and non-traditional backgrounds such as commercial music, world music, and technology.

INTRODUCTION

For many years, as a student and as a teacher, I have had the strong belief that music education should be as egalitarian as possible, and also have held the growing concern that it is not. A perusal of music education literature showed me that I was not alone in my concerns; others held the same concern about elitist tendencies in music education (Hoffer, 1989; Gerber, 1989; Fowler, 1986). In Fowler's words:

> For decades, amid slogans such as 'Music for every child, every child for music' and 'All arts for all the children' many arts teachers have been content to reach just the talented, the gifted, and the already interested. Hypocrisy not withstanding, music teachers who agree philosophically that music programs should serve all students have often in practice focused primarily on developing new generations of musicians

and music teachers, leaving the education of the masses largely to chance. Music education, particularly at the secondary level, has been elitist. By and large, music teachers have not reached the general high school student nor have they wanted to. (Fowler, 1986, p.10)

Things have not changed much since Fowler's 1986 analysis. We are still not reaching the "masses." What barriers are standing in the way of making music education egalitarian on the secondary level? What would happen if educational values shifted and music became a required subject for all students? Are secondary level ensemble directors willing and prepared to teach the general high school student Fowler mentions? There is an educational counter-part to music already in place that could serve as a model for our "what if" questions. I will argue here that coaches of elite sport teams who also teach required physical education (PE) will serve as that model. I will also argue that the institutional, teacher training, and personal needs problems that are examined in PE and coaching literature are also effectively preventing music educators from reaching the masses.

When the "general high school student" Fowler refers to has an interest in taking a music class or needs to fulfill a fine arts graduation requirement, the choices in schools are often limited. We still find that, in the United States, not all high schools have general music or music appre-ciation classes and most instrumental programs are not structured to start beginners on the high school level. Consequently, despite having little or no background and a limited interest specifically in choral music and its traditions, the only choice for many is a non-select choir.

Imagine if you will, Mr. Smith, a typical high school choir director in the U.S. (he could also easily be a band or orchestra director), specifically trained and socialized from an early age to the role of a performing musician. He is a superb conductor of an elite performing group and deals well with all the pressures of frequent performances and is very successful in competitive events.

Now, let us place Mr. Smith in two scenarios. In the first, Mr. Smith is standing in front of a class of surly high school students who are required to take music appreciation in order to fulfill their fine arts graduation credit. In the second, Mr. Smith is standing in front of a non-select choir. In this case it is the type of non-select choir directors clandes-tinely refer to as "the zoo choir," or the guidance counselor's "dumping ground" for stu-dents who are struggling academically and/or looking for "an easy A."

Neither scenario presents a pleasant picture. Even though on the surface, the non-select choir would seem like a better match for Mr. Smith because these students will actually be participating in the performance of music, their motivation for being in choir and the wide range of their talent make these students more similar to the music appreciation class than they are to the students in Mr. Smith's select group. Mr. Smith does not share the same musical taste as these students, he doesn't share the same norms and values, and what's more, it is likely that he doesn't care that he doesn't. Why? This paper will suggest that he has been socialized as a performing musician, and is probably a content-centered rather than pupil-centered teacher. He wants to be doing what he has been trained to do: conduct a choir of talented students who want to perform and perfect "good" music.

Mr. Smith also has other product-oriented assessment and competition pressures that complicate his ability and his will to address the non-performing students' diverse needs. Many ensemble directors avidly support competition as a means for keeping standards high and motivating students to excellence (Ponick, 2001). Some directors in competition driven-states in the U.S. find that competition no longer serves that single function; it is also becoming an assessment tool for a band or choir director's competence. Administrators with a minimal musical background may understand the sporting aspects of a first place rating, while a great listening lesson, development of student's creative improvisational ability or a very musical performance may be beyond their capacity to perceive and evaluate.

Many secondary level band and choir directors in the U.S. find themselves involved in competition to the extent that it can be argued that they are actually involved in "musical sport." Sport is "institutionalized competitive activity involving two or more opponents and stressing physical exertion by serious competitors who represent or are part of formally organized associations"(Nixon, 1984, p.13). This definition of sport implies that an activity can be considered sport if it has persistent patterns of social organization, contains competitions whose outcome is not pre-arranged, stresses skill and occurs in an organized framework that includes such elements as teams, coaches, sponsorship, rule books and regulatory bodies (Nixon, 1984).

Table 1 examines each aspect of this definition from the perspective of a competitive high school music program. The comparisons suggest that many music programs are in fact involved in "musical sport."

Table 1
Comparisons of Sport and Musical Equivalents

Aspect of Sport as described by Nixon (1984)	Musical Equivalent
Persistent patterns of social organization	Musical instruction begins quite early; students begin their training in elementary school and sometimes even younger. The socialization process occurs concurrently with training.
Contains competitions whose outcome is not pre-arranged	Judges listen to and evaluate performances and determine the results of music competitions, contests, and festivals.
Stresses skill	Just as in sports, where knowledge does not make one an athlete, knowledge about music does not mean one has the skill to be a musician. The kinesthetic training and practice process of skill building are similar in the two fields.
Occurs in an organized framework which includes: teams, coaches, sponsorship, rule books and regulatory bodies	Most high school music departments in the U.S. are organized in band and choirs that are stratified by ability. This is a mirror of sport practice. In fact many schools use such sport terminology as varsity choir, junior varsity choir, and non-varsity. These musical "teams" share such sports concepts as tryouts/auditions and uniforms.
	It is now common to see schools with large music departments hiring head directors and assistant directors in a mirror of the sport practice

of head and assistant coaches.

It is also common to see "booster organizations" that raise money and solicit sponsors who take out ads in concert programs, etc. The original concept behind these support groups comes from high school sports.

In the U.S. many states have broadened their interstate athletic regulatory bodies to include all types of competition, including such activities as music contests, speech and debate contests, etc. These regulatory bodies publish rulebooks and guidelines.

The more competitive the band or choir program, the greater is the similarity that exists between the football team coach and the "band team" director. If we accept that musical competition has enough in common with sport that it can legitimately be termed "musical sport," we can compare the situation of Mr. Smith with that of his colleagues who both teach physical education (PE) and coach interscholastic teams: "teacher/coaches." Sport sociologists estimate that over 70% of college level coaches teach PE in addition to coaching (Sage, 1987, p.17). Odenkirk (1986), hypothesizes that the percentage of teacher/coaches on the high school level is probably higher.

High school music and athletic programs both require extensive training, practicing, coaching-teaching, discipline, performances, and are important to the participant's identity as well as a source of prestige among adolescents (Synder & Sprietizer, 1978, p.344). Both high school ensemble directors and coaches deal with a performance-oriented elite. However, teacher/coaches in the United States reach almost all high school students through compulsory PE classes whereas ensemble directors rarely reach more than a small percentage of a high school's student population.

There are some highly effective high school general music programs taught by dedicated and talented teachers, but these programs are comparatively rare, with high school ensemble directors who are enthusiastic about teaching general music even rarer. Mr. Smith, the teacher/director, is by and large hypothetical at this time. But what would happen if educational values shifted and, instead of music being offered only for skilled performers, it was deemed as essential as PE for every student's education? If high school music for all students became a common practice, teacher/directors like Mr. Smith would be as common as teacher/coaches. By looking at how teacher/coaches cope with balancing the pressures and role conflicts of coaching elite sport teams and heavy competition schedules with teaching PE and by comparing those findings with related music studies, we can get a sense of how Mr. Smith might fare as a teacher/director.

SOCIOLOGY OF SPORT: THEORETICAL BASIS

The majority of sociological studies in sport have been constructed from social learning theory, which is used to examine the characteristics of the coaching role, role preference, and role conflict existing in the teacher/coach role (Foon, 1987). Sport roles are acquired from exposure to role models and reinforcement from significant others. Social learning theory suggests that are three main influential elements: personal attributes, significant others, and socialization situations (Kenyon & McPherson, 1976).

Personal Attributes

Personal attributes are studied because social learning theory postulates that people with certain attributes are drawn to the coaching role, which then reinforces these characteristics. According to Sage (1980), "Trait theory is based on the assumption that personal attributes are relatively stable and consistent, exert fairly generalized effects on behavior, and are so enduring that they override situational or environmental influences."

Teacher/coach personal attributes literature provides the following descriptions: coaches as a group are aggressive, highly organized, rational, practical, display a high amount of psychological endurance, persistence and inflexibility, they dislike change and tend to be very conservative politically, socially, and attitudinally (Ogilvie & Tutko, 1971; Scott 1969). Edwards (1973) found that the evidence is inconclusive as to whether the demands of the coaching role operate to weed out non-authoritarian-type personalities, or whether experiences while training to become a coach or fulfilling the coaching role condition people to react in an inflexible manner.

Music studies suggest that social pressure to appear normal and conventional leads to a tendency for music teachers to be conservative (Kemp, 1982, 1996, 1997; Roberts, 1991c; Wubbenhorst, 1994). White (1967) suggests that the profession attracts or selects conservative individuals while simultaneously reinforcing their conformist tendencies. Less conventional students are probably discouraged from pursuing public school music teaching careers (Woodford, 2002).

Significant Others and Socialization Situations

Teacher/coaches are a product of a highly complex, long-lasting socialization process. The family provides primary socialization by being the significant initiator of sports involvement, not the school (Kelly, 1974; Armour & Jones, 1998). The school, however, plays an important role in reinforcing and expanding the earlier patterns of sports socialization through its interscholastic athletic programs (Kelly, 1974).

Former coaches are often credited with influencing students to enter the profession (Templin, Woodford & Mulling, 1982; Templin, Sparkes & Grant, 1994; Bain & Wendt, 1983; Doolittle, Dodds & Placek, 1993; Stroot, Collier, O'Sullivan & England, 1994). The better coaching positions are normally obtainable only when the applicant has support from significant others who comprise the membership of an occupational subculture. This reference group acts as a referral system to vested interest groups like booster clubs. The aspiring teacher/coach gains this help by conforming to the expected values and norms of the subculture.

Anderson (1972) found that the most frequent reason given for selecting physical education as a college major (72%) was experience in competitive sports. Kenyon (1976) found that intense socialization to athletic participation and coaching is so different from the socialization taking place in other academic areas that undergraduate physical education majors have little in common with students in other majors and still less in common with students who are in teacher preparation programs.

DILL BRUENGER

Like their athletic counterparts, music education majors attribute their interest in music teaching to the positive influence and encouragement of family and former school or private music teachers (Beynon, 1998; Cox, 1997; Duling, 2000; L'Roy, 1983; Roberts, 2000a). When Cox (1997) surveyed 310 Arkansas music educators she found that 50% had at least one musician-parent and 20% also had a parent who was a teacher. Mark (1998) reported 90% of his pool of 200 active Austrian music educators had at least one musician-parent.

Even more importantly, music educators also share socialization patterns with their athletic counterparts that influence them more toward performance rather than teaching (Cox, 1997; L'Roy, 1983; Roberts, 1991a, 1991b, 1991c). Cox found that subjects reported more people influencing them as musicians than as future teachers. For example, former school music teachers encouraged and praised musical performance skill but not verbal skills or potential talent as a teacher (Cox, 1997 pp. 117).

Role Preference

Many teacher/coaches are more capable of performing one role than the other. This is because different preparation, abilities, and attitudinal disposition are required for each role. Physical educators who are not interested in coaching find the outlook for employment quite dismal. Most secondary and even some elementary schools hire only those physical educators who have expertise and interest in coaching. This forces prospective physical educators into the dual roles of teacher and coach (Bain and Wendt, 1983). However, studies indicate that the majority of teacher/coaches prefer the coach role (Segrave, 1980; Rupert & Buschner, 1989; Edwards, 1973; Ojeme, 1988). More recent research has found a gender difference where men expressed a preference for the coaching role more often than women (Macdonald, D., Kirk, D. & Braiuka, S., 1999; Yalcin, 2000). Why does a group of educators prefer an extra-curricular assignment to teaching? Because, for most, coaching was the original motivation for becoming a teacher/coach (Sage, 1987, Segrave, 1981). Professional sports and major universities provide about the only opportunity for full-time coaching employment in the United States. Since these opportunities are relatively scarce, if an athlete wants to earn a living coaching he must be employed somewhere in the educational system, which requires teaching in addition to coaching.

Like the teacher/coaches, music education students also identify more with the performer role than the teacher role. The training received by the majority of students in North American universities places a significant emphasis on performance. A belief shared by both university teachers and music education majors is that music teaching is a function of musicianship (Roberts, 1991b, p.32). Thus, Roberts found a sense of teacher identity lacking in music education students. The students in his studies saw themselves as performers or "well rounded musicians" even when they realized that they could not compete on the same level as performance majors.

Since the physical education literature referenced thus far emphasizes the competitive aspects of the job, in other words the coaching role, it will be beneficial to look at the characteristics of the coaching role in some detail before considering what effects coaching competitive teams might have on the teaching role.

Characteristics of the Coaching Role

Coaches' duties vary, but decision-making responsibilities are a characteristic found on all levels of the coaching hierarchy. The coaching role emphasizes a rational and practical approach to decision making (Edwards, 1973). This rational decision making ability is juxtaposed to a real aspect of uncertainty in the game situation, which demands the use of intuition and the ability to make educated guesses. "Coaches demand dedication, obedience, and loyalty for they are held responsible for losing, not the team members. Success is expected of them through their leadership behavior and decision making power" (Ogilvie & Tutko, 1971).

In the U.S., and perhaps more generally, it is a commonly held belief that the success or failure of an athletic team depends almost entirely upon the competence or incompetence of its coach. This belief persists even when there are obviously things that happen in all games that are beyond the control of a coach. A coach's work and preparation for a sporting event is rarely evaluated by an impartial judge who concludes that he/she did the best they could with the talent available. Ultimately, coaching effectiveness is measured in terms of winning. This lack of control over events results in coaches trying to control the things they can. Sometimes this affects events not directly related to the sporting event resulting in acts that could be seen from an outsider's view as irrational, for example, dictating the style of their athlete's hair (Calhoun, 1987, p. 178).

High school ensemble directors have a similar concern with control. If a band plays poorly at a contest or concert it is the director's responsibility. Contest judges have no way of knowing that the first clarinet player just broke up with her boyfriend or the first trumpet player recently got braces on his teeth. In the U.S. high schools are stratified for competition purposes by the size of the student body, not by access to other resources. So the high school choir in a poor community, where parents do not have the means or the inclination to pay for private lessons, is evaluated by exactly same standards as a more affluent high school choir where more than half of the students are studying privately.

Control issues manifest in two music director behaviors which could be considered questionable from an educational practices standpoint: (a) Selecting music that keeps the amount of challenge firmly within control, and then drilling it over and over until both students and directors are tired of it is, unfortunately, all too common. Yet from the standpoint of the factor of challenge in motivation theory, it is a questionable competition strategy (Maehr, 1983); and (b) Thirty states in the U.S. have instituted a version of "no pass, no play," which was originally enacted in Texas in 1984 (National Association of State Boards of Education, n.d.) to restrict student participation in "extracurricular" activities, including sport and music competitions, if they do not maintain their grades. In many states this is tabulated on a six week basis, which means it is possible for students to lose eligibility to perform at an extra-curricular event such as a music competition if they fail, for example, just one history exam. Being a student teacher supervisor, I have on a number of occasions observed classroom situations where music "teacher/coaches," worried about contest ratings, try to wrest a degree of control over the "no pass, no play" ruling by "benching" those who lost eligibility. This practice did not only take place in extra-curricular, after-school rehearsals; it happened during regularly scheduled class time. I have witnessed this when as many as one third of the class were ineligible! Instead of being allowed to participate, because the director wanted to rehearse with the same balance with which they would go to contest, the ineligible students were either given theory worksheets or study hall until after the contest performance.

Clientele

Although competitive sport and physical education co-exist in schools and sport is a major component of physical education, the learning outcomes of these activities are largely different due to the differences in clientele. The clientele differ in that students are required to take PE and they exist in large numbers with wide-ranging skill levels and diverse attitudes, whereas highly skilled team sport athletes are participating voluntarily, exist in comparatively smaller numbers, and are highly motivated (Kneer, 1987).

Coaches are interested in athletes who will help them win. Talamini (1973) discovered that school athletic programs emphasized interscholastic competition more than intramural sports so that high school athletics were oriented toward the athletic elite rather then the less talented.

In ideal situations teacher/coaches have different goals for PE and team sports. A frequently stated goal of physical education classes is the development of lifelong physically active lifestyles in students of all skill levels (Siedentop, 1994). Whereas the goals of coaching are to assist athletes to enhance their skills and knowledge of sport so they can fulfill their potential individually and as a member of a team. Unfortunately there is evidence of a lack of ideal situations. For example, coaches, in a study by Locke and Massengale (1978), were concerned because their interest and abilities as coaches were not well suited to the demands of teaching a physical education class where the numbers, ability, and motivation of students were different than the varsity situation.

High schools that offer general music classes are comparatively few. Whether or not clientele differ between competition-oriented elite musical performing groups and non-select performing groups depends on the school system. There are two commonly seen scenarios in the United States:

(1) In highly competitive school districts competition for ratings begins at the middle school level. Those who are not able to join the "choir team" by demonstrating the proper attitude and/or skill either quit of their own volition or are weeded out before they get to high school. Administrators in these districts, like administrators who work with coaches who demand as much control as possible over their clientele, support the band and choir directors' inclination to remove or not accept students who aren't team players or whose skills are not up to team standards. Because the attitude-impaired and the unskilled have been weeded out in middle school, the high school non-select group in this situation will have much the same clientele as the select group, only younger and less experienced. Non-select groups in this situation usually compete on the junior varsity level. The choir/band director in this environment, although working in a highly competitive situation, has much less in common with the coach who is teaching large numbers in compulsory PE because the choir/band director is not responsible for addressing the needs of all types of students.

(2) One can find large numbers of students with differing skill levels and attitudes in the type of non-select choir that teachers refer to as "my zoo choir" in districts where competition culture is not as highly institutionalized. Many of these students are present simply to fulfill a fine arts credit or because the counselor decided they could probably pass the choir class. Typically only the varsity choir competes, making this situation very similar to that of the teacher/coach.

The training music education students receive to work with the type of diversity described in the second situation has been found wanting by some writers. These authors have begun to question undergraduate music training in musical idioms outside of the mainstream curriculum of Western European classical music. This kind of training is being proposed to be increasingly essential to be successful in today's diverse classrooms (Bowman, 1994; Roberts, 1998, 2000c; Rose, 1990).

Assessment of teacher/coaches

Researchers have found that coaches perceive a difference in the way academic teachers and teacher/coaches are awarded job security. Teacher/coaches believe that academic subject teachers are awarded job security when they demonstrate teaching adequacy whereas teacher/coaches do not have this benefit. If a teacher/coach wants job security he or she has to win. Therefore, teacher/coaches usually perceive their primary responsibilities as coaching and winning and sometimes perceive coaching and winning as the only real responsibilities (Sage, 1987; Figone, 1994; Edwards, 1973).

In seeking jobs, many teacher/coaches look primarily for coaching positions. When coaching vacancies occur, high schools often advertise for and hire the coaching position first, giving secondary consideration to the teaching competencies of the applicants (Sage 1989). Teacher/coaches are normally hired as faculty members but the actual job descriptions and their occupational roles vary greatly from what the school expects from other teachers. Teacher/coaches are expected to produce competitive results. They are seldom fired for teaching inadequacy if they are a winning coach and teaching expertise seldom substitutes for losing. Non-coaching teachers do not face this problem (Massengale, 1977). When teacher/coaches are held accountable for winning, they demand the complete authority to make any decision they deem necessary to succeed. Since they aren't treated like other teachers they do not have the same need to conform to policies, procedures, and regulations that affect non-coaching teachers.

While school districts typically have official teacher assessment instruments, competition can be used as a measurement tool for a band or choir director's competence. It is interesting to note that 56% of all secondary-level principals in the United States are former coach/athletic directors (Gruber, Wiley, Broughman, Strizek, and Burian-Fizgerald, 2002). As stated earlier, administrators with a minimal musical background, usually understand the sporting aspects of a first place rating, when other aspects of a music teacher's role may be beyond their capacity to perceive and evaluate.

In the U.S., in states such as Texas, competition is so integral to school music programs that it is clear that music teachers perceive it to be an important component of the evaluation of their competence. I have recently talked to a teacher in my geographical area that claims to have been terminated on the basis of low scores in musical competition. I contacted the administrators involved and they could not validate this claim because they were forbidden by privacy laws from discussing the case. I have found no music teacher/coach dismissal studies to back up the assertion that teacher dismissal on the basis of low competition ratings exists. Privacy laws make acquisition of data on this subject difficult to obtain so at this point there is mostly conjecture and hearsay. A study surveying teachers to ascertain if they believe their job is in jeopardy if they do not produce first place ratings would provide interesting data. Even if the phenomenon of teacher dismissal on the basis of low ratings does not exist or simply cannot be verified, the perceived threat of reprimand or dismissal could still have an effect on music teachers.

I have also talked to two school district music supervisors who ascertain the competitive drive of music teacher applicants as a prerequisite to a job offer. Those found to be lacking in competitive drive were not hired. I validated this information by talking both to teachers who applied in these districts as well as the supervisors who asked the questions. This information is based on only two administrators in two school districts in one particular geographical area and, therefore, cannot be generalized. However, it does validate that this behavior does indeed exist.

Role Conflict

Role conflict has been cited as one of the reasons for physical education teacher turnover in the United States (Rupert & Buschner, 1989). Role theory maintains that most people engage in multiple roles, for example, family roles, professional roles, recreational, or religious roles. Role conflict occurs when a person is exposed to contradictory expectations at the same time. Many studies on teacher/coaches explore the role conflict inherent in the position. The following have been cited as causing differences in the expectations for the two roles of teacher and coach: clientele, rewards, value differences, role requirements in the school organization, low status, and blocked career aspirations (Kneer, 1987). Balancing the demands of these roles can be problematic. Walters and Crook (1990) maintain that people resolve multiple role conflict by either compartmentalizing the most salient roles, negotiating, or withdrawal from one or more of the roles.

Effect of Teacher/Coach Role Conflict on Teaching

Templine (1987, p.66) found that teacher/coach role conflict affects the teaching role more than the coaching role for two reasons: (a) Many future physical educators enter the field with coaching as their primary orientation, but they are required to obtain a teaching certificate despite their lack of interest in teaching. (b) Identification with the coaching role is "reinforced by our society's emphasis on sport and the athletic hierarchy found in most schools. The community in general has more interest in and values the football team more than the p.e. class."

Cox (1987) provides us with an example of how the value differences between the teacher role and the coach role may affect the teaching of physical education. During an average basketball season the coach will spend 30 hours a week in coaching responsibilities. This is in addition to the 35 hours spent in the classroom. Many teacher/coaches maintain this schedule for the entire school year, which leaves them concerned about the detrimental effect that lack of time to prepare for teaching has on their physical educa-tion instruction. When time becomes a factor and the teacher/coach must make a choice, the area of physical education suffers most (Chu, 1981; Macdonald, 1999).

Cox believes teaching and coaching should be the same except for the fact that the clien-tele is different in skill level and interest. He believes that the cause of role conflict is rooted in values of the teacher/coach and the values of the school, which result in a prob-lem with time. He states that "the problem with the teacher/coach role rests with the teacher/coaches who believe p.e. is 'recess.' A reduced load will not solve this problem. The solution to this problem requires separating teaching and coaching"(1987, p.27).

How do teachers who primarily see themselves as coaches teach? Research indicates that the higher the competitive situation, the more coaches were concerned about the outcomes of player action. Also practicing PE teachers tended to take a product-orient-ed stance with success being measured by how happy, busy, and well behaved their stu-dents were (Chaumeton & Dud, 1988; Placek, 1983).

Bain discovered that teaching behaviors in PE class differed from those in a coaching sit-uation. There was more specificity and instructional achievement emphasis in coaching situations. Coaches made verbal comments, gave directions towards skills and knowl-edge, and used more praise and criticism in their responses to athletes. A PE student was more likely to be treated as a member of a group than as individual and was afford-ed less privacy than the athlete (1978).

Thomas Templin, in his review of physical education literature provides several descriptions of how PE is taught by teacher/coaches. "Physical education in our schools can be described as: Supervised recreation, glorified recess...a criminal waste of time...an irrelevant learning setting where there are no teacher or curriculum effects...a setting where custodial, inequitable teacher behavior is normative...a setting where accountability for teaching and learning is minimal, if not non-existent" (1987, p.56). In sum, if we look to teacher/coaches' work in the PE class to predict the effect of music directors' effectiveness in dealing with general music students or non-elite performing students we have cause for concern.

Bouij (1998) suggests that students entering music education tend to be predisposed to be pupil-centered or content-centered in their approaches to teaching. Content-cen-tered teaching implies an objective approach to musical subject matter while pupil-cen-tered teachers tend to emphasize interpersonal relationships and make it a priority to educate the whole child through music. Students who primarily see themselves as per-formers tend to become content-centered teachers whereas students who see them-selves as "all-round musicians" tend to become pupil-centered teachers. Roberts (2000b) surmised that undergraduates who identify themselves as "performers" may be more likely to end up as high school teachers whereas those who see themselves as "general musicians" may pursue elementary level teaching. Hence we can predict that high school music directors will probably be content-centered teachers.

The question now becomes how do music educators who identify with the performer role and thus tend to become content-oriented in their approach to teaching deal with the students found in a stereotypical non-select or "counselor's dumping ground" choir?

Bruenger (1999) found that the choir director in her study of student motivation in a non-select "counselor dumping ground" type choir had essentially the same teaching plans for both her highly competitive, award-winning choir and her non-select group, which included warm-up and vocal pedagogy exercises, sight reading and the singing of mostly Western European "classical"-style literature. The students in her select group tended to share the teacher's values and enjoyed this type of curriculum and the choral traditions that go with it, whereas the majority of the students in her non-select group had significant problems. This teacher treated her "varsity" choir differently than her non-select choir by asking questions demanding higher order thinking skills frequently in the select group but never in the non-select group; by giving positive reinforcement and useful feedback in the select group and very low level feedback and minimal positive reinforcement in the non-select group; by giving students more privileges in the select group than the non-select group; and by giving the select group more opportunities to take ownership in the experience while giving the non-select group no opportunities for autonomy. Because this was a case study the results are not generalizable, but it does point out the need for studies of the way teachers approach the teaching of non-select and non-performing groups.

From the discussion above we can suppose that our hypothetical Mr. Smith has been socialized to a role that emphasizes performance over teaching, thus increasing the probability that he will be content rather than pupil-centered, and a product rather than process-oriented teacher. One could argue that a content-centered, product-oriented teacher/director would probably be highly adaptive in a competition-based culture and might find pressure to compete from administrators and booster clubs to be stimulating.

Competition for ratings is an integral part of the music education culture in the United States. Many ensemble directors avidly support it. Administrators support it. Winning "first place" ratings garners prestige for the institution, motivates many students to excel, and undoubtedly works to improve and sustain performance standards. However, Fowler reminds us that music directors have not reached the general high school student nor have they wanted to, thus making music education elitist (1986, p.10). The culture of competition encourages an emphasis on elite performing ensembles, the members of which accrue most of the benefits derived from competition. Students not among the "talented, the gifted, and the already interested" benefit relatively little (Fowler, 1986). A course specifically in music is still not a graduation requirement in most states because it is still not considered a core subject. In order to be a core subject, music would have to address the needs of every student, which is not an important component of competition-based programs.

Despite the positive benefits of competition for elite performers and the preference of directors for working primarily with the already interested and talented, ignoring the music education of the masses marginalizes music's place in the curriculum. Why then do music educators persist in behavior that could be considered self-defeating? An examination of how athletic teacher/coaches find professional and personal validation can provide insight into this behavior.

Low Status

Low status can lead to results that make the physical education role seem less attractive than coaching. Koslow (1988) studied college students' perceptions of physical education and discovered that not only was an undergraduate degree in physical education viewed as the degree that is least difficult to earn, it was also rated as the least prestigious.

Once teacher/coaches begin their professional life they find that: (1) large classes; (2) insufficient space, time, and equipment; (3) the assignment of menial supervisory tasks; and (4) the stigma of the "muscular matron" and "dictatorial coach" image make teaching physical education difficult and less than satisfying (Kneer, 1987; Wilcox, 1987). O'Sullivan, Siedentop, and Tannehill (1994) found evidence to suggest that physical educators perceive a lack of pressure to improve physical education as well as feel a lack of instructional challenges. They believe this explains why physical education teachers sought self-worth and challenge in coaching.

The physical education literature also suggests that the impossibility of meeting the demands of both teaching and coaching roles simultaneously is compounded by powerful social and personal incentives such as increased kudos and financial gain that make the coaching role pre-eminent (O'Connor & Macdonald, 2002).

Rose (1986) summarized the effects of the relative status of sports and the ideal teaching of physical education. He maintains that the main purpose of competitive athletics is not related to education or entertainment but rather the achievement of deference or respect. The competition for respect permeates athletics and becomes vital to the entire school. On the other hand, ideally, learning how to perform in physical education is done for its own sake as an end in itself.

Like their counterparts in physical education, North American music education students also experience the effects of low status. A number of studies have outlined how significant others have influenced music education students more toward performance rather than teaching (Cox, 1997; L'Roy, 1983; Roberts, 1991a, 1991b, 1991c). Various studies in the formation of music teacher identity have found that music education students perceive an institutional hierarchy of musical types and social roles that ranks performance of primary importance and high social status. Since practicing music teachers as well as music education majors have been found to agree that music teaching is a function of musicianship (Roberts, 1991b, p.32), music education majors are compelled to compete with performance and other majors for recognition and social status. Since their professional identity is tied up with their perceived social status as musicians and not with music education tasks, many music education students feel stigmatized by the label, music educator (L'Roy, 1983; Roberts, 1991c).

Music education students struggle to compete with performance majors for social status by acquiring a performance reputation while they are acquiring the knowledge and other skills needed to teach (Roberts, 1991c). L'Roy (1983) suggests that those who have been denied status on the basis of marginal performance skills may develop motivational problems, which hinder their commitment to proper preparation for the teaching profession. "If music education majors invest too much of themselves in performance at the expense of other aspects of their professional preparation and identity, and if they fail to achieve the level of performance desired or expected, they may be needlessly setting themselves up for role conflict and failure" (L'Roy, 1983, p. 47).

Cox (1997) concludes that due to their socialization as performers, music education students are not prepared to assume a music teacher professional identity until they actually begin teaching. That conclusion brings us back to our hypothetical Mr. Smith. Does this experienced teacher label himself as a teacher or does he still identify more with the performance identity? Cox's (1997) survey of 310 experienced teachers showed that even experienced music educators identify more strongly with the role of musician than that of teacher.

Undergraduate music education majors also attach more status to the performance of "classical" music than other types of music. Being associated with other types of music means incurring a reduction of status (Roberts, 1991c).

In reference to the development of music teacher identity and successful teaching, Bouij (1998) suggests that failed performers do not easily turn into pupil-centered teachers. So chances are our Mr. Smith, like many high school choir directors, strongly identifies himself as a musician rather than a teacher. He directs choirs for the opportunity to challenge himself, to receive validation for his musicianship, as well as to be a gatekeeper of choral masterworks. In terms of his training, preferred work environment, and self-validation Mr. Smith, like PE teacher/coaches, does not aspire to teach all the students.

CONCLUSIONS

North American music schools graduate music educators who perceive that they have worth only so far as their musicianship skills take them. Hence, music student teachers want to be seen primarily as "good musicians." Because of this, their feelings of self-worth depend on external validation of their performance ability (Rose, 1998).

Maslow's hierarchy of needs theory (1970) maintains that esteem is one of the deficiency needs that must be met before a person can act unselfishly. There are two types of esteem needs: self-esteem resulting from competence or mastery of a task and the need for recognition from others. Since music education students have been denied social status because they did not measure up to performance majors and since they have not been accorded commensurate status for the development of their teaching skills they quite naturally seek external validation until they receive the status they need. How is this status achieved for the working music teacher? I propose that for many this need is met through directing a choir, band, or orchestra that earns the validation the director needs from the judges, and the status of a first place rating, which can be shared with the school community.

We do a good job of reaching all students on the elementary level. It is in early adolescence when students are beginning to feel vulnerable about their limitations that many students lose interest in making music. Motivation scholars have found that task involvement (wanting to demonstrate to oneself that one can do something for its own sake) rather than ego involvement (wanting to be better than the next person) is the best indicator for continued motivation and persistence over the long run (Covington, 1983; Nichols, 1983). Students start to realize that ability means capacity in early adolescence. If they perceive that they are not doing well in music because they are not as talented as others they may decide that it is not worth their while to keep trying (Nichols, 1984). This is when middle schools start the ensemble selection process whereby students discover that their skills are deficient and many teachers who are socialized and trained as Western European classical-style performers fail to meaningfully engage the non-elite musicians in alternative music classes.

Also, how does competition for acceptance into select groups and competitions for ratings at solo and ensemble contests affect the students who just want to play or sing, the students who simply want to participate for "the fun of it," not because they see music as a possible vocation? Maehr in his address to the Ann Arbor symposium predicts:

[handwritten annotation: → focus on music ed should not be to satisfy the egos of its teachers]

> The problem comes for the merely interested and merely good. As noted earlier, the ego goal situation is known to create an avoidance pattern in those whose sense of competence is ambivalent at best, negative at worst. In music, as in any other domain if the definition of success or the goal of performance is primarily one of determining who is the best among the competitors, most are doomed to failure and, therefore, also doomed to be turned off by the task. One does not create enduring motivational patterns by showing people that they are incompetent. Insofar as an activity is structured to do that, it will be a motivational failure for the large majority of the participants. (Maehr, 1983, p.10)

How does the possible harm competition does by discouraging those Maehr (1983) referred to as "merely good" or those without a strong sense of competence in music balance against the possible benefits of competition for the musically elite? By looking at the construction of the majority of high school music programs in the U.S. we see that concern for the education of the masses does not balance the music director's need for the validation from winning the first place ratings they can only earn from working with the talented elite. The hierarchy of needs theory supports the conclusion that until music directors meet their validation deficiency need it will be very difficult to act unselfishly. Meeting the musical needs of the masses in general music classes or non-select performing groups is indeed selfless, as there are no awards or applause to be earned from these activities.

This discussion began by asking what would happen if it were decided that every student must be musically educated when they graduate? Evidence has been presented that indicates that in general, athletic teacher/coaches have not been successful in balancing the dual roles. Would music director/coaches be any more likely to be successful teaching the general population in music classes than the teacher/coaches are at teaching compulsory physical education?

If the above comparisons between athletics and music mean anything, the answer is no. One cannot assume that every high school ensemble director will be an acceptable general music instructor just because they excel at directing an ensemble. Teaching general music is a completely different role with different clientele and a completely different set of expectations.

Four possible solutions to role conflict found in teacher/coach literature are: (a) Staff scheduling assigned to eliminate simultaneous teaching while coaching, (b) Hiring teachers and coaches separately, (c) Hiring part-time experts with physical education training, (d) Removing sports from school control may help those teachers whose livelihood depends on their success as a coach (Templin, 1987; Kneer, 1987).

These solutions may seem far-fetched for music, but one that might work would be to hire teachers, either full or part-time, specifically trained to teach high school general music classes separately from ensemble directors. This would necessitate the addition of secondary level general music certification and a secondary general music track at the university level to prepare general music teachers with training in the needs of the general high school student and musical skills that include music outside the Western European classical canon. Adding an additional track for such non-traditional music educators seems a far more possible venture than changing the passionately held beliefs of the standard musical academy. This new track could also accommodate students who at present are not accepted in many programs because their socialization, skills, and interests do not fit the standard profile: the student striving to perfect the performance of Western European classical music. This could open up opportunities in music education for individuals with such varied interests and skills as: the diverse styles of world drumming, the many genres of popular music, or the vast spectrum of music from many different cultures.

A new track could also make use of the many music technology resources available today. Adolescents want music in their life and they also have an interest in computers. Music technology can help students learn to become producers of culture instead of merely reproducers of the work of others.

If we hold to our current training standard, how will our hypothetical Mr. Smith's non-select choir or general music teaching fare in comparison with teacher/coaches in PE? If Mr. Smith's teaching approach in choir is pupil-centered and comprehensive, if he is as interested in the process of music making as he is in the final product, and if he has received training in the teaching of students with diverse interests and needs in a general music or non-select performing group situation, his experience of role conflict and its effect on his teaching will probably be minimal. Adjusting to a difference in clientele, and the value differences between varying clientele might still be a factor, but the comprehensive process-oriented approach to teaching an ensemble suggests director-held values that will transfer to the teaching of general music. If, however, Mr. Smith is a product-oriented director, whose main interest is producing a first rate performance of "quality" music, his role conflict will probably be as great as that of most teacher/coaches.

How could the standard musical academy be adjusted to produce a pupil-centered, process-oriented high school music director who identifies with the teaching role as much as the musician role? The answer is, with much difficulty. Music education professors are not nearly as influential on undergraduate music education majors' identity as are their private instructors and other members of the faculty (L'Roy, 1983). The performance faculty of a university music department is highly unlikely to change their values about the importance of performance. Therefore, in order to gain more influence, a music education faculty would need to find ways to reach these students before their last two years when they typically begin their methods classes. Since music education professors are themselves a product of the culture that emphasizes musicianship over teaching ability, they will have to examine their own validation issues to avoid transmitting the same assumptions to their students. Then, given the opportunity to reach music education students in time to affect their role identity and socialization process, the music education faculty should extend their influence beyond the standard teaching of methodology in order to encourage students to critically examine all of the social and ethical implications and consequences of the actions music directors take to sustain our revered traditions.

References

Anderson, F.W. (1981, December). *A study of selected reasons for majoring in physical education.* Paper presented at the Annual Convention of the Texas Association for Health, Physical Education and Recreation, Austin, TX.

Armour, K. & Jones, R. (1998). *Physical Education Teachers' Lives and Careers: PE, Sport and Educational Status.* London: Farmer Press.

Bain L. L. (1978). Differences in values implicit in teaching and coaching behaviors. *Research Quarterly,* 49, 5-11.

Bain, L.L. (1983). Teacher/coach role conflict: Factors influencing role performance in teaching in physical education. In T.J. Templin (Ed.), *Teaching in physical education.* (pp.94-101). Champaign, IL: Human Kinetics.

Bain, L. & Wendt, J. (1983). Undergraduate physical education majors' perceptions of the roles of teacher and coach. *Research Quarterly for Exercise and Sport,* 54, 112-118.

Beynon, C. (1998). From music student to music teacher: Negotiating an identity. In P. Woodford (Ed.), Critical thinking in music: Theory and practice [Monograph]. *Studies in music from the University of Western Ontario,* 17 (pp. 83-105).

Bowman, W. (1994). Sound, sociality and music. *Quarterly Journal of Music Teaching and Learning,* 5(3), 50-67.

Bouji, C. (1998). Swedish music teachers in training and professional life. *International Journal of Music Education,* 32, 24-31.

Bruenger, S. D. (1999). *The relationship of selected personal investment behaviors to the meaning members attach to their choral experience.* Unpublished doctoral dissertation, North Texas State University, Denton.

Calhoun, D. W. (1987). *Sport, culture, and personality.* Champaign, IL: Human Kinetics.

Chaumeton, N. R., & Duda, J.L. (1988). Is it how you play the game or whether you win or lose?: The effect of competitive level and situation on coaching behaviors. *Journal of Sport Behavior,* 11, 157-174.

Chu, D. (1981). Origins of teacher/coach role conflict: a reaction to Massengale's paper. In S. L. Greedorfer and A. Yiannikas (Eds.), *Sociology of sport: Diverse perspectives.* NewYork: Leisure Press.

Covington, M.V. (1983). Musical chairs: Who drops out of music instruction and why? In *Ann Arbor Symposium III on the application of psychology to music teaching and learning: motivation and creativity.* Reston: Music Educators National Conference.

Cox, K. E. (1987). The physical education/athletics problem in secondary schools. *Journal of Physical Education, Recreation and Dance,* 58, 27.

Cox, P. (1997). The professional socialization of music teachers as musicians and educators. In R. Rideout (Ed.), *On the sociology of music education* (pp. 112-120). Norman: University of Oklahoma.

Doolittle, S., Dodds, P. & Placek, J. (1993). Persistence of beliefs about teaching during formal training of pre service teachers. In S. Stroot (Ed.), Socialization into physical education [Monograph], *Journal of Teaching in Physical Education,* 12,(pp. 355-365).

Duling, E. (2000). Student teachers' descriptions and perceptions of their mentors. *Update: Applications of Research in Music Education,* 19(1), 17-21.

Edwards, H. (1973). *Sociology or sport.* Homewood, IL: Dorsey Press.

Foon, A.E. (1987). Reconstructing the social psychology of sport: An examination of issues. *Journal of Sport Behavior,* 10, 223-230.

Fowler, C.B. (1986). Music for every child, every child for music. *Musical America,* 36(5), 10-13.

Figone, A.J. (1994). Origins of the teacher-coach role: Idealism, convenience, and unworkability. *Physical Educator,* 51 (3),148-156.

Gerber, T. (1989). Reaching all students: The ultimate challenge. *Music Educators Journal,* 75(7), 36-39.

Gruber, K.J., Wiley, S.D., Broughman, S.P., Strizek, G.A. & Burian-Fizgeral, M. (2002). U.S. Department of Education, National Center for Education Statistics, schools and staffing survey, 1999-2000: overview of the data for public, private, public charter, and bureau of Indian affairs elementary and secondary schools. NCES 2002-313., Washington, DC: 2002.

Hoffer, C.R. (1989). Reaching all students: The ultimate challenge. *Music Educators Journal,* 75(7), 33-35.

Kelly, J.R. (1974). Socialization toward leisure: A developmental approach. *Journal of Leisure Research,* 6, 181-193.

Kemp, A.E. (1982). Personality traits of successful music teachers. Psychology of Music [Special issue]. Proceedings of the *Ninth International Seminar on Research in Music Education,* 72-75.

Kemp, A. E. (1996). *The musical temperament: Psychology and personality of musicians.* Oxford: Oxford University Press.

Kemp, A.E. (1997). Individual differences in musical behavior. In D.J. Hargreaves & A. C. North (Eds.), *The social psychology of music* (pp. 25-45). Oxford: Oxford University Press.

Kenyon, G.S. & McPherson, B.D. (1976). An approach to the study of sport socialization. In W.N. Widmeyer (Ed.), *Physical activity and the social sciences*, (pp. 194-205). New York: MSS Information.

Kneer, M.E. (1987). Solutions to teacher/coach problems in secondary schools. *Journal of Physical Education, Recreation and Dance*, 58(2), 28-29.

Koslow, R.E. (1988). College students' perceptions of physical education: Reasons for concern. *The Physical Educator*, 45(2), 100-102.

Locke, L.F. & Massengale, J.D. (1978). Role conflict in teacher/coaches. *Research Quarterly*, 49, 162-174.

L'Roy, D. (1983). *The development of occupational identity in undergraduate music education majors*. Unpublished doctoral dissertation, North Texas State University, Denton.

Macdonald, D. (1999). The professional work of experienced physical education teachers. *Research Quarterly for Exercise and Sport*, 70(1), 41-54.

Macdonald, D., Kirk, D. & Braiuka, S. (1999). The social construction of the physical activitgy field at the school/university interface. *European Physical Education Review*, 5(1), 31-51.

Maehr, M.L. (1983). The development of continuing interests in music. In *Documentary report of the Ann Arbor Symposium on the Applications of Psychology to the Teaching and Learning of Music: Session III* (pp. 5-11). Reston, VA: Music Educators National Conference.

Mark, D. (1998). The music teacher's dilemma: Musician or teacher? *International Journal of Music Education*, 32, 3-22.

Maslow, A. (1970. *Motivation and Personality*. (2nd ed.), New York: Harper &Row.

Massengale, J.D. (1977). Occupational role conflict and the teacher/coach. *Physical Educator*, 34, 64-49.

National Association of State Boards of Education. (n.d.). No pass, no play: eligibility requirements for extracurricular activities. NASBE Policy Update 7 (12), Policy Information Clearinghouse. Retrieved December 15,2 003 from http://www.nasbe.org/Educational_Issues/Policy_Updates/7_12p.html

Nichols, J.G. (1983). Task involvement in music. In *Documentary report of the Ann Arbor Symposium on the Applications of Psychology to the Teaching and Learning of Music: Session III*. Reston, VA: Music Educators National Conference.

Nichols, J.G. (1984). Conceptions of ability and achievement motivation. In C. Ames and R. Ames (Eds.), *Research on motivation in education* (Vol.1). San Diego: Academic Press.

Nixon, H. L. (1984). *Sport and the American dream*. New York: Leisure Press.

O'Connor, A. & Macdonald, D. (2002). Up close and personal on physical education teachers' identity: Is conflict an issue? *Sport, Education and Society*, 7(1), 37-54.

Odenkirk, J.E. (1986). High school athletics and the shortage of qualified coaches: An enigma for the public schools. *The Physical Educator*, 43, 82-85.

Ogilvie B. & Tutko, T. (1970). Self-perception as compared with measured personality of selected male physical educators. In G.S. Kenyon (Ed.), *Contemporary psychology of sport*, (pp. 73-78). Chicago: Athletic Institute.

Ojeme, E.O. (1988). Perceived and actual role of secondary school physical educators. *Journal of Teaching in Physical Education*, 8 (1), 33-45.

O'Sullivan, M., Siedentop, D. & Tannehill, D. (1994). Breaking out: Codependency of high school physical education. *Journal of Teaching in Physical Education*, 13, 421-428.

Placek, J.H. (1983). Conceptions of success in teaching: Busy, happy and good? In T. J. Templin & J.K. Olson (Eds.), *Teaching in physical education*, (pp. 46-56). Champaign, IL: Human Kinetics.

Placek, J., Dodds, P., Doolittle, S., Portman P., Ratcliffe, T. & Pinkman, K. (1995). Teaching recruits' physical education backgrounds and beliefs about purposes for their subject matter. *Journal of Teaching in Physical Education*, 14, 246-261.

Ponick, F.S. (2001). Competing for ratings: Is it a good idea? *Music Educators Journal* 8(6), 21-25.

Roberts, B.A. (1991a). *Musician: A process of labeling*. St. John's: Memorial University of Newfoundland.

Roberts, B.A. (1991b). Music teacher education as identity construction. *International Journal of Music Education*, 18, 30-39.

Roberts, B.A. (1991c). *A place to play: The social world of university schools of music*. St. Johns: Memorial University of Newfoundland.

Roberts, B.A. (2000a). Gatekeepers and the reproduction of institutional realities: The case of music education in Canadian universities. *Musical Performance*, 2(3), 63-80.

Roberts, B.A. (2000b). A North American response to Bouij: Music education student identity construction revisited in Sweden. In R.R. Rideout & S.J. Paul (Eds.), *On the sociology of music education II* (pp. 63-74). Amherst: University of Massachusetts.

Rose, A.M. (1998). Exploring music teacher thinking: A reflective and critical model. In P. Woodford (Ed.), Critical thinking in music: Theory and practice [Monograph]. *Studies in Music from the University of Western Ontario*, 17, 23-44.

Rose, D.A. (1986). Is there a discipline of physical education? *Quest*, 30(1), 1-21.

Rupert, T.A. & Buschner, C. (1989). Teaching and coaching: A comparison of instructional behaviors, *Journal of Teaching in Physical Education*, 14, 246-261.

Sage, G.H. (1980). Sociology of physical educator/coaches: Personal attributes controversy. *Research Quarterly*, 51, 110-121.

Sage, G.H. (1987). Considering the future of physical education. In J.D. Massengale (Ed.), *Trends toward the future in physical education.* (pp.9-24). Champaign, IL: Human Kinetics.

Sage, G.H. (1989). Becoming a high school coach: From playing sports to coaching. *Research Quarterly*, 60(1), 81-92.

Segrave, J.O. (1981). Role preferences among prospective physical education teacher/coaches. *NAPHE Annual Conference Proceedings II*, 53-61.

Siedentop, D. (1994). Curriculum innovation: Toward the 21st century, *ICHPER Journal*, 30(2), 11-14.

Snyder, E.E. & Spreitzer, E. (1978). Socialization comparisons of adolescent female athletes and musicians. *Research Quarterly*, 49, 342-350.

Stroot, S., Collier, C., O'Sullivan, M. & England, K. (1994). Hoops and hurdles: Workplace conditions in secondary physical education. *Journal of Teaching in Physical Education*, 13, 342-360.

Talamini, J. (1973). School athletics: Public policy versus practice. In J. Talamini & C. Page (Eds.), *Sport and society: An anthology.* Boston: Little and Brown.

Templin, T.J. , Woodford, R. & Mulling, C. (1982). On becoming a physical educator: Occupational choice and the anticipatory socialization process. *Quest*, 34 (2), 119-133.

Templin, T.J. (1984). Developing commitment to teaching: The professional socialization of the pre-service physical educator. In H.A. Hoffman and J.E. Rink (Eds.), *Physical Education professional preparation: Insights and foresights* (pp. 119-131). Reston, VA: American Alliance For Health, Physical Education, Recreation and Dance.

Templin, T.J. (1987). Some consideration for teaching physical education in the future. In J.D., Massengale (Ed.), *Trends toward the future in physical education* (pp. 51-68). Champaign, IL: Human Kinetics.

Templin, T., Sparkes, A. & Schempp, P. (1994). Matching the self: the paradoxical case and life history of a late career teacher/coach. *Journal of Teaching in Physical Education*, 13, 274-294.

Walters, M. & Crook, R. (1990). *Sociology one.* Melbourne: Longman Cheshire.

White, H.G. (1967). The professional role and status of music educators in the United States. *Journal of Research in Music Education*, 15(1), 3-10.

Wilcox, R.C. (1987). Dropouts: The failing of high school physical education. *Journal of Physical Education, Recreation and Dance*, 58, (6), 21-25.

Woodford, P.G. (2002). The social construction of music teacher identity in undergraduate music education majors. In R. Colwell & C. Richardson (Eds.), *The new handbook of research on music teaching and learning.* New York: Oxford University Press.

Wubbenhorst, T. (1994). Personality characteristics of music educators and performers. *Psychology of Music*, 22, 63-74.

DILL BRUENGER

SECTION 4:

QUESTIONING WHOM WE SHOULD BE TEACHING

FRED SEDDON
INCLUSIVE MUSIC CURRICULA FOR THE 21ST CENTURY

LEE BARTEL
MUSIC MAKING FOR EVERYONE.

CHAPTER FIFTEEN

Inclusive Music Curricula for The 21st Century

FRED SEDDON

Abstract

Music education practices that focus on the acquisition of instrumental performance skill in the Western classical tradition favour and perpetuates a 'talent' or exclusive orientated view of music education. Changes in music curricula that include music composition and a wider range of musical styles and genres considered appropriate for inclusion have gone a long way to promoting inclusive music education. However, these positive changes in curricula are often circumvented by teacher interpretations of these proposed changes that adhere to their personal musical skills, which are often grounded in instrumental skills based on music literacy. Proposals designed to make music education more inclusive are presented in this chapter. These include focusing on the acquisition of composition, improvisation and aural skills through learning techniques adopted by popular musicians. Suggestions are also made for employing music technology and e-learning environments to assist learning and changes in the recruitment and training of music educators

Introduction

The first section of this chapter will argue that in Western society music is universally regarded as being a specialised activity only to be engaged in by music specialists with 'talent.' It will describe how focusing on teaching musical skills and literacy that are measured by the evaluation of the product of such musical activities perpetuates this specialist perception of music. It will indicate that 'experts' who expect product to conform to criteria they have come to regard as 'appropriate' usually undertake product evaluation. It will further argue that this situation has resulted in the alienation of many individuals potentially capable of engaging in rewarding musical activity. These individuals have been alienated by feelings of inadequacy or exclusion largely generated by current music education practices.

The second section of the chapter will propose alternative inclusive curricula designed to enable individuals to engage in rewarding, valuable, life-long musical activity regardless of the nature of their musical interest and aspirations. It will present current and future technological applications that facilitate individual and collaborative creative music making by developing aural skills through progressive schemes of work which offer 'scaffolding' for the participant. It will focus on the importance of both self and peer-evaluation of the process of music making.

Support for the proposed notion of specialist perception of music education will be provided from relevant current research literature and previous research conducted by myself in collaboration with Susan O'Neill in the areas of 'perceived self-competence,' 'adolescent computer-based composition,' and 'evaluation criteria.' Proposals for alternative curricula will draw from current research in collaborative music making and my current research with Chris Bachelor investigating 'modes of communication during creative music making' and with Gisle Johnsen, Yrjan Tangenes, and Mathilda Joubert investigating 'effects of computer mediation on creative music making in cyberspace.'

The specialisation of music making

In most Western cultures music performance has undergone a process of specialisation which has resulted in a steady decline in amateur performances in favour of 'live' and recorded expert performances (Green, 2001; Paynter, 2002). This process of specialisation contributes to a decline in amateur music making and a rise in music listening with music making being considered the realm of the professional (Green, 2001).

Over the past 40 years there have been many changes in the way music is taught in schools and colleges (Pitts, 2000; Sloboda, 2001; Green, 2001; Cook, 1998; Small, 1998;). These changes reflect changes in society, for example widening the number of styles and genres considered appropriate for music education (Green, 2001; Vulliamy & Lee, 1976; 1982) and a move towards developing a more 'inclusive' music curriculum (Bray, 2000). Despite these changes it is true to say that many countries around the world have developed systems of formal music education that are largely based upon the conventions of Western classical music (Green, 2001; Sloboda 2001). This means that from primary schools through to conservatories a major focus of music education is on the teaching and learning of musical instruments (including voice).

During the last three or four decades the variety of 'acceptable' musical styles regarded as appropriate for inclusion in music curricula has increased to include 'pop,' 'jazz' and 'blues' (Green, 2001). Although this broadening of acceptable styles could be interpreted as an attempt to make music education more 'inclusive' it is problematic. It is not possible to insert alternative musical styles into a set of classroom practices that have been developed to deal with classical music. Musical sub-cultures are more than just the style of music they use, they are context-dependent, have different purposes and interact with inter-personal relationships that give rise to specific meanings (Sloboda, 2001). Many classroom teachers are unable to address adequately issues relating to these styles of music as they lack specific understanding of and exposure to the style and its role for its habitual users (Sloboda, 2001).

In the last two decades much larger proportions of children have had the opportunity to learn musical instruments but despite the broadening of acceptable musical styles many of these children give up playing instruments before they reach adulthood, often during adolescence (O'Neill, 2003; Lamont, 2003; Green; 2001; Sloboda, 2001). This dropout rate is not as a result of losing interest in music per se as music remains central to the lives of most adolescents (North, Hargreaves & O'Neill, 2000). Adolescent dropout rate can be attributed to earlier perceptions of playing an instrument as a 'hobby' which can be 'grown out of,' instruments being perceived as less important than 'academic' subjects, expressions of adolescent autonomy and lacking 'purpose' in adolescent related activities and goals (Sloboda, 2001). Transition from primary to secondary school also leads to adolescents making choices of subjects to study at examination level. For example, in the UK adolescents continuing with music to General Certificate of Secondary Education (GCSE) are as low as 6.8% (Bray, 2000). It can also be argued that many adolescents would only consider themselves to be 'musical' if they were having formal instrumental music tuition. Lamont found that 48% of the 1800 children between the ages of 5 and 16 years she interviewed described themselves as 'non-musicians' because they didn't have instrumental lessons and didn't play a musical instrument even though teachers reported that the same children did play instruments in classroom activities (Lamont, 2003).

Creative music making through composition and improvisation has now been included in many music curricula. All of these changes are welcome attempts to extend the appeal and relevance of music education. However, there is still a tendency for music education to be regarded as the process of delivering to the student a body of musical knowledge that reflects acceptable boundaries of taste and preference. Furthermore, having 'musical talent' often displayed through instrumental performance, is usually regarded as an indication of more 'serious' musical intention. Performance of music from the 'Western classical repertoire' on a traditional acoustic instrument is still probably regarded as being more 'serious' than performance of music from the 'pop' or 'rock' repertoire on a synthesiser.

Support from research studies

In Western cultures being a 'musician' often means being able to play a musical instrument (O'Neill, 2003). Children's attitudes about whether or not they are musical is often reinforced by teacher distinctions between 'musical' and 'un-musical' children based largely upon their ability to play musical instruments (Lamont, 2003). Attitudes to musical self-competence can have consequences when children and adolescents engage in musical activities other than instrumental performance, e.g., computer-based music composition. → Or can encourage...

In two studies conducted with Susan O'Neill we found that child and adolescent self-evaluations of their own computer-based compositions were influenced by their self-perceived musical competence which was related to their prior experience of formal instrumental music tuition (FIMT) (Seddon & O'Neill, 2001 & Seddon & O'Neill, under review). In the first study (Seddon & O'Neill, 2001), 32 children (aged 10 years) formed two groups based on whether or not they had 2 years prior experience of FIMT. The children self-evaluated the computer-based compositions that they produced and the compositions were also evaluated by 8 experienced teachers. The self-evaluations of the children with FIMT were found to be significantly higher than the self-evaluations of the children without FIMT. In contrast to the children's self-evaluations teacher evaluations revealed no significant differences between the compositions based on whether or not the children had or did not have prior experience of FIMT. We interpreted these results to indicate that children with and without FIMT perceived a link between FIMT and their ability to compose which influenced their self-perceived competence in composition when self-evaluating their compositions. Alternatively, we speculated that 2 years prior experience of FIMT wasn't a long enough period of time for the tuition to significantly effect the outcome of composition or that possibly children apply different evaluation criteria than teachers when evaluating compositions.

In order to test the possibility that 2 years prior experience of FIMT was not a long enough period of time for the instrumental tuition to significantly effect the outcome of composition, the second study (Seddon & O'Neill, under review) replicated the first study but this time with adolescents (aged 13-14 years). In this second study 48 adolescents formed two groups based on whether or not they had 4 years prior experience of FIMT. The adolescents self-evaluated the computer-based compositions that they produced and the compositions were also evaluated by 7 experienced teachers. As in the first study, the self-evaluations of the adolescents with FIMT were found to be significantly higher than the self-evaluations of the adolescents without FIMT. Teacher evaluations again revealed no significant differences between the compositions based on whether or not the adolescents had or did not have prior experience of FIMT. These results seemed to support our interpretation that the adolescents in the second study, like the children in the first study, perceived a link between prior experience of FIMT and their ability to compose which effected their self-perceived competence levels when self-evaluating their compositions.

The results of our two studies supported other prior studies that indicated instrumental expertise does not necessarily produce greater composition skills (Webster, Yale & Haefner, 1988; Hickey, 1995 & 2003; Webster, 1990; Folkestad, 1998) yet it appeared that their self-perceived competence levels influenced our participants' self-evaluations. This suggested that children and adolescents believe they can only be 'musical' if they play a musical instrument even when engaged in musical activities like computer-based composition that don't necessarily require instrumental skills.

A further study (Seddon & O'Neill, in press) was conducted in order to test the possibility that adolescents may apply different evaluation criteria than teachers when evaluating musical compositions. This study employed Q-methodology (McKeown & Thomas, 1988) to reveal the criteria adolescents, with and without prior experience of FIMT, use when evaluating musical compositions and compared it to criteria considered important by specialist music teachers. In this study 32 adolescents (aged 13-14 years) formed two groups based on whether they had between 2-4 years prior experience of FIMT or had no prior experience of FIMT. The adolescents participated in a Q-sort procedure that involved rank ordering forty-six Q-items. The Q-items were formulated from four sources: specialist music teacher interviews, adolescent focus group discussions, music curriculum documents, and academic papers investigating the assessment of music composition. Findings from this study indicated that overall the adolescents tended to value different evaluation criteria than specialist music teachers but there was a greater level of agreement between adolescents with prior experience of FIMT and specialist music teachers than between adolescents without prior experience of FIMT and specialist music teachers. Findings also suggested that specialist music teacher evaluations tended to be based on criteria linked to their music training, which was primarily focused on the acquisition of instrumental performance skills.

Summary

The three studies described above indicate how child and adolescent perceptions of the importance of instrumental skill can influence levels of self-perceived competence when engaged in tasks not directly related to instrumental skill. These perceptions are very important when we consider that one of the reasons for including musical activities like computer-based composition was to attempt to broaden music curricula and make them more inclusive. This attempt to make music curricula more inclusive is being undermined by the importance placed on instrumental skill by traditional attitudes to music education.

Instrumental tuition has tended to reflect and reinforce the 'talent' concept of music education. Expert instrumentalists who have learned their craft from other expert instrumentalists in a master/apprentice relationship still deliver the majority of instrumental tuition. Most instrumental tutors have not received any professional teacher education and consider their instrumental skills the only prerequisite required to enable them to teach their pupils effectively. Musical literacy plays a central role in measuring success as an instrumentalist. Progression through public examination grades or promotion through hierarchical positions in bands is also an indicator of success. Engagement in these evaluative activities is impossible without being able to read traditional music notation. As this pattern of music education repeats itself from generation to generation the perception of the requirement of 'talent' and musical literacy is reinforced in the minds of pupils and their parents. The outcome of this situation is that the prevailing perception in society is that music is a specialised activity only to be engaged in by specifically trained individuals.

Like Adams musicals

Despite of the strong perception that music in Western society is a "specialist" pursuit, there is an "informal" involvement with music that focuses on the learning of musical performance and composition through the development of aural skills (Green, 2001; Toynbee, 2000; Vulliamy & Lee, 1976 & 1982). These aural routes often employ a range of technology from the copying of professional musicians' performances to composing original music on computer using specially designed software. Instrumental and vocal parts are learned by listening to CD recordings and copying them. Once the parts are learned it is possible to collaborate with others in the performance of this music. Rapidly developing computer technology has enabled engagement in computer-based music composition that ranges in complexity from the relatively simple juxtaposing of pre-recorded musical samples (e.g., Dance eJay) to the complex production of fully orchestrated pieces created in the home (e.g., Sibelius). Evaluation is usually self- or peer-orientated with no requirement for expert, norm referencing evaluation. Motivation for continuing involvement with music making in these informal settings results from feelings of satisfaction and fulfilment achieved through experiencing musical and social interaction during the process rather than external evaluation of the product (Green, 2001; Toynbee, 2000; Vulliamy & Lee, 1976 & 1982).

If music education is to become more inclusive it is important that learning styles associated with aurally based methods are adopted. This will require teachers to become facilitators rather than providers. The potential advantages of modern technology should be applied to challenge the view that only talented musical experts can benefit from music education. Music education should embrace a more inclusive philosophy enabling everyone to engage in the creative process of music making, developing skills that are relevant to their personal goals using current and future technologies. yes.

Proposals for the future

If the problems discussed above are to be resolved, we need to examine music education provision in three directions: (1) what are we hoping to achieve with any changes implemented, (2) how can music curricula be made more inclusive without weakening existing good practice, and (3) the implications of 1 & 2 on music teacher education.

First, we need to establish some fundamental criteria that form the basis of what it means to be musically educated, without focusing on performance skills. Second, we need to focus on the teaching and learning of musical skills for the majority of pupils and students that do not necessarily require performance skill on a specific musical instrument. This should be done without dismantling the excellent systems already established to support the minority of pupils and students who wish to follow the established conventional routes. Some technological and non-technological solutions are presented below with supportive evidence from research studies. Third, recruitment of trainee teachers should draw from a broader section of the musical community to include individuals with alternative musical skills, e.g., music technology, recording studio technicians, and disc jockeys. Programs of in-service training should be introduced for existing teachers who wish to learn additional skills. Recruiting trainee teachers with a wider selection of musical skills and promoting the concept that such a diverse domain as music cannot be delivered in an educational establishment by one or two narrowly trained individuals even with peripatetic (itinerant) support. Each of the above will be examined in more detail in the following sections.

Hopeful signs exist that some of the improvements in music education described above are being addressed and it should be noted that major improvements in developing inclusivity through curriculum change have been implemented in many countries world-wide. For example, *Music in the National Curriculum* in the UK can be interpreted to allow for the inclusion of much of what has and will be recommended in this chapter. However, teachers who, understandably, do not feel confident engaging in music education practices that fall outside of their own areas of expertise often unintentionally impede this potential inclusivity. They do this by interpreting the curriculum in such a way as to focus on their personal musical skills, which are often a product of a traditional musical training. Also, limited financial resources prevent teachers from recruiting professional assistance or receiving additional in-service training in areas outside their personal expertise.

Music in the National Curriculum in the UK recognises and promotes the interrelated skills of performing, composing and appraising (for detail see http://www.nc.uk.net/nc/contents/Mu-home.htm). If we perceive these three skills as the basic core of music education and they are interpreted in a broad sense they can form the basis of an inclusive programme of music education. Performance can mean performance on anything from a traditional acoustic instrument to, electronic instruments, samplers and the sound-mixing desk. Composition can be anything from a string quartet in the style of Beethoven, to a computer-produced 'soundscape' or film score and a DJ sample mix produced on CD. Appraising (i.e. self-appraisal) during the creative process is a natural consequence of engaging seriously with any of the latter activities and product will inevitably be self-appraised. Teachers should be in a position to facilitate a learning environment where learners can focus on acquiring manipulation skills on their chosen sound producing apparatus. Learners would be given the opportunity to produce imaginative compositions in the style and genre of their choice through media that match their individual skills and style choice. Learners would also develop sophisticated appraisal skills through self, peer, and expert evaluation of their musical process and product. For this scenario to be successful in making music education, more inclusive and effective teachers would have to be comfortable with facilitating experiences beyond their specific expertise. They also need to ensure that interactions with pupils do not project any hierarchical bias towards one experience over another by expressing implicit or explicit value judgements.

Technological solutions

In order to implement the changes described above, without diminishing existing good practice, teachers would require additional resources. Peripatetic (itinerant) instrumental teachers would still need to be provided to support the traditional routes to specialist music school and conservatories. It is unrealistic to propose the provision of unlimited resources to provide experts in all the areas described above (e.g., music technology experts, sound engineers, and disc jockeys). Projects that bring professional musicians and composers from a variety of genres into schools to work with pupils (e.g., composer in residence) can initiate pupil interest and provide motivation for projects but motivation can decline when the expert leaves. ICT employing Internet communication is a potential answer to resource and teacher expertise problems in some circumstances as it can facilitate virtual collaboration between teachers, experts, and students that would be difficult and expensive to offer 'in reality' (Rees, 2002). Pupil motivation and inclusivity is also enhanced by the introduction of this virtual collaboration (Cosenza & MacLeod, 1998). There are collaborative music composition systems available on the Internet e.g. Composers in Electronic Residence (CIER) (Rees, 2002; http://www.edu.yorku.ca/CIER/Page2.html) and The Vermont MIDI Project (Cosenza & MacLeod, 1998; http://www.vtmidi.org/) (for more detail see Rees, 2001).

Evidence from research projects

My own interest in virtual collaboration began with a research project conducted with colleagues in 2003 (Seddon, Joubert, Johnsen & Tangenes, 2003). This exploratory research project investigated the effects of computer mediation, prior musical experience, and culture on the process and product of collaborative computer-based music composition. The study linked a school in the UK with a school in Norway to engage in computer-mediated collaborative composition via e-mail using 'Music Interactive' a music sequencing software program with an integral text and email facility (see http://www.Musit.com).

In this study participants were grouped into composing pairs (one from each country) balanced for prior musical experience. Prior musical experience in the study was based on whether or not the participants had received a minimum of four years formal instrumental music tuition (FIMT). There were eight participants (4 Norwegian, 4 English) aged 13-14 years and they formed 4 composition pairs one from each country. Pair 1 were both non-FIMT, Pair 2 were both FIMT, Pair 3 were one FIMT (UK) one non-FIMT (Norway) and Pair 4 were one FIMT (Norway) one non-FIMT (UK). Each composing pair had 6 composition sessions (3 in each country). After each composition session the evolving collaborative compositions were saved in separate files and emailed between the UK and Norway until completion. This process produced six music and six embedded text files for each composing pair.

Semi-structured interviews were conducted with individual participants pre- and post-composition in order to gain the participant's perspective and to provide support for researcher interpretations of musical and text dialogue. The main findings were, all 4 composing pairs were successful in producing a composition that 'pleased' both members and they all reported high levels of motivation, enjoyment, and the willingness to continue working with their partners. Communication on both musical and 'text' levels was revealed and 'adolescent preferences' were reported more often than 'cultural influences' as reasons for effective collaboration. Prior experience of FIMT was linked to extended and complex musical dialogue, critical engagement with musical ideas, and producing an 'exploratory' environment. No prior experience of FIMT was linked to uncritical and descriptive dialogue and a 'cumulative' environment. The most productive pairings had at least one participant having had prior experience of FIMT.

These results indicate that collaborative virtual environments can be useful and can produce high levels of motivation for both FIMT and Non-FIMT students. Also pairing FIMT and Non-FIMT students can result in more effective, 'exploratory' composition processes. This was a particularly interesting finding as it contradicted previous findings which reported links between FIMT and less 'exploratory' composition processes (Seddon & O'Neill, 2003; Folkestad, 1998). These less 'exploratory' processes were also found to be linked to compositions with more 'fixed ideas' about crafting music (Webster, Yale & Haefner, 1988; Hickey, 1995 & 2003; Webster, 1990; Folkestad, 1998). The contradiction between the results might be attributable the virtual environment in the Seddon, Joubert, Johnsen & Tangenes (2003) study. Contradictions might result from the fact that in the virtual study the participants were not aware of each other's prior musical experiences, but in the other studies conducted in 'reality,' the participants probably would have been aware of each other's musical experience. More research is required comparing computer-based composition in the two different environments.

Teacher intervention

Computer-based composition makes it possible for students to compose music without first having to learn to play a musical instrument or learn traditional music notation. It also allows students to manipulate sounds that are associated with their everyday musical environment and are part of their culture. However, will merely engaging with computer-based composition individually or collaboratively necessarily improve students' composition skills? Is intervention by teachers required? If so, what form should this intervention take?

One view is that intervention should be a dialogue between the student and the teacher based upon reflexive evaluation. The teacher would encourage the students along a path (or through a spiral) towards a goal that is grounded in recognised, good composition practice based on Western classical values (Hickey, 2003; Rees, 2003; Webster, 2003; Younker, 2003). In order to promote this view specific composition tasks should be set. These tasks must reach a balance between being too 'closed,' promoting low levels of intrinsic motivation and creativity resulting in 'rule-bound' composition, and being too 'open' which, although it can promote potentially higher motivation and creativity, may run the risk of resulting in chaotic 'noise' (Hickey, 2003). This view appears to be based upon the assumption that, because of their training and experience, teachers know what makes a 'good' composition and it is their responsibility to pass this knowledge on to the student by teaching composition. It also impacts upon the evaluation process and criteria employed (see Hickey, 2002; Hickey, 2001; Webster & Hickey, 1995). This view suggests that student compositions should be regarded as relatively naïve offerings that can be shaped and improved by applying conventional tried and tested techniques of past successful composers (e.g., ABA and Rondo form repetition, augmentation and diminution, timbre combinations etc.). Unfortunately, many teachers lack confidence in teaching composition because they did not receive training in composition during their musical studies and they are not practising composers.

An alternative view is that students have a natural musicality (Paynter, 2003) and they acquire musical knowledge through the process of enculturation (Sloboda & Davidson, 1996) meaning that there is no such thing as a musically naïve adolescent (Folkestad, 1998). Students' natural musicality manifests itself in making up music (Paynter, 2003) much in the way that across the ages music has been made up, invented, and performed by untutored people (Paynter, 2003). Paynter also believes that composition, which he prefers to refer to as making up music, is a natural process that just requires opportunity and encouragement (Paynter, 2003). Central to the difference between these two viewpoints is assessment or evaluation (see Paynter, 2003; Ross, Radnor, Mitchel and Bierton, 1993).

Increasing pressure during the second half of the twentieth century for schools to provide evidence of their efficacy can promote the acceptance of the former view as the passing on of an agreed body of knowledge makes it easier to evaluate pupils progress and provide efficacy of teaching (Paynter, 2003). It could be that exercising imagination, creative response, and the expression of independent views while making up music may be assessed but cannot be evaluated (Paynter, 2003). Paynter's view on evaluation is that teachers should respond to student compositions by commenting purposefully and encouragingly involving the student composer and his or her peers on how the composer's idea was fulfilled.

There are many similarities between these two opposing views but there does seem to be a fundamental difference that may be grounded in what may be described as music education being regarded as aspiring to be 'inclusive' or 'exclusive.' Teachers may lack confidence in making evaluations of children's music compositions because they are not practising composers and not only doubt their own ability but also doubt student's potential to respond. It is not my intention to promote one view over the other but to accept there is validity in both viewpoints. What is of concern to me is how technology can be developed to support the teaching of music regardless of the view teachers ascribe to.

Music e-learning environments

During the last decade much progress has been made in developing music e-learning environments (for excellent reviews see Webster, 2002; Rees, 2002). A good example of a music e-learning environment The Vermont MIDI Project (Cosenza & MacLeod, 1998) can be found at http://www.vtmidi.org/ . The exploratory study (Seddon, Joubert, Johnsen & Tangenes, 2003) examined collaborative computer-based composition via email employing 'Musit Interactive.' From this study we developed the idea of extending the collaborative communication process within an Internet based e-learning environment to involve further collaborative, creative music making activities. We believed that moving from an email-based collaboration to an Internet-based e-learning environment would produce greater flexibility for creative collaboration. An interactive, collaborative Internet-based music e-learning environment 'MusicLAB Online' (http://www.MusicLABonline.com) was commissioned from Musit A.S. (the Norwegian music technology company that supplied 'Music Interactive' for the previous study). This newly developed e-learning environment will facilitate international online communication between educational establishments and has been designed specifically for musical collaboration. A future international study to be conducted between educational establishments in the UK, Ireland, Norway and the US has been initiated to test the efficacy of this music e-learning environment. Researchers will also record and evaluate emergent modes of communication and teaching strategies as they develop in the e-learning environment. It is anticipated that new and effective modes of communication will be developed by the participants to mitigate the perceived restrictions of such environments e.g. the disembodiment of the learning process (Dreyfus, 2001) and restricted social interaction (Kreijns, Kirschner & Jochems, 2003). It is also anticipated that new teaching strategies, based on the emergent, effective modes of communication, will be developed to take advantage of music e-learning environments. The proposed study will offer participants the opportunity to engage in creative music making within the e-learning environment. Where it will differ from other Internet collaborative composition sites is musical activities will not be restricted to composition or rely mainly upon mentoring and evaluation by experts in the 'Western Classical Tradition.' It is anticipated that increased flexibility in the music e-learning environment will accommodate teaching styles based on both alternative viewpoints discussed above. It is anticipated that over time professional musicians from all sections of the world-wide musical community, music teachers, pupils and students from schools, colleges and universities will become members of online communities and will interact to provide expertise across a broad range of music and musical activity. In future if pupils and students wish to embark upon a musical activity that is outside the experience of their teacher they can enter a music e-learning environment and seek 'others' who have experience in the activity or wish to collaborate to acquire it. The 'others' may be other students or teachers who have acquired expertise or professional artists in the chosen field. While developing 'MusicLAB Online,' Musit AS has found many professional artists willing to make their work available to students and teachers within this educational e-context and in some cases become more directly involved. Teachers will have to be prepared to accept the change in their role from instructor to facilitator but will not have to relinquish organisational responsibility. They will have total control over student access to the various areas of the e-learning environment and be able to organise their own grouping of students. Assessment procedures will be based on self and peer assessments with teachers always able to assess progress made by students in any musical activity based upon improvements in the interrelated skills of performing, composing and appraising provided their interpretations of the skills are broad enough.

Music e-learning environments will also be able to provide students with opportunities to receive support in teaching themselves to play musical instruments. Young musicians can learn to play music they identify with by listening to recordings and copying them and exchanging knowledge and skill with their peers (Green, 2001). One example of how this could be achieved in music e-learning environments is through pre-prepared musical 'loops' (i.e. small sections of music that can be played and re-played in a music-sequencing software package). These 'loops' could be made available for students to download from the e-learning environment. These 'loops' can be from any style of music the student is interested in learning to play and on any instrument. Once downloaded, the student selects the 'loop' and hears the 'loop' by inserting it in the music sequencing software within the e-learning environment and pressing play. The student can then attempt to copy the 'loop' on his/her chosen instrument. The 'loop' can be repeated as many times as necessary for the student to learn to play it, computers have infinite patience. When the student thinks that the 'loop' has been learned on the musical instrument he/she could then record their performance of the 'loop' in the music-sequencing program (via MIDI or microphone) and re-play the recording comparing the original 'loop' to his/her recording. Not only is this learning to play or perform on the instrument it also incorporates a natural appraisal process. This process includes decision making on the accuracy of the pitch, rhythm, style and timbre. All this activity can then be saved in music files designated to the individual for future appraisal by the teacher. The advantage of this system is that the student must rely upon self-appraisal prior to saving the file for the teacher's appraisal. This process may begin with a very simple 'loop' e.g. a single note moving to a 3 or 4 note 'loop' with stepwise movement and simple rhythm with the length and complexity increasing as the student's aural and performance skills improve. The benefits of this mode of learning to play an instrument is that the student selects the music to be learned, learns at a pace that is suitable for the individual and can be engaged with at a time and in a place to suit the individual. The teacher will be able to access the saved files, also at a convenient time, to monitor the student's progress in performance and appraisal skills which will be apparent to the teacher regardless of whether or not the teacher is experienced in the style of music chosen. As student skill levels in playing an instrument and manipulating the technology develop the teacher may monitor composing skill as the student begins to use the music sequencing program to compose original pieces of music. These pieces can be exchanged with other students within the e-learning environment forming collaborative works. Recording instrumental parts to synchronise with existing parts is beneficial for acquiring ensemble playing skills also appraisal skills can be developed during the process of finalising a piece by adding electronic effects such as 'reverberation,' 'chorus' and 'distortion.' The whole process of how popular musicians learn to play (see Green, 2001) can be carried out in a music e-learning environment without the teacher having to have personal experience in the style of music chosen by the student.

Non-technological solutions

Music education in the Western world largely focuses on teaching written notation and teaching students how to perform the European cannon (Sawyer, 1999). This focus on notation and performance of pre-composed works has shifted attention away from the important music-making practise of improvisation. If more attention were paid to teaching improvisation prior to notation more students would continue with their music education as many students find learning notation tedious and undermines their confidence (Sawyer, 1999). Western classical music holds a privileged position in that it is claimed to be spiritual, intellectual and unique in the world's musical cultures (Small, 1998) yet it appeals to a tiny minority of people even in Western industrial societies as evidenced by recorded music sales (Small, 1998; Green, 2001). Music should be regarded as an 'activity' rather than a 'thing' by focusing on music making e.g. improvised conversations (Sawyer, 1999) or musicking (Small, 1998) rather than the realisation by musicians of a pre-composed musical piece. Why do we find fulfilment and satisfaction in improvised music making especially when collaborating with others?

Evidence from research project

In a recent study conducted with my colleague Chris Bachelor (Jazz musician and educator) we investigated our proposed concept 'empathetic creativity' which is based on the concept 'empathetic intelligence' (Arnold, 2003). Empathetic creativity in collaborative, creative music making is analogous to empathetic intelligence as each music collaboration can result in enhanced musical experience (i.e. learning). As with empathetic intelligence in the pedagogical context empathetic creativity in collaborative, creative music making also requires collaborating individuals to interact empathetically. This is achieved through musical communication that facilitates attunement and mirroring creating a preparedness for exploration, risk taking, concentration and rapport taking into account shifts in intra-subjective and inter-subjective experiences resulting in a creative act (Seddon, forthcoming). We believe empathetic creativity is the aspired to outcome of all collaborative improvisatory music making (Seddon and Bachelor, 2003; Seddon, forthcoming). In our study, six undergraduate jazz students were interviewed, observed and videotaped during rehearsal and performance. The initial interviews were conducted using a constructivist elicitation technique developed by Denicolo and Pope (1990) and applied in a study by Burnard (2000). The participants were asked to reflect upon and relate critical incidents they felt helped shape their musical development. None of the participants referred to learning music in school being a significant influence on their musical development, most found it irrelevant and did not engage, yet they all now aspire to be professional jazz musicians. They all cited later informal, untutored, collaborative, improvisation sessions as positive motivational experiences that inspired them to return to formal music education in the context of the jazz course they were currently pursuing. The content of the school music curriculum did not motivate these highly intrinsically motivated musicians and they were forced to seek their music education outside the formal education system in order to prepare them to re-enter the system at university level.

Analysis of the videotape recordings of rehearsal and performance revealed a form of non-verbal communication that began with 'attunement' (Arnold, 2003) and developed into 'empathetic interplay' (Arnold, 2003) which could produce 'spontaneous musical utterances' (Davidson & Good, 2002) which was interpreted as 'empathetic creativity' (Seddon & Bachelor, 2003). During retrospective verbal protocols (Richardson & Whitaker, 1996) stimulated by viewing videotaped recordings of rehearsals and performance participants supported researcher interpretations of their modes of communication. Additional support for researcher interpretations was obtained in post-analysis interviews with participants when results and interpretations were presented to and discussed with participants. All participants described empathetic interplay as desirable but not always achievable. There is a view that this form of musical communication is only available to individuals who have already achieved high levels of musical expertise (Berliner, 1994; Monson, (1996). Some hold the view that it is found naturally in very young children and can be developed in an appropriate atmosphere that is 'safe' and facilitates preparedness for exploration, risk taking, concentration and rapport (Sawyer, 1999; Burnard, 2000; Kenny & Gellrich, 2002; Paynter, 2003; Young, in press). If music education is to be made more inclusive, then performance should focus on music making through collaborative improvisation using musical instruments appropriate to the individual's instrumental skill level in order to make this activity possible, enjoyable and communicative. Music education will remain an exclusive domain if the focus of performance continues to focus on teaching written notation and showing students how to perform the European cannon (Sawyer, 1999; Paynter, 2003). Undoubtedly there is a minority demand for the conventional exclusive pathway through music education, which has been provided historically. This pathway should be preserved but providing an inclusive music education for the vast majority of pupils should now become a priority. Inevitably, this will mean greater resources will be required for music education but this is not an argument for maintaining the status quo.

Music Teacher education

Most trainee music teachers are recruited into teacher education programs at university after having progressed through conventional music education systems where they will have gained high levels of performance skill on their chosen instrument(s). They will also have passed exam entry requirements (e.g. GCSE and A-level in the UK) that involve examination courses based on performance, musical literacy, musical analysis, theory and some may include composition. Their studies will mainly have centred on music from the Western classical tradition. Some trainee teachers will receive instruction on music technology and be encouraged to learn about a broad range of musical styles from 'pop,' jazz and blues to 'world music' but generally they will not have first hand experience of performing in these styles or have experienced how they are learned. Other music teachers will be recruited from the ranks of graduates from music conservatories who have not, for one reason or another, embarked upon a full time career in performing. Instead, they will have taken a teacher education program (postgraduate certificate in education, PGCE in the UK) to acquire teaching skills to prepare them for entering music education. Either route to becoming a music teacher in school will usually have found them spending the major part of their study time perfecting their instrumental performance and music literacy skills towards a 'concert platform' level. A recent survey of 750 heads of music in the UK (York, 2001) found that 78% of respondents had degrees based in classical music with 50% being either classical pianists, organists, or singers. Many music education courses are examined, at least in part, by a formal instrumental performance at the end of the course and are impossible to pursue without a relatively high level of music literacy and performance skill. Very few require musicians to be able to play an instrument by ear, improvise or compose. Once employed as music teachers in schools, teachers usually spend the majority of their time teaching general classroom music to pupils between the ages of 5-14 years and the minority of their time teaching examination courses which a small minority of students have elected to pursue. The number of occasions that music teachers will need to draw on their high levels of instrumental performance skills acquired during their teacher education in relation to the time spent acquiring them brings into question the educational justification for focusing on such high levels of instrumental performance skills in music teacher education. This requirement of relatively high levels of performance skill (on a conventional, orchestral instrument in the Western classical tradition) for most music education courses restricts the recruitment of people with other valid expertise (e.g. music technologists, sound recording engineers, disc jockeys, 'pop,' jazz and blues musicians with improvisation and composition expertise). It also plays a part in perpetuating the 'talent' orientated and 'exclusive' student-perception of music (Wright, 2002). A fundamental change in music teacher recruitment criteria coupled with change in curriculum for music teacher education and an increase in in-service training is required if music teachers are to be able to teach music in the way it is often outlined in current worldwide national music curricula. One example of required change would be to take into account the availability of new technology like e-learning environments that are usually asynchronous learning environments. Such asynchronous learning environments will require different teaching techniques to take into account the diminished social interaction created by communicating via the Internet (Dreyfus, 2001). Current research into the efficacy of these e-learning environments investigated the feasibility of incorporating their application into music teacher education and have reported resulting improvements in teaching techniques (Reese, 2001). Without changes of this nature in music teacher education music teachers will continue to resort to interpreting new curricula in a way that relates to their existing areas of expertise instead of the requirements of the curriculum and their students (Johansen, 2002; Paynter, 2003). This will require less emphasis on unnecessarily high levels of instrumental skill to allow more time for emphasis on how to adopt the role of facilitator and co-learner in technological and non-technological collaborative learning environments.

Summary

As we progress through the 21st Century it is time we closely examined how we should promote the activity of music making in our education systems. There will be those who would argue for the supremacy of the Western classical tradition and conventional curriculum on the grounds that they have served us well so far. Without doubt the largely exclusive nature of music education world wide has provided us with musical experts that have enriched the lives of many people. It is arguable however that these people form a minority and their involvement with music is evolving into a relatively passive form of engagement through listening to expert professional recordings and performances rather than engaging in active amateur music making. If this trend to passivity is to be halted and reversed we must make music education inclusive. This will entail having a broader interpretation of what constitutes a musical performance in a formal music educational context, encouraging collaborative, creative music making in real and virtual environments and encouraging self and peer appraisal of musical activity. It is only by giving individuals the confidence to self-appraise their musical activities we can hope to promote lifelong involvement in music making. Much work is needed if these proposed changes are to be brought about and as argued above it is not enough to just change curricula. Attitudes and beliefs will have to change to ensure that changes in curricula are implemented in the schools, colleges and universities in the way they were intended. Change in music teacher education is required to ensure entry into the profession reflects a broader cross section of musical society and provides teaching skills relevant to inclusive music education curricula. Teachers should be equipped to lend support to students as they learn their skills through 'learner-centred' education. Music education should celebrate, understand and promote access to the diversity of music within each society if it is to realise the musical potential of the individuals it is meant to serve (Welch, 2001).

References

Arnold, R. (2003) Empathetic Intelligence: The Phenomenon of Intersubjective Engagement. Paper presented at the *First International Conference on Pedagogies and Learning*, 1-4th October 2003, University of Southern Queensland.

Berliner, P.F. (1994) *Thinking in Jazz: The Infinite Art of Improvisation*, The University of Chicago Press: Chicago.

Burnard, P. (2000) How Children Ascribe Meaning to Improvisation and Composition: rethinking pedagogy in music education, *Music Education Research*, Vol.2, No.1, p.7-24.

Bray, D. (2000) An examination of GCSE music uptake rates, *British Journal of Music Education*, Vol. 17, pp. 79-89.

Cosenza, G. & MacLeod, S. (1998) Vermont MIDI distance learning network: a model for technology in classroom music. In S.D. Lipscomb (Ed.), *Proceedings of the fifth international Technological Directions in Music Learning conference*, San Antonio, TX: Institute for Music Research, pp. 137-138.

Cook, N. (1998) *Music: a very short introduction*, Oxford University press: Oxford.

Davidson, J.W., & Good, J.M.M. (2002) Social and Musical Co-ordination Between Members of a String Quartet: An Exploratory Study, *Psychology of Music*, Vol.30, No.2, p.186-201.

Denicolo, P. & Pope, M. (1990) Adults Learning – Teachers Thinking. In Day, C., Pope, M. & Denicolo, P (Eds.), *Insight into Teachers' Thinking and Practice*, p. 155-169. Basingstoke: Falmer.

Dreyfus, H.L. (2001) *On the Internet*, London: Routledge.

Folkestad, G. (1998) Musical learning as cultural practice: as exemplified in computer-based creative music making. In B. Sundin, G.E. McPherson, and G. Folkestad (Eds.), *Children composing: research in music education*, Malmo Academy of Music: Lund University pp. 97-134.

Green, L. (2001) *How popular musicians learn: a way ahead for music education*, Ashgate Publishing: Aldershot, England.

Hickey, M. (2003) Creative Thinking in the Context of Music Composition. In M.

Hickey (Ed.) *Why and how to teach music composition: a new horizon for music education*. MENC, The National Association for Music Education, pp.31-53.

Hickey, M. (2002) Creativity research in music, visual art, theatre, and dance. In R. Colwell & C. Richardson (Ed.s) *The new handbook of research on music teaching and learning*, Oxford: Oxford University Press, Ch. 23, pp.398-415.

Hickey, M. (2001) An application of Amabile's consensual assessment technique for rating the creativity of children's musical compositions, *Journal of Research in Music Education*, Vol. 49, No. 3, pp. 234-244.

Hickey, M. (1995) Qualitative and quantitative relationships between children's creative musical thinking processes and products,' *unpublished doctoral dissertation*, Northwestern University, Evanston, Il.

Johansen, G. (2002) The challenge of change in music education. In I.M. Hanken, S.G. Nielson & M. Nerland (Eds.) *Research in and for higher music education: festschrift for Harald Jorgensen*, NMH-publikasjoner, 2002:2, Norway: Oslo, pp135-148.

Kenny, B.J., & Gellrich, M. (2002) Improvisation. In Parncutt, R. & McPherson, G.E. (Eds.) *The Science & Psychology of Music Performance: Creative strategies for teaching and learning* (pp. 117-134) Oxford University Press: Oxford.

Lamont, A. (2003) Musical identities and the school environment. In MacDonald, A.R., Hargreaves, D.J., and Miell, D. (Eds.) *Musical Identities*, pp. 41-59, Oxford: Oxford University Press.

Monson, I. (1996) *Saying Something: Jazz Improvisation and Interaction*, The University of Chicago Press: Chicago.

McKeown, B & Thomas, D. (1988) *Q Methodology*. London. Sage Publications.

O'Neill, S.A. (2003) The self-identity of young musicians. In MacDonald, A.R., Hargreaves, D.J., and Miell, D. (Eds.) *Musical Identities*, pp. 79-96, Oxford: Oxford University Press.

Paynter, J. (2002) Music in the school curriculum: why bother? *British Journal of Music Education*, Vol. 19, No. 3 pp215-226.

Pitts, S. (2000) *A century of change in music education: historical perspectives on contemporary practice in British secondary schools*, Ashgate Publishing: Aldershot, England.

Rees, F. J. (2002) Distance learning and collaboration in music education. In R. Colwell & C. Richardson (Eds.) *The new handbook of research on music teaching and learning*, Oxford: Oxford University Press, Ch.16, pp. 257-273.

Rees, S. (2001) Integration of on-line composition mentoring into music teacher education, *Contributions to Music Education*, Vol.28, No. 1, pp. 9-26.

Richardson, C & Whitaker, N. (1996) Thinking about think alouds in music education research, *Research studies in music education*, Vol. 6 pp.38-49.

Ross, M., Radnor, H., Mitchell, S. & Bierton, C. (1993) *Assessing achievement in the arts*, Open University Press: Buckingham, Philadelphia.

Sawyer, R.K. (1999) Improvised conversations: music, collaboration and development, *Psychology of Music*, Vol. 27, No.2, pp.192-216.

Seddon, F. A. (forthcoming) Communication during collaborative, creative music making. In Miell, D and

Littleton, K. (Eds.) *Collaborative Creativity*, Free Association Books: London.

Seddon, F.A., & O'Neill, S.A. (2001) An evaluation study of computer-based compositions by children with and without prior experience of formal instrumental music tuition,' *Psychology of Music*, Vol. 29 (1): pp.4-19.

Seddon, F.A. & O'Neill, S.A. (2003) Creative thinking processes in adolescent computer-based composition: an analysis of strategies adopted and the influence of formal instrumental music training,' *Music Education Research*. Vol.5, No.2, pp.125-138.

Seddon, F.A. & O'Neill, S.A. (in press) The application of Q-Methodology to the study of criteria used by adolescents in the evaluation of their musical compositions, accepted for publication by *Musicae Scientiae* October 2003.

Seddon, F.A. and O'Neill, S.A. (under review) How does formal instrumental music tuition (FIMT) impact on self- and teacher-evaluations of adolescents' computer-based compositions? *Psychology of Music*.

Seddon, F.A. and Bachelor, C. (2003) Modes of communication during collaborative creative music making an exploratory study, *proceedings of the Third International Research in Music Education Conference* (RIME) 2003, 8-12 April at The University of Exeter.

Seddon, F.A., Joubert. M.M., Johnsen, G. and Tangenes, Y. (2003) The effects of computer-mediation on cross-cultural collaborative music composition, *proceedings of the 5th Triennial Conference of the European Society for the Cognitive Sciences of Music* (ESCOM), Hanover University of Music and Drama, September 8-13, 2003.

Sloboda, J.A. (2001) Emotion, functionality and the everyday experience of music: where does music education fit, *Music Education Research*, Vol. 3 pp. 243-253.

Sloboda, J.A. & Davidson, J.W. (1996) The acquisition of musical performance expertise: Deconstructing the "talent" account of individual differences in musical expressivity. In K.A. Ericssion (Ed.) *The road to excellence: the acquisition of expert performance in the arts and sciences, sports and games*, Lawrence Erlbaum, pp. 107-126.

Small, C. (1998) *Musicking: the meanings of performing and listening*, Wesleyan University press: Hanover.

Vulliamy, G & Lee, E. (Eds.) (1976) *Pop music in school*, Cambridge University Press: Cambridge.

Vulliamy, G & Lee, E. (Eds.) (1982) *Pop, rock and ethnic music in school*, Cambridge University Press: Cambridge.

Webster, P. (2002) Computer-based technology and music teaching and learning. In R. Colwell & C. Richardson (Eds.) *The new handbook of research on music teaching and learning*, Oxford: Oxford University Press Ch. 24 pp. 416-438.

Webster, P. (1990) Study of international reliability for the measure of creative thinking in music (MCTM), *paper presented at the general poster session of the MENC National Conference*, Washington DC.

Webster, P., Yale, C., & Haefner, M. (1988) test-retest reliability of measures of creative thinking in music for children with formal music training, *paper presented at the poster session, 1988 MENC National In-Service Meeting*, Indianapolis, Indiana.

Webster, P. & Hickey, M. (1995) Rating scales and their use in assessing children's music compositions, *The quarterly journal of music teaching and learning*, Vol. 6, No. 4, pp. 28-44. University of Northern Colorado School of Music.

Welch, G. (2001) *The misunderstanding of music*, The Institute of Education, University of London: London

Wright, R. (2001) Music for all? Pupil's perceptions of the GCSE Music examination in one South Wales secondary school, *British Journal of Music Education*, Vol. 19, No. 3, pp 227-241.

York, N. (2001) *Valuing School Music: a report on school music*, London: University of Westminster and Rockschool Ltd.

Young, S. (in press) The Interpersonal Dimension: a Potential Source of Musical Creativity for Young Children, *Musicae Scientiae*.

Chapter Sixteen

Music-Making for Everyone

Lee R. Bartel

Abstract

This chapter focuses on junior and high school music and argues that at this level music education is essentially practiced as orchestra, band, or choir. There are departures from this but most music teachers resent and neglect these alternatives. The problem with "non-performance" music, meaning usually "general music," is that it lacks the scope and sequence clarity of performance music, and usually consists of students who lack the attitude and discipline valued in performance ensemble participants. After examining the problems with non-music-making "general music," it looks at the difference between performance and music-making, and explores music making possibilities in "general music." It argues that alternative ways to make music in the classroom, like guitar, steel pan, African drumming, gamelan, composition and improvisation, can be considered "general music" because they are accessible by students who lack the years of consistent instruction needed for high school band or orchestra. The chapter argues that music education has an obligation to reach all students, even in junior and senior high school. The means proposed to accomplish this is a variety of socially and culturally relevant forms of music-making. However the "musical" content of music class is only part of the solution to the exclusivity of music classes. The "pedagogical" content is equally if not more important. The chapter concludes with an appeal for an emotionally sensitive, child-centred pedagogy that develops greater student responsibility in collaborative small group contexts and features abundant tact, thoughtfulness, and playfulness.

Introduction

Should school music be for everyone? Most would say it should, for the first seven or eight years of schooling. But, after that there is no agreement. Those supporting traditional music programs do not really want "everyone" – they only want those talented, motivated, or well-disciplined students who make good ensemble members. Those music educators who have accepted the concept of music as one of the basic intelligences may theoretically believe music education for all students beyond eighth grade is a good idea, but are conflicted about the pragmatics of accommodating those with less motivation, those with less skill and aptitude, and those with inadequate preparation for the level of attempted entry. But the problem is not just one of "talent" and motivation, it is now also one of cultural relevance. In 1981 StatsCan identified only six "ethnic enclaves" in Toronto, Vancouver and Montreal. In 2001 StatsCan identified 254 "ethnic enclaves" in those same three cities (Toronto Star, September 27, 2004, p. A6). Part of the problem is knowing what to do with those students who do not fit neatly into the traditional performing programs dominated by both the musical and pedagogical tradition of western Europe. The solution tried most often is "general music."

"General music" as a class that basically listens and talks about music is conceptually appealing to music educators as an alternative to performing ensembles because it does address one of the main problems of performance-based programs – limited access points to the program and the need for pre-requisite knowledge. A student who has not begun to play an instrument at the starting point for the instrumental track will probably not start later. The student moving from an area without an instrumental program to a school with one, will probably not start mid-stream. The access problem is accentuated by economics, culture, and regional and international mobility. But the very concept of "general music" is a problem. Bennett Reimer (1994) observes:

> "That music educators have not achieved a carefully constructed and widely shared concept of general music is attested to by our dissatisfaction with the name. No one is very happy about the name "general music," but no good alternative has presented itself. This is not a trivial matter easily fixed... it reflects nothing less than our inability as a field to answer many of the most fundamental questions underlying general music education(p. 3).

Determining what "general music" does mean today is not simple. Is it everything other than band, orchestra, and choir? The Society for General Music (SGM) within the Music Educators National Conference (MENC) includes teachers of classes from K -12, teachers of Orff and Kodaly programs, teachers of Junior High guitar classes, and teachers of non-performance college preparation music courses. Each teacher may call what s/he is doing general music. Is general music all of this?

At its broadest, general music can be described the way Eloise Haldeman (1988) does as:

> a larger framework that encompasses comprehensive, in-depth and quality musical learning; that allows those in performing ensembles to study and to become acquainted with music that is beyond their performance ability; that can be adapted within a pluralistic society to fit the needs of local areas and populations; that leads all learners, within their abilities to develop understandings, appreciations, and aesthetic sensibilities–not only in music, but also in other arts and in the humanities–that will continue to grow during their lifetimes." (p.4)

In this definition general music is viewed as an over-arching concept of music education. It is an educational ideal focused less on performing than on "understandings, appreciation, and aesthetic sensibilities." It is not specific to any one type of program. Band, orchestra, or appreciation classes could all be pursuing this form of "general music."

For some educators "general music" refers to music instruction when it is given to all students in the school as a required part of the curriculum. This then refers specifically, in most places, to music instruction in elementary K-6 classrooms.

Many educators use a narrower definition for "general music" – a definition that deals more with the structural school realities of who is in the class and why rather than the content of the classes. The most common is to classify all music classes that are not part of a band, orchestra, or choir program as "general music." In addition, it is often used as a classification only for those levels where band, orchestra, or choir programs are available. These performance programs enrol the really "serious" students (at least those serious about school band, orchestra, or choir) and those who are not as serious about music (i.e. typical school music) are then left for "general music" classes which then, in most schools where there are no opportunities outside of orchestra, band, or choir, become non-performance classes.

Paul R. Lehman (1988) points to the need for music classes in high school for the "general student." "By 'general student' I mean the student who for lack of interest, ability, or time, or for whatever reason, does not participate in the school's performing groups" (p.79). The hegemony of the orchestra, band, or choir is daunting indeed, and the disparaging designation of "general student" for someone who may be very serious about some form of popular music or world music but is assume by the music education establishment to "lack ... interest [or] ability" is disturbing.

Thomas Regelski, in his book *Teaching General Music*, focuses on middle and high school classes that engage primarily in active creating, exploring, or listening to music sounds. That essentially means classes other than orchestra, band, or choir. He recommends instruction be planned to meet specific behavioural objectives related to the development of conceptual knowledge. Action oriented learning is planned to illustrate and reinforce these conceptual learnings. Teachers engaged in doing this are teaching general music.

I reluctantly use the term "general music" with the most common definition—music classes in middle and high schools for students not in orchestra, band, or choir; music classes for the differently-motivated students; music classes for students who may lack interest in the kind of music performed by the traditional performing ensembles.

What Are The Problems With Non-Music-Making "General Music"?

Teachers now teaching general music with the primary objectives of developing conceptual knowledge and aesthetic response are experiencing problems. In a survey done almost 20 years ago of the Georgia chapter of the Society for General Music (Monsour, 1988), the two most critical problems identified were (1) "setting realistic goals," and (2) "motivating students in music." Although elementary teachers were involved in this survey, the problems identified are keenly experienced by teachers of middle and high school general music. In 1998 Irma Collins concludes that "major issues for reform of general music identified in 1987 are still true today" (p. 7).

The first problem, "setting realistic goals," is basically a problem of what should be learned in music class. When the assumption is that students will not systematically learn to make music, what is to be learned becomes a difficult question. What should be learned about music? Should students in 10th grade first be taught to: (1) understand the concept that a melody is a string of tones organized in time or (2) develop an awareness of rhythm in nature? The problem is that there is no natural sequence of conceptual learning. Responding to the "MENC Goals for 1990" call for a K-12 curriculum that is "balanced, comprehensive, and sequential," Bennett Reimer (1988) points out a problem of general music.

He asks, "How does one achieve a `sequential' program if one is not clear about (a) what to sequence, and (b) how to sequence it?" p.82) Consequently, the teacher setting out what is to be done in music class and what is to be learned is faced with the difficult challenge of setting realistic learning goals for students with differing experience with music and balancing this with time constraints and motivation levels.

The music-making solution to this problem is simple. What is to be learned in music class is music-making. Music teachers are generally experienced and skilled at recognizing the music-making level of students and consequently can determine what needs to be taught first. The sequence of instruction is then determined by the pieces selected to be played or sung. The selection of pieces becomes the critical act of long-range instructional design but what is to be learned is always clear you meet the musical challenges of the piece. Is conceptual learning then irrelevant? Not at all. But the sequence of conceptual learning flows from the core of music class – music-making. The concepts verbalized, the listening done, the notation analyzed are all determined by what enhances or extends the making of the music under study or soon to be studied. If a particular bit of information, analysis, or verbal reflection does not contribute to an enhanced experience with making music it is irrelevant.

The second problem identified by the Georgia general music teachers was student motivation. It is linked to the first. When what is to be learned in music class is not clear to teachers it is even less clear to students. Without clearly identifiable content deemed important in relation to the students' existing culture or conscious needs, motivation derived from subject material will be lacking.

To make the situation worse, if the teacher's agenda in class seems irrelevant or runs counter to the students' desires or expectations, motivation for the subject matter is decreased. Most, if not all students, in our schools are active listeners to the music of their culture before they come to music class. The connection between "music class" and the student's music culture is often not apparent (O'Toole, 2000). And, when it is apparent it is frequently a relation of conflict. The typical goals of school music education are to a great extent the goals of a particular socioeconomic and cultural subgroup of western society. To verbalize critical reaction to the sequential intervallic structure of the second phrase of a musical composition by a European composer of 200 years ago, may not seem culturally, intellectually, socially, or psychologically relevant to a recent immigrant to Toronto. It may seem just as irrelevant to an adolescent who has always lived in the U.S Midwest. When there is not a closely related application of music within the culture experienced by students, motivation to learn is understandably a problem. To compound the problem, when music instruction is not essentially musical, motivation suffers further.

Motivation to enrol in music class can be apart from the content of music class or its apparent relevance to the student's life. If this is the case, the content will at best capture the interest with time or at worst the content will be distasteful and the student will become disruptive to the class. Requirements of an arts credit course in high school may bring students to music class who would not otherwise be there. These students with little intrinsic motivation present a challenge to teachers in as much as the teacher has an opportunity to expand the students' interest in music and enrich their lives through music-making. Engaging students in the heart of music - music-making – affords them the best possible opportunity to enjoy music and to experience it as culturally relevant.

Although our concern often is restricted to those "in music class," we must become more conscious of those not in music class. The question is, why are they not in music class? Do we feel any obligation to make music class appealing and appropriate for ALL students, not just for the talented, motivated, compliant, and disciplined "music students"?

The music-making approach to music education addresses the problem of motivation by creating experiences for students that are culturally relevant and situated at the centre of music as human activity—music-making. A student living immersed in Soca music may find an appreciation class focused on the music of Bach and its structural relation to gothic architecture boring, irrelevant, and highly unmotivating. But the opportunity to play steel pans in music class may result in enthusiastic participation and an openness to many other learnings. The satisfaction of playing familiar tunes valued by peers and "getting into the feeling" of the music is satisfying and highly motivating.

A third problem of general music is related to the first two problems. Bennett Reimer (1988) describes the problem like this:

> there are some high school performance directors who take such courses seriously, enjoy them, and give them their best shot. But there are many more who disdain them, are threatened by them because they have never been helped to learn how to deal with them, and regard them as an imposition on their time and energies. (p.82)

Important reasons high school music teachers dislike non-performance general music courses are, of course, that the "talking" content is not clearly musically worthwhile, not clearly determined, not clearly sequential and, consequently, not appealing and motivating to students. Music teachers became music teachers because they first like to make music and they prefer to teach others how to make music. When they begin a course with the assumption that the students are not capable of or interested in making music, teachers understandably lack enthusiasm. It is also not simply a dislike of "non-performance" music classes. Most music teachers feel most comfortable with rehearsal-performance oriented band, orchestra or choir. Other forms of music making like guitar, steel pans, class piano, or even computer or synthesizer- based music making are considered less worthwhile. If they begin with the assumption that "classical" or traditional "school" music is really the only music worthy of class time, they will communicate a cultural elitism that implicates students' "cultural inferiority" and quickly and effectively alienates them. Of course it also diminishes a teachers' enthusiasm. Other reasons for teachers' lack of enthusiasm are obviously possible, but will not be examined in detail here.

The solution to the general music teacher's lack of enthusiasm is to encourage the music teacher to make music-making the central feature of music class for ALL students. The level of music-making will not be equally advanced with all students but ought to be as musically competent as possible with all. This may appear to be an argument for what Regelski (1997) seems to condemn as "...trends that either deny any value to music education that does not involve ensembles or aim to make general music class largely into ensembles" (p. 5). What Regelski's "Action" approach argues for is "to get general music students to be musically intentful or mindful in creating music – which is to say, to bring music into being as performers, composers, and listeners" (p 8). The confusion seems to be between being "performers" and being an "ensemble." The difference is between "performance" and "music-making."

Difference Between Performance And Music-Making

By music performance we generally mean a form of music-making. But, performance has the implication of music-making for someone. A performance music program generally focuses on the learning and rehearsing of music to be performed at a concert. However, not all music learned or made in class or in rehearsal has to be performed publicly. The notion that music-making has its highest fulfilment is formal public performance is one of the cultural developments of the past few hundred years that has created the separation of stage and audience (Bartel, 2000), that constructs musicians as unique and talented, that disenfranchises the music potential of many people, and that removes music from its most potent form as community builder.

Music-making can fill most of the time in music class but the students in that class may rarely perform for an audience other than themselves or each other. If the class itself is developed as a social community, such sharing of music-making is a meaningful experience. Music-making is an enjoyable and rewarding activity for the music-maker apart from sharing that activity with an "external" audience. Music-making can be the "intentful or mindful" activity that is the core around which creating and listening find meaning. So I would like to define general music as an approach to music education where music-making is the primary occupation of music class but may not be intended for public performance. I would like to call this "community music" but that term has been associated with music performance outside of the school.

What Are Music-Making Alternatives In General Music?

To be a viable alternative to non-performance general music, the content of a music-making course must meet several requirements. First, it must be accessible to all students regardless of previous music experience. One of the features of traditional, ability-level-grouped, lock-step, large-group-instruction-based, performance programs, particularly orchestra and band, is the limited number of entry points. For example, a student reaching 10th grade, who for some reason has not been in orchestra up to that point, will find joining the orchestra in most schools impossible because of inadequate ability. Even choral programs are intimidating to students who lack early experience with music, who are not fully inducted into the style of western art music, or who have not sung through the middle school years. Music-making alternative courses should be open to ALL and should be designed to attract ALL. The instruction level must accommodate the student who may not read standard notation, who is not familiar with the musical language of "classical" music, or who cannot vocally match a pitch. The "class culture and climate" must be welcoming and supportive for the student for whom these may be first attempts. In other words, instruction must accommodate EVERYONE.

Secondly, a music-making course must offer the possibility of satisfying musical experience in a relatively short time. If the student in high school takes music class for only one year or semester, there is no point in beginning instruction that would lead to satisfactory performance in another 2 or 3 years. The student wants and needs to experience satisfying music-making within that year or semester.

Thirdly, a music-making course must have potential cultural relevance to the students' experience. For students to be attracted to a course and motivated by the content, the music that is made in class ought to resonate positively with the music valued in their culture. In some cases students develop an interest in a type of music because of curiosity or the appeal of the exotic or because someone they know likes the music. The musical language they have heard in the first years of life will be easier for them to learn, but a musical sound or style associated with an admired person or valued group will have particular appeal. More important than pre-existing preferences, however, is having a positive music-making experience with music worthy to be shared.

What kind of music-making meets these requirements? Of course, no one type of music-making will meet these requirements in all settings. In fact, many schools may need to offer several types. Some of the possibilities include: guitar, steel pans, drumming, handbells, MIDI/computer, folk instruments, gamelan, various world musics, and orchestral percussion-based classes.

What Is The Need For These Alternatives In The Schools?

I just argued that music-making alternatives to orchestra, band, choir, and non-performance courses are needed in all schools, and that these need to be accessible to all students regardless of previous music experience, offer the possibility of satisfying musical experience in a relatively short time, and have potential cultural relevance to the students' experience. Why are courses that meet these criteria needed? Basically they are needed because of the realities I perceive in the schools today.

The first reality is essentially political. I have already pointed out that in most high schools in North America, students are now required to take at least one course in the arts before graduation. This has created new opportunities and challenges related to students not involved in traditional performance programs. But, connected to this fact is the increased requirements students face in the curriculum with the result that more students who in the past might have taken a traditional performance stream are now looking for only a single unit in music. This means, of course, that a satisfying musical experience in a relatively short time is an important factor in course design. The tendency is, however, for administrators to urge that the single credit course be "academic" and, therefore, consist of talking about music and its role in culture. Courses that can involve students in an authentic performance experience as well as the examination of related musical and cultural issues are most urgently needed.

A second reality in today's schools is economic. Many schools face shortages in funding with obvious deterioration in quality performance music programs. One of the features of many of the course alternatives advocated here is that they are relatively inexpensive. For the cost of a tuba and set of tympani a classroom can be equipped with enough guitars or steel pans for 25 students.

A third reality in many communities is cultural diversity. The traditional performance programs do not connect in a relevant manner to the lives of many students. Increasing cultural diversity in our schools necessitates an examination of the musical content of our classrooms. The performance alternatives suggested here have cultural adaptiveness.

A fourth reality in our society is the relatively small percentage of students who are engaged in music-making in junior and senior high schools. General music classes have attempted to reach those not in traditional performance programs but have failed to involve students in authentic music performance. Performance alternatives can help to increase the proportion of students engaged in music-making. All students have musical intelligence and, therefore, musical potential. As music educators we have an obligation to contribute as much as possible to the development of everyone's musical potential, not just those we see as "talented."

How Is Alternative Music-Making General Music In The Broad Sense?

You will have noticed so far that I am describing a particular kind of music teaching – music-making as central activity that is not orchestra, band, or choir at the middle or high school level. I am arguing for music-making around which listening, responding, creating, and the development of conceptual knowledge is organized. So is it "general music"? Yes, it is general music. Music for everyone. Music for the person who may be in orchestra but wants an additional experience. Music for the person without an extensive background in music. Music for the person with little interest in traditional music class. Music for the student who will only take one credit in music.

If this approach to music class is about making-music, is it still about general music in the broadest sense as described by Eloise Haldeman as "a larger framework that encompasses comprehensive, in-depth and quality musical learning"? (full quote above). Yes, it most certainly is and this becomes clear if music-making is understood adequately. Helping students learn to make music is general music education in the broad sense. How so? Music-making is not a simple skill merely involving fingers pressing the right keys at the right time. If it were, the chicken pecking out a tune on the xylophone at the carnival would be called a musician. Rather, music-making is a thoughtful and knowing act that involves a music-maker in musical and contextual cognition.

Too often traditional general music classes have attempted primarily to develop conceptual knowledge about music in the hope that this will lead to listening ability and appreciation. The development of this type of knowledge apart from meaningful music-making is not music education—it may be education about music but it is not music education. The flip side of this is the public performance-oriented program that focuses on the behavioural "skills" of performing with little attention to the development of holistic musical understanding and experience. The music director who thinks of nothing but competition success and takes no time to invite students to reflect, question, experiment, take responsibility for musical decisions may well be guilty of training performance skills and not doing music education.

The intention of all music instruction should be for the student to become a thoughtful and knowing music-maker—a musician—and a sensual and reflective music "experiencer." Music instruction should develop musicianship in all students whether in orchestra, band, choir, guitar, steel band, handbell choir, MIDI class, jug and blues band, fiddling ensemble, or piano class. That is not to say that a student will become a fully developed musician in a single credit course in, say, guitar, but the process of development should be underway. More importantly, the teacher must see musicianship as the goal and, therefore, facilitate its development with the "social climate" in the class, the questions asked and invited, the reflective thinking encouraged, and the insights con-

BARTEL

tributed. But, at the same time as developing the abilities and various forms of knowledge to be a music-maker, music class needs to provide opportunity to "just listen," to experience the magnificent sensual delight of sound, without any obligation to analyze, label, identify, or replicate. Simply to revel, to enjoy, to love, to respond.

All students who will be educated musically must be involved in authentic music-making – music-making in a context where robust questions (where the teacher does not already know the RIGHT answer) are asked and invited, where reflective thinking is encouraged, where insights from music-making are contributed, and where conceptual knowledge is developed to inform music-making decisions. This type of music-making should not be restricted to the gifted and committed musicians in traditional performance programs. Such music-making situations should be available to any student in the school. Situations for the development of musicianship must be appropriate to the existing level of the student's musicianship. Although musicianship is a complex of knowledges, it exists at levels of development. At whatever level, however, the context must be authentic music-making with musical challenges appropriate to the students in the class.

The 'Tone' Of Teaching Music-Making

One of the arguments that I have tried to develop is that music education has an obligation to reach all students, even in junior and senior high school. As a means to this I have proposed is a variety of socially and culturally relevant forms of music-making such as guitar and steel pan classes. However the "musical" content of music class is only part of the solution to the exclusivity of music classes. The "pedagogical" content is equally if not more important.

How should music be taught to students in general music classes? A better question is, How should students be taught? But even that is not the best question, because education is not so much about teaching as about learning. So an even better question is, How can we help students learn? Now this question does not say "learn music." If we could restrict classroom learning to only subject matter, we might concentrate the question on 'learning music' but that is not possible. The subject matter cannot be all that is on our minds.

In learning situations students shape their own self-perceptions and self-esteem, form concepts of others, develop attitudes toward the intended subject of learning, develop or lose competencies, gain increased or decreased curiosity, gain or lose energy and excitement, find their "souls" growing or shrivelling, and become more human or less human in the process. John Dewey (1938) in *Experience and Education* wisely says that each "experience" in learning lives on in future experiences in a helpful or harmful way. A teacher's focus then cannot be so much on content to be learned as on the overall learning experience with the designated content.

The question "How can we help students learn?" is still not asking the question quite correctly. That question would be, "How can we help Jim learn?" "How can we help Yolanda learn?" How can we help Gagan learn?" If we see only the class we are not seeing the ones who learn. Individuals learn. Real people learn. Each person will extract different learnings from the situation. As teachers we must see Jim and Gagan and Yolanda as persons. Especially easy in performance-oriented music is to see only the class or only the ensemble. Directions are given to the ensemble or section and if one person is not playing the correct notes the whole performance is marred—the music suffers and since perfect performance of the music is the goal the group fails and the teacher's disappointment and maybe even anger is justified. No! No!! No! !! There are only individual people in the room and in the ensemble—people with differing goals and needs and desires and motivations. People are the focus of teaching, not perfect performance!

If perfect performance is not the top priority in a general music class, what is? I had a general music class in a school situated in a neighbourhood riddled with ethnic and language-related animosities, unemployment, the social degradation of reliance on government social assistance, and unstable family relationships. Several of my students in the seventh grade guitar class were being monitored by probation officers. Most of the students in the class took the guitar option because music was required and it was the least distasteful choice. Did they want to be in school? No! Did they want to be in band? No! Did they want to be in guitar class? Maybe. Was perfect performance my top priority? No! But did I engage the students in music-making? Yes! What was my primary priority? It was involving these students in music-making challenges they were able to meet successfully in such a way that they enjoyed the experience. They gained satisfaction and a substantial boost to their self-concept from the success. But, that reward would have been completely negated and perhaps been unattainable if the process of learning had not been enjoyable. Allan would come back to the music room to show me a new guitar chord he learned, before going to meet his probation officer. He was proud of his ability to pick locks. Now he was developing another, more acceptable, source of pride.

Music class must create an environment where all students are invited to experience music-making in a way that supports first attempts, that legitimizes musical exploration, that expects passions and preferences to surface, and that aims, above all, to open to students the joy, release and energy of life through music.

How is this done specifically? Perhaps I could tell you what to do but it is much more a matter of who you are. It is a matter of attitudes, perspectives, and qualities which you possess. A fundamental perspective needed is to see that students are not there for you, you are there for the students. Therefore, what goes on in the class must be for the students' growth, not your reputation, merit pay increase, or satisfaction. You need an attitude that celebrates students and their achievement and not yourself. This attitude requires that you first see each student as valuable, able to learn, curious if curiosity meets with revelation, and as a feelingful individual experiencing life not by semesters or weeks or days but by the moment.

In dealing with people in our frequently stressful and frightening world you need to embody an attitude of hope. Max van Manen in a wonderful little book entitled, *The Tone of Teaching*, says,

> This experience of hope distinguishes a pedagogic life from a non-pedagogic one. It also makes clear that we can only hope for children we truly love, in a pedagogic sense. What hope gives us is this simple confirmation: "I will not give up on you. I know you can make a life for yourself." Hope refers to all that gives patience, tolerance and belief in the possibilities for our children. Hope is our experience of our child's

possibilities. It is our experience of confidence that a child will show us how life is to be lived, no matter how many disappointments we may have experienced. Thus hope gives us pedagogy. Or is it pedagogy that gives us hope? (Manen, 1986, p.28.)

This attitude of hope, however, is not merely demonstrated in a set of behavioural objectives. Such objectives, encouraged by the industrial model of schools, appear at first glance to be statements of expectation for the student, statements of hope. But you see on close observation that they are primarily focused on "doing" for the future, not on "being" now. Yet "being" with students in an attitude of hope is immensely important. Hope versus sterile sets of expectations makes a difference also in the learning encounter. Max van Manen says,

> "Having measurable objectives" differs from "having hope." Expectations and anticipations easily degenerate into desires, wants, certainties, predictions. Thus teachers close themselves off from possibilities that lie outside the direct or indirect vision of those expectations. To hope is to believe in possibilities. Hope strengthens and builds. (Manen, 1986, p.28).

Engaging students in music-making who may not have done so before high school, who have been told by a previous teacher that they are not good at it, or who have very different interests than those exemplified by the school orchestra, requires the teacher to believe in possibilities. Students quickly sense the presence of possibility in the classroom. It is this to which they respond with engagement and achievement.

Look with me for a moment at a music class I visited recently. The school is located in an area of the city where cabs sometimes refuse to drive to at night. The school is in an area known for government assisted housing and for a drug dealing problem. In the school the band program died several years ago. A keyboard class attracts some students. But the real attraction is the steel pan class. We are looking at one of these classes.

Mr. Bowen the tall, elegant, brightly dressed teacher leans against the large glass window between hallway and classroom as he chats with lingering students from a previous class. A few guys dressed in baggy clothes sit on a counter over a storage cabinet at the back of the room. A few students drop their books at the side of the room as they enter and walk over to one of the soprano pans in the front row. They pick up the small sticks with rubberband tips and play a short repeating pattern on the pan. Their arms verily dance as they follow the across-the-pan scale pattern. It looks like the same muscular joy as I saw in the guy shooting a basket on the school courtyard when I arrived at the school. A familiar easiness that feels good. Wrists loose, arms easy, right hand circling the top, left hand following the bottom circle. Soon two girls are huddling over the set of bass pans in the back. They share the mallets that look like they are constructed of rubber bouncing balls and sticks. They alternate bouncing the mallet to draw out the rich warm bass tones. Soon a repeating walking bass pattern is evident and the students at the soprano and alto pans slowly merge into the music as they apparently search for and find the appropriate tune or motive to go with the bass pattern.

Mr. Bowen has been giving winks, smiles, nods, thumbs-up signs or high fives to every student that has walked in. Some drop off notes on his desk. Some seem to collapse in fatigue at the side of the room. Some hover around him for a word. But most have found their way to the pans. One person shows him a tenser on her wrist and he asks about it in concern and hands her one thin drum stick and gestures toward the brake drum on a stand at the side of the room. She goes over to it and with her good hand tries some rhythms. After a few gentle words to the ones around him, a pat on one student's back, and a signature on another's note, Mr. Bowen holds his hand with thumb, index finger, and pinky in the air for a moment. The playing at the pans subsides and he announces a song title. He gives a gesture of invitation to the two students reclining at the side of the classroom and points them to a tenor pan. He walks to a pan, picks up a set of mallets, taps his foot four times and starts to play. The students now play with enthusiasm what they were practising individually just a moment ago. As they play he walks around to watch. He raises his hand and stops the class briefly to say, "remember when we learned this pattern on the board? There was a spot nine counts in where we gave a moment of silence for the swallow with the broken wing flying on its side? Don't forget the moment of silence for the quarter rest." He starts the class playing again. He steps in beside a girl who has apparently forgotten the note sequence. He takes her mallets and shows her in slow motion and hands them back to her and she joins the section. He walks over to the two students at the tenor pans who were evidently very tired earlier. They are looking a little mechanical in their movements and he starts to dance energetically. They laugh and play with more joy. He walks over to another student and teasingly pulls the pan off to the side while the student pretends alarm and strains to stay with the music. He then picks up a set of maracas and takes them over to one of the guys still sitting at the back of the room. He is obviously not a member of the class and is given the invitation to stay and play or apparently a suggestion to leave. He takes the maracas and plays the rhythm he has been shown.

The music fragment that has been repeated over and over is becoming cleaner and tighter rhythmically and the students relax technically and start to move their knees or hips with the beat being laid down by the bass pans and the drummer. Mr. Bowen shimmies to the front of the group, holds up his hand for an ending and claps his approval to the group. A few `spectators' outside the classroom window applaud.

The basic qualities other than excellent musicianship I see important in music teachers who will be able to engage all students in music-making are thoughtfulness, tact, and playfulness. When I looked at Mr. Bowen I first saw thoughtfulness. He saw each individual. That is he actually noticed, looked at, responded to the person. Each person mattered to him—they were not just another class to teach for 55 minutes. They were real people with real lives and with real problems and with real hopes and dreams and with real potentials and with real feelings. He was inviting real people to learn and play. He was thoughtful in relation to the specific needs and problems. One person had an injured wrist but he found a way to invite her to participate. Some students were tired and did not feel like participating but he encouraged them and asked them in and boosted their attitudes. Some students were eager to play and learn and he simply allowed them to do it. Some students were wanting to be part of the class and he did not chide them but made it clear that being in class required participation. All of this demonstrates thoughtfulness. Max van Manen calls thoughtfulness a special kind of knowledge. I think it is a knowledge particularly required in teachers of general music.

Thoughtfulness has the related attribute of tact. Tact is the knowledge of what will be a particularly appropriate and useful action in a specific situation. It is "the ability to appreciate the delicacy of a situation and to do or say the kindest or most fitting thing" (Morris, 1970). A teacher needs to see each student, needs to be thoughtful in every circumstance, and needs to say or do the kindest and most fitting thing in every situation. There are times when a brief dance with a student is more tactful than a word of encouragement, when a gesture is more tactful than a verbal instruction, when one word is more helpful than a sentence, when silence is more fitting than talk. What I saw in Mr. Bowen was tact.

Play is a word with various dimensions of meaning. We play basketball. We play with toys. We play instruments in music class. We play instead of work. Play implies amusement or recreation. It implies an activity that is done for its own enjoyable sake rather than for the practical benefit that comes from it. But professional athletes or professional musicians earn their living "playing." Play can be a very serious activity indeed. But "playfulness" captures the "fun" aspect of play more effectively. It seems to contain the meaning play has for children—an innocent absorption in the joy of the making and doing itself rather than in the product. It implies good humour and lightheartedness. It suggests high spirits and frolic in action or speech. But it does not have to mean "frivolous" or "silly" or "mischievous." Playfulness does not mean always trying to be funny or telling dumb jokes. Students tire very quickly of that. Playfulness is a fundamental quality of enthusiastic life.

Music class ought to be playful as well as engaging students in musical play. That does not mean the students are not to gain specific and important knowledge. It does not mean music class is merely an entertainment for students. It does not mean that there is not rigorous hard work involved in learning to play music. But the process of making music should be play at its best—playful in its spirit. The joy of making music is what we want to share with students. It is the joy and playfulness of music that captures the soul of the general student and prepares them for a lifetime of musical enjoyment.

Mr. Bowen was playful in class. His dance, his teasing, his clapping, his reference to a swallow with a broken wing. All were demonstrative of his joy and of his pleasure in making music even at the basic level of a beginning pan class. It was evidence that he enjoyed being with those particular students at that time. He was interacting with music and the students in a way that communicated to them, "I like you and I like making music with you." Music-making is fundamentally about joy. Joyful music is best made by joyful people.

References:

Bartel, L. (2000). Separation of audience and stage. *Orbit*(1)31, p. 13.
Dewey, J. (1938). *Experience and education*. New York: Company.
Eloise Haldeman (1988). in *Readings in General Music*, MENC, Macmillan Publishing University Press.
Lehman, Paul R. (1988). in *Readings in General Music*, MENC Macmillan Publishing University Press.
Van Manen, Max. (1986). *The Tone of Teaching*. Richmond Hill, Ontario: Scholastic-TAB Publications Ltd.
Monsour, Sally. (1988) in *Readings in General Music*, MENC, Macmillan Publishing University Press.
Morris, W. (Ed.) (1970) *The American Heritage Dictionary of the English Language*. New York: Houghton Mifflin Company.
O'Toole, P. (2000). Field report on music in the schools. *Orbit*(1)31. pp 34-36.

Perlmutter, M. L. & Perkins, D. N. (1982). *A model of aesthetic response. In S. S. Madeja & D. N. Perkins Eds.), A model for aesthetic response in the arts* (pp. 1-29). St. Louis, MO: CEMREL, Inc.

Regelski, Thomas (1981) *Teaching General Music*, Collier MacMillan Publishers, London.

Regelski, T. (1997). A critical pragmatism of creativity for general music. *General Music Today* 10(3) pp 5-9

Reimer, Bennett (1988). "The continuing problem of high school non-performance courses." in *Readings in General Music*, MENC Macmillan Publishing University Press.

Reimer, B. (1994) Thinking globally about a research agenda for general music. *General Music Today* 7(2) pp 3-12

SECTION 5:

QUESTIONING OUR ASSUMPTIONS AND STRUCTURES

Pamela Burnard
Reflecting On Music Learning And Rethinking Contexts

Bina John
Relating Music And Affect: An Alternative Model For Structuring Music Instruction

Adam Adler & Scott Harrison
Swinging Back The Gender Pendulum: Addressing Boys' Needs In Music Education Research And Practice

Elizabeth Gould
Philosophy In Music Education: Relevance, Re-Vision, Renewal

CHAPTER SEVENTEEN

Reflecting On Music Learning And Rethinking Contexts

PAMELA BURNARD

Abstract

Educational researchers examining transfer of primary pupils to secondary school emphasise the impact of factors affecting transfer on pupil attainment, attitudes and learning. These limiting factors most affecting the move to the 'big school' include the lack of curriculum continuity between primary and secondary school, the limiting effects of the relatively inflexible secondary school timetable, the lack of primary-secondary liaison by subject specialists (or subject leaders), the misreading of students' ability, unfamiliar routines, unchallenging demands or abrupt change of teaching methods and ways of working between primary and secondary phases. What lessons can we learn from what musically matters to children when they move from primary to secondary school and to teacher trainees becoming teachers and to experienced teachers?

The first and most obvious change needed is that both teachers and pupils should reflect on and exchange musical beliefs and experiences as an important part of the curriculum, particularly at points of transition and transfer. The second issue which needs to be taken seriously by teachers concerns the fact that what pupils encounter in their primary and secondary school music lessons impacts significantly upon pupil perceptions of their own musical learning potential and ability. It is within the teacher's control to influence, develop, and indeed change student beliefs about their own music learning and its potential. Third, the widening and reconfiguring of educational contexts is of crucial significance for music education practices in the twenty-first century. Whether within schools, across institutions, in the larger community, or cross-culturally, we know that music educators must allow for encounters of different kinds, for professional and cross-disciplinary collaborations to occur in contexts and across sites and with resources different from the ones we are presently used to. This is the vision and challenge of preparing music educators for twenty-first century schools.

Change And Continuity In Teacher Practice

With progressively greater emphasis on efficiency, accountability, and curriculum reform, there is a new highlighting of and interest in research on the changes that face educators in the twenty-first century. In music education many of these challenges relate to:

(1) the effectiveness of music in schools (Lamont, Hargreaves, Marshall and Tarrant,

2003; Lamont, 2002; Mills, 1996; Harland et al., 2000);
(2) curriculum reform (Green, 2001; Berkley, 2001; Kushner, 1999; Swanwick, 1999);
(3) pedagogical appropriateness (Stålhammar, 2003, 2000; Kushner, 1999;
Hargreaves & Zimmerman, 1992);
(4) how and to what extent teachers develop or change their knowledge and beliefs
(Upitis et al, 1999; Yourn, 2000; deVries, 2000; Mark, 1998; Cox, 1999; Pitts,
2000a/b; Green, 2002; Dolloff, 1999; Drummond, 2001); and
(5) teacher-pupil cultural dissonance (York, 2000; Green, 2001; Sloboda, 2001;
Burnard, 2004), to name a few.

It is a widely held view that the assumptions we hold about music education need challenging with key educationists calling for a "rethink of music education practices" and "a significant paradigm shift from what music educators have been used to" (Leong, 2003, p. 153).

Professional development and teaching quality is strongly linked with the significant shift towards the use of frameworks that facilitate standardization in education. For example, in the USA there are "National Standards for Arts Education"; in Britain, there is "The National Curriculum for England"; in Australia, there is a "Curriculum and Standards Framework." Although music education practices are influenced by regional variants in philosophical, cultural, and contextual commitments to education, continuity in educational values has been identified. For example: "all learners should have the opportunity to grow in musical knowledge, skills, and appreciation so as to challenge their minds, stimulate their imaginations, bring joy and satisfaction to their lives, and exalt their spirits" (International Society for Music Education, 1994, p. 49). Corresponding examples of teacher transformation, where significant changes to teacher practices have occurred and been identified are peppered throughout the literature (see for example, Upitis, Smithrim and Soren, 1999).

Along with this, a commitment to school improvement remains, for many teachers, a factor which determines not only to what extent teachers develop or change their beliefs about musical learning, but also the factors which influence this development or change. The concern to enhance learning and achievement is something we share in education all around the world (Stoll and Fink, 1996). Approaches to school improvement have included changing teacher practice and, more recently, through listening to and acting on what students have to say about learning in school (Rudduck and Flutter, 2000) and in particular their impressions and experiences of coping with transitions from primary or middle to secondary or upper school being one of the most important and eventful episodes that occurs during a pupil's career.

The Importance of Transitions in Student Learning

Although educational theorists argue that learning should be seen as a continuum, the issue of transition, that is, what learners actually encounter in the school and at transitional points in their education (and as phases which occur across a lifetime), although promoted as a key element in improving teaching *and* learning in both primary and secondary schools (Rudduck and Flutter, 2000 amongst others), remains a persistent problem which has yet only recently attracted widespread interest (Hargreaves and Galton, 2002). The highlighting and impact of transitions—whereupon development or change of beliefs occur cumulatively from experience—continues to intrigue researchers, teachers, and parents alike. We are all interested in the navigation of developmental transition to and leaving childhood and adolescence through to adulthood; for indeed, the success of education, in general, depends upon the understanding of the skills, motivations, and purposes that underlie learning experiences. But as in this country, the day-to-day practice in primary and secondary (elementary and high schools), is more often to operate as islands. This is a concern by no means confined to Great Britain; it occurs within a world-wide context (Parkyn, 1962).

Educational researchers examining transfer of primary pupils to secondary school emphasise the impact of factors affecting transfer on pupil attainment, attitudes, and learning (Hargreaves and Galton, 2002). These limiting factors most affecting the move to the "big school" include the lack of curriculum continuity between primary and secondary school, the limiting effects of the "relatively inflexible" secondary school timetable (p. 192), the lack of primary-secondary liaison by subject specialists (or subject leaders), the misreading of students' ability, unfamiliar routines, unchallenging demands, or abrupt change of teaching methods, and ways of working between primary and secondary phases. What students say about the first year after transfer suggests that whilst some pupils want everything to be new and exciting and very different from their previous school, others do not. These differences "may also influence the ways in which pupils who are 'at risk' as the result of transfer often remain unidentified and supported" (p. 195).

Researchers examining the musical worlds of young people have made some meaningful progress (Sloboda, 2001; O'Neill, 2002; Campbell, 2002; Hargreaves & Marshall, 2003; Hargreaves *et al* 2003). Insights into the nature of the problem have been found in the work of Stålhammar (2000, 2003) whose comparative examination of young people in the United Kingdom and Sweden focused on the incongruence between young people's musical experience and music teaching. It appears, we have a limited understanding of teachers' *and* pupils' musical beliefs and about what musically matters in classrooms according to pupils. Until recently students were usually omitted from the consultation process about school reforms and the teachers who ran the classrooms seldom asked how the students themselves perceive music and music learning in their school. We still know relatively little about why so many turn away from music education or how young people today are responding to school music. What students say about music learning and its potential speaks to the problems they have in trying to commit themselves to learning in the face of "devastating misconceptions about people's learning potential: that music is a talent that is only possessed by a few" (Bartel, 2000, p. 37).

Listening To Learners

The significance of listening to learners' accounts of critical incidents and views of their critical cross-phase learning experiences has become a common theme in much research on learning in general (Woods, 1993; Entwistle et al, 1989; Flutter et al, 1999; Cooper & McIntyre, 1996; Richardson, 1996) and musical learning in particular (Mills, 1996). What teachers and researchers are finding out is that young people *are* observant, reflective, and capable of presenting their own musical beliefs and experiences in an analytic and constructive way, and usually respond well to the responsibility, seriously entrusted to them, of helping to identify aspects of transfer and transitions in schooling that strengthen or get in the way of their learning.

In considering these challenges we come to reflect upon: (a) the impact of developmental transitions on learning; (b) about the blind adherence to outmoded dogmas about what musically matters to people's perceptions of their learning potential; and (c) how slowly music education is to recognise this.

In this chapter, I will address aspects of what musically matters to children when they move from primary to secondary school and to teacher trainees becoming teachers and to experienced teachers. The results of previous empirical research, which uses a critical incident charting technique to reflect on prior musical encounters (see Musical Rivers in Burnard, 2000, 2004), will be reported as drawn from datasets comprising interviews with young people aged between 12 and 16 and with pre- and in-service teachers. Examples of significant musical encounters (or critical incidents in learning) will be discussed. The chapter will conclude with a list of the challenges to the profession with ways music educators can become more connected, genuinely transformative, and defined by the ideals of learner agency, reflexivity, and equity.

Trouble with Transitions: Moving Musically from Childhood to Adolescence

There seems to be a general acceptance that a sharp decline in participation in school music occurs over the primary-secondary transition (Harland and Kinder, 1995; Harland, Kinder and Hartley, 1995; Ross, 1995; O'Brien, 1996; Sefton-Green, 1999; North and Hargreaves, 1999; Kushner, 1999; Harland et al, 2000). Recent research suggests that school music receives a low rating for enjoyment compared with art and drama at secondary school (Harland, et al, 2000); and that pupil enjoyment and involvement in formal music declines as they progress through their teens (Sloboda, 2001).

We know that many young people find the transition from primary to secondary—or the "big" school—challenging (Hargreaves and Galton, 2002). We also know that the musical journeys of young people in out-of-school settings engage them in musical learning of the kind not experienced in school (Stålhammar, 2003, 2000). Very often music in school is perceived as allowing little or no input from the young people themselves or with much scope for choice and self-determination (Glover, 2003; Green, 2001). For many young people, the long-standing problems of transfer in the lower secondary school continues to contribute to a sharp decline in school participation (Lamont, Hargreaves, Marshall and Tarrant, 2003; Hargreaves et al, 2003; Lamont, 2002; Harland et al., 2000).

What follows are two cases (Sidin and Tim) drawn from a two-phase study of eighteen young people who were individually interviewed at 12-years (see Burnard, 2000) and again at 16-years (Burnard, 2004) for the purpose of identifying the key factors shaping participations in school music over the primary-secondary transition. Both primary and secondary schools had good reputations for music each of which was located in West London. Each interview lasted between 45 and 60 minutes and was tape-recorded, transcribed, and thematically analysed. What follows is a description of the procedural tool for reflection which was used on each occasion. The method used was a critical incident technique, with one single question framed as follows:

Visualise your musical life as a winding river in which each bend in the river's path marks a critical moment. Think back and reflect on key moments (positive and negative memories) that have influenced the direction of your musical lives. What are the first most significant memories, persons, events or pivotal moments that you recall about your musical journey (or career path, or your develop-ment as a teacher)?

Locate each important episode on a different bend along the length of a winding river where each bend represents a critical moment or turning point. Tell the story (or recall it in your mind) of this important episode. Label the story (e.g. 'Singing with Nursery, brownies, camps'; Terrible at clarinet, Grade 8'; 'Told at school to mime').

Go on mapping your recollections and chart the complete journey of your musical life (or on becoming a teacher or your development as a teacher or experience of teaching) by recalling, listing, and labelling each critical incident on each bend.

Reflect on the whole picture and see what patterns start to emerge. Note where and when the watersheds, sudden swerves, turning points, currents, memorable moments or marker events occur in your career path (development). This now becomes a navigable river representing a narrative of personal (and professional) significance that does not necessarily have to, but can, be sorted into a chronological sequence or an autobiographical timeline. The purpose is not necessarily to rearrange the pieces but rather to visualise and draw our own musical journey as a mighty winding river and to reflect upon what discoveries have marked your particular path (either as a musical learner or teacher). The technique of discovering emerging patterns of personal meaning within one's self and seeking and creating connec-tions allows us to reflect upon the meanings of experi-ences in our past lives and to potentially set out on a new voyage.

For many school children, feeling anxious about taking part in musical activities is the norm because they often do not read and play music. Based on the charted summa-ry of critical musical incidents (see Figure 1) recalled by Sidin, a 12-year-old girl, with no formal training on an instrument nor instruments at home, an understanding of the complex interrelation-ships between students' beliefs about their musical learning potential and musical

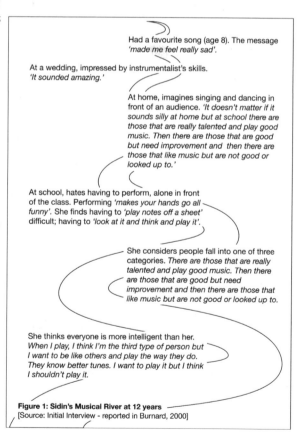

Had a favourite song (age 8). The message *'made me feel really sad'.*

At a wedding, impressed by instrumentalist's skills. *'It sounded amazing.'*

At home, imagines singing and dancing in front of an audience. *'It doesn't matter if it sounds silly at home but at school there are those that are really talented and play good music. Then there are those that are good but need improvement and then there are those that like music but are not good or looked up to.'*

At school, hates having to perform, alone in front of the class. Performing *'makes your hands go all funny'.* She finds having to *'play notes off a sheet'* difficult; having to *'look at it and think and play it'.*

She considers people fall into one of three categories. *There are those that are really talented and play good music. Then there are those that are good but need improvement and then there are those that like music but are not good or looked up to.*

She thinks everyone is more intelligent than her. *When I play, I think I'm the third type of person but I want to be like others and play the way they do. They know better tunes. I want to play it but I think I shouldn't play it.*

Figure 1: Sidin's Musical River at 12 years
[Source: Initial Interview - reported in Burnard, 2000]

meanings (as the knowledge of culture from outside) and from within the school context, can be identified. At primary school, Sidin aspired to play music yet despite her musical enthusiasm and engagement with music at home, she believed music was not a talent she possessed. The overwhelming impression, four years later, was that she still held this belief.

Four years later, when asked to reflect upon the critical incidents of moving up to the "big school"; about events and experiences which she felt had had some bearing upon her present involvement in music in school, Sidin shared examples (see Figure 2) of situations in which she felt unable to make the musical transition, and afraid of losing face if she failed musically, and increasingly less willing to pursue her musical interests. All musical involvement had stopped. Sidin was "at risk" prior to and remained so after transfer. Why this happened is clearly evident from the interview conducted at 16-years-old in which, as with many interviewees, the perceived musical barriers were too many and so she decided it was better to give up than to try to catch up. Figure 2 tells us a great deal about they way some pupils view the transfer to new schools, how they make choices about opting in or out of music at secondary school, and about the development of beliefs about musical learning potential.

What mattered musically and what was offered at the secondary level represents a challenge for many young people (Lamont et al, 2003; O'Neill *et al.*, 2002). As with Sidin (and reported by Lamont *et al* 2003 as occurring more with girls than boys), her level of participation declined dramatically in secondary school.

Unlike Sidin, at 12 years, Tim had a solid musical background in the form of five years formal instrumental tuition. He achieved Grade 5 piano, Grade 4 theory and Grade 3 violin (British Conservatory Examination system). His musical commitment was attributed to and evident after several successful experiences and musical achievements coupled with having a highly supportive musical family.

At 12 years Tim valued his own musical achievements that emanated particularly from the supportive musical learning environment enjoyed at home. At 16 years, Tim continued to show positive attitudes to music after making the transition to

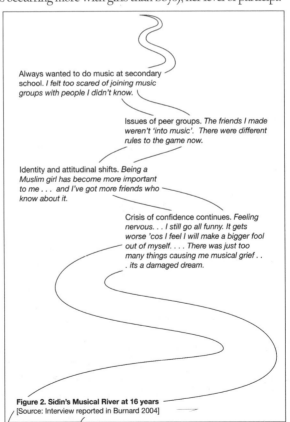

Always wanted to do music at secondary school. *I felt too scared of joining music groups with people I didn't know.*

Issues of peer groups. *The friends I made weren't 'into music'. There were different rules to the game now.*

Identity and attitudinal shifts. *Being a Muslim girl has become more important to me . . . and I've got more friends who know about it.*

Crisis of confidence continues. *Feeling nervous. . . I still go all funny. It gets worse 'cos I feel I will make a bigger fool out of myself. . . . There was just too many things causing me musical grief . . . its a damaged dream.*

Figure 2. Sidin's Musical River at 16 years
[Source: Interview reported in Burnard 2004]

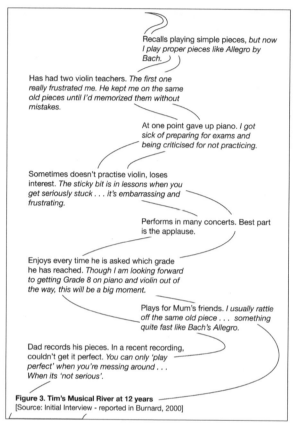

Recalls playing simple pieces, *but now I play proper pieces like Allegro by Bach.*

Has had two violin teachers. *The first one really frustrated me. He kept me on the same old pieces until I'd memorized them without mistakes.*

At one point gave up piano. *I got sick of preparing for exams and being criticised for not practicing.*

Sometimes doesn't practise violin, loses interest. *The sticky bit is in lessons when you get seriously stuck . . . it's embarrassing and frustrating.*

Performs in many concerts. Best part is the applause.

Enjoys every time he is asked which grade he has reached. *Though I am looking forward to getting Grade 8 on piano and violin out of the way, this will be a big moment.*

Plays for Mum's friends. *I usually rattle off the same old piece . . . something quite fast like Bach's Allegro.*

Dad records his pieces. In a recent recording, couldn't get it perfect. *You can only 'play perfect' when you're messing around . . . When its 'not serious'.*

Figure 3. Tim's Musical River at 12 years
[Source: Initial Interview - reported in Burnard, 2000]

secondary school, and the subject specialisation that characterises secondary school, seeing the move as providing more opportunities to make music, to identify with and to musically progress (see Figure 4). But with Sidin, as with many students moving from primary, secondary school can end in fragmented notions of the subject, disappointment, and decline in participation (Lamont et al, 2003). For Tim, however, secondary school was a place where he flourished musically, making self-determined choices to initiate and widen opportunities for musical interaction in forming bands, using technology, and concert going.

Tim appeared to resent the number of music teachers he encountered. Some of the challenges Tim elaborated (see his reference to having "many teachers") was of "sussing" and "sizing up" new teachers and resenting the number of music teachers which came and went during the four years he had been in the school (a current recruitment and retention problem in Secondary music teaching).

This comparison of 16-year-olds, as illustrated by the case of a very high and low level of interest and enjoyment of class and school music in the early secondary years, shows that students' development or change of beliefs about music learning seem to be above all personal and to follow different patterns. Young people who do care deeply about music, who want to get involved musically and make music in their lives, but who feel scared that they will be humiliated or "shown up" by teachers, or feel they don't have the skills or are not willing to "*practice hard enough,*" seem to, above all, find it difficult to transcend their own situation individually and to find, either informally or within a school context, positive sources or agency for change.

So, how can the current challenges of school music be better understood? One way forward is to consider the developing musical self as tracked along both pupils *and* teachers career paths, that is, to examine beliefs about the causes of success and failure in music from people of different ages, interests, and music experience. It may be then that the role of institutional contexts in preventing engagement with music becomes clearer.

Trouble with Transitions: Moving Musically from School to University to Teaching

The development of professional identity—in this case, of pre-service trainee teachers and of in-service primary and secondary teachers—and understanding how we learn to become teachers from examination of teacher's career histories, is well documented (Woods, 1993; Tripp, 1993).

Identifying transitions in pre-service teachers' career charts. What follows are summarised critical incident charts of two student teachers *written* reflections on the directions along which they have musically moved and now see themselves. Based on their reflections on critical musical events as recalled from their personal histories, we can compare the contrasting experiences at each bend in the winding rivers of these two primary generalist (non-specialist) teacher trainees and how the factors of opportunity and rejection at various points in their musical lives have influenced how confident, or not, they now feel about teaching music in school. We witness how positive (see Figure 5) and negative critical incidents (see Figure 6) lead to positive and negative musical identities. By examining such incidents we gain insight into the processes by which identities are built by individuals at various points in their lives and how this then invokes seeing and labelling themselves as sufficiently musically confident to teach or not.

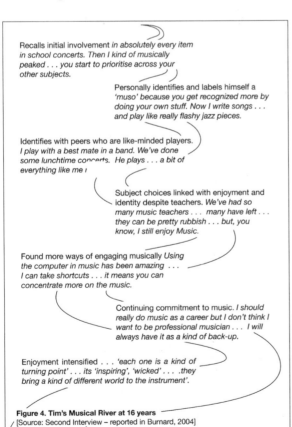

Recalls initial involvement *in absolutely every item in school concerts. Then I kind of musically peaked . . . you start to prioritise across your other subjects.*

Personally identifies and labels himself a *'muso' because you get recognized more by doing your own stuff. Now I write songs . . . and play like really flashy jazz pieces.*

Identifies with peers who are like-minded players. *I play with a best mate in a band. We've done some lunchtime concerts. He plays . . . a bit of everything like me ı*

Subject choices linked with enjoyment and identity despite teachers. *We've had so many music teachers . . . many have left . . . they can be pretty rubbish . . . but, you know, I still enjoy Music.*

Found more ways of engaging musically *Using the computer in music has been amazing . . . I can take shortcuts . . . it means you can concentrate more on the music.*

Continuing commitment to music. *I should really do music as a career but I don't think I want to be professional musician . . . I will always have it as a kind of back-up.*

Enjoyment intensified . . . *'each one is a kind of turning point' . . . its 'inspiring', 'wicked' . . . .they bring a kind of different world to the instrument'.*

Figure 4. Tim's Musical River at 16 years
[Source: Second Interview – reported in Burnard, 2004]

Here we witness the recollection of incidents of high musical achievement and pleasure along with a self-rating of confidence about teaching music. This response shows a clear relationship between feedback and high levels of confidence.

In Figure 6, we witness the consequence of a series of negative feedback and unsuccessful efforts to get involved in music making contexts. This student teacher remembers negative encounters only and describes herself as not sufficiently confident to teach music.

Clearly, each student teachers' belief about her own music learning locate the principal sources of pleasure in or unease with music as a reaction to experiences from their own school days. This self-knowledge is experien-

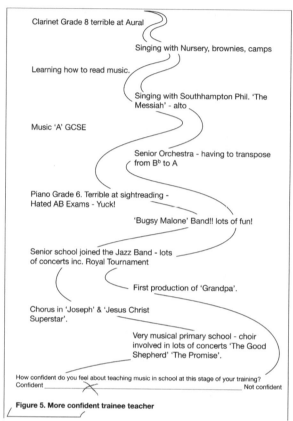

Clarinet Grade 8 terrible at Aural

Singing with Nursery, brownies, camps

Learning how to read music.

Singing with Southhampton Phil. 'The Messiah' - alto

Music 'A' GCSE

Senior Orchestra - having to transpose from B♭ to A

Piano Grade 6. Terrible at sightreading - Hated AB Exams - Yuck!

'Bugsy Malone' Band!! lots of fun!

Senior school joined the Jazz Band - lots of concerts inc. Royal Tournament

First production of 'Grandpa'.

Chorus in 'Joseph' & 'Jesus Christ Superstar'.

Very musical primary school - choir involved in lots of concerts 'The Good Shepherd' 'The Promise'.

How confident do you feel about teaching music in school at this stage of your training?
Confident _____X_____ Not confident

Figure 5. More confident trainee teacher

tial, highly contextualised, personal, and is acquired with direct help from others.

Identifying transitions in in-service music teachers' career paths. A teacher's own biography and career path into Primary or Secondary teaching also provides insightful indicators of the ways in which we build up experience and beliefs about music learning. In the course of time, teachers integrate the information from a range of principal sources (recollections located mainly from their own school days) into an experiential knowledge base that we use within our own practice.

What follows are exemplars of critical incident charts drawn from the musical life history of a primary music specialist (see Figure 7 for James) and secondary music teacher (see Figure 8 for Fiona).

For James, his teachers form the origins of his beliefs about musical learning in which contextual elements play an important role in understanding who he wanted to be and a professional identity, which explains who he has become – that is, having a dual identity as musician and teacher.

For Fiona (see Figure 8), whose musical instrumental family provided specialist interests, skills and performance opportunities; we can see how meaning is embodied differently in the musician/ music teacher who sees herself "as musician *before* teacher."

What can we learn from these transitions in music learning?

From analysis of these and the previous telling musical lives of 12- and 16-year-old learners, as inductively drawn from interviews and written reflections, presented here as summarised critical incident charts, three themes emerge which link primary-secondary transitions with the development and change of beliefs about music learning.

● Musical identity We can identify how positive (see Figures 3-4, 6-8) or negative (see Figures 1-2, 5, 7-8) feedback from significant others (such as teachers, parents and peers) invoke a series of choices. The *initial critical incident* (i.e. a surprise or shock) is followed by a *counter incident* (which signals and confirms the direction or decision taken). It acts as the turning point that helps to crystallise ideas, attitudes, and beliefs as they are being formed. For example, whilst Tim (see Figure 3 at 12 years) recalled initial incidents involving frustrations with "violin teachers" and getting "sick of preparing for exams" these incidents were followed by counter incidents of successful concert performances, graded exam results and affirming experiences with "Mum" and "Dad." Whilst for Fiona (see Figure 8), the significance of "failing" a practical examine during her undergraduate specialist degree was that it invoked consideration of the motivation and vocational

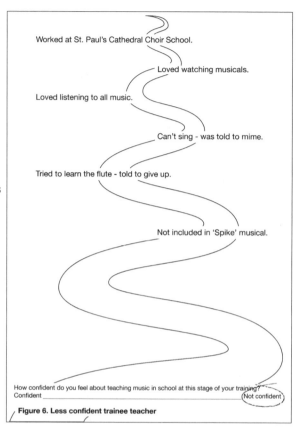

Worked at St. Paul's Cathedral Choir School.

Loved watching musicals.

Loved listening to all music.

Can't sing - was told to mime.

Tried to learn the flute - told to give up.

Not included in 'Spike' musical.

How confident do you feel about teaching music in school at this stage of your training?
Confident _____ Not confident

Figure 6. Less confident trainee teacher

path dilemma of becoming a teacher or professional musician. Thus, reflecting on critical and counter incidents can help us to gain insights into processes by which beliefs are developed or change and identities are built at particular points in life.

● **Barriers to involvement** These include a perceived lack of confidence, ability, skills, talent, opportunity, and support. By reflecting on music experiences we may identify 'at risk' learners whose feelings of uncertainty, dissatisfaction, and uneasiness connected with musical decisions on how to act as perceived by individuals wishing to keep securely within a comfort zone where personal meanings are not expected to be made public in their schooling.

● **Music beliefs** These differ in the extent to which learners unconsciously or consciously change or build up their beliefs about music learning. This is inextricably linked with perceived levels of musical achievement or lack of positive feedback from significant others.

From what people know and say, it is clear that music learning is a complex activity in which very personal and contextual elements play an important role. More attention needs to be paid to what causes shifts in values about musical learning.

What are some of the issues (and dilemmas) that confront music teachers?

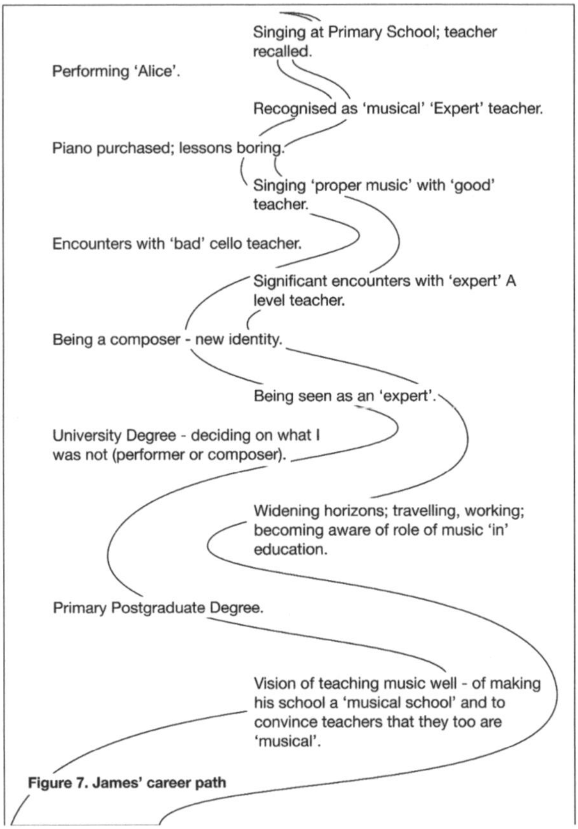

● **Identification of moral as well as musical commitments.** As teachers, we are presently required to differentiate between the ethical responsibility for not exploiting the dependency relationship to the "more musical pupil" and for the strong commitment and responsibility that all classroom music teachers are supposed to give to "all" pupils the same musical opportunity. This is an aspiration which is, in reality, not achieved (or achievable).

● **Idealisations of practice.** As teachers, we are supposed to be aware of the musical potency of our actions in relation to students. We are expected to be careful about prescribing musical ideals in

Figure 7. James' career path

teaching practice. Neither are the ideals of sufficient space and time provided, to take music teachers' and their pupils' own judgements into account. Having the space and time to find the arena of reflection in our classrooms and to explore alternative answers to the question of why some teachers neglect their musical responsibilities towards "all" pupils remains an educational conundrum.

● **Contexts and conditions for an inclusive musical landscape.** As teachers, we are presently trained to reflect on our own practice but not to act. We accept difference and divergence in our classrooms and yet what we appear to lack is not the willingness but the means to create the contexts and conditions to move reflexively from a rule-governed understanding of music learning to an opening up, discussion, testing, and celebration of the many possible musical meanings found in our classrooms.

Changing Schools - Changing Practices

Although I do not claim to generalise from these eight cases, or the findings from the small-scale studies from which they originate, they do, nevertheless, yield some potentially useful knowledge which adds new information to the perception gaps in teaching

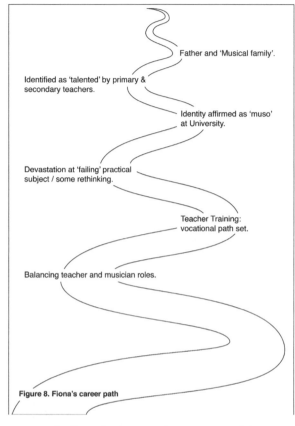

Father and 'Musical family'.

Identified as 'talented' by primary & secondary teachers.

Identity affirmed as 'muso' at University.

Devastation at 'failing' practical subject / some rethinking.

Teacher Training: vocational path set.

Balancing teacher and musician roles.

Figure 8. Fiona's career path

and learning and school music provision in the primary and secondary classroom through the eyes of the learner.

The first and most obvious recommendation in terms of how things should be changed is that both teachers and pupils should reflect on and exchange musical beliefs and experiences as an important part of the curriculum, particularly at points of transition and transfer. The unpopularity of music in school, particularly at junior secondary levels (reported by both pupils and teachers reflections on school days), is well documented but the reasons for that unpopularity are less certain.

The second issue which needs to be taken seriously by teachers concerns the fact that what pupils encounter in their primary and secondary school music lessons impacts significantly upon pupil perceptions of their own musical learning potential and ability. It is within the teacher's control to influence, develop, and indeed change student beliefs about their own music learning and its potential. When this aspect is not explicitly focused on, no positive changes are likely to occur. More attention needs to be paid to issues like these in future studies.

Third, the widening and reconfiguring of educational contexts is of crucial significance for music education practices in the twenty-first century. Whether within schools, across institutions, in the larger community, or cross-culturally, we know that music educators must allow for encounters of different kinds, for professional and cross-disciplinary collaborations to occur in contexts and across sites and with resources different from the ones we are presently used to. This is the vision and challenge of preparing music educators for twenty-first century schools.

References

Bartel, L. (2000). Music education's pedagogic model. *Orbit*, 31 (1), 35-41.

Berkley, R. (2001). Why is teaching composing so challenging? A survey of classroom observation and teachers' opinions. *British Journal of Music Education*, 18 (2), 199-138.

Burnard, P. & Younker, B.A. (2004). Problem-solving and creativity: insight from students' individual composing pathways. *International Journal of Music Education*, 22 (1) 59-76.

BURNARD

Burnard, P. (2000).How children ascribe meaning to improvisation and composition: rethinking pedagogy in music education. *Music Education Research*, 2(1), 7-23.

Burnard, P. (2004). A damaged dream? Adolescent realities and changing perspectives on school music. In P. Shand. (Ed) *Music in Schools and Teacher Education in the 21st century, International Society for Music Education* (ISME), University of Western Australia Press, pp.104-114.

Campbell, P. (2002). The musical cultures of children. In L. Bresler & C. Thompson (Eds.) *The arts in children's lives: Context, culture and curriculum*, 57-69. Dordrecht: Kluwer.

Cooper, P. & McIntyre, D. (1996). *Effective teaching and learning: Teachers' and pupils' perspectives*, Buckingham: Open University Press.

Cox, G. (1999). Secondary school music teachers talking. *Music Education Research*, 1 (1), 37-46.

DeVries, P. (2000).Learning how to be a music teacher: an autobiographical case study. *Music Education Research*, 2 (2), 165-180.

Dolloff, L. (1999). Imagining ourselves as teachers: the development of teacher identity in music teacher education. *Music Education Research*, 1 (2), 191-208.

Drummond, B. (2001). 'The classroom music teacher – inspirations, aspirations and realities. The evidence from Northern Ireland. *British Journal of Music Education*, 18 (1), 5-25.

Entwistle, N., Koseiki, B. & Tait, H. (1989). Pupils' perceptions of school and teachers *British Journal of Educational Psychology*, 59, 326-339.

Flutter, J., Rudduck,J., Addams, H., Johnson, M & Maden, M. (1999). *Improving learning: the pupils' agenda*. A report for secondary schools supported by the Nuffield Foundation, 1997-1998.

Glover, J. (2003).*The Creative journeys of young people taking part in youth music projects*. Paper presented at the East Anglian Researchers (EARS) in Education Forum. University of Cambridge, November.

Green, L. (2001). *How popular musician learn: A way ahead for music education*. London and New York: Ashgate Press.

Green, L. (2002). From the Western classics to the world: secondary music teachers' changing attitudes in England, 1982 and 1998. *British Journal of Music Education*, 19 (1), 5-32.

Hargreaves, D. J. & Zimmerman, M.P. (1992). Developmental theories of music learning. In: R. Colwell (Ed) *Handbook of Research in Music Teaching and Learning*, 372-91. New York: Schirmer.

Hargreaves, D., Welch, G., Purves, R. & Marshall, N. (2003). The identities of music teachers. In R. Kopiez, A.C.Lehmann, I.Wolther and C. Wolf (Eds.) Conference Proceedings of the 5th Triennial ESCOM Conference, Hanover University, Germany, 178-181.

Hargreaves, D.J. & Marshall, N. (2003). Developing identities in music education. *Music Education Research*, 5 (3), 243-54.

Hargreaves, L & Galton, M. (2002). *Transfer from the primary classroom: Twenty years on*. London: Routledge

Harland, J. & Kinder, K. (1995). *Buzzes and barriers: young people's attitudes to participation in the arts*. Children and Society, 9 (4), 15-31.

Harland, J. et al (2000). *Arts education in secondary schools: Effects and effectiveness*. Slough: National Foundation for Educational Research (NFER).

Harland, J., Kinder, K., & Hartley, K. (1995). *Arts in their view: A study of youth participation in the arts*. Slough: NFER.

International Society for Music Education (1994). Declaration of beliefs for worldwide promotion of music education. *International Journal of Music Education*, 24, 47-51.

Kushner, S. (1999). Fringe benefits: Music education out of the national curriculum. *Music Education Research*, 1(2), 209-218.

Lamont, A. (2002). *Musical identities and the school environment*. In R.A.R. MacDonald, D.J.Hargreaves and D.E.Meill (Eds.). Musical Identities. Oxford: Oxford University Press, 41-59.

Lamont, A., Hargreaves, D., Marshall, N. & Tarrant, M. (2003). Young people's music in and out of school. *British Journal of Music Education*. 20 (3), 229-242.

Leong, S. (Ed.) (2003). *Musicianship in the 21st century: Issues, trends and possibilities*. Nedlands: University of Western Australia.

Mark, D. (1998). The music teacher's dilemma – musician or teacher? *International Journal of Music Education*, 32, 3-23.

Mills, J. (1996). Starting at secondary school. *British Journal of Music Education*, 13 (1) 5-14.

North, A. & Hargreaves, D. (1999). Music and adolescent identity. *Music Education Research*, 1 (1),75-92.

O'Brien, J. (1996). *Secondary school pupils and the arts: Report of a MORI research study*. London: ACE.

O'Neill, S.A. (2002). The self-identity of young musicians. In R. MacDonald, D.J.Hargreaves & D.Meill (Eds.) *Musical identities*. Oxford: Oxford University Press.

Parkyn, G.W. (1962). The transition from primary to secondary school in UNESCOI World Survey of Education, UNESCOI, Paris, France.

Pitts, S. E. (2000a). *A century of change in music education: Historical perspectives on contemporary practice in British secondary school music*. London: Ashgate.

Pitts, S.E. (2000b). Reasons to teach music: establishing a place in the contemporary curriculum. *British Journal* of *Music Education*, 17 (1), 33-42.

Richardson, V. (1996). The role of attitudes and beliefs in learning to teach. In Skula, J., Buttery, T., & Guyton, E. (Eds). *Handbook of research on teacher education.* (2nd ed.102-119. New York: Macmillan.

Ross, M. (1995). What's wrong with school music? *British Journal of Music Education*, 12 (3), 185-201.

Rudduck, J.& Flutter, J (2000). Pupil participation and pupil perspective: carving a new order of experience. *Cambridge Journal of Education*, 30 (1),75-89.

Sefton-Green, J. (Ed.), (1999). *Young people, creativity and new technologies.* London: Routledge.

Sloboda, J. (2001). Emotion, functionality, and the everyday experience of music: Where does music education fit? *Research in Music Education*, 3 (2), 243-54.

Stålhammar, B. (2000). The spaces of music and its foundation of values: Music teaching and young people's own music experience. *International Journal of Music Education*, 36, 35-45.

Stålhammar, B. (2003). music teaching and young people's own musical experience. *Music Education Research*, 5(1), 61-68.

Stoll, L. & Fink, D. (1996). *Changing our schools.* Buckingham: Open University Press

Swanwick, K. (1999). *Teaching music musically.* London: Routledge.

Tripp, D. (1993). *Critical incidents in teaching: developing professional judgement.* London: Routledge.

Upitis, R., Smithrim, K., & Soren, B. (1999). When teachers become musicians and artists: teacher transformation and professional development. *Music Education Research*, 1(1), 23-36.

Woods, P. (1993). *Critical events in teaching and learning.* London: Falmer.

York, N. (2001). *Valuing school music: A report on school music.* London: University of Westminster and Rockschool.

Yourn, B. (2000). Learning to teach: perspectives from beginning music teachers. *Music Education Research*, 2(2), 181-192.

CHAPTER EIGHTEEN

Relating Music and Affect: An Alternative Model for Structuring Music Instruction

BINA JOHN

Abstract

Current music education practice often reveals a narrow focus on musical skill acquisition that overlooks the vital connection between affect and musical development. There is a dire need to address not only the cognitive and perceptual aspects of music making, but the affective aspects as well. One cannot ignore the fact that music making is human action, with all of its 'chaotic' variables, such as the emotional needs and desires of children. The focus of music instruction should be on the integration of children's musical and affective development by means of especially caring teacher-student relationships in the music teaching/learning context. When children are given authentic opportunities to extend their musicianship, their musical understanding deepens and their self-esteem is enhanced. The potential for developing empathetic musical relationships in a music classroom is particularly promising if we conceive and carry out music as ritual, in which artistry, community, and caring combine.

Introduction.

Sarah: A Bright and Shining Star

Many years ago, I was introduced to a lovely, passionate, young singer who exhibited an unusually high level of musical intelligence. Not only could Sarah master complex repertoire within a very brief period of time, she performed her songs with artistry and bravado. Audiences were always moved by her ability to express herself musically in such a profound manner. Her musical abilities so intrigued me that I decided to examine her potential in other areas of musical performance. I introduced Sarah to a well-reputed flute instructor, who immediately became quite enthralled with this nine-year-old's natural inclination to the mechanics of the flute. After a few lessons, she was playing far beyond her developmental level. Sarah's musical abilities were clearly out of the ordinary. Her verbal-linguistic and logical-mathematical abilities, however, were weak in comparison. She experienced great difficulty in processing language and understanding abstract thought. Fortunately, Sarah's primary music teacher ensured success for her students by focusing soley on musical engagement. She personally connected with Sarah, by providing her with the real thing...real music, authentic choral experiences, and a genuine sense of belonging. When music making was the focus in the music class-room, Sarah shone with her peers. Naturally, Sarah received glowing assessments from her primary music teacher, who provided Sarah with the affective and musical means to go beyond her disabilities. The huge successes that Sarah was able to enjoy through her music making would undoubtedly see her through the more challenging areas in her life. The possibilities seemed endless. One thing was certain. Whenever Sarah was engaged in music making, she was a bright and shining star.

The following year, Sarah moved to another school. Her new music teacher inadvertently managed to suppress any form of emotional and musical engagement by structuring all of her classes around musical concepts and music theory. Sarah's tasks in music class included writ-ing reports on famous composers, filling out music theory sheets, reading rhythm cards, and taking musical dictation. In her first-term report, at her new school, Sarah failed music. True, Sarah did not have the verbal intelligence to write a major report on Johann Sebastian Bach, but did the teacher know that she could sing 'Bist Du Bei Mir' artistically, and with ease? True, Sarah could not read an isolated rhythm pattern on a randomly chosen rhythm card, but did the new teacher appreciate that she could play authentic Ghanaian rhythms on the djembe, without missing a beat? Sarah could not identify the six musical intervals that were blasted into her ears from an ear-training computer program, but her ability to listen to, and understand musical relationships were demonstrated whenever she played her flute. It was obvious that the teacher had no idea of Sarah's musical potential. By choosing concept-driven curricula and musical skill acquisition as the major foci of her classroom, the music teacher was, in fact, depriving Sarah of her human right to joyfully exhibit her musical intelligence through her inspired music making. In this all-too-familiar music education scenario, Sarah would always fail in music. She could never be a bright and shining star. It broke my heart.

As reflected in Sarah's story, two distinct, yet philosophically similar approaches perme-ate current, traditional elementary music education practice. Many elementary music education classes are comprised of verbally based formal music instruction designed to transform children into cultured consumers of music. Another very common model embraces a conglomeration of various methodologies intended to turn out quasi music-literate children. Neither approach, however, adequately addresses one vital aspect of musical development; the significance of emotions and affect in music making.

The singular focus on musical skill acquisition combined with music appreciation activ-ities disregards the critical relationship between emotions and music. The majority of elementary music education textbooks embrace an absolute expressionist stance that explores the relation between music affect and music's effect on human beings, thereby differentiating between an absolute orientation (in which musical meaning is said to lie exclusively within the musical work itself) and a referentialist position (in which musi-cal meaning is said to refer to the 'extramusical' world of actions, concepts, and emotion-al states). Mind and affect are two separate entities of which affect is not a necessary precondition for making music. Absolute expressionism assumes a relationship between musical structure and musics' expression of and contribution to human feeling. The role of emotions is to inform a disengaged understanding of music's form.

However, the role of emotions and music lie much deeper than appreciating the struc-tural subtleties of a musical work. Affect exists as an independent entity of consciousness that enables the very actions of music making and music listening. The relationship between music and emotions must be examined from the essence of which it is born; the affective-based musical interactions that occur between human beings.

Musical development—a natural, human process—always takes place with a significant other. The basis for this musical relationship is both neurobiological and affective. The musical actions of making music with others, as well as listening to a musical performance, require the emotional capacities of being calm, attentive, and relating to others in a nonverbal manner. Musical development and emotional development are, therefore, deeply intertwined. We must then examine the nature of this relationship when considering how to structure music instruction.

This chapter will focus on the nature of musical relationships and the significance of emotions and affect on these relationships. I will then present an alternative model for structuring music instruction that incorporates the vital role that emotions and affect play in the human actions of music making.

The Musical Relationship

The musical relationship that develops between the child, the music teacher, and his/her peers is a critical element that is often ignored in present elementary music curriculum models. "Music is a medium through which individual brains are coupled together in shared activity" (Benzon, 2001, p. 23). We cannot ignore the fact that music acquisition occurs within a human context. The first musical sound a fetus hears is his/her mother's, thus beginning a shared, musical journey that continues with other primary caregivers, teachers, and so forth. The spirit of this collective journey should be recaptured in musical instruction.

According to Rochat (2001), all forms of development in infancy and childhood are dependent on the relationship between the child's self, other people, and physical entities (p. 23). The physicalized musical object that comes alive through the shared actions of music making underscores what Rochat (2001) refers to as "inseparable pillars" of self that support and hold the child's musical world. Children interact with other human beings through the musical object that enables unique, nonverbal communication between the self and others. The more children learn to read nonverbal forms of communication, the more likely they will be able to understand the fundamentals of human interactions. Most of the intuitive learning in early childhood, according to Greenspan (1993) "comes from what we learn from relationships . . . If children haven't the fundamental ability to relate, much of their learning is going to be undermined and sabotaged" (p. 19). Greenspan observes that children who are able to comprehend and assess basic non-verbal human interchanges tend to be better students in school.

The gesture of music enables children to communicate through their bodies. The ability to understand and respond to gestural communication, such as music, plays an "enormous part in a child's ability to socialize and to learn during the school-age years" (Greenspan, 1993, p. 20). Music making in the elementary classroom, whether through the actions of singing, dancing, or musical play, requires young children to coordinate their "thinking-in-action" with the actions of their peers. This biomusical ability is facilitated through synchrony. Normal interactions involve a matching of movements that set up an interactive space for communication. Benzon (2001) asserts that this space enables "a coupling between two brains in which each can affect the other's internal states" (p. 27). The extents to which synchronized interactions occur over the first decade of a child's life determine, in part, the extent to which the cerebral cortex develops (Benzon, 2001, p. 27). The gestural essence of music not only increases brain capacity, but the musical relationship that occurs as a result of shared music-making is entrained in the brain during the critical period of early childhood.

The first years of elementary school are characterized by a very active interchange between a child's internal and external world, revealing a very fragile relationship between the child and his/her environment. A major task for a young music student is to understand his/her role in larger contexts. The child must understand what s/he needs to perform within a specific context and what codes to follow. The relational nature of music can be witnessed and better understood in the context of the numerous rituals that young children are exposed to. Christopher Small (1998) points out that just as music is not a thing, but something people do, rituals also involve human actions— something that people do. Rituals, such as music making, "are more potent means of teaching about relationships in all their complexity and of impressing them by the emotions they arouse than are words" (Small, 1998, p. 133).

The choral experience, in particular, can be an empowering process that requires groups of children to simultaneously engage in the ritualistic behaviour of singing. Choral singing requires an awareness of how one's own musical actions merge with the musical actions of others. Deeply intertwined within this relational phenomenon, is an affective experience. This feeling of what happens when children sing is often an overwhelmingly bonding experience for both the choir and the audience members.

It is this felt sense of musical consciousness that intrigues me the most (John, 2002). Music making obviously involves more than sensory/motor integration. Music making, especially through the actions of choral singing, is sustained through affective integration at the highest level. This may explain why some children may or may not remember the particular song they sang at a concert, long after the event, but they most probably will remember whom they sang with, and how they felt! One possible explanation for these phenomena could be attributed to the role affect and emotions play in musical development.

Emotions and Affect

Emotions, in the context of this paper, refer to the complex feeling states made up of somatic, psychic, and behavioural components that relate to affect and mood (Kaplan, Sadock & Greb, 1994). Affect refers to the expressed emotions that can be observed by others (Kaplan, Sadock & Greb, 1994). According to Dr. Stanley Greenspan (1997), emotions and affect are the basis for cognition. Contrary to the belief that emotions are cognitive in nature (Elliott, 1995), perhaps it is cognition that is affective in nature. If so, the inherent nature of music making during the early years presents an ideal context for securing the emotional foundations of young children in the elementary music classroom. Emotional milestones (Greenspan, 1993) such as the abilities to be attentive, to relate to, and communicate with others can be fostered through the musical relationships that develop in the classroom in the musical actions of singing, dancing, playing, and so forth.

A child's ability to develop secure relationships within his/her environment depends on numerous factors, a major factor being his/her insight on matters of affect. Before a child can relate to others, s/he must first possess an inner state of calm and attentiveness that allows her/him to enter into a caring relationship. Nurturing relationships can be ideally fostered in a musical context by helping secure healthy emotional development for children in their first few years of schooling.

Only human beings can communicate and understand the affective states of self and others. It is intersubjectivity (a sense of shared experience) that fosters not only the affective understanding of infants and children but musical understanding as well. The shared essence of musicianship provides children with a unique way of knowing. I propose we extend Elliott's (1995) cognitive view of affect by acknowledging the affective nature of musical understanding. If music cognition is affective in nature, then, one of the consequences of developing musicianship could be the development of an empathetic awareness of others.

The Corollary Development of Empathy

Musicing, according to Freeman (2000), activates brain mechanisms that foster social bonding that is a precondition to the development of empathy. Collaborative music making has the potential to influence a child's ability to sustain secure and caring attachments through the development of musical intelligence and empathy. The elementary music classroom could resemble an infant/caregiver dyad in which the human relationships that develop in this unique context, through the actions of music, enable affective integration in a mutual, caring environment. It is here, I propose, that music relocates its roots from the womb (Silverman, 1988) to another resonant and nurturing environment such as the music classroom.

One of the most powerful contexts in which empathy is fostered is within the practice of Music (John, 2002). Music making, in essence, is a cooperative effort requiring a dynamic relationship between the players and the conductor/teacher. The evidence of children's intrinsic ability to make music in the early years challenges the notion that music is purely a matter of perceiving and cognizing sonic patterns. Music is remembered as a feeling of what happens when human beings come together in the actions of a musical performance. These co-operative acts involve deriving affect and meaning from and within the music and the music makers.

Colwyn Trevarthen's (2000) extensive research on the "innate musicality" of infant communication provides profound insight into the affective and social nature of music that has important implications for music educators who want to foster empathetic relationships in the classroom:

> All such acts of co-operation in getting at meanings require genuine human understanding and confluence of emotional activity—they require relationships of trust, admiration, respect or obedience, and so forth. In a word, they require a responsive empathy of the kind that *music* [italics added] exercises and celebrates. (Trevarthen, 2000, p. 195)

Empathy, according to Nussbaum (2001), is essentially a creative reconstruction of another person's experience (p. 302). Understanding social relationships requires an understanding of the emotions, affects, and intentions of others (Rochat, 2001, p. 128). The human ability to make music is "intimately linked with the unique intensity of the human need to make, learn and transmit meaning in the experience of acting in common social experience" (Trevarthan, 2000, p. 165). Choral singing enables children to creatively reconstruct their musical actions in response to the conductor's musical gesture.

The gestural, nonverbal essence of music making provides a unique understanding of this very human experience. Nussbaum's (2001) misguided appreciation of how the song "Twinkle, Twinkle Little Star" invokes feelings of wonder that foster the development of empathy is based solely on the non-musical aspects of words and meaning. I propose the contrary; it is singing, with or without words, that creates an inner state of awe. Singing, a "distinctively human act" (Cumming, 2000, p. 25), enables an empathetic awareness of others.

One of my student teachers was attempting to teach a song to my primary choir, that she had not yet mastered herself. She attempted three times to teach the song, each attempt becoming more disastrous than the first, until, finally, she broke down and sobbed in front of thirty, very surprised children. Before I could even conjure up a rescue plan for my student, a few children ran up to the distraught teacher, reassuring her with helpful comments, such as: "It's OK, it will be better next time," "Try again...you can do it," and "Would you like to teach another song?" Clearly, there was every opportunity for these children to stand back and laugh at the student teacher, but instead they felt her pain and took action by offering whatever support they could.

The emotionally charged actions, followed by the highly empathetic reactions, support Elizabeth Tolbert (2001)'s observations that "music arises in social situations that are emotionally motivated-situations that are the product of both subjective and intersubjective processes of meaning formation" (p. 85). Within this sociocultural phenomenon, the emotions that arise from these actions are part of the same core brain mechanisms that act simultaneously in making music. Music, according to Rochat's (2001) eloquent observations, "is an auditory analog of the feelings perceived from inside and choreographed by the musician in the act of playing" (p. 42).

The choral experience, in this scenario, provided an ideal context for empathetic interactions to take place. The ideal choral experience in an elementary setting is one that fosters both affective and musical development. Through the ritual of choral singing, musicianship becomes the basis for constructing and sharing meaning among the choir members and the choral conductor (John, 2002).

Structuring Music Instruction Revisited: Addressing Emotions and Affect

The picture that emerges from the collective narrative of musical development in the early years reveals young children who exhibit highly developed skills of auditory perception, song and musical skill acquisition, and musical movement skills (John, 2002). The conventional image of children with limited capacities of musical acquisition combined with a narrow, or non-existent view of affect prolong a philosophical orientation that favours a linear, stage-model approach to music education. The sole focus on formal elements of a musical work or teaching music literacy epitomizes epistemological solipsism (Freeman, 2000), which is a theory of knowledge that upholds the belief that "only oneself and one's experience exists" (Blackburn, 1994, p. 356). The development of formal musical knowledge, such as knowing about rhythm, melody, and harmony, serves only to isolate one human being from another because this formal-verbal knowledge does not need to be shared. Furthermore, the more formal knowledge a child amasses, the more her brain grows apart from her classmates, "because of the uniqueness of the knowledge that is constructed within each one" (Freeman, 2000, p. 411).

On the other hand, music can be defined as an affective, cognitive, bodily, and socially situated form of knowledge that develops within a community of music makers (Elliott, 1995). Such an orientation serves to dissolve the solipsistic barrier by supporting the view that musical knowledge increases only in the corporate musical actions that occur among music makers. In other words, the musical knowledge that develops in the communal actions of music making and music listening results in a shared understanding of musical knowings that reinforce the bonds among the music makers.

Consequently, all components of the music teaching-learning environment should be considered in relation to the multidimensional aspects of musicianship and aspects relating to affect. Music is one of the most complex biological, neurological, bodily-kinaesthetic, spiritual and, therefore, affective experiences that young children engage in. The development of affect and musical cognition enables children to make music. And it is affect that *sustains* children in their actions of music making (John, 2003).

An Alternative Model for Structuring Instruction

The majority of elementary music curricula are based on outdated models of child development that do not take into account emotional or affective issues that provide the foundation for all musical learning. In light of the research conducted regarding the emotional significance of music education, we require a major departure from traditional approaches to curriculum making that resemble teacher- proof curricula. Many elementary music textbooks are designed in such a way that anyone could teach a music lesson. Instruction is based on a sequence of concepts focusing exclusively on the structural elements of music: melody, harmony, rhythm, timbre, form, and styles of musical works. The primary aims of such curricula are that students will grasp the techno-rational aspects about music and not necessarily learn how to make music. Lessons proceed in a step-wise manner designed to advance conceptual skills in a prescribed and predictable way.

Several problems arise from these approaches to curriculum making, especially in artistic disciplines such as music. Musical experience is one of the most complex biological, neurological, bodily-kinaesthetic, spiritual, and affective of human experiences. There need not be any artificial separation between music making, listening, and teaching. The key is to conceive music education as the process of inducting all students into the affective, social-cultural practices we call "music."

Practical Solutions

How then do we address the affective, social, as well as cognitive, and perceptual elements of music making when structuring musical instruction? First, I suggest that we accept the fact that music making is human action, with all of its characteristically "chaotic" variables, such as the emotional needs and desires of young children. Musical knowings cannot exist in and of themselves. Nor can these forms of knowings be thought of as natural or objective. If we adopt Bowlby's (1951) claim that emotional development is the basis for all forms of learning, then we must acknowledge that each of these knowings is infused with affective corollaries. Musical meaning is highly individual, multilayered, and fluid. For most children, this meaning is dominantly affective.

Secondly, children should be allowed musical opportunities that will enhance their emotional well-being. The ultimate state of healthy emotional development is the ability to monitor and regulate one's emotional thinking and reactions. Singing in a choir requires cooperative actions of musicianship, which in turn require (to a certain degree) the ability to "monitor, adjust, balance, manage, oversee and otherwise regulate" (Trevarthen, 2000, p. 195) one's emotional states in the context of a larger group. A caring teacher could tap into the choir's metacognitive knowledge of affect by encouraging corporate support instead of disapproval. The challenge of choral blending, for example, requires children to be aware of, and sensitive to, each other's voices. In such a setting, where every child's effort is to be valued, the refusal of a child to contribute to a unified sound could be a sign of distress, or a plea for help. The emotional knowledge-in-action of the choir could serve as a safety net if they affirm and redirect the child's emotional state within. As children learn to master musical challenges, such as vocal blending, their musical understandings deepen and their self-esteem is enhanced. Subsequently, through these positive, affective musical experiences, children increase in their knowledge of others, and more importantly, can begin to empathize with others.

Finally, instruction should be set up in such a way that the child learns how to use his or her emotions to enhance his or her musical experiences. The "feeling" for playing and singing depends on the "feeling" for musical action. The nature and value of music making is best understood in affective-kinaesthetic terms. The abilities to have emotional ideas and think emotionally can be ideally fostered by addressing the affective experience in elementary music curriculum making, particularly when addressing basic issues such as the music learner, the music teacher, and the music teaching/learning process.

Music Learners

A child's emotional self is undoubtedly determined by two factors: the events that take place in his/her early life and his inborn temperament. As evidenced by brain research, the impact of positive, nurturing, early experiences can alter one's genetically determined predispositions. Even though some of a child's emotional abilities are already formed in infancy, within the critical relationship between mother and child, the ability to regulate one's emotional state continues to develop in early and middle childhood. When structuring musical instruction, the learner must be viewed as not only a potential music maker, but as child whose affective state can be nurtured through his/her experiences within the musical classroom. The power of the musical context is that emotional meaning can be transmitted, not through words, but through the non-verbal, gestural modes of music making.

The child's implicit memory determines what skills and capacities s/he will learn. Outward manifestations of his behaviour reveal the emotional climate that s/he is exposed to. These responses can develop into patterned behaviours that become embedded in adulthood. The emotional, cognitive, and bodily components of these behaviours are often formed in early childhood. If these patterns of behaviour need to be altered or reversed, it must ideally take place in early childhood, within a positive emotional environment, and through actions that merge emotion, cognition, and body. The multidimensional nature of musicianship, which incorporates a multimodal way of knowing, feeling, and body, is one of the most potent means by which children can learn to regulate and sustain positive emotional experiences. The multifaceted nature of the young musical apprentice must be explored in light of the multidimensional nature of musicianship. We must provide children with authentic musical opportunities that will inform their musical actions. To nurture and extend the musicianship of our students is to ensure both musical and affective development that transcends time and place—the only restrictions are those imposed by the music teacher.

Music Teachers

If musicianship is multidimensional and affective in nature, then, in a radical sense, the music teacher is not just a mentor in the domain of music but in the domain of affect as well (John, 2002). In other words, just as music teachers need to adopt an apprentice model that reflects the nature of music making, teachers also need to adopt the model of a significant caretaker in their musical practice. The music teacher is no longer just the choir or band director. The role of a significant caregiver must also be considered. What children need, both emotionally and musically, resemble the very processes that occur between mother and child. It is during this stage that children need caring and empathetic "others" to direct their emotional development. Children need significant others to regulate their early experiences. A child's feelings are very much influenced by the way in which s/he thinks and the belief systems s/he is exposed to. Children need to know that their feelings are understood by significant others.

Teachers have the capacity to act as "emotional shields" (Music, 2001, p. 25) by helping children manage their feelings and modulate their experiences of the world. Ultimately, children need caring teachers who help to regulate their feelings in the hopes that children will be able to develop some capacity to process their own emotional experiences and manage their own emotional states.

Infants often appreciate the music in their mother's voice with infectious delight. Likewise, young school children may also eagerly attend to the music in the voices of other important people in their lives. Significant caregivers during this period of time of early childhood extend from the nucleus of the family into the potentially beneficial realm of the school.

Young music students readily respond to positive emotional experiences. In the same spirit of the mother-child bond, children are naturally drawn to the musical expressions of a caring teacher "as part of their elaborate adaptations to co-operate with and benefit from the strong messages of care, concern and love" presented by the music teacher (Trevarthen, 2000, p. 194). A teacher's intuitive musical and affective pedagogy is of prime importance for a child's musicianship to flourish.

In the dyadic musical relationship between music-affect mentor and apprentice, teachers must learn to communicate musically (nonverbally) with games and gestures that allow a child to become aware of his relationship with others. Furthermore, as Smithrim & Upitis (2004) suggest, "teachers must themselves be so engaged to allow music to attain its transforming power." This will lead to true musicianship, specifically in the cultural awareness and learning of different musical practices. A teacher's positive affect, combined with a high level of artistry, will further enhance a child's musical "self and other" awareness. Finally, if the teacher establishes a sense of community in the classroom, then children become active and contributing partners in the music making process.

The Music Teaching-Learning Process

Every music classroom should focus on active musicianship. Music is experienced through all of the senses of hearing, seeing, touching, smelling, and feeling in our bodies. The presence of feeling in music is an essential aspect of music education that overrides structure and technique. Musical consciousness is realized and can only be expressed in the bodily and affective actions of music making. Through the cooperative actions of music making, the change that takes place between self and object enables a growth in musicality, resulting in a nonverbal form of communication. The object and self engage in a musical dialogue that contains affective messages. Children can learn to express themselves through shared musical experiences in the classroom. Attachments are therefore formed and developed within a human, musical context.

The range of children's expressive powers is enhanced through immersing children in musical practices that require the musical expression of emotions as well as the musical expressions of cultural-ideological meanings. When this range of opportunities for musical expression and creativity is combined with opportunities presented by the text and music of choral music (in particular), music makers gain numerous ways of giving artistic form to their powers of thinking, knowing, valuing, evaluating, believing, and feeling, challenging their conscious power and musical understandings (Elliott, 1995, 2000).

If we accept music as ritual, then music making is not just a means to achieving an aesthetic experience. Music making and music listening both involve the socially and emotionally meaningful presence of significant others. Musical learning, therefore, depends on the musical-social relationships that form in the elementary music classroom. This shared "building" of musicianship is a critical factor in music education. The music classroom should reflect the magical bonding that begins in utero through music. As Elliott aptly suggests, music may be the "first art" (Elliott, 1995). Music making offers a direct way to engage the basic human need to be loved and nurtured. The development of musicianship in the music classroom is the ideal environment in which to foster healthy, musical, and empathetic relationships. Consequently, all components of the music teaching-learning environment should be considered in relation to the multidimensional aspects of musicianship and aspects relating to affect.

Conclusions

The nature of musical experiences in early childhood is affective, cognitive, and relational. In other words, music making occurs in a dyadic/social context and gradually extends to relationships outside the family, into school and society in general. The affective nature of music informs consciousness through the powerful emotional bonds that occur between the child (the music maker) and important caregivers (music teachers). Musical consciousness is a socially and emotionally situated phenomenon that begins as an awareness of one's self and grows into an awareness of the relationships that develop between one's self and significant others.

Affect influences musical consciousness by motivating actions that sustain positive experiences, including music making. Affective experiences not only motivate a child to pursue further music making, they affirm his/her relationship to significant others, thereby confirming the true social significance of musical endeavours (Bowman, 2000). Even though children are innately musical, the young musical mind does not develop in isolation. Rather, musicianship develops within human relationships in social contexts. "Every particular musical moment has a context; each is embodied in human experience of some kind" (Yob, 2000, p. 72). A child's musical mind will flourish when this relationship is built on empathy and caring. The affective experience of music making will ultimately determine the quality of the musical experience. Affect plays a critical part in determining all forms of purposeful activity, revealing the interrelational aspects of musicianship, consciousness, and emotions (Trevarthen, 2000, pp. 164-165).

The value of teaching children to make music transcends the notions of developing musically literate students, or carefully crafted consumers of music. The value of music is the affective experience that emanates from musical consciousness and impacts the whole child and his/her relationship to others. The musical classroom provides an empathetic environment that facilitates musical and emotional development.

I propose that emotions not only accompany the primary values of music; emotions, in fact, enable musical consciousness (John, 2002). We nurture musicianship by developing music making and music listening in balanced relation to exemplary musical challenges. Simultaneously, we contribute to the overall emotional development of the child, which includes his/her self-esteem, self-identity and, subsequently, his/her ability to relate to others in a healthy manner. The relationship between musical and emotional development should be the fundamental focus of all music instruction models. Sarah's story should not have ended on such a tragic note. Sarah could have been a bright and shining star, if only her music teacher had acknowledged this intimate connection between music and affect.

References

Benzon, W. L. (2001). *Beethoven's anvil.* New York: Basic Books.
Blackburn, S. (1994). *The Oxford Dictionary of Philosophy.* Oxford: Oxford University Press.
Bowlby, J. (1951). *Maternal care and mental health.* Geneva: World Health Organization.
Bowman, W. (2000). In dialogue. *Philosophy of Music Education Review,* 8 (2), 111-112.
Bowman, W. (2000). A somatic, "here and now" semantic: Music, body and self. Bulletin of the Council for *Research in Music Education,* Spring, 2000 (144), 45-60.

Cumming, N. (2000). *The sonic self.* Bloomington: Indiana University Press.

Elliott, D.J. (1995). *Music matters: A new philosophy of music education.* New York: Oxford University Press.

Elliott, D.J. (2000). Music and affect: The praxial view. *Philosophy of Music Education Review,* 8 (Number 2), 79-88.

Freeman, W. (2000). A neurobiological role of music in social bonding. In N. Wallins, Merker, B., & Brown, S. (Ed.), *The origins of music.* (pp. 411-424). Cambridge: MIT Press.

Greenspan, S. (1993). *Playground politics.* New York: Addison Wesley.

Greenspan, S. (1997). *The growth of the mind: and the endangered origins of intelligence.* Reading, Mass.: Addison Wesley.

John, B.A. (2002). *Music in early childhood: A philosophical analysis of intersections.* Doctoral Dissertation, University of Toronto.

John, B.A. (2003). Music in early childhood: A philosophical analysis of intersections. Paper presented at Research in Music Education Conference at Exeter University, April 2003.

Kaplan, H., Sadock, B. & Grebb, J. (1994). *Synopsis of psychiatry.* (Seventh Ed.). Baltimore: Williams & Wilkins.

Music, G. (2001). *Affect and emotion.* Cambridge: Icon Books.

Nussbaum, M. C. (2001). *Upheavals of thought.* Cambridge: Cambridge University Press.

Rochat, P. (2001). *The infant's world.* Cambridge: Harvard University Press.

Silverman, K. (1998). *The acoustic mirror.* Bloomington: Indiana Press.

Smithrim, K. & Upitis, R. (2004). Contaminated by peaceful feelings: The power of music. In Lee Bartel, (Ed) *Questioning the music education paradigm.* CMEA

Small, C. (1998). *Musicking.* Hanover: Wesleyan University Press.

Tolbert, E. (2001). Music and meaning: An evolutionary story. *Psychology of Music,* 29, 84-94.

Trevarthen, C. (2000). Musicality and the intrinsic motive pulse: Evidence from Human psychobiology and infant communication. *Musicae Scientiae Special Issue,* 1999-2000, 155-215.

Yob, I. (2000). A feeling for others: Music education and service learning. *Philosophy of Music Education Review,* 6(1), 67-78.

JOHN

Chapter Nineteen

Swinging Back the Gender Pendulum: Addressing Boys' Needs in Music Education Research and Practice

Adam Adler & Scott Harrison

ABSTRACT

Gender has been a focus in music education research for at least 25 years. Sex-stereotyping, participation rates by each sex, the gendering of musical roles and the role of patriarchy have been investigated at length. Green (1993) and Conway (2000) acknowledge that most of this research has concentrated on the needs of girls. This chapter focuses on issues related to boys' participation in music, the social forces which influence that participation, and our profession's responsiveness to the issue. Present practices are critically examined to assess the role of our profession in the facilitating or preventing boys' participation in music activities in school. Taking a post-feminist perspective that acknowledges that males and females are disadvantaged by the present day gender order, the role of the construction of masculine identity in western society with regard to music learning and music making is investigated. By using this framework the needs of boys are addressed, at the same time acknowledging that girls are also disadvantaged by gendering social forces. The aim is to provide equitable and just experiences of music for both sexes.

The maintenance of male gender role rigidity through homophobia is a key concept in the shaping of boys' musical choices. It has been found by the authors to effect participation in a variety of musical activities, and is particularly significant in boys' disengagement from vocal music. The meanings and values which boys attach to musical participation, and the strategies which they apply to facilitate their participation in or avoidance of music activities, are examined.

A review of the existing literature is fused with the authors' experiences and research to provide some realistic initiatives for improving male engagement through philosophical, political, and practical means.

Introduction

The GRIME (Gender Research in Music Education) organisation was inaugurated in 1991 at the first Feminist Theory and Music Conference (Lamb, Dolloff, and Howe, 2002), with a "mission... to provide leadership, advocacy, professional contacts, and a

strong research agenda for gender researchers in music education" and with "the purpose...
to provide a forum for promoting scholarship that addresses gender issues in music education; to share research and classroom materials that focus on gender issues in music education; and, to work towards establishing a climate within the music education discipline
that addresses issues, concerns and scholarship pertinent in any way to gender." [1] Gender
research in music education began in the 1960s with research on sex stereotyping as perpetuated in pedagogical practices and resources in our field. Since the early 1990s, gender
research in music education has been significantly influenced by feminist theory, and has
moved away from broader issues of gender [2] to a focus on issues of girls' and women's needs
and experiences in music education (Green, 1993; Conway, 2000). This shift demonstrates
a "pendulum swing" away from male-centred academic study, which was necessary to
address issues of the inclusion and representation of girls and women in our field. It is our
assertion, however, that the "pendulum" has swung too far for too long, and has resulted in
the subordination and exclusion of males in gender research in music education.

This chapter marks a recognition (or a re-recognition) of the value of gender research in
music education that focuses on issues which span a gender spectrum which includes
"female" but is not limited to it; and on male gender research in music education – both
male-centred research and gender research conducted by male researchers. It is our goal
to focus on issues of gender as they affect males in music education. For this we make no
apology; the pendulum has swung too far, and we intend to move it back to the centre.
There are boys in our classrooms and in our ensembles, as well as male teachers and
researchers whose voices and experiences are as deserving of recognition as any.

Our first step will be to critically examine gender research in music education as it has
developed since the early 1990s. Taking a post-feminist stance, we will problematize the
impact of feminist theory on music education research as it relates to the subordination
and exclusion of males, with a view to establishing our stance as a *critical genderist perspective* [3]. We will discuss issues of gender and identity as they relate to males' engagement
in education and music. We will problematize schooling and music education from a
critical genderist perspective, with a view to illuminating structures and practices that
contribute to a gendered social hierarchy that negatively affects the participation of both
males and females in music and the arts. Finally, we will discuss practices that may aid
in building a gender-equitable music education experience for all students.

A note about our "problematizing" aspects of the field of music education related to gender: In the case of our discussion of feminism and gender research, it is not our purpose
to devalue what has gone before, but rather to seek a broader, more critically reflective
awareness of thinking and acting as we move forward as researchers in music education.
And in the case of our discussions of schooling and of music education practices and
paradigms, it is not our purpose to call the musical or educational value of common
practices into question, but rather to illuminate the issues of gender that are embedded
in them, with a view to understanding the experiences of their participants.

Problematizing Feminism, Feminist Research, and Gender Research in Music Education

In their chapter dedicated to feminism, feminist research, and gender research, Lamb,
Dolloff, and Howe (2002) provide a detailed discussion of the relationship between of

feminism, feminist theory, and gender studies; in so doing, the content and structure of their chapter maintains a clear distinction between feminist research and gender research. Feminist research in education emerged from second wave feminist education theory, which sought to examine issues of gender as they affected the participation of females in education. Emancipatory research in particular focused on the restrictions of gender to girls' and women's equal access to opportunities and social and political power. This field of study became "feminist studies" within the broader category of "women's studies," for which distinct academic programs dedicated to the study of girls' and women's experiences were established. Emerging with the development of third wave feminism was a change of focus to research on intra- and inter-gender differences "in a post-modern world" amidst the complex influences and interactions of race, ethnicity, social class, and sexuality which became known as *gender studies* (Lamb, Dolloff and Howe, 2002:650). Gender studies also included an examination of the roles and experiences of males within a critical feminist perspective. Feminist studies remained a concrete entity, but within it emerged a discussion of valuing women's ways of knowing, feeling, and operating. Both the gender studies movement and the "valorization of an ethics of caring" (Lamb, Dolloff and Howe, 2002:651, citing Gilligan, 1982) were not fully accepted by some feminists, who maintained concern that the original emancipatory purpose of feminist studies would be lost.

Examined critically, the content and structure of Lamb, Dolloff and Howe's chapter demonstrates the subordinate place of gender studies to feminist studies, and the resulting invisibility of male gender studies within gender studies. The term "feminist," attached to words such as "theory," "studies" and "education," dominates the chapter, while the term "gender" takes a decidedly secondary place. Masculinity studies are mentioned in only two or three places, and when discussed appear to be categorized as outside of gender studies; only 3 paragraphs in a 20 page chapter are dedicated to the discussion of research on males in music education, and even this section categorizes existing M-GRIME (male gender research in music education) as largely compensatory in nature. Lamb, Dolloff, and Howe explain that the primary differences between feminist studies and gender studies are their breadth of focus and basis in second- or third-wave feminism theory; we assert that, in practice, the central focus of both areas remains girls and women. Technically, gender studies should include any studies of gender, including studies of femininity, masculinity and male gender issues; but in practice, male gender studies remain outside of gender studies because they do not focus on the experiences of girls and women. Further, we find the reference to male-centred gender research as "masculinity studies" to be problematic: First, because such a reference conveys a two-dimensional view of male gender issues, whereby any study of male gender issues necessarily focuses on the issue of masculinity. In post-modern terms, we recognize that a continuum of gender exists, and that all individuals – whether gendered male or female through still sex-related categories – experience and exhibit aspects of both masculinity and femininity.

Just as feminist studies have the potential to examine issues of females' femininity and masculinity (alongside the more commonly explored issues of social and political empowerment), male-centred gender research could just as much focus on males' femininity as on their masculinity. Second, we find that the reference to male-centred gender research as "masculinity studies" is linguistic evidence of the purposeful marginalization of male-centred research and male researchers from the field of gender studies. At once, some feminists refuse to "come to the (gender studies) table" by maintaining feminist studies as distinct from gender studies, while others have simply rebottled feminist studies (as with the rebottling of "sex" as bipartite gender) as gender studies. At the same time, both camps appear to linguistically and philosophically marginalize male-centred research as being outside of gender studies altogether, while the term "gender" has been appropriated to be synonymous with girls' and women's issues. To some, "gender studies" has become a neutral zone in which nothing really significant exists, which serves to further separate studies centred on females or males, and yet at the same time it has become third wave feminist research; GRIME, by any other name, is FRIME [4].

This relatedness-yet-apartness is problematic for male-centred research in music education. By politicizing the discussion of gender, and by limiting the discussion of male gender issues to being a backdrop against which women's experiences are perpetually compared and denigrated, any discussion of male gender issues in their own right has become politically incorrect. While feminists such as Hanley and Montgomery (2002:131, cited in Lamb, Dolloff and Howe, 2002:649) praise (feminist) research for "assuring equitable education for all students," that field continues to produce writing that marginalizes males' experiences in education. Such writing cannot serve the needs of male students, because it at once prioritizes the needs of girls in education, while making invisible the needs of boys. It also fails to recognize and celebrate girls' successes in music and education, and perpetuates the idea of girls as victims and as passive recipients of mistreatment by males in education and in life.

Approaching all gender research through the lenses of critical feminist thinking and pedagogy is problematic. The generalizability of critical thinking across subjects remains an issue (Younker, 2002). We must question: Are feminist studies, gender studies, and male-gender studies separate subjects worthy of their own brands of critical thinking? It is our view that because both feminist studies and male gender studies examine issues of gender in context, they follow the same type of critical thinking in which decisions are delayed "until solutions are considered" (Younker, 2002:163, citing McPeck, 1981) and in which re-learning, re-critiquing, and re-evaluating are practiced (Younker, 2002, citing Paul, 1993). We recognize that the emancipatory goal which continues to dominate feminist studies necessitates a focus on girls and women, and that this research is not intended to directly improve the experience of males in education. We do find, however, that critical feminist thinking not only makes invisible the experiences of males, at times it categorizes and marginalizes them. If the basis of critical thinking is generalizable, then we would expect that feminist research and pedagogy conducted critically would not practice the same categorization and marginalization of males which it criticizes as being done to females. Further, Younker (2002:163, citing Dewey, 1938) discusses the inclusions of "students in the formation of the purposes that direct their activities in the learning process." We assert that male students would not support their own marginalization, either in gender research or in pedagogy. While the critical thinking involved in the study of gender should be neutral, the highly political nature of critical feminist thinking has obstructed the process of re-learning, re-critiquing, and re-evaluating, and thereby blinded it to its own gender transgressions.

We propose that a broader, post-feminist construct is required for examining issues of gender in music and general education. The term *critical genderist thinking and action* [5] describes the process of examining issues of gender across the entire gender spectrum. It allows us to examine the experiences of individuals or groups while still valuing and understanding that those experiences do not negate the experiences of other individuals or groups, and while illuminating the interconnectedness of differing experiences. It would place FRIME in the valued context where it deserves to be, and re-establish GRIME as the field it should be. This shift is essential if we are to stop the violent, self-marginalizing, blaming, and devaluing rhetoric that has slowed the growth of our discipline, and the trust of our work in the larger educational research community. The adoption of this principle as the central procedural tool of GRIME would facilitate interaction and cooperation among gender researchers of both genders; it would provide a common basis for communication, for the sharing of experiences and observation of the complex interconnectedness of individuals' teaching and learning experiences; and it would allow male researchers to claim equal citizenship in the GRIME community.

IDENTITY, MASCULINITY, AND GENDER TRANSGRESSIONS

Males experience social challenges to their attempts to cross gender lines. The restriction of gender role development and expression, with its consequent denial of the experience and expression of cross-gender traits, emotions, and actions, is called *gender role rigidity* (Archer, 1993). Gender transgressions are challenged by peers, teachers, and family through the enactment of social punishments; these often take the form of negative verbal and physical reactions which demonstrate disapproval and rejection, and which isolate individuals from their support groups as negative incentive to conform their traits, emotions, and actions to social expectations for appropriate gender role behaviour. This conforming action is termed *gender intensification* (Colley, Comber and Hargreaves, 1994) and is strongest during the middle years (Adams and Marshall, 1990) when status and identity are uncertain.

Gender transgressions are more negatively viewed in boys than in girls (Jackson and Sullivan, 1990). While Helgeson (1994) proposes that gender traits are only perceived as socially desirable when gender role and gender are the same, evidence suggests that females are encouraged and rewarded for crossing gender lines in school or the workplace, while males are not. According to McCreary's (1994) *social status hypothesis*, the expression of femininity and cross-gender behaviours are punished in males due to the lower social status of female behaviours. McLaren (1995) explains that perception and valuation are also socially constructed to serve specific interests, which in this case would be a patriarchal power system to which both genders are encouraged to subscribe.

Social and cultural definitions of masculinity, cross-gender behaviour, and homosexuality remain powerful determinants of boys' life choices. Mac an Ghaill (1994, citing Arnot, 1984) suggests that femininity is ascribed by others as a tool for social control. Adler (2002) asserts that male femininity is ascribed based on a different set of perceptions and values than female femininity, which are linked to homophobia and not misogyny. The cultural definition (enhanced by popular stereotype) that aligns effeminacy and homosexuality is not supported in empirical research. There is evidence to suggest that homosexuals are not more likely than heterosexuals to posses a greater degree of cross-gender traits. Phillips (2001:201) comments that feminine characteristics in males do not necessarily indicate homosexuality; there is no direct relationship between how "feminine" a man might appear to be and his sexual orientation. McCreary's (1994:517) *sexual orientation hypothesis* "predicts that, for males, there is a stronger perceived link between gender roles and sexuality and that a male acting in a feminine way is more likely to be considered a homosexual than a female acting in a masculine way." For boys who exhibit cross-gender behaviour, social punishments include labels of homosexuality, which can follow them through school and limit their personal and social growth. Adler (2002) found homophobic labelling to be the most frequently used form of social lowering in the middle school, where homophobic labels surpass their more common usage as casual slurs for social positioning within social groups, and "stick" to some recipients as markers which limit their social interactions and their acquisition of social esteem and power. Harrison (2001:36) commented: "Of all the terms used in verbal bullying and sexual harassment, it [homophobic labelling] is the most serious, damaging, and long lasting, because of the stigma attached to it."

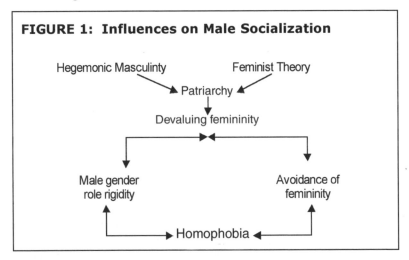

FIGURE 1: Influences on Male Socialization

Individuals are socialized in complex person-social contexts, with multi-dimensional and interactive influences to their construction of identity (Figure 1). According to Mac an Ghaill (1994), boys are more prone than girls to construct and use *gender categories*. Individuals respond to systems of social and institutional rewards and punishments by constructing identities that will gain them the best possible social security and mobility in their social contexts. The purposeful investment of time and energy in activities or actions by which individuals self-identify, and are identified by others is referred to as *identity capital* (Coté, 1990; Evans and Eder, 1993). By contrast, Adler (2002) describes the potential of an individual's actions or conveyed traits to result in a negative social response as *identity liability*. Activities that might highlight socially undesirable traits are avoided (Evans and Eder, 1993). Because singing (and many other musical pursuits) is viewed as feminine, many men are not involved in such activities. Lehne (1995:334) confirms the popular notion that interrelated concepts of gender role rigidity and homophobia limit areas of male interest:

An appreciation of many aspects of life, although felt by most men in different times of their lives, cannot be genuinely and openly enjoyed by men who must defend their masculinity through compulsively male-stereotyped pursuits. Fear of being thought to be a homosexual thus keeps some men from pursuing areas of interest, or occupations, considered more appropriate for women or homosexuals.

Definitions of masculinity are context and class-dependent (Mac an Ghaill, 1994, et al). Identity construction, perceptions of gender and gender role congruence, as well as perceptions of identity capital and liability are socially and culturally determined. Given the diversity of cultures and socio-economic classes in western countries, it is difficult to define occurrences of gendering behaviour beyond common trends that are observed or enacted in the public sphere, through public contexts such as schooling that bring together the multiple aspects of our society. We are reminded that as gender researchers and educators, we must be cognizant that the inter-relatedness of context, culture, class, and gender may support or limit our attempts to address gendered social values according to our own ideas of gender equity.

PROBLEMATIZING SCHOOLING FROM A CRITICAL GENDERIST PERSPECTIVE

Schools operate on hierarchical systems that reward specific behaviours, actions, and successes. Observe any junior high or high school commencement ceremony, and the subjects and activities that are valued by the institution become immediately clear. Success in athletics and the "harder," "academic" subjects such as mathematics, sciences, and technologies receive greater visibility and rewards than the "softer" subjects – languages, social studies, lastly the fine arts. Fullerton and Ainley (2000:14) report that in Australian schools, males dominate the areas of mathematics, physical sciences, technical studies, computer studies and physical education while females dominate in the areas of English, humanities, social sciences, biological sciences, the arts, languages other than English, home sciences and health studies. This holds immediate implications for students who choose to engage in the humanities and the arts, for whom less institutional significance translates to lower social- and self-esteem. Academic streaming, semestering, and limiting of academic choices by school and/or government-mandated curricula to some extent determine access to subject areas, the amount of time that students spend in each subject, as well as the academic weight of each subject in terms of its significance towards academic promotion to higher levels of study. Schools reinforce this hierarchy by allotting greater resources (equipment, facilities and personnel) to more highly valued subjects and activities.

Students make academic and activity choices in a gendered social context in which their choices will directly affect their social- and self-esteem and social power. Further, students may choose activities that enact an "ideal self-portrait" to their community(s). The Gender Hierarchy of School Subjects and Activities (Figure 2) illustrates the implicit system of rules and expectations for individuals' behaviour and investment of time that influences students' decision-making in school. Subjects valued "masculine" reflect competitive and/or violent, hyper-masculine (and, primarily by inverse association – heterosexual) archetypes such as the soldier, the successful capitalist-industrialist entrepreneur, the science-and-technology pioneer, and the corporate executive. Subjects valued "feminine" reflect cooperative, nurturing, and/or creative archetypes such as the humanist/philanthropist, the artist, and the mother. The further a subject is from any relation to the masculine archetypes (and from any contribution to a career which matches these archetypes) [6], and the closer it is to the female archetypes, the less valued it is in society and, therefore, in school. In the case of music, Koza (1990) comments that the ornamental or peripheral status has been given to all subjects (including music) taught at female academies in the 19th century has persisted. Swanwick (1988) also refers to this occurring in the United Kingdom at the turn of the 20th century. Subjects which present the most masculine associations also carry the greatest identity capital. Conversely, subjects which present the most feminine associations carry the greatest identity liability, and are increasingly avoided by both males and females who are increasingly competitive for places of social and academic power in school and beyond. For males, these subjects also reflect the distinctly male femininity that is associated with homosexuality, and therefore, carry additional identity liability.

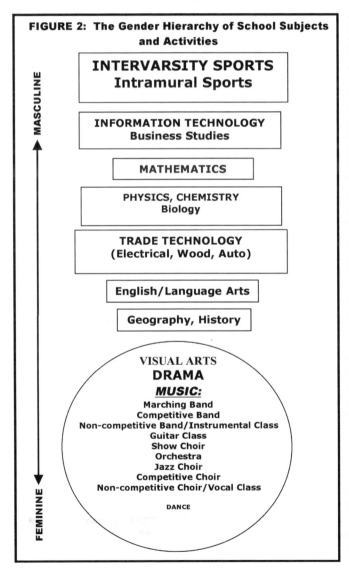

FIGURE 2: The Gender Hierarchy of School Subjects and Activities

MASCULINE

INTERVARSITY SPORTS
Intramural Sports

INFORMATION TECHNOLOGY
Business Studies

MATHEMATICS

PHYSICS, CHEMISTRY
Biology

TRADE TECHNOLOGY
(Electrical, Wood, Auto)

English/Language Arts

Geography, History

VISUAL ARTS
DRAMA
MUSIC:
Marching Band
Competitive Band
Non-competitive Band/Instrumental Class
Guitar Class
Show Choir
Orchestra
Jazz Choir
Competitive Choir
Non-competitive Choir/Vocal Class

DANCE

FEMININE

The focus of the feminist movement in education on female emancipation, and its rejection of "the valorization of an ethics of caring" and "women's ways of knowing" (Lamb, Dolloff and Howe, 2002:651, citing Gilligan) have resulted in the central goal of gaining social and political power in the public sphere for girls' and women. Ironically, this goal ultimately represents the valorization of things masculine, and the adoption of a patriarchal value structure by women. In educational terms, this has resulted in "equity projects which [have] promoted the inclusion of women in the curriculum... as well as investigating ways to encourage girls to study the higher levels of math, science, and technology and participate in sports" (Lamb, Dolloff and Howe, 2002:651). Girls and women are rewarded for rejecting self-associations with traditional femininity, and for enacting a male mantle of patriarchy, while boys and men are punished for not "rising" to meeting social expectations for masculinity, in an increasingly violent and competitive world.

While we do not consider the feminist movement to be responsible for the establishment of the gendered hierarchy of school subjects and activities, we do assert that the valorization of the masculine in the curriculum has contributed to the exodus of male and female students from the arts, and from music in particular (Gates, 1989), as well as to the social devaluation of a liberal arts post-secondary education, towards an emphasis on education as preparation to function in a competitive, capitalist industrialist, hyper-technological system. If our purpose is to bring music and the arts to a greater place of social value, and to encourage as many individuals as possible to engage in music making, then continuing to engage in research which seeks to perpetuate a masculinist curriculum will not achieve our goal.

PROBLEMATIZING THE MUSIC EDUCATION PARADIGM FROM A CRITICAL GENDERIST PERSPECTIVE

Swanwick (1988) explains how students (male and female) view participation in music: Between the ages of 8 and 15, music is the subject that exhibited the single greatest decline in interest, excepting religion. Solie (1993) was one of the first researchers to claim that music is gendered feminine. Harrison (2002) and Adler (2002) found that gender role rigidity, the avoidance of femininity, and homophobia all inhibit boys' participation in music. Green (1997:185) comments on boys' attitudes and their preference for sport over music, and reiterates the notions that boys succumb to heavy peer pressure against school music, and that certain musical activities are avoided because they are seen to be "sissy" and "unmacho." She explains – "For a boy to engage in slow music, or music that is associated with the classical style in the school – to join a choir, to play a flute – involves a taking a risk with his symbolic masculinity."

As with the hierarchy of school subjects and activities, music education programs are also socially valued based on their gender associations. Music education programs can also enact and perpetuate gender role rigidity in ways that maintain a gender hierarchy, with consequent implications for social security and social power within the context of schooling. The Gender Hierarchy of Music Programs in the Current Music Education Paradigm (Figure 3, hereafter referred to as GHMP) not only demonstrates the gendered reality of the music education paradigm, but also reflects patterns of challenge in recruitment and retention: the higher a music program is on this scale, the less difficulty practitioners experience in recruitment from the body of students who would choose music as an activity. As with the hierarchy of school subjects and activities, higher placement on this hierarchy also indicates institutional valuing as demonstrated through the deployment of resources (equipment, facilities and personnel), as well as by opportunities for competition, performance, and public visibility.

Lamb, Dolloff, and Howe, (2002:661) discuss Gould's (1992) *legitimation theory* in music, whereby leadership or "implemental" behaviours are legitimate for males, while "expressive" behaviours are legitimate for females. Since music activities exist on a gender con-

FIGURE 3:
Gender Hierarchy of Music Programs in the current Music Education Paradigm

MASCULINE

Marching Band

Competitive Band

Non-competitive Band/Instrumental Class

Guitar Class

Show Choir

Orchestra

Jazz Choir

Competitive Choir

FEMININE

tinuum, they can also be described as being "implemental" or "expressive." Band by definition is implemental, because it involves the use of instruments as "implements" – tool usage that distances the participants from their musical engagement. Choir is by definition "expressive," because we sing with our authentic voices, and thereby risk sharing ourselves with the individuals around us. The valorization of the masculine in the curriculum has lead our field to continually call for the masculinization or "implementalization" of music – and singing in particular – in order to improve recruitment and retention. Music education is increasingly "sold" to administrators and parents for its "implemental" value – its extra-musical relevance and contribution towards the building of intelligence and employment skills. This direction has not improved either long-term recruitment or retention, because it has pandered to the gendered personal/social fears of students and the public at large – to the general quest for personal-social elevation through the acquisition and enactment of masculine social power.

Instrumental Music Education

There are numerous accounts acknowledging the value of learning instruments and playing in ensemble dating back to Plato, who considered musical order to be analogous to moral order: a child who studied music would be emotionally stable enough to study philosophy. Boethius (in McKeon, 1929) espoused that mathematics, including music, should be used to prepare for the study of philosophy and that music could inspire men to higher learning and bring them closer to true reality. More recently Campbell (1997) in his works on the Mozart Effect, claims music can improve learning and development in young children. With regard to children, music is a tool to improving language, movement and emotional skills, as well as providing an opportunity for creativity, imagination, and self-expression. According to Campbell (1997), music is also thought to have a role assisting students in coping with autism, attention deficit disorder, learning disabilities and sensory processing disorders. As males are more likely to suffer from such disabilities and disorders, the therapeutic value of music should not be underestimated.

The stereotyping of musical instrument choice has also been thoroughly researched in recent years (Abeles and Porter, 1978; Griswold and Chroback, 1981; Delzel and Leppla, 1992). Since the early 1990s, the gendering of instrumental participation has been investigated, though, as pointed out above, this has taken place from a limited viewpoint. In the last few years, the role of men and boys has begun to be analysed more closely. For example, Pickering and Repacholi (2001:642) conclude: "The perceived risk associated with playing, or even just circling, a gender-inappropriate instrument [on a survey] was probably much greater for the boys than for the girls." Conway (2000) supports the notion of females crossing gender lines more easily than males. Her research in part, addresses the issue of permission (rather than talent) preventing participation. She found that "All of the students who were asked whether or not they would allow a daughter of theirs in 20 years to play a low brass instrument responded that the child should play what ever she would like. When asked that same question in regards to a son playing the flute, many of the students expressed concern about the teasing that child might experience" (Conway, 2003:13). Harrison (2001) found that over 73% of tertiary students surveyed indicated that flute was feminine while over 80% thought that trombone and drums were masculine. The full range of instruments (including voice) tested in this study appears in Figure 4:

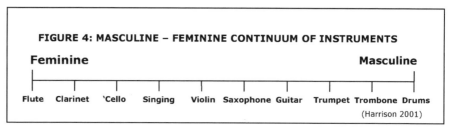

FIGURE 4: MASCULINE – FEMININE CONTINUUM OF INSTRUMENTS

Feminine — Masculine

Flute Clarinet 'Cello Singing Violin Saxophone Guitar Trumpet Trombone Drums

(Harrison 2001)

We have positioned wind band – and marching band in particular – at the top of the GHMP (Figure 3). The very nature of the school wind band as a cultural tradition carries hyper-masculine associations with a 19th and early 20th century military past; marching bands effectively evoke images of lines of soldiers and military parades. The marching band became associated with socially valued team sports, which replaced soldiering as the proving ground for masculinity in the post-war years of the 20th century. While playing in a marching band may not be perceived as being as masculine as participating in organised sport, it becomes more masculine by association, and by the continuing evocation of images of soldiering through the sound and the regimented organisation and manoeuvres which marching bands enact.

Humphreys, May and Nelson (2000:654, citing Burnsed and Sochinski, 1983, and Rogers, 1985) found that "most of the benefits of marching band competition, as perceived by students, directors, parents, and administrators, are extramusical." The competitive nature of wind band and marching band is itself inherently masculine; success in terms of "beating" others (we note the linguistic irony of this term) in competition fulfils the same purpose as fighting – to subordinate others through superior physical ability. Competitive musical activities are gendered more masculine because they provide the opportunity for individuals, groups, and institutions to rank themselves, thereby raising individual and collective esteem and reinforcing in-group valuation. Competition is a gatekeeper of participation in music activities, because it necessitates audition and selection. We assert that audition and selection are also inherently masculine because they fulfill the same competitive purpose of ranking individuals by skill, and by defining a "losing" class of individuals or groups. Competitive and selective activities perpetuate a success/failure binary that determines the identity capital or liability of activities for individuals considering participating. Individuals tend to avoid activities in which they project possible failure; males in particular avoid such activities, because the prospect of the loss of public esteem that accompanies failure often carries with it a sentence of homophobic labelling.

The centrality of public performance in musical activities can be a deterrent for individuals who would otherwise enjoy participating in them. Public performance, while an important part of musicianship, places musicians in "competition" against a publicly held aesthetic standard, which is based upon our prior experiences of professional performances. For amateur musicians, this standard is a difficult one to be compared to, because it sets success in the public esteem beyond their reach. Again, the fear of failure and accompanying fears of lowered social esteem and homophobic labelling compel some individuals to avoid musical activities. Some individuals choose more individualized music paradigms such as keyboard or guitar class, which allow individuals to participate in music without direct fear of competition. These activities also remove the necessity of public performance, which can also be a deterrent for some would-be musicians.

We have positioned guitar class in the middle of the GHMP. Guitar class facilitates musical participation without direct fear of either competition or necessity of public performance. A strength of this program is its individualization; as with keyboard class, participants can often work at their own pace, on separate and personalized material, and are somewhat freed from the in-class competition which can arise in a band class. Unlike keyboard class, however, the guitar's connections to the highly hetero-sexualized world of rock music also facilitate the building of a masculine public identity, which further serves to aid in recruitment. While this paradigm's individualized nature and heterosexual association are strengths in terms of recruitment, they are also problematic from a critical genderist perspective. The individualized nature and removal from competition and performance reflect the cults of isolation and perfection that dominate our society. Individuals – and males in particular – are expected to distance themselves from others both physically and emotionally; to succeed independently and profit individually. In order to achieve this, individuals maintain their authentic selves as "private," while they develop "public" personae to operate in their lived contexts. Authentic interpersonal connection is perceived as a sign of weakness, and in males is defined as gay. Guitar class facilitates musical participation while maintaining interpersonal distancing by removing expectations for making music with others. By removing the need for public performance, participants are protected from public judgement and the possibility of failure and its consequent social lowering. Further, the recruiting "strength" of this paradigm is problematic because capitalizes on students' needs for opportunities to publicly enact popular images of masculinity and heterosexuality, and thereby creates an environment that does not nurture a broad spectrum of gender possibilities.

The gender associations of the orchestral paradigm are complex. As discussed by Harrison (2001) the feminine-gendered perceptions of most orchestral instruments mean that individual participation in an orchestra is more likely to be gendered feminine than masculine; the few positions available to individuals who play the masculine-gendered instruments also places those individuals in positions of public visibility, and provides opportunities for the defence of their masculinity. However, the positioning of the orchestra at the apex of the largely male-dominated Western Classical tradition, with its consequent traditional male hegemony and undemocratic power structure, means that as an ensemble the orchestra is gendered masculine in the public perception.

Vocal Music Education

O'Toole (1995) explored the power relations of choral rehearsals through critical feminist lenses. According to O'Toole, girls are particularly disadvantaged in the traditional undemocratic and teacher-dominated choral rehearsal, which at once asks for their singing voices while silencing their personal voices. We assert that the continued focus on the disadvantaging of girls makes invisible the disadvantaging of boys. Any examination of contexts which are teacher-centred through critical feminist lenses necessitates a focus on the disadvantaging of girls, despite the fact that the power-disadvantaging which students experience in the "undemocratic" context of traditional choral rehearsals is shared by girls and boys. We propose that, despite any power inequities that are experienced by students who are already in choral activities, students are not deterred from joining because of them. Rather, a re-examination of choral activities through post-feminist, critical genderist lenses reveals that the gender issues arising from individual and social perceptions of singing and choir activities are more relevant in terms of recruitment, retention, and individuals' abilities to make singing a part of their continuing lives.

We have positioned singing at the "feminine" end of the GHMP. Gates (1989), Hanley (1998) and Green (1997) agree that singing is perceived as feminine, but that it is also undertaken by a disproportionate number of women, enhancing the existing stereotype. According to Hanley (1998), boys and girls share musical experiences, though girls are considerably more successful at singing than boys. She states – "singing is viewed a feminine activity – boys who engage in singing are feminine by implication" (Hanley 1998:58). Some of Hanley's subjects reported a negative view of male participation in singing because male peers view singing as "girls' stuff," one respondent relating that "they're hung up on the image that boys don't sing and those who do are gay or sissies or whatever – weak anyway" (Hanley 1998:57). Harrison (2002) found that 80% of those involved in singing at primary school are female, while in high school that proportion increases to 90%. Green (1997) suggests that women can become successful singers because the voice is completely lacking in technology and/or the woman singer can be perceived as either a singer of lullabies and picture of maternal care or the sexually available temptress. Solie (1993) refers to the voice (that is song, music, and sound in general) as identified with the maternal, with a state of being that is irrational, inarticulate and marked female." Koza (1993:50) suggests that boys' reticence to sing is based on "discursive binaries that construct females, femininity and homosexuality in the 'undesirable other' category."

Gates (1989:32) traced the incidence of male and female public singing in America back to the seventeenth century, and found that from that time to the present "there has been a marked shift from male to female predominance in public singing interest." Gates explains that the decline in male participation in public singing in the late 20th century is in part due to the fact that the social and political advantages gained in the past by singing adolescent and adult males were no longer applicable. Examined through Gould's *legitimation theory*, this gender shift is the result of a change in the social attribution of implemental value to public singing. Adler (2001) explains that since singing does not construct or defend masculinity it carries with it gender-incongruent and therefore homophobic labels; this is supported by Hanley (1998), who states that while some girls might want to be like boys, boys do not want to be like girls. As a result, more girls are joining traditionally male ensembles like wind and jazz bands, but boys are not increasingly attracted to choir. Koza (1993) notes that if reliance on rigid definitions of masculinity and femininity continue, along with a devaluation of things feminine, there might be dire consequences for choral programs.

Show choir remains problematic from a critical genderist perspective, despite its being a vocal paradigm that encourages (and secures) participation by both males and females. In terms of its gender values, show choir shares more in common with traditional competitive instrumental paradigms and auditioned musical theatre than it does with traditional choirs. Show choir is by nature selective and competitive, both of which cater to the masculine cults of perfection and competition. Through the performance of music choreographed with male-female interaction to emphasize heterosexual romantic lyrics, show choir enacts heterosexist values in a highly visible public venue. The devotion of large portions of schools' music budgets to sustain show choirs – which involve the minority of their music student population, and therefore privilege those individuals in terms of their student-resource ratio – is evidence that these ensembles fulfil institutional goals and reflect institutional values, which by demonstration must include the elevation and promotion of heterosexuality. The selective and heterosexist nature of this paradigm facilitates participation by males; because the activity is highly selective and highly visible, participation raises participants' public esteem; and, despite being a "singing" paradigm, show choir facilitates the defence of public heterosexuality, and is therefore acceptable to more males than traditional choirs might be.

The masculinization of choral activities through competition and selection may be an immediate strength in terms of recruiting and retention, but at the same time remains problematic from a critical genderist perspective. While competition and selection may aid in recruitment in the short term, they also reinforce gendered social attributions to choral singing, thereby contributing to the problem of male avoidance. As with competitive and selective instrumental music, competitive and selective choir activities facilitate participants' rationalization of their participation through implemental and extra-musical means, and thus their maintenance of preferred public gender image. Humphreys, May and Nelson (2000:662) stated – "a positive rehearsal setting, a relaxed music-making atmosphere, and a sense of cooperative spirit leads to higher-quality public performances. If competition is the goal of the activity, then a relaxed music-making atmosphere and sense of cooperative spirit will be supplanted by the quest for technical perfection in a competitive spirit. Adler (2002) found that, for boys who participated in voluntary choir activities, choir represented a much-needed escape from the masculine proving ground of the playground and sports, and from the constant quest for higher grades to prove self-worth to parents. The masculinization of choir through competition and selection may therefore be an obstacle to some boys' participation in choral singing.

How do boys experience singing in school?

According to White and White (2001:41) "recruiting, training and retaining of male singers may be the toughest challenge music teachers face." Green (1997:185) suggested that "boys are willing to sing in stage productions, because the stage provides a mask and an audience" and "boys will sing in rock groups." In both cases, participants are able to rationalize their singing through implemental and extra-musical means: singing on stage entails their enacting a role that distances them from the act of singing; singing in a rock group defends their masculinity and heterosexuality, immunizing participants from homophobia and social lowering. Harrison (2001) found support for this from his subjects, one of whom commented: "In year 11 and 12 with school productions, suddenly music, acting and singing were accepted by the majority of students." This subject also raises the issues of perseverance: students who "survived" until the final years of schooling could be rewarded for their efforts. The experience of other students in the study presented a contrary view:

> My school wasn't really the place for a singer because it wasn't considered normal for a young man to sing. The accepted pursuits for young men were sports... because I enjoyed singing the large majority of students thought I was homosexual. I couldn't sit through lunch hour or recess without people screaming things at me and throwing pieces of food at me. For a while it was terrible (Harrison, 2001:34).

A study by Adler (2002) marked the first in-depth examination of the experiences of singing boys in the middle school [7]. He states: "Boys perceive singing as two separate but concurrent acts: the **bodily-aesthetic act** by which they engage with the music, and in which they use their bodies to produce singing sound; and the psycho-social act in which they engage with each other in music making, as well as in the experience of being singers within the social environment of school" (2003:14). Of these two acts, the psycho-social act is more significant in boys' decision-making around singing; partly because boys view the bodily-aesthetic act itself in terms of the public use and public judgement of their bodies, and. therefore, as a quasi-psycho-social act; and partly because the participants viewed schooling as a primarily personal-social experience.

Adler also uncovered a social hierarchy of masculinities that colour the meanings that boys attach to their educational and musical experiences, which influences their decision-making and strategizing around singing and other activities in and out of school. Singing boys are more likely to be satisfied with delayed gratification and intrinsic rewards than are non-singing boys; this is particularly important for survival/retention in light of a lack of institutional or community recognition of their singing success. Boys who possess or enact androgynous self-concepts and who rely primarily on internal processes of self-esteem maintenance and support are able to participate in choir with greater ease than their more masculine peers. Some boys with more masculine self-concepts develop multiple identities in order to facilitate and to rationalize their engagement in differing and sometimes gender-conflicting activities.

One of the strongest determinates of boys' participation in any activity is whether the activity is co-educational or single-sex. Given that boys and girls have different expectations of schooling (Gates, 1989; Mahoney, 1998) and the differences in their experience seems to be great, the question of whether a single-sex or a co-educational learning environment is better for either sex has been the source of debate. The primary reasons for single-sex schooling – the ability to address gender-specific learning and developmental needs, aided by the removal of strongly sexualized social and behavioural pressures – can also be applied to the activity of singing in school. Adler (2003:16) explains:

> The creation of a Boys' Choir at Valleyfield proved to be highly successful in recruiting and maintaining boys' participation in singing. The Boys' Choir provided a venue in

which the boys' unique developmental needs could be addressed, and an environment free from the social and behavioural pressures which can accompany a mixed choir. Some of the participants perceived the Boys' Choir as a sanctuary where they could participate free of social limitations and controls: where *The Jocks of Singing* could shed their constructed context-specific identities; and where *The Social Isolates* could emerge from their shields of purposeful overachievement, to interact with their peers and with the music as their most authentic selves, free from peer criticism and homophobic harassment. Once the place of singing was elevated at Valleyfield through a succession of successful performance projects and recordings, the boys found that they experienced homophobic harassment less frequently, and with less intensity.

BEST PRACTICES: SUPPORTING PARTICIPATION IN MUSIC

Why should students take music?

Music plays a part in socializing people, transmitting ideologies and shaping patterns of thought and perception through epistemological constructs. Music does not merely reflect social and cultural values – it plays a part in shaping them (Louise, 1997). As music educators we are continually challenged by the innate power of the art form we deal with; the effect of music on the listener appears to be direct and unmediated. According to Altenmuller et al (2000:51) the workings of the brain are affected by music education, concluding, "it seems reasonable to assume that large networks tried and trained during music learning may be utilized for other tasks in daily life." That said, music education must have value in its own right. Hennessy (2001) supports the view that music education is needed for its own sake, i.e. the intense pleasure it can generate for listeners and makers, and the centrality to so many cultures and communities in defining, refining, challenging and celebrating their identities. Donaghy (1997) also recognizes the need for a political agenda that focuses education less on the economic and more on the community.

Changing the gender order: Best Practices

Creating a sense of community is central to the process of changing the gender order in music education. An approach that involves the entire school community is required in order to effect change in an educational setting: policy makers, administrators, teachers, students and parents need to be aware, supportive and active. As music educators, we must recognize the value in the creation of communities of learners, in which we strive to educate not only the students, but also parents, administrators, and other teachers, about the goals and values of our art. The changed community would be one where a sense of ownership exists and where artificial masculinization of the arts has removed and replaced with more conducive structures.

Forsey (1990) provides some guidelines for identification and reversal of the constraints placed on males by artificial masculine ethos. These include identifying the limitations of sex-role expectations; developing skills in co-operation, sharing, intimacy and caring; devising strategies for dealing with conflict, peer pressure and aggression, and encouraging an acceptance and expression of feelings, thought and aspirations. Such attributes can only take place in a safe environment where the element of risk has been removed.

In order to remove risk, Shores (1995) advocates the use of non-judgemental language and attitudes while Pallotta-Chiarolli (1995) further suggests that this type of work is achieved within a framework of social justice that deals with issues of marginality, prejudice and discrimination. Adler (2002) suggests that student engagement in music class and ensembles is increased when the risk of musical task failure is decreased. Cameron and Bartel (2000) argue that engagement is the central pedagogical goal in education and that conditions for learning must be created to facilitate this, including student responsibility for what is learned, freedom to approximate the goal, and a tactful response to student efforts. Music educators – particularly at the middle school level – must understand that students' abilities to demonstrate their musical skills and understandings are sometimes constrained by the temporary limitations of rapidly changing bodies; consequently, despite their best efforts, they may not be able to physically demonstrate their musical understandings to a set standard. By basing musical success on students' engagement in the musical process, rather than on their demonstration of standardized levels of practice, students perceive less risk in the musical activity and are encouraged to engage in the music learning process.

An elaboration of Pallotta-Chiarolli's call for social justice can be found in Jorgensen (2003:144) who advocates the need to base any change in education on basic principles of justice, goodness, fidelity and mutuality while Rudduck (2003) claims that there needs to be a better fit between young people and the structures of school. This requires music educators to take a more collegial view of the students – we are no longer the holders of knowledge we once were rather partners on the lifelong learning journey. Student knowledge and expertise needs to be valued and student/staff interaction reassessed. Such an approach may prove to make music more inclusive and less exclusive and achievement-driven, thereby altering perceptions of musical success. Success should perhaps be measured less in terms of standards (though these are important) and more on the principles Jorgensen suggests above. Cox (2002) proposes a redefinition of roles in order to enhance musical experiences. Finney and Tymoczko (2003) stress that an important aspect of this redefinition is the need for students need to be more than consulted, but rather to actively participate in the teaching-learning process.

Understanding structures such as competition and selection that increase perceived risk of musical task failure, and inhibit involvement in musical activities, is central to supporting students' participation in the arts. Competition can stifle men's co-operative and vulnerable behaviour, bringing with it an inability for men to play, to enjoy themselves, to suspend self-consciousness and to let go. Pollack (1999) points out that there is a negative side to competition that can promote intolerance and the idea that ethics can be supplanted by the need to win at any cost. More specifically, an investigation by Stollak and Stollak (1996) of music programs that focused on sport-like elements of competition (to the detriment of other factors) offers some insights. In particular, their investigation of the notion of "team" versus "family" in choir and the emphasis in winning as a "team" in competition reveals that, at times, this short-term team "winning" goal was chosen instead of giving students a life-long love of the art.

A re-evaluation of the culture of schooling is required to support engagement in the arts through balanced academic programs and academic credit that do not favour one academic area over another, and through scheduling, timetabling, and alternatively organised

student groupings (including mixed-age/grade and single-sex organisation) that facilitate participation and success in a variety of activities. As proposed by Adler (2002,
2003), there is much to be gained from single sex activities. Further investigation of
assessment practices, and greater attention to increasing public and institutional valuing
and rewards for music and the arts remain crucial to stopping the exodus of students.
The questions underpinning any change should be: Are we addressing students' learning
and personal development needs? Are the students better off because of this change?

Finally, we challenge music educators to reflect on their own practices and beliefs.
Teacher education programs should support pre-service and in-service teachers in the
development of reflective practice; the ability to critically reflect, and to plan and act
based on those reflections, is crucial to this process. Teacher education and in-service
training programs should address practical issues such as addressing gender issues
through teaching practices, and school policies and structures, to save both beginning
and experienced teachers the stress and confusion of having "re-invent the wheel" in the
field. Once these issues are substantially addressed, teachers will have a foundation from
which to reflect on their experiences and observations, and will be better able to
respond constructively to address the needs of their students.

References

Abeles, H.F. and Porter, S.Y. (1978). The sex-stereotyping of musical instruments. *Journal of Research in Music Education*, 26, 65-75.
Adams, G. R. & Marshall, S. K. (1990). A developmental social psychology of identity: Understanding the per son-on-context. *Journal of Adolescence*, 19(5), 429-441.
Adler, A. (2001). Male gender issues in music education: a three dimensional perspective. Paper presented at Research in Music Education Conference at Exeter University, April 2001.
Adler, A. (2002). *A case study of boys' experiences of singing in school*. Doctoral Dissertation, University of Toronto.
Adler, A. (2003). Let the boys sing and speak: masculinities and boys' stories of singing in school. Paper presented at the Sharing the Voices Symposium, June 2003 in St. John's, Newfoundland.
Altenmuller, E., Gruhn, W., Parlitz, D., and Liebert, G. (2000). The impact of music education on brain net works: evidence form EEG studies. *International Journal of Music Education*, 35, 47 – 63.
Archer, J. (1993). The organisation of childhood gender roles. In H. McGuirk (Ed.), *Contemporary Issues in Childhood development*. London: Routledge.
Cameron, L and Bartel, L (2000).Engage or disengage: An inquiry into lasting response to music teaching. *Orbit* 31(1), 22-25.
Campbell, D. (1997). *The Mozart effect*, Harder Headline, Sydney.
Colley, A., and Comber, C., and Hargreaves, D. J. (1994). School subject preferences of pupils in single sex and co-educational secondary schools. *Educational Studies*, 20(3), 379-385.
Conway, C. (2000). Gender and musical instrument choice: a phenomenological investigation. *Bulletin of the Council for Research in Music Education*, 146, 1-15.
Coté, J. E. (1990). Sociological perspectives on identity formation: the culture-identity link and identity capital. *Journal of Adolescence*, 19, 417-428.
Cox, G. (2002). *Living music in schools*. Aldershot, Ashgate.
Delzell, J. and Leppla, D.A. (1992). Gender association of musical instruments and preferences of fourth-grade students for selected musical instruments. *Journal of Research in Music Education*, 40, (2),93-103.
Donaghy, B. (1997). *Leaving early: youth suicide: the horror, the heartbreak, the hope*. Harper Collins, Sydney.
Evans, C., and Eder, D. (1993). No exit: Processes of social isolation in the middle school. *Journal of Contemporary Ethnography*, 22(2), 130-170.
Finney, J. and Tymoczko, M. (2003). Secondary school students as leaders: examining the potential for trans forming music education. *Music Education International*, 2003 (2), 36-50.
Forsey, C. (1990). *The making of men*. West Education Centre, Footscray.
Fullerton, S. and Ainley, J. (2000). *Subject choice by students in year 12 in Australian secondary schools*. Australian Council for Educational Research, Canberra.
Gates, J. T. (1989). A historical comparison of public singing by American men and women. *Journal of Research in*

Music Education, 37(1), 32-47.

Green, L. (1993). Music, gender and education: A report of some exploratory research. *British Journal of Music Education*, 10, 219-253

Green, L. (1997). *Music gender education.* Cambridge University Press, Cambridge.

Griswold, P.A. and Chroback, D.A. (1981). Sex-role associations of musical instruments and occupations by gender and major. *Journal of Research in Music Education*, 26, 57-62.

Hanley, B. (1998). Gender in secondary music education in British Columbia. *British Journal of Music Education*, 15 (1), 51-69.

Harrison, S. D. (2001). Real men don't sing. *Australian Voice*, 7, 31-36.

Harrison, S. D. (2002). Devaluing femininity: Its role in determining musical participation by boys. Paper presented at International Society for Music Education Conference, August 2002 in Bergen, Norway.

Harrison, S. D. (2003). A male flautist, female drummer: the persistence of stereotypes in musical participation. Paper presented at Research in Music Education Conference, April 2003 in Exeter, UK.

Helgeson, V.S. (1994). Prototypes and dimensions of masculinity and femininity. *Sex Roles*, 31(11/12), 653-682.

Hennessy, S. (2001). In C Philpott, and C Plummeridge, C (eds.), *Issues in music teaching.* Routledge Falmer, New York.

Humphreys, J.T., May, W., and Nelson, D. (2000) . Research on Music Ensembles. In Colwell, R. (2000). *The Handbook of Research on Music Teaching and Learning.* New York: MENC/Schirmer.

Jackson, L. A., and Sullivan, L.A. (1990). Perceptions of multiple role participants. *Social Psychology Quarterly*, 53, 274-282.

Jorgensen, E. (2003). *Transforming Music Education.* Bloomington and Indianapolis, Indiana University Press.

Koza, J.E. (1990). Music instruction in the 19th Century: view from Godey's Lady's Book, 1830 – 77. *Journal of Research in Music Education*, 3 (84), 245-257.

Koza, J.E. (1993). The 'Missing Males' and other gender issues in music education: evidence from the Music Supervisors' Journal, 1914 – 1924. *Journal of Research in Music Education*, 41(3), 212-232.

Lamb, R., Dolloff, L.A., and Howe, S. (2002). Feminism, Feminist Research, and Gender Research in Music Education: A Selective Review. In Colwell, R., and Richardson, C. (eds.) (2002). *The New Handbook of Research on Music Teaching and Learning.* 648-674. New York: Oxford.

Lehne, G. (1995). Homophobia among men: supporting and defining the male role. In M Kimmel and M Messner (eds.), *Men's lives*, Allyn and Bacon, Needham Heights, MA.

Louise, J. (1997). Gendered difference in music, feminist and feminine aesthetics in the music of Mary Mageau, Sarah Hopkins and Betty Beath. Unpublished Masters thesis, Griffith University.

Mac an Ghaill, M. (1994). *The making of men: Masculinities, sexualities and schooling.* Buckingham, Open University Press.

Mahoney, P. (1998). Girls will be girls and boys will be first. In D Epstein, J Elwwod, V Hey, and J Maw (eds.), *Failing boys: issues in gender and achievement*, Open University Press, Buckingham.

McCreary, D. (1994). The male role and avoiding femininity. *Sex Roles*, 31(9/10), 517 – 531.

McKeon, R. (1929). *Selections from medieval philosophers.* Scribner, New York.

McLaren, P. (1995). Moral panic, schooling, and gay identity: Critical pedagogy and the politics of resistance. In G. Unks (Ed.), *The Gay Teen: Educational Practice and Theory for Lesbian, Gay, and Bisexual Adolescents* (pp. 105-123). New York: Routledge.

O'Toole, P. (1995). *Re-directing the choral rehearsal: A feminist, post structural analysis of power relations in three choral settings.* Doctoral dissertation, University of Wisconsin-Madison.

Pallotta-Chiarolli, M. (1995). Can I use the word 'gay'? In R Browne and R Fletcher (eds.), *Boys in schools: addressing the real issues – behaviour, values and relationships*, Finch Publishing, Sydney.

Phillips, W. (2001). *Developing manhood: the testosterone agenda*, New Holland, Sydney.

Pickering, S. and Rapcholi, B. (2001). Modifying children's gender-typed musical instrument preferences: the effects of gender and age. *Sex Roles*, 45, (9/10), 623 – 642.

Pollack, W. (1999). *Real boys*, Holt, New York.

Rudduck, J. (2003). The transformational potential of consulting young people about teaching learning and schooling. *Scottish Education Review*. In Print.

Shores, D. (1995). Boys and relationships in schools. In R Browne and R Fletcher (eds.), *Boys in schools: addressing the real issues – behaviour, values and relationships*, Finch Publishing, Sydney.

Solie, R. (ed.) (1993). *Musicology and difference.* University of California Press, Berkeley.

Stollak, G. and Stollak, M. (1996). Competition in choral education: adults' memories of early choir experiences. *Choral Journal*, August, 21 –27.

Swanwick, K. (1988). *Music, mind and education.* Routledge, London.

White, C. and White, D. (2001). 'Commonsense training for changing male voices', *Music Educators Journal*, May 2001, 39-53.

Younker, B.A. (2002). Critical Thinking. In Colwell, R., and Richardson, C. (eds.) (2002). *The New Handbook of Research on Music Teaching and Learning*, 162-170. New York: Oxford.

[1] Taken from the GRIME Mission Statement and Statement of Purpose, GRIME website http://qsilver.queen-su.ca/~grime/#mission

[2] For the purposes of this chapter, we define gender as the social construction, definition, and ascription of masculinity and femininity

[3] Adler, 2003

[4] We must credit Kevin Bieman (2003), a music educator with the Peel District School Board in Ontario, Canada, for this observation.

[5] Adler, 2003

[6] We assert that the intersection of class and gender has also resulted in the social raising of the 'hard' academic subjects which are perceived as leading towards these fundamentally middle-class masculine archetypes, while the traditionally masculine trade subjects have been socially lowered because they do not achieve this goal. As a consequence of this middle-class 'academic inflation' the trade subjects have also been devalued in terms of their potential contribution to the construction and defence of masculinity, and are thus placed lower on the Gender Hierarchy of School Subjects and Activities.

[7] Previous studies had focused primarily on the reasons for boys' avoidance of singing, but had failed to develop solutions for supporting the recruitment and retention of male singers.

CHAPTER TWENTY

Philosophy In Music Education: Relevance, Re-Vision, Renewal

ELIZABETH GOULD

Abstract

For the past 35 years, philosophy in North American music education has been used chiefly as advocacy. Both music education philosophies, music education as aesthetic education and praxial music education, have claimed to espouse a single, unified philosophy on which the profession should be based. Traditional and totalizing in approach, however, each of them is grounded in linear logic, theory, and power that are irrelevant in and irreducible to the lived experiences of music educators. Alternatively, philosophy as experience describes ways in which music educators create philosophy as they solve musical problems in their everyday lives. These educational practices become philosophy when teachers and students mindfully create concepts, experiment with possibilities and solutions, and affirm connections. Because it cannot be sustained in rationalistic philosophies and pedagogical methods that depend or rules or codified ways of thinking, philosophy as experience requires pragmatic, bold, and playful approaches that make room for fluidity and dynamic vitality.

Introduction

For the past 35 years, philosophy in North American music education has been used chiefly as advocacy, as a means for justifying the necessity of teaching music in the public schools. This goal was considered to be so important that inhered within it was the imperative for the profession to espouse only a single, unified philosophy, one which everyone, regardless of what or where they taught music, could use to defend their program. That philosophy came to be known as music education as aesthetic education (MEAE). During the past decade, a second music education philosophy, known as praxial music education (PME), has been promulgated not as an alternative to MEAE, but as a replacement for it, again leaving the profession with a single philosophy, and a unitary statement of purpose.

While many philosophers and music educators during the middle part of the 20th century explored a variety of approaches for developing a philosophy of music education in North America (for reviews outlining them, see McCarthy & Goble, 2002; Panaiotidi, 2002; Walker, 2001), Bennett Reimer codified the position of MEAE with the publication of the first edition of his book, *A Philosophy of Music Education* in 1970. Subsequent editions appeared in 1989 and 2003. Philosophies based on praxis in music education have similarly been explored by a variety of philosophers (see, for instance Alperson, 1991; Regelski, 1996), but it was David Elliott who codified his version of the position with the 1995 publication of his book, *Music Matters: A New Philosophy of Music Education*. With the latest edition of Reimer's book, the two philosophies continue to assert their individual claims as the definitive philosophy of music education, irrespective of Reimer's assertion of incorporating useful and relevant aspects of many viewpoints—including Elliott's praxial philosophy of music education—in his so-called new "synergistic" experience-based philosophy.

Traditional Philosophy and Music Education

My purpose here is not to address the issues surrounding the use of philosophy as advocacy, or the relative merits of music education's competing philosophies, but to instead highlight that they are examples of traditional philosophizing, what Panaiotidi (2002) describes as a "substantive (or essentialist) approach" (p. 231). Each of the two philosophies consists of hierarchical, representational, and analogical concepts that have "a shared, internal essence: the self-resemblance at the basis of identity" (Massumi, 1987, xi), dependent on linear or circular ways of thinking. In their pursuit of truth, and their concern with identity and rationality through resemblance and negation, the philosophies are built on so-called rational, propositionally based arguments reflecting modern power relations that privilege some groups while sanctioning others. These power relations reflect the structure of modern society in which reality can be known only partially, based on each group's perspective or positionality. Further and more to the point, the philosophies are irrelevant in and irreducible to the lived experiences of music education practitioners.

In the context of philosophy of art or aesthetics, [1] these essentialist theories offer wide-ranging, all-inclusive philosophies of music education that "purport to offer a clarification of the nature and value of music" (Panaiotidi, 2002, 231). Vogt (2003) argues, however, that philosophies of music education based on aesthetics or a philosophy of art as a starting point are logically flawed, rendering them not only impossible to write, but unnecessary, as they ignore ethical issues associated with pedagogy and education in general. Instead of dealing with "the concept of musical experience and its implications for music education" (p. 21), he argues that philosophies of music education should be directed toward local issues, what he calls "the more mundane, but nevertheless philosophical questions concerning the reality of music education" (p. 19), asking questions such as, "the Deweyan question, How is education in a modern society possible?" (p. 20).

MEAE and PME, consequently, as they are practiced in music education, do not connect with or are responsive to the everyday lives of music educators. They require ways of thinking and being that exclude the music educators they claim to address—not because practitioners are incapable of understanding them, but because the philosophies do not address problems of material life and cannot account for difference[2] in perspective and values. The inevitable outcome of these philosophies which use the traditional, substantive approach, then, is a "search and struggle for 'the only true' philosophy of music education" (Panaiotidi, 2002, 242). This claim that each formalized philosophy is the only tenable philosophy on which the profession may be based renders the function of each in music education not as philosophy, but rather, as ideology.

Alternative Approaches To Philosophy And Music Education

In contrast to substantive, ideological approaches to philosophy, Wayne Bowman (1992) offers an analytical approach (Panaiotidi, 2002) that rejects the notion of philosophy as a body of immutable truths. He argues instead that

> philosophy is a *process* of exploration of inquiry (whose outcomes may well be secondary in importance to that process); and philosophy takes as its object not so much facts or essences, not so much immutable or eternal truths, as human *beliefs* and the *practices* in which they are both embedded and which tend to shape them. (p. 3, emphasis in original)

This analytical approach is pragmatic in that it "construes philosophy as a quest for clarity and consistency in thought and action" (p. 3) that "holds its 'truths' provisionally" (p. 5). Further, it is located in terms of its positionality(ies), and is consequently, "limited in what [it] can tell us about music" (Bowman, 1998, 16) and music education. Characteristics of analytical philosophy include "the ardent pursuit of clarity and understanding, . . . respect for theory and for ideas . . . that [demonstrate] their resilience to critical scrutiny" (Bowman, 1992, 5). The (analytical) philosophical mind is persistently curious and characterized by "adherence to rigorous philosophical method. . . . independence of thought. [It is] discriminating and critical, ... committed to reflective inquiry , ...[and] strives to understand the perspective of others" (p. 5). ·

Bowman (1992) also integrates criticism into his analytical approach, noting, "philosophy is to belief as criticism is to music" (p. 9). For Bowman, musical criticism is "exploratory and descriptive" as opposed to finding fault or judgmental, and is an important instructional tool in developing philosophical habits of mind. While (analytical) philosophy is concerned with conceptions, criticism focuses on perceptions through language. Similarly, where philosophy is more "rational/conceptual," criticism is more "perceptual and sensory" (p. 9). Philosophy and criticism, then, exist in a "dialectical interplay" (p. 13) that complement each other in their "similar ways of exploring the realms of human belief and meaning" (p. 9).

The analytical approach is vulnerable to criticism because of its dependence on linguistics and propositional logic (Panaiotidi, 2002), a criticism that, of course, may be directed just as easily to substantive approaches to philosophy. In addition, Panaiotidi suggests that Bowman's analytical approach tends to eschew methods of evaluation and contextualization, even while seeking to be more inclusive. The analytical approach, then, like the substantive approach, may be considered to be incomplete, and unable to account for the perspectives or positionalities of those who practice it. Noting that analysis is integral to the two codified substantive philosophies of music education, Panaiotidi proposes a third philosophical approach that is "characterized by permanent interconnection of analysis and theory-building" (Panaiotidi, 2002, 251). Although she suggests that Elliott's (1995) and Koopman's (1997) work are representative of this approach, Panaiotidi (2002) is forced to concede that "Elliott's approach is substantive par excellence in that it amounts to a particular philosophy" (p. 245), and Koopman's (1997) position is that of an "analyst's since he places emphasis on the analysis" (p. 245). Neither philosophical approach, apparently, is able to successfully combine theory-building with analysis. Her definition of an approach to philosophy of music education, then, is "*as a process of dialectical interplay of theory-building and analytical inquiry, i.e. synthesis and analysis*" (p. 245, emphasis in original).

Bowman's (1992) "dialectical interplay" (p. 13) and Panaiotidi's (2002) "interconnection of analysis and theory building" (p. 251) are similar to Jorgensen's (2001) distinction between what she calls the "*synoptic and analytic*" (p. 19, emphasis in original), represented respectively by the metaphors of architect and building inspector. In her dialectical approach to transform music education, Jorgensen (2003) is careful to avoid creating dualisms between the alternatives she combines in terms of the possibilities between them. Yob describes this as a "*this-with-that solution*" (Yob [1998] 2004, 1, emphasis in original) that "multiplies the strengths . . . [while] it also multiplies the weaknesses" (p. 1), an approach she nevertheless supports. For Bowman, the interplay is between philosophy and criticism; for Panaiotidi, it is between synthesis and analysis; for Jorgensen, it is between any two concepts considered dialectically. While useful in providing a variety of perspectives, all three approaches potentially run the risk of trying to reconcile what may not be able to be reconciled, and can appear to be unconnected from everyday life. If grounded in lived experiences that involve both music teachers and students in nondiscursive as well as discursive modes, however, they could, perhaps, be incorporated into an approach to practicing philosophy that includes a way of thinking with which music education practitioners may question and inform their own practices.

Philosophy as Experience

Philosophy in music and music education that has been connected to everyday life (feminism, queer theory, and postmodernism) has been denigrated as being political; that is, concerned with special interests (see, for instance, Miles, 1999; Reimer, 1995; Reimer, 2003; Woodford, 1999). Indeed, inspite of Gramsci's (1971) observation that "everything is political, even philosophy . . . and the only 'philosophy' is history in action, that is, life itself" (p. 357), some music education philosophers have created a philosophy/politics dualism in which philosophy is privileged above politics and politics is defined as not-philosophy (Bowman, 1998; Reimer, 1995; Woodford, 1999). Failing to recognize that politics are inhered in all aspects of lived experience, the philosophy referred to in this dualism, of course, consists of the substantive approach (which may include the analytical), and represents traditional, modernist, and exclusionary ways of thinking.

Alternative ways of thinking are demonstrated in the writings of philosopher Gilles Deleuze and psychoanalyst Félix Guattari, and demonstrated by Rosi Braidotti (1994) in her modification of their concept of the nomad (Deleuze & Guattari, 1987). Concerned with change and changing conditions exemplified in 1968 by students and workers demonstrating in the streets of Paris, Deleuze and Guattari co-authored several works during the decade between 1970 and 1980. In his individual writings, as well as those he completed with Guattari, Deleuze conceives of philosophy as a type of nomadic wandering in which philosophers embark on a conceptual trip without a map (Rajchman, 2001, 22). The destination of this trip is unknown, and arriving at it involves crossing borders, and abandoning traditional discourses in a type of deterritorialization of selves, identities, and ways of thinking that "releases [us] from such borders and becomes light . . . like a tent put down by nomads" (p. 95). This way of thinking focuses on possibilities and affirmation in terms of connections and experimentation, and involves trust or confidence in the world and logic related to life that does not rely on propositional logic, but rather is intuitive in nature and conceived in relationship to specific, lived problems (p. 6).

Philosophy, then, is not about seeking truth—higher or otherwise—but about working out problems that exist in lived reality—nomadically, outside of traditional (substantive and traditional analytical) philosophy. For Deleuze and Guattari (1994), philosophers work out these problems uniquely by creating concepts; indeed, "philosophy is the art of forming, inventing, and fabricating concepts" (p. 2). While these concepts are always new, they already have histories because they are related to other concepts (p. 18). Indeed, concepts literally "extend to infinity" as they overlap with each other in "zones, thresholds, or becomings" (p. 20). It is important to note that concepts are not fixed, because philosophers are always changing them in response to new problems. In fact, concepts and problems are dependent on each other in that concepts cannot exist independently of problems, and problems are understood only in terms of the solutions (concepts) that philosophers create for them (Deleuze & Guattari, 1994). These problems (and their solutions) raise still more questions which require still new ways of thinking. Indeed, philosophy in this sense may be described as a kind of "detective story with concepts for characters, intervening to resolve local problems, then themselves changing as fresh questions emerge and new dramas take shape" (Rajchman, 2001, 21).

Concepts are not discursive, however; that is, they do not lend themselves easily or naturally to verbal expression. Rather, they "freely enter into relationships of nondiscursive resonance . . . . [T]hey all resonate rather than cohere or correspond with each other" (Deleuze & Guattari, 1994, 23). Consequently, philosophy is not conceived in terms of propositions, but instead, in terms of a "series' or 'plateaus' into which the conceptual pieces enter or settle along the web of their interrelations" (Rajchman, 2001, 21). This results in philosophy that does not involve contemplation, reflection, or even communication.

> It is not contemplation, for contemplations are things themselves as seen in the creation of their specific concepts. It is not reflection, because no one needs philosophy to reflect on anything. . . . Nor does philosophy find any final refuge in communication, which only works under the sway of opinions in order to create "consensus" and not concepts. . . . Philosophy does not contemplate, reflect, or communicate, although it must create concepts for these actions or passions. (Delueze & Guattari, 1994, 6)

The concepts that constitute philosophy, then, are dynamic, constantly changing, and related in terms of connections that do not necessarily reflect traditional, discursive logic. They constitute a philosophy of doing, of experimentation, of affirmations, and connections in a "mad zone of indetermination and experimentation from which new connections may emerge" (Rajchman, 2001, 9).

Experimentation, as well, refers to new ways of thinking. "To think is to experiment" (Deleuze & Guattari, 1994, 111), and experimentation itself is philosophical. It consists of no set method, no rules by which it is carried out. Focused on what is yet to be, this thinking/experimentation is very much connected to the world through its basis in affirmation which "requires a belief or trust in the world and what may yet transpire in it, beyond what we are 'warranted' to assert" (Rajchman, 2001, 76). Further, "to affirm is not to assert or assume, but to lighten, to unground, to release the fresh air of other possibilities" (p. 13). Because they do not already exist, connections must be made, and involve "work[ing] with other possibilities, not already given" (p. 6). This clearly implies trust—in the world and in the possibilities resulting from those connections; hence, affirmation. Indeed, this thinking/experimentation/affirmation/connection is "always that which is in the process of coming about—the new, remarkable, and interesting that replace the appearance of truth and are more demanding than it is" (p. 111). The goal, then, of this philosophy is not to correct, dispel or critique—but to "make new forces visible, . . . inciting a kind of experimental activity of thinking around them" (p. 45).

Affirmation is expressed in terms of both becomings and difference. Becoming is the space between, in terms of both (all) directions at once, eliding the present. As Deleuze (1993) notes, "becoming does not tolerate the separation or the distinction of before and after, or of past and future" (p 39). Indeed, pure becomings encompass entire spectrums of time, quantities, actions/thoughts, and results, even while transcending their limits. Becoming is also related to difference, which for Deleuze and Guattari is an integral aspect of reality that makes possible the conditions for philosophy as experience. Described in terms of the outside, they note, "There is no becoming-majoritarian; majority is never becoming. All becoming is minoritarian" (Deleuze & Guattari, 1987, 106). It should be noted that minor and minority are not quantitative concepts, but rather refer to transformative potential (Boundas, 1993, 16). Minoritarian, because it is becoming, is inhered with transformative potential. Conversely, majoritarian, because it is not becoming, is not inhered with transformative potential. As a way of doing philosophy of difference, Deleuze and Guattari "replace Being with difference" (Boundas, 1993, 4), which, however, "is not foundational" (Kiefte, 1994, 162). According to Deleuze (1990) difference "engulfs all foundations, it assures a universal breakdown (*effondrement*), but as a joyful and positive event, as an un-founding (*effondement*)" (p. 263).

As an integral aspect of feminist theory, difference is understood in relationship to a matrix of interlocking oppressions, such as sexism, racism, classism, heterosexism, ageism, and discrimination based on physical, cognitive, and emotional disabilities, all of which must be dismantled. Similar to Deleuze and Guattari's language, joyfulness associated with difference has been described in terms of "affirmation" and "positivity" (Braidotti, 1994, 100), "no longer *different from* but *different so as to bring about alternative values*" (p. 239; emphasis in original). Indeed, the importance of feminism(s) and its relevance to music education may be understood in terms of difference (Gould, 2004).

Philosophy of Music Education as (Nomadic) Practice(s)

Philosophy as experience, then, does not consist of higher knowledge—but rather as a type of nomadic roaming. Not only do philosophers embark on conceptual journeys, they also borrow ideas from other disciplines, and deliberately subvert or de-territorialize the hierarchies on which they are organized (Braidotti, 1994, 37), connecting the theoretical and political, including experiences from everyday life, conflating so-called high and low culture, and mixing expressive modes. Indeed, Deleuze conceives of philosophy itself as nomadic, a type of "outsiders' art" (Rajchman, 2001, 21) external to other disciplines (Deleuze, 1995). It should be noted that insiders always attempt to appropriate and assimilate nomads. When forced inside, though, nomads bring with them "lines of flight" (Boundas, 1993, 14) which allow them to escape and transform themselves. These lines of flight, then, constitute paths of resistance and becomings that can only be accomplished by nomads on the outside.

Music educators may understand themselves and/or their practices as nomadic in a variety of contexts. First, they are nomadic in relationship to society, the profession of education, and the nature of schooling. Teachers in North American have been held in low regard for literally centuries (Gould, 1992), demonstrated by their low salaries, particularly when compared to those of other professionals, and the high level of control that is exerted over them professionally. Similarly, the place of music in public school curricula has been in doubt literally since it was first introduced in the 19th century. Second, music educators are nomadic in relationship to the profession of music, and some music educators are in a nomadic relationship within the profession of music education itself (Gould, 1992; Gould, 2003). The discrepancy in status between musicians and music educators has existed virtually since the founding of the school-based music education profession. Among music educators, band directors, for example may be considered to be in a nomadic relationship with the profession of music education. Although the vast majority are men, giving their group high social status and a disproportionate amount of power in the profession (Kanter, 1977), band directors have been described as belonging to a "truculent fraternity" (Britton, [1961] 1985, 225) through which they work to legitimate their bands as viable musical ensembles and blunt criticism from the profession that has historically undermined the status of bands relative to other musical organizations, most specifically, orchestras. Third, music educators are nomadic in relationship to traditional music education philosophers who have created and promulgated their own music education philosophies since the middle of the twentieth century, at least two of which are purported to be the only legitimate philosophy for the entire music education profession. How, then, may the lives and work of music educators be construed as philosophy as experience?

Music education practitioners create their own music education philosophy as they solve the problems of their everyday lives. Their practices become philosophy when they enact them mindfully, create concepts concerning them, experiment with possibilities and solutions, and affirm connections in their material reality in terms of teacher and student identities and subjectivities. This involves intentional ways of thinking and acting that do not necessarily demonstrate any consistent method or approach associated with any particular doctrine or school (Rajchman, 2001). Like the concepts they create, it is, literally, unique to each music educator, making possible the creation of other philosophies, each of which consists of sprawling interconnected images of thought (Deleuze, 1990; Rajchman, 2001). Indeed, Deluze (1995) notes that this is an artistic process, "It's the image of the thought that guides the creation of concepts.... [C]oncepts are like songs (p. 148). Most notably, the philosophy created by music education practitioners is not written down or codified in any way.

This process occurs for music educators in the very act of teaching and learning, in each interaction with students and music. In teaching/learning situations that are constructive in nature, teachers and students in music address learning by identifying, confronting, and solving musical problems. This social constructivism process of education (Vygotsky, 1978; Wiggins, 2001) results in socially constructed knowledge (concepts). Teachers and students work together to select specific issues for attention, formulate possible solutions in relationship to them, experiment with those solutions and other possibilities, and then modify them as necessary. This constitutes an ongoing process of dancing with students, literally, a dance of becoming (C. L. Matthews, personal communication, 13 January 2004). As they create knowledge (concepts), they mindfully apply them as singing, moving, playing instruments, creating, analyzing, evaluating, and knowing music. Students' part in this process, of course, is related to their nomadic relationship to teachers, schools, and music when the last is approached as something that must be transmitted to or learned by students, as if it existed separately from them. Just as problems are an integral component of solutions, students play an integral part in creating music education philosophy.

In this context, the role of music education philosophers in philosophy as experience is rather different from what it is in traditional substantive and traditional analytical approaches to philosophy. First, music education philosophers may provide alternative perspectives to both theoretical and real life problems. They can broaden and inform the positionalities of specific music educators, students, and music education situations. Second, they may help to identify new problems and implications of problems to extend current concepts, solutions, and possibilities in order to stimulate new ones. Third, and perhaps most importantly, they may help validate the creation and experimentation process of music educators and students. By asking questions of the questions, music education philosophers may potentially enrich the philosophy as experience process for those who are living it in their classrooms. This is a profound responsibility, and not one to be confused with writing substantive philosophies that purport to provide definitive answers. Deleuze and Guattari (1994) note, "Communication always comes too early or too late, and when it comes to creating, conversation is always superfluous" (p. 28). The role of music education philosophers, then, is not to discuss philosophies (concepts)—their own or those of music education practitioners and students—but to provide the impetus for the creation of more philosophies (concepts). This can only be done by asking questions, posing problems, participating in the experimentation of possibilities, literally, creating philosophy as experience.

(Some) Related Becoming-Concepts

Not surprisingly, "humor, play, and ruse" (Rajchman, 2001, 52) are integral to philosophy as experience. They are a function of the uncertain nature of nomadic wandering: border-crossings that are accomplished through making connections and elicit "not so much hope as a kind of trust or confidence—a belief-in-the-world" (p. 6). Based on a logic of sense and event (Deleuze, 1990) that is about "the relations between thinking and life itself" (Rajchman, 2001, 51), philosophy as experience is created only in relationship to the world, and is concerned with "a 'practical' question about life" (p. 51). Those who practice it "want to *do* something with respect to new uncommon forces, which we don't quite yet grasp, [and] have a certain taste for the unknown, for what is not already determined by history or society" (p. 6); literally, those who are nomadic. Fortunately, this describes music education practitioners and students who are actively and joyfully involved in making and learning music together.

Feminism(s) provides one of the means by which philosophy as experience may be approached. It is concerned with dismantling sources of oppression based on difference in which all individuals teaching and learning in music education may benefit, as it troubles long-held assumptions, disrupts dualistic concepts and traditional ways of thinking, accepting nothing as given. Indeed, feminist theory "fracture[s] the line of fault hidden underneath the everydayness of music teaching" (Lamb, 1994, 69). In its concern with those who participate in music education, feminism(s) reveals new possibilities and alternative ways of looking at the profession as well as the world as it embodies the practice of philosophy as experience by challenging its own beliefs and practices.

Philosophy as experience, then, is inhered with delight in uncertainty, joy in the unexpected, excitement in change. It requires ways of thinking that are at once pragmatic, bold, and full of possibility. Initiated through asking questions of and seeking solutions for issues and problems of material reality, it makes room for fluidity and dynamic vitality. It cannot be sustained, however, in rationalistic philosophies and approaches to teaching and learning that depend on a particular methodology, set of rules, or codified way of thinking. Literally, it cannot be sustained in the substantive philosophies of music education as aesthetic education or experienced-based music education, and praxial music education as they are currently conceived. Further, to write about it in this way is to negate the idea of philosophy as experience. What I must do, then, is become engaged in the everyday lives of those who read this, those who practice philosophy as experience in the material reality of their everyday lives in music education.

References

Alperson, P. (1991). What should one expect from a philosophy of music education? *Journal of Aesthetic Education*, 25(Fall), page numbers.

Boundas, C. V., (Ed.). (1993). *The Deleuze reader.* New York: Columbia University Press.

Bowman, W. D. (1998). *Philosophical perspectives on music education.* New York and Oxford: Oxford University Press.

Bowman, W. (1992). Philosophy, criticism, and music education: Some tentative steps down a less-travelled road. *Bulletin of the Council of Research in Music Education*, 114(Fall), 1-19.

Braidotti, R. (1994). *Nomadic subjects: Embodiment and sexual difference in contemporary feminist theory.* New York: Columbia University Press.

Britton, A. P. [1961] (1985). Music education: An American specialty. In P. H. Lang, (Ed.), *One hundred years of music in America,* (pp. 211-229). Reprint. New York: Da Capo Press.

Deleuze, G. (1993). *The Deleuze Reader.* C. V. Boundas, (Ed.). New York: Columbia University Press.

Deleuze, G. (1990). *The logic of sense.* C. V. Boundas, (Ed.); M. Lester with C. Stivale, (Trans.). New York: Columbia University Press, 1987.

Deleuze, G. (1995). *Negotiations, 1972-1990.* M. Joughin, (Trans.). New York: Columbia University Press.

Deleuze, G., & Guattari, F. (1987). *A Thousand Plateaus: Capitalism and Schizophrenia.* B. Massumi, (Trans.). Minneapolis and London: University of Minnesota Press.

Deleuze, G., & Guattari, F. (1994). *What is philosophy?* H. Tomlinson, G. Burchell, (Trans.). New York: Columbia University Press.

Elliott, D. J. (2001). Modernity, postmodernity and music education philosophy. *Research Studies in Music Education*, 17, 32-41.

Elliott, D. J. (1995). *Music matters: A new philosophy of music education.* Oxford and New York: Oxford University Press.

Gould, E.. (2003). Cultural contexts of exclusion: Women college band directors. *Research and Issues in Music Education*, 1(1), http://www.stthomas.edu/rimeonline/vol1/gould.htm.

Gould, E. (2004). Feminist theory in music education research: Grrl-illa games as nomadic practice (Or how music education fell from grace)." *Music Education Research*, 6(1), 67-80.

Gould, E. (1992). Music education in historical perspective: Status, non-musicians and the role of women. *College Music Symposium*, 32, 10-18.

Gramsci, A. (1971). *Selections from the Prison Notebooks*, Q. Hoare and G. N. Smith (Trans). London: Lawrence and Wishart.

Humm, M. (1990). *The dictionary of feminist theory.* Columbus: Ohio State University Press.

Jorgensen, E. R. 2003. *Transforming music education.* Bloomington and Indianapolis: Indiana University Press.

Jorgensen, E. R. 2001. What are the roles of philosophy in music education? *Research Studies in Music Education*, 17, 19-30.

Kanter, R. M. (1977). *Men and women of the corporation.* New York: Basic Books.

Kiefte, B. (1994). Gilles Deleuze: The ethics of difference and the becoming-absent of community. In E. M. Godway, G. Finn, (Eds.), *Who is this 'we'? Absence of community,* (pp. 159-184). Montréal and New York: Black Rose Books.

Koopman, C. (1997). *Keynotes in music education: A philosophical analysis.* Nijmegen: Mediagroep Katholieke Universiteit.

Lamb, R. (1994). Feminism as critique in philosophy of music education, *Philosophy of Music Education Review,* 2(2), pp. 59-74.

Massumi, B. (1987). Translator's foreword: Pleasures of philosophy. In *A thousand plateaus: Capitalism and schizophrenia,* (pp. ix-xv). B. Massumi, (Trans.). Minneapolis: University of Minnesota Press.

McCarthy, M., & Goble, J. S. (2002). Music education philosophy: Changing times. *Music Educators Journal,* 89(1): 19-26.

Miles, S. (1999). The limits of metaphorical interpretation, *College Music Symposium* 39, 9-26.

Panaiotidi, E. (2002). What is philosophy of music education and do we really need it? *Studies in Philosophy and Education,* 21(3), 229-252.

Rajchman, J. (2001). *The Deleuze connections.* Cambridge, MA: MIT Press.

Regelski, T. A. (1996). Prolegomenon to a praxial philosophy of music and music education.' *Musiikkikasvatur: Finnish Journal of Music Education,* 1, 23-38.

Reimer, B. (1995). Gender, feminism, and aesthetic education: Discourses of inclusion and empowerment, *Philosophy of Music Education Review,* 3(2), 107-124.

Reimer, B. (1970). *A philosophy of music education.* Englewood Cliffs, NJ: Prentice Hall.

Reimer, B. (1989). *A Philosophy of Music Education, 2nd ed,* Englewood Cliffs, NJ: Prentice Hall.

Reimer, B. (2003). *A Philosophy of Music Education: Advancing the Vision, 3rd ed,* Upper Saddle River, NJ: Prentice Hall.

Vogt, J. (2003). Philosophy—music education—curriculum: Some casual remarks on some basic concepts. *Action, Criticism, and Theory for Music Education,* 2(1), http://mas.siue.edu/ACT/v2/Vogt03.pdf.

Vygotsky. L. S. (1978). *Mind in society: The development of higher psychological processes.* M. Cole, V. John-Steiner, S. Scribner, E. Souberman, (Eds.). Cambridge: Harvard University Press.

Walker, R. (2001). The rise and fall of philosophies of music education: Looking backwards in order to see ahead. *Research Studies in Music Education,* 17, 3-18.

Wiggins, J. (2001). *Teaching for musical understanding.* New York: McGraw-Hill.

Woodford, P. G. (1999). Living in a postmusical age: Revisiting the concept of abstract reason, *Philosophy of Music Education Review,* 7(1), 3-18.

Yob, I. M. [1996] (2004). Can the justification of music education be justified? *In Philosophy of Education 1996,* (pp. 237-240). F. Margonis (Ed.). Urbana, IL: Philosophy of Education Society.

[1] It is important to note that Elliott (2001), Reimer (2003), and Bowman (1998) all argue that philosophy of art and aesthetics are not the same. My point is that either or both may be implicated in a philosophy about the nature and value of music.

[2] In terms of feminism(s), difference is both a political term and a social concept, referring to diverse and alternative perspectives that are a function of oppression in terms of experience and voice. Because of its potential to transform society, difference is conceived in terms of affirmation. See, for instance, Humm (1990).

Brief Biographies of Contributing Authors

Adam Adler, a specialist in choral conducting and music education, Adam Adler holds degrees from the universities of Western Ontario, New Brunswick, and Illinois; in June 2002, he became the first graduate of the PhD program in music education at the University of Toronto, with a research focus on male gender issues in choral music education. He has taught music in schools across southern Ontario, and is active as a consultant, clinician, and composer/arranger. His compositions and arrangements have been performed across Canada and abroad. In 1999, he founded *The Margarita Project* – a performance-based collaboration between folk artists and choirs to encourage the choral performance of previously unpublished and unperformed folk music. Dr. Adler is the founding conductor of the Toronto-based community choir Just Singers; he also performs as a soloist and professional chorister throughout the Greater Toronto area.

Bernard W. Andrews, Faculty of Education, University of Ottawa, teaches music certification for beginning teachers and graduate curriculum and program evaluation courses. Bernie has experience at elementary and secondary settings, and is past president of the Arts Researchers and Teachers Society (ARTS). He is widely published in the leading education journals. His research interests include examining the generative processes of musical composition, evaluating the effectiveness of arts education programs, assessing gender differences in arts instruction, probing the parameter of pedagogical composition, and postulating alternate forms of curriculum inquiry based on musical metaphors (e.g., Integrated Inquiry based on the composer metaphor; Responsive Inquiry based on the notion of the studio musician).

Lee R. Bartel is Associate Professor, Coordinator of Graduate Music Education at the University of Toronto and Director of the Canadian Music Education Research Centre and the Sonic B.R.A.I.N. Laboratory. He teaches research methods, music and the brain, evaluation, social psychology, choral music, and alternative methods in secondary music. He is the Senior Editor of the CMEA "Research to Practice" biennial book series, edits the monograph series, *Research Perspectives In Music Education*, and is former editor of the *Canadian Music Educator* and the *Canadian Journal of Research in Music Education*. He has presented academic papers and workshops around the world. His varied publications include research articles on music response, curriculum, and pedagogy; edited books on philosophy of music and curriculum; and a guitar text, *Get into Guitar*, and 39 cd's in several series including Music for Your Health, SonicAid, and Fisher Price. He has served as anchor for evaluation for an educational reform project in Central Asia under the United Nations. He adjudicates Canadian and U.S choral, vocal, and instrumental music festivals. Current research includes the "Face the Music" project focused on music, dance, and artistic gymnastics, and several music and brain studies.

Pamela Burnard is a senior lecturer in Music and Arts Education in the Faculty of Education at the University of Cambridge, England where she works on undergraduate and postgraduate courses along with the supervision of PhD students. She is co-editor of International Journal of Music Education, an associate editor of Psychology of Music, on the editorial boards of British Journal of Music Education, and Music Education Research, and on the international editorial boards of International Journal of Arts and Education and the Asia-Pacific Journal for Arts Education. Her research interests include creativity, creative thinking, arts and artistic practices, pupil voice, teacher education, and teacher thinking.

Susan Bruenger is an Assistant Professor of music education at the University of Texas San Antonio. She has 22 years of experience teaching choral and general music K-12. Her education includes degrees from Southern Illinois University and both a Masters and Ph.D. in Music Education from the University of North Texas. Prior to teaching at UTSA, she taught at Webster University, St. Louis University, and Northwestern State University of Louisiana. At UTSA she teaches general and choral music education classes and supervises student teachers. Dr. Bruenger also offers recorder, elementary composition, high school musical workshops and non-select choir clinics. Her research interest is in non-select performing groups.

Linda Cameron is Associate Professor of Education at the Ontario Institute for Studies in Education, University of Toronto. She is a specialist in educational psychology, early childhood education, language and literacy development, parenting, theory of play, and play therapy. She is widely known for her media work in the past and is currently a consultant, writer, and producer for the Fisher Price children's music series. She has eight published books on the development of language and literacy, and has written numerous academic and professional papers on play, parenting, ESL issues, teacher education, music and literacy connections, and special education concerns. Dr. Cameron has consulted on education across North America, Pakistan, South Africa, England, Vietnam, the five Central Asian countries, and Early Childhood Education projects through UNICEF working with leaders from the five countries of the Persian Gulf.

Katie Carlisle is completing her PhD in music education at the University of Toronto, Faculty of Music. She holds a Master of Music Education from VanderCook College of Music in Chicago and a Bachelor of Music in Jazz Performance from the University of Toronto. Publications include: Nimmons Talks About Community (*Canadian Music Educator*). Katie has taught music to pre-school through post-secondary students in a wide variety of educational settings. Her dissertation research explores the social climate of high school music programs offering progressive approaches to music education. Katie lives in Burlington, Ontario with her husband and son, Sasha.

Colleen Conway is Associate Professor and Director of Graduate Studies in Music Education at The University of Michigan in Ann Arbor. Her scholarly interests include instrumental music education, preservice music teacher education, qualitative research, and the mentoring and induction of beginning music teachers. She has presented at national and international conferences and has published over 40 articles on these topics in all of the major music education journals. She is currently on the editorial board of *Update: Applications of Research in Music Education*. Her edited book entitled *Great Beginning for Music Teachers: A Guide to Mentoring and Induction* was released in October 2003 by MENC.

Elizabeth Gould is Associate Professor of Music Education at the University of Wisconsin-Madison and teaches graduate and undergraduate courses in music education history, philosophy, and foundations. She was Visiting Associate Professor at the University of Toronto from 2002 – 2004, and previously served on the music education and conducting faculty of Boise State University, and as Director of Bands at the University of Wisconsin—Marshfield/Wood County, and Associate Director of the Community Music School at Michigan State University. Her research focuses on philosophical and gender issues in music education, and has been published in *Philosophy of Music Education Review, College Music Symposium, Update, Research and Issues in Music Education, and Music Education Research* (forthcoming).

Betty Hanley teaches music education at the University of Victoria. She chaired the 1998 National Symposium on Arts Education in Victoria and the Symposium on Musical Understanding in 2001. She co-authored The State of the Art: Arts Literacy in Canada (1993), and co-edited Looking Forward—Challenges to Canadian Music Education (2000) and Musical Understanding: Perspectives in Theory and Practice (2002). Co-author of a chapter in The New Handbook of Research on Music Teaching and Learning (2002), she continues to contribute to numerous journals. She has been working on arts policy, especially towards drafting the 'Policy Guidelines for Arts Education in Canadian Schools.'

Scott D Harrison's career as an educator spans almost 20 years. He has taught classroom music in state and private schools and singing to students in primary, secondary and tertiary environments. A graduate of Queensland Conservatorium, Australia, he was Director of Music and Expressive Arts at Marist College Ashgrove from 1988 to 1997, after which he was appointed Lecturer in Voice at Central Queensland Conservatorium of Music, Mackay. Scott is currently Director of Performing Arts at Clairvaux MacKillop College, Brisbane, Australia. Dr Harrison lectures in music education and voice at Griffith University and maintains an active performance profile with Opera Queensland. Recent publications have focused on music, gender and teacher identity.

Bina John is an Instructor at the Faculty of Music, University of Toronto and the Director of Choral Programs at Montcrest School, Toronto. Dr. John teaches courses in Psychology and Music, Foundations of Music Education and a new course called 'Music in Early Childhood: From Philosophy to Practice.' Conference presentations include the International Music Education Conference at the University of Exeter and the ISME Conference in Barcelona, Spain. She has a Bachelor of Music (Piano Performance) from the University of Alberta. She completed her Ph. D. in Music Education, at the University of Toronto, in 2002. Bina John lives in Toronto with her husband and two children, Saira and Paul.

Mary Copland Kennedy is an Assistant Professor in music at Rutgers University where she teaches undergraduate and graduate courses in music education in addition to conducting the Voorhees Choir. Dr. Kennedy holds Bachelor of Music and Master of Education Degrees from the University of Victoria, Canada, and a Doctor of Philosophy in Music from the University of Washington in Seattle. Research interests involve three main areas: creative process, choral music, and music in community. Dr. Kennedy has published articles in the *Journal of Research in Music Education, British Journal of Music Education, Journal of Historical Research in Music Education, Choral Journal, Research Studies in Music Education, Music Education Research,* and *Music Education International.*

Richard Marsella is the president of Music Roots Seminars Inc., which engages students in constructing their own musical instruments, composing their own music, and recording their work for further reflection. He has worked with such important Canadian artists as R. Murray Schafer, Mendelson Joe, and The Nihilist Spasm Band. As a composer he has written and produced music for 3 seasons of MTV's *The Tom Green Show.* He has composed and produced 7 full-length CDs, and has been featured on CBC Radio One (3 documentaries for Outfront), CBC Radio Two (continuous airplay on Brave New Waves and RadioSonic), TFO (VOLT) and Muchmusic (Muchnews, BradTV). He also worked for three years at Metalworks Studios, working with such artists as Busta Rhymes, SUM41, and LEN. Also known as 'Friendly Rich,' he is the founder and director of the Brampton Indie Arts Festival, an annual event which promotes underground artists. Friendly Rich recently finished building his own barrel organ and began touring across Canada in September 2004.

Jennifer Peters is a teacher and performer in Toronto. She has performed regularly with the Calgary Philharmonic Orchestra, including several CBC broadcasts and CD recordings. Jennifer has also appeared in recital across Canada with her duo partner, guitarist Mathew Peters. After spending a year in residence at the Banff Center, where she was a member of *Music Makers* - a performance team that tours schools in support of music programs in rural and disadvantaged areas, Jennifer completed a Masters of Music in Performance with Doug Stewart, at the University of Toronto. She has also completed a Master of Music in Music Education at the U of T. She has a special research interest in Children's Television and has several published by papers in the *Canadian Music Educator*.

Bennett Reimer is the John W. Beattie Professor of Music Education Emeritus at Northwestern University, Evanston, Illinois. His professional interests include philosophy of music education, curriculum theory, research theory, and intelligence theory. He is the author and editor of some 15 books and has written over 125 published articles, chapters, reviews, etc. His most recent book is *A Philosophy of Music Education: Advancing the Vision*, 2003, a 90% revision of the 1970 and 1989 editions. Several other books are in the initial phases of creation.

Fred Seddon is currently a research lecturer in Psychology at the Open University, UK. He formerly worked as a Head of Music in secondary school and as an instrumental tutor. He studied Music Psychology at the University of Keele, UK between 1997-2001. His PhD (completed in 2001) investigated adolescent computer-based composition in relation to instrumental experience. He has published several articles in international peer reviewed journals and has also presented his work at international conferences during the past five years.

Eric Shieh holds undergraduate degrees in Instrumental Music Education and English, with an emphasis in multicultural theory, from the University of Michigan, Ann Arbor. As a music educator, he has worked extensively with a number of orchestras in the Ann Arbor area, has opened music workshops in a number of area prisons with the Prison Creative Arts Project, and coordinates the Music and Social Change initiative at the University of Michigan. He has recently been published in the *Philosophy of Music Education Review* and has presented at the *New Directions in Music Education* conference at Michigan State University on music education and social change

Joseph Shively joined the faculty in the Department of Music, Theatre, and Dance at Oakland University in Michigan in 2004. His previous experience was at Kansas State University and at The University of North Carolina at Greensboro. He holds degrees from Limestone College and the University of Illinois. At Illinois he served as Associate Editor of the *Bulletin of the Council for Research in Music Education* and Coordinator of Band Programs for the Office of Continuing Education and Public Service in Music. As an educator he taught band at several schools in South Carolina. Dr. Shively has served as an adjudicator, arranger, clinician, drill designer, and program consultant for concert, jazz, and marching bands and orchestras throughout the United States. Recent publications include chapters on constructivist learning approaches in *Dimensions of Musical Learning and Teaching* (MENC) and *Musical Understanding*. His research interests include constructivist learning and teaching, instrumental music, teacher education, technology, and philosophy.

Katharine Smithrim (Ph.D Eastman) is Associate Professor of Music Education at the Faculty of Education at Queen's University. She teaches pre-service teachers and graduate students, specializing in topics related to arts education. Dr. Smithrim has created and taught both private and school music programs for all ages, from parents and infants, to graduate students and teachers. Current research interests include music in early childhood, rhythm, teacher transformation through the arts, and the spiritual dimension in teaching and learning. She is co-author of the book *The Arts as Meaning Makers: Integrating Literature and the Arts Throughout the Curriculum* (2001).

Yaroslav Senyshyn is an Associate Professor of philosophy of music and aesthetics at Simon Fraser University. He has published extensively in the *Philosophy of Music Education Review, Interchange,* the *International Society for the Study of Music Education,* the *Journal of Educational Thought,* the *Canadian Journal of Education, Educational Leadership,* and other venues. As well his classical performances in concert halls throughout the world include Washington's Kennedy Center, New York's Carnegie Recital Hall, Toronto's St. Lawrence Centre and Massey Hall, and the Moscow Conservatory's Bolshoi Hall. The Washington Post referred to him as a pianist of "enormous power" and "sophisticated finger work."

Rena Upitis (Ed.D, Harvard) is the former Dean of Education at Queen's University, and currently a Professor of Arts Education at Queen's. A musician and composer, Dr. Upitis has worked as a music teacher in inner-city schools in Canada and the United States and her two books on music teaching explore possibilities for teaching music through children's improvisation and composition in regular classroom settings. She is also co-author of a book on elementary mathematics teaching. Her various SSHRC and NSERC and contract research projects have explored teacher transformation through the arts, the impact of the arts on elementary students, and the use of electronic games in mathematics and science education

Renate Zenker is a private music educator, independent researcher, and educational consultant in Vancouver, British Columbia. She brings a background of 21 years of private teaching to her research in appreciation, understanding, and the lifelong learning of music. In 2000 she earned her Ph.D. from the University of British Columbia, the same institution from which she earned her Masters. She also holds conjoint music and music education degrees from the Memorial University School of Music. She spends her free time playing her 1895 Bluethner, studying the history of the piano, and climbing mountains.